Environmental Law in India

Fourth Edition

Mohammad Naseem
Saman Naseem

This book was originally published as a monograph in the International Encyclopaedia of Laws/Environmental Law.

Founding Editor: Roger Blanpain
General Editor: Frank Hendrickx
Volume Editor: Kurt Deketelaere

Wolters Kluwer

Published by:
Kluwer Law International B.V.
PO Box 316
2400 AH Alphen aan den Rijn
The Netherlands
E-mail: lrs-sales@wolterskluwer.com
Website: www.wolterskluwer.com/en/solutions/kluwerlawinternational

Sold and distributed by:
Wolters Kluwer Legal & Regulatory U.S.
920 Links Avenue
Landisville, PA 17538
United States of America
E-mail: customer.service@wolterskluwer.com

ISBN 978-94-035-3386-5

e-Book: ISBN 978-94-035-3726-9
web-PDF: ISBN 978-94-035-3736-8

This title is available on www.kluwerlawonline.com

Environmental Law in India

The Author

Mohammad Naseem was born and brought up in Sardarnagar, Pilibhit, India. He is a science graduate and has a Master of Laws with a specialization in Mercantile Law from the Aligarh Muslim University, India. He is the former General Manager (Legal) of ONGC Limited, where he joined in 1985. He was also the Vice President in ONGC-Videsh Limited, an overseas arm of ONGC, for seven years. At present, he is the Chairman and Managing Partner of Global Law and Liaison Services, New Delhi. In his professional career spanning over more than three decades, he has dealt with a large number of high-value commercial matters, domestic and international arbitration and litigation. He has been a part of many negotiation teams having successfully negotiated various types of contracts worth billions of dollars including acquisition of petroleum properties in a number of countries. He has travelled extensively throughout the world in relation to negotiations and conducting training programmes. He has spoken in seminars organized by IBC Asia Limited in Singapore, Oil and Gas IQPC, Bangkok, Thailand; Kuala Lumpur, Malaysia; and Tehran, Iran, in a seminar conducted by OIPF, Iran. For conducting negotiations, he has visited different parts of the world, including Myanmar, Vietnam, Iran, Iraq, Syria, Kuwait, Qatar, Egypt, Sudan, Libya, Russia, Turkmanistan, Singapore, Japan, South Korea, Hong Kong, Thailand, UAE, Jordan, Turkey, South Sudan, Italy, Kazakhstan, Denmark, the Netherlands, Switzerland, France, United Kingdom (UK), United States, Canada, Ecuador, Uzbekistan and Venezuela. He is the author of the monograph/book on *Energy Law of India*, *International Energy Law*, *Sports Law of India*, *Environmental Law of India*, *International Environmental Law*, *Medical Law of India*, *International Medical Law*, *Islamic Law of Contracts and Religion and Law in India* of Wolters Kluwer, the Netherlands and has to his credit a number of papers published in national and international journals of repute. He is the coauthor of *Fuel and Energy II (Petroleum and Natural Gas)* of Halsbury's Laws of India Series (Volume 21) published by LexisNexis Butterworths India Limited. Edward Elgar Publishing Limited has published a paper authored by him, by the title 'World Petroleum Regimes' in the Hand Book on International Energy Law and another article on 'Natural Gas Provisions in Host Government Contracts – Regulatory and Contractual Aspects in India' published by Oil, Gas and Energy Law Intelligence, UK. He is visiting faculty and guest expert speaker for the Indian Academy of International Law and Diplomacy, University of Petroleum and Energy, Dehradun and the Indian School of Petroleum, New Delhi.

The Author

With more than thirty years of varied practical and on-the-job legal experience in drafting, negotiation, interpretation and vetting of legal documents and dealing with arbitration and litigation on the one hand and acting as a trainer, speaker and author on the other, M. Naseem has been part of an exclusive team of trainers, negotiators, advisers and strategists and is a legal luminary of international repute in his own right.

Email: naseem_md@yahoo.com.

Coauthor

Ms Saman Naseem holds her post-graduation in Commercial Law from the Aligarh Muslim University, with her graduation from Symbiosis International University and is a founding partner of Global Law and Liaison Services, a firm providing professional advice in the field of law. She is an active participant in seminars and conferences and has presented research papers on various topics. She is the coauthor of monographs on *Energy Law*, *International Energy Law*, *International Environmental Law*, *Environmental Law of India*, *International Medical Law*, *Medical Law of India*, *Sports Law of India*, *Islamic Law of Contracts* and *Religion and Law in* India of Wolters Kluwer, the Netherlands. Edward Elgar Publishing Limited has published an article coauthored by her, by the title, 'World Petroleum Regimes' and another article 'Natural Gas Provisions in Host Government Contracts – Regulatory and Contractual Aspects in India' published by OGEL, UK. She is associated with a non-governmental organization, namely the Madad Foundation and supports various social causes like Leprosy Eradication Drive by the Indian Leprosy Foundation and collection of funds for Help Age India, the poor, the needy and for the blind to name a few.

Email: saman1492@gmail.com.

Coauthor

Table of Contents

Table of Contents

List of Abbreviations

AAQ	Ambient Air Quality
AERB	Atomic Energy Regulatory Board
AIR	All India Reporter
AIS	Automotive Industry Standard
AQI	Air Quality Index
AR	Annual Report
AWBI	Animal Welfare Board of India
BFDAs	Brackish Water Fish Farmers Development Agencies
BIS	Bureau of Indian Standards
BOD	Biological Oxygen Demand
BSI	Botanical Survey of India
CAEPPR	Chemical Accidents (Emergency Planning, Preparedness and Response)
CAF	Compensatory Afforestation Fund
CAMPA	Compensatory Afforestation Fund Management and Planning Authority
CAZRI	Central Arid Zone Research Institute
CBD	Convention on Biological Diversity
CDM	Clean Development Mechanism
CEA	Central Electricity Authority
CECs	Central Empowered Committees
CEPI	Comprehensive Environmental Pollution Index
CETP	Common Effluent Treatment Plant
CFCs	Chlorofluorocarbons
CGWB	Central Ground Water Board
CITES	Convention on International Trade in Endangered Species
CLC	Convention on Civil Liability
CNG	Compressed Natural Gas
CPA	Critically Polluted Areas

List of Abbreviations

CPC	Civil Procedure Code
CPCB	Central Pollution Control Board
CPR	Common Property Resources
CrPC	Criminal Procedure Code
CRZ	Coastal Regulation Zone
CSD	Commission on Sustainable Development
CSE	Centre for Science and Environment
CSIR	Council of Scientific and Industrial Research
CTC	Carbon Tetrachloride
CZA	Central Zoo Authority
CZM	Coastal Zone Management
DAE	Department of Atomic Energy
dB	Decibels
DDA	Delhi Development Authority
DDP	Desert Development Programme
DFE	Directorate of Forest Education
DNA	Deoxyribo Nucleic Acid
DO	Dissolved Oxygen
DoE	Department of the Environment
EAC	Expert Appraisal Committee
EEZ	Exclusive Economic Zone
EF	Exceedance Factor
EIA	Environment Impact Assessment
EMF	Electromagnetic Field
EMP	Environment Management Plan
ENVIS	Environment Information System
EPA	Environment Protection Act
EPR	Extended Producer Responsibility
ESM	Endangered Species Management
ESS	Environmental Surveillance Squad
ESZ	Eco-Sensitive Zone
EV	Electric Vehicles
FAC	Forest Advisory Committee
FAO	Food and Agricultural Organization
FDA	Forest Development Agency
FRA	Forest Conservation Rules
FSI	Forest Survey of India
GDP	Gross Domestic Product
GEAC	Genetic Engineering Approval Committee

GEF	Global Environment Facility
GFFA	Global Forum for Food and Agriculture
GHG	Greenhouse Gases
GIPIP	Good International Petroleum Industry Practice
GMOs	Genetically Modified Organisms
GOI	Government of India
GoM	Gulf of Mannar
GPI	Grossly Polluting Industries
GRP	Green Rating Project
GSP	Global Soil Partnership
HCFCs	Hydrochlorofluorocarbons
HFCs	Hydrofluorocarbons
HRD	Human Resource Development
HSMD	Hazardous Substances Management Division
HTL	High Tide Line
HW	Hazardous Waste
IAEA	International Atomic Energy Agency
ICE	Internal Combustion Engines
ICFRE	Indian Council of Forestry Research and Education
ICG	Indian Coast Guard
ICIMOD	International Centre for Integrated Mountain Development
ICMBAs	Important Coastal and Marine Areas
IIFM	Indian Institute of Forest Management
IIT	Indian Institute of Technology
IPC	Indian Penal Code
IPCC	Intergovernmental Panel on Climate Change
IPIRTI	Indian Plywood Industries Research and Training Institute
IPM	Integrated Pest Management
ISFR	India's State of Forest Report
ISI	Indian Standard Institute
IWDP	Integrated Wasteland Development Programme
IWMP	Integrated Watershed Management Programme
JFM	Joint Forest Management
JFMC	Joint Forest Management Committee
KLIS	Kaleshwaram Lift Irrigation Project
LCA	Life Cycle Assessment
LOI	Letter of Intent

List of Abbreviations

LPG	Liquefied Petroleum Gas
LTL	Low Tide Line
MAB	Man and Biosphere
MAP	Marine Protected Area
MIC	Methyl Isocyanate
ML	Mining Lease
MLP	Multilayered Plastic
MNP	Marine National Park
MoEFCC	Ministry of Environment, Forest and Climate Change
MoP&NG	Ministry of Petroleum and Natural Gas
MOPIP	Modern Oilfield and Petroleum Industry Practices
MoWR	Ministry of Water Resources
MPA	Marine Protected Area
MSIHC	Manufacture, Storage and Import of Hazardous Chemicals
NAAQS	National Ambient Air Quality Standards
NAEB	National Afforestation and Eco-development Board
NBA	National Biodiversity Authority
NBAP	National Biodiversity Action Plan
NCAP	National Clean Air Programme
NCEP	National Committee on Environmental Planning
NCEPC	National Committee on Environmental Planning and Coordination
NCR	National Capital Region
NCT	National Capital Territory
NEAA	National Environment Appellate Authority
NEAMA	National Environment Assessment and Monitoring Authority
NEERI	National Environmental Engineering Research Institute
NEP	National Environment Policy
NFAP	National Forestry Action Programme
NFDB	National Fisheries Development Board
NFP	National Forest Policy
NGO	Non-governmental Organization
NGP	Namami Gange Programme
NGT	National Green Tribunal
NH3	Ammonia
NITI Aayog	National Institution for Transforming India
NLCP	National Lake Conservation Plan
NMCG	National Mission for Clean Ganga

NNRMS	National Natural Resources Management System
NOC	No Objection Certificate
NO_2	Nitrogen Dioxide
NPC	National Productivity Council
NPCA	National Plan for Conservation of Aquatic Eco-systems
NPP	Nuclear Power Plant
NRAA	National Rainfed Area Authority
NRCD	National River Conservation Directorate
NRCP	National River Conservation Plan
NTFP	Non-timber Forest Produce
NWDB	National Wasteland Development Board
NWMP	National Water Quality Monitoring Network
NZP	National Zoological Park
PCB	Pollution Control Board
PCC	Pollution Control Committee
PEL	Petroleum Exploration Licence
PIC	Prior Informed Consent
PIL	Public Interest Litigation
PISFR	Pre-investment Survey of Forest Resources
PM	Particulate Matter
PMKSY	Pradhan Mantri Krishi Sinchayee Yojana
POPs	Persistent Organic Pollutants
PPP	Polluter Pays Principle/Public-Private Partnership
PSC	Production Sharing Contract
RCGM	Review Committee on Genetic Manipulation
RCs	Regional Centres
RD&GR	River Development & Ganga Rejuvenation
RDAC	Recombinant DNA Advisory Committee
RVNL	Rail Vikas Nigam Limited
SAARC	South Asian Association for Regional Cooperation
SAL	Social Action Litigation
SBB	State Biodiversity Board
SBCC	State Biotechnology Coordination Committee
SCC	Supreme Court Cases
SDG	Sustainable Development Goals
SEAC	State Expert Appraisal Committee
SEIAA	State Environment Impact Assessment Authority
SFS	State Forest Services
SPAs	Severely Polluted Areas

List of Abbreviations

SPCB	State Pollution Control Board
SPM	Suspended Particulate Matter
SPS	Sanitary and Phyto-Sanitary Measures
SSI	Small-Scale Industries
ST	Schedule Tribe
STP	Sewage Treatment Plant
SWM	Solid Waste Management
TC	Total Coliform
TDS	Total Dissolved Solids
TOI	*Times of India*
TPN	Thematic Programme Network
TPP	Thermal Power Plants
TTZ	Taj Trapezium Zone
TWG	Technical Working Group
UCIL	Union Carbide India Limited
ULB	Urban Local Body
UN	United Nations
UNCCD	UN Convention to Combat Desertification
UNCED	United Nations Conference on Environment and Development
UNCHE	United Nations Conference on the Human Environment
UNCLOS	United Nations Convention on the Law of the Sea
UNDP	United Nations Development Programme
UNEP	United Nations Environment Programme
UNESCO	United Nations Educational, Scientific and Cultural Organization
UNFCCC	United Nations Framework Convention on Climate Change
UT	Union Territory
WDC	Watershed Development Component
WHO	World Health Organization
WII	Wildlife Institute of India
WMC	Waste Minimization Circles
WQM	Water Quality Monitoring
WRI	World Resources Institute
WWF	World Wide Fund for Nature
ZSI	Zoological Survey of India

Preface

This description of Environmental Laws of India and views expressed herein are in the personal capacity of the author and coauthor and do not represent in any way any organizations with which they are associated in one capacity or other.

Acknowledgements

We would like to thank and express our sincere gratitude to Mrs Rana Naseem and Mr Faraz Naseem who have not only spared the time out of their share but also collected material on Environmental Law, provided typographic help and in all other respects supported for the successful completion of this task.

Acknowledgements

General Introduction

Chapter 1. General Background

§1. Geography and Population

1. India lies in the southern peninsula of the Asian Continent and has a triangular shape tapering southwards to the Indian Ocean. It has an area of approximately 3,287,580 km^2 with the Bay of Bengal to the east, the Indian Ocean to the south and the Arabian Sea to the west. A mountain range, the Himalayas, lies to the north. India may be divided into four main regions, namely, the great mountain zone, the Ganges and Indus Plains, the desert zone and the southern peninsula. Its neighbours are Myanmar and Bangladesh lying in the east; China, Nepal and Bhutan to the north; and Afghanistan and Pakistan to the northwest. Sri Lanka lies to the south, separated from India by the Palk Straits. There are several varied ecological and climatic zones. India has the highest snowbound mountain range of the world, the Himalayas and humid tropical forests on the southwest coast, the fertile Brahmaputra valley, low mangrove swamps of the Sunderbans and the Garo Hills of Meghalaya, which is the wettest spot on the universe, lying to the east.

2. The population of India was 1,403,606,220 as of 31 March 2022, based on Worldometer elaboration of the latest United Nations data. This population is equivalent to 17.7% of the total world population. India ranks second after China in the list of countries (and dependencies) by population. The population density in India is 464 per km^2. Yet, it is still lower than the population density in South Korea (526), Taiwan (669) and the Netherlands (507). The total land area is 2,973,190 km^2. 35.0% of the population is urban (483,098,640 people in 2020). However, the rate of growth has started steadily declining. This massive growth in population eats away the fruits of development, thereby keeping down the growth in per capita income and is considered not only contributing to but also accelerating environmental degradation. Reaching such densities of population presents monumental problems for India on the environmental front. India started its population control programme on a large scale early in the 1950s, but it relies only on publicity and persuasion except for a brief period in 1975–1977 during the emergency. An interesting development has taken place in Haryana, one of the States of India where any person having more than two children is disqualified from standing for the election of Sarpanch (a local body functionary) and this has been upheld by the Supreme Court of India. Bihar, Assam, Himachal Pradesh, Madhya Pradesh, Rajasthan,

Haryana, Andhra Pradesh, Odisha, Chhattisgarh, Gujarat, Maharashtra and Uttarakhand have also at some point implemented the two-child policy for state government employees.

3. Indians belong to diverse ethnic groups, and India presents the most diverse mixture of races. The five major racial types, Australoid, Caucasian, Europoid, Mongoloid and Negroid, find representation among the people of India. Various phases of Indian history show waves of invaders and settlers, including the Aryans, Greeks and Central Asians coming into the country, intermingling religions, settling and merging with the local population. This historical process explains the racial, linguistic, and cultural variety and diversity of India.

4. India is a vast and one of the oldest civilized countries endowed with diverse physical features of the land, ecological and climatic zones, fauna and flora, culture, religions, languages, climate, etc. The land consists of snowbound peaks, beautiful hills, fertile river valleys, lush and green plains, tropical rainforests, blistering deserts and breathtakingly beautiful long coastal areas. India lies entirely in the northern hemisphere, the mainland extending between latitudes 8°4' and 37°6' North and longitudes 68°7' and 97°25' East and measures about 3,214 km from north to south between the extreme latitudes and about 2,933 km from East to West between the extreme longitudes. With a land frontier of 15,200 km and a mainland coastal line of 6,100 km and those of the Lakshadweep group of Islands and Andaman and Nicobar group of islands of about 1,516.5 km, India is rightly called a subcontinent.

5. The Ganga and Yamuna emerge from mountains and flow into the Gangetic plain. These rivers cause constant erosion, thereby building the vast alluvial Gangetic plains. The Brahmaputra river forms the world's largest and most fertile delta, the Brahmaputra valley, before flowing into the Bay of Bengal. A series of low mountain ranges lie between the Deccan Plateau and the Gangetic plain like the Aravallis and Vindhyas. The plateau has the Eastern and Western Ghats flanking its sides. The Western Coastal Plain is uneven, and rivers flowing through it form beautiful lagoons and backwaters. On the western side of India are the Lakshadweep Islands in the Arabian Sea and on the eastern side lie the Andaman and Nicobar Islands in the Bay of Bengal. Because of these islands, India shares its border with Indonesia.

6. India has three major seasons, namely summer, winter and rainy season (monsoon). Summer months are generally hot and humid in most parts of India. Summer is experienced between the months of March to May. Winter months fall between the months of mid-November to early March and are pleasantly cool for most parts of India but severe in the northern plains and the areas around the Himalayan range. India experiences two monsoon spells, the southwest monsoon from June to September and the northwest monsoon from October to early December.

7. There is a wide variety of natural vegetation in India that ranges from the tropical to tundra regions. India can be divided into four major vegetation regions namely: (1) the Himalayan region, (2) the tropical wet evergreen and semievergreen forests, (3) the tropical deciduous forests, and (4) the thorn forests and shrubs.

8. There are over 1,223 species of birds, which include varieties of pheasants, quails and wildfowl, mostly found in the Himalayan region. Storks, cranes, flamingos and kingfishers can also be found in certain regions of the country. The most spectacular and exquisite of all the birds is the peacock, the national bird of India, which is found throughout the country. There are over 500 species of mammals, which include elephants, rhinoceros, bears, lions and tigers just to name a few. A large variety of marine life is found in rivers and seas around it. India's natural resources (agriculture, livestock, forestry and fishery), ignoring minerals, contribute to nearly one-third of its domestic production and provide raw materials for many of its pharmaceuticals, both in western and indigenous herbal-based medicines.

§2. Legal and Political Structure

9. After Independence, India adopted a parliamentary form of democracy. On 26 January 1950, the Constitution of India, drafted by a Constituent Assembly, was enacted which is in force and in practice. It makes India a Union of States with a strong federal centre and declares India a Sovereign, Socialist, Secular and Democratic Republic. The Constitution closely follows the British Parliamentary model with the difference that in India the Constitution is supreme, whereas in England, Parliament is supreme. The laws in existence at the time of promulgation of the Constitution or passed thereafter must conform to the Constitution. In case any law is inconsistent with or derogates from the constitutional provisions, such law shall be void to the extent of such inconsistency or derogation. Indian courts are vested with the authority to adjudicate on the constitutionality of laws. The Constitution guarantees fundamental rights to the citizens, for example, the right to equality, the right to freedom, the right against exploitation, the right to freedom of religion, cultural and educational rights for minorities, etc. These rights are enforceable against the State. The right to enforce fundamental rights and to seek judicial remedies against the State through issuance of writs is also a fundamental right.

10. The Constitution also prescribes fundamental duties such as the duty to respect the Constitution, national flag and national anthem; to develop scientific awareness; to strive towards excellence in all spheres of individual and collective activity so that the nation constantly rises to higher levels of endeavour and achievement, etc. The Directive Principles of State Policy contain principles to be kept in view by the State while framing laws and policies of the State, but these are not binding and enforceable against the State. However, courts have selected certain Directive Principles, which are identifiable with fundamental rights and have treated them as fundamental rights too.

11. The Parliament in Delhi is the central legislative body. It comprises the President and two Houses, namely the Lok Sabha (House of the People) and the Rajya Sabha (Council of States). The President is the Executive Head of the State and the Supreme Commander of the Armed Forces (Article 53 of the Constitution). The President is elected from an Electoral College consisting of: (a) elected members of both Houses of Parliament and (b) the elected members of the Legislative Assemblies of the States (Article 54). The President holds office for a period of five years and can be re-elected for a further period of five years (Articles 56 and 57 of the Constitution).

12. There is a clear-cut demarcation of power between the Centre and States with respect to framing of laws and their implementation. The Constitution contains three lists, namely the Union List, the State List and the Concurrent List. The Union List contains matters on which Central Government has the exclusive right to make laws. The State List includes items over which the State Government has the power to make laws, and the Concurrent List contains items over which both the Centre and States have authority to make laws. The Centre deals with and enacts laws on income tax, defence, foreign policy, railway, postal department, telecommunication, etc. The subjects of police force, education, public health, local taxes, agriculture and industry fall under the State List and are reserved for the State.

13. The country is divided into twenty-eight states[1] and nine centrally administered Union Territories (UT). Each state has an elected legislature headed by a Chief Minister. The Governor is the Head of the State Government, appointed by the President for a term of five years. The Chief Minister, assisted by a cabinet, looks after day-to-day administration of the State Government. The Parliament, State legislatures, local bodies and other legally constituted authorities enact the laws falling within their respective spheres. The States have been divided into districts, districts into subdivisions, and subdivisions into basic units called *taluks* or *tehsils*. Large cities have corporations led by a mayor with authority to make rules on certain local matters.

14. India has a well-developed judicial system. There is a Supreme Court in New Delhi, the capital of India and High Courts in each of the capitals of the States barring few exceptions. There are district courts in every district which function under the administrative control of the respective High Courts. The court procedure is based on the Anglo-Saxon system, which is slow and cumbersome. There is a separation of the judiciary from the executive. Various recognized alternative modes of resolution of commercial disputes are in use, such as sole expert, conciliation and arbitration. Conciliation has been accepted and given legal recognition through enactment of the Arbitration and Conciliation Act of 1996, which is largely based on the Model Law of the United Nations Commission on International Trade Law. It has brought arbitration law in India in conformity with international law on commercial arbitration and international practices.

1. The State of Jammu and Kashmir has been converted into two Union Territories in 2019.

§3. ECONOMIC CHARACTERISTICS

15. India is emerging as the fifth-largest economy in the world and a prominent developing country. It has launched a strategy of planned development since 1950, starting with a mixed economy and subsequently moving towards a market economy. Yet, there is widespread poverty, and the country faces threats to its rich and diverse natural resource environment from vehicular, industrial and other pollution and degradation of land. Starting with the First Five Year Plan in 1951, the plans were implemented up to the Twelfth Plan (2012–2017 partially). In January 2015, the Planning Commission was dissolved, and in its place the National Institution for Transforming India (NITI Aayog) was constituted. The different Five Year Plans have accorded top priorities to different sectors; for example, the First Five Year Plan accorded the highest priority to agriculture, the second to industrialization, the third to self-sustaining growth, etc. These plans were the main tools for planned development of the country up to 2015.

India is reasonably well endowed with a variety of natural resources. The economy is largely self-sufficient in spheres like agricultural produce. The quality and sophistication of Indian skills best illustrate the economic power of the country. A major part of income comes from the export of manpower. The Indian market is widely diversified and sophisticated, with considerable industrialization made possible by its own machine-building industry. India is a large emerging and open market for international trade.

16. India has the know-how and capacity to produce atomic energy from nuclear reactors designed indigenously. Industries like textiles, sugar and cement largely run on machinery made in the country. India has attained such sophistication and degree of skill that it can design and build large steel mills entirely on its own and has designed and put on the market its own supercomputer. Despite all these achievements, parts of the economy have not changed, while others are right at the forefront of technology.

§4. SOCIAL AND CULTURAL CHARACTERISTICS

17. The culture of India is varied and diverse as evident from various forms of art and architecture, music, dance, handicrafts, theatre and cinema. India has eighteen nationally recognized languages and some 844 different dialects. The Sanskrit of the Aryan settlers merged with Dravidian languages to give rise to new unique languages; therefore, most of the Indian languages are Sanskrit based. Notable exceptions are Urdu and Kashmiri, the scripts of which are based on Persian and Arabic but with a basic structure similar to that of Hindi. Tamil has a distinctive Dravidian background. The languages of the northeastern hill tribes find their roots in Chinese and Tibetan. Hindi is the national language, which is spoken by around 44% of the population, while English remains the main language used for commerce and official communication by the Central Government and the majority of State Governments. The main religions practised and followed are Hinduism, Islam, Jainism, Buddhism, Sikhism and Christianity.

18. The history of paintings in India dates back to the frescoes of the Ajanta and Ellora caves and the manuscripts of Buddhist and Jain teachings. Religion has also played an important role in the early Indian paintings. The Muslim period saw the influence of Persian origin, while the Ragini paintings depict the influence of musical modes and Hinduism. The modern art of India is influenced by Europe, and painters like Rabindranath Tagore laid its foundation. Similarly, sculptures of India are famous the world over, for example, the carvings of Khajurao pictured on the rocks.

19. Development of architecture in India can be traced back to the Indus Valley civilization. Hindu temples adorned with beautiful intricate sculptures, evidence of which can be found at the Badami rock-cut caves in Karnataka and the shore temple at Mahabalipuram, are part of important milestones in the development of Indian architecture. Great monuments like the Qutub Minar, Taj Mahal, Agra Fort, Jama Masjid, Humayun's Tomb, Charminar and many more depict the Islamic style of architecture. The British laid the foundation of modern architecture by bringing the western style of architecture to India. This is evident in the style of the Victoria Memorial in Calcutta and to some extent in the President's House (Rashtrapati Bhavan) in Delhi.

20. There are two prominent forms of classical music in India – the Hindustani style of the north and the Carnatic style of the south. Folk music is another very popular form, the roots of which lie in the rural areas of India. There is an ancient tradition of classical dance dating back to 2 BC. Important classical dance forms are Bharat Natyam, Kathakali, Kathak, Manipuri and Odissi. Bharat Natyam is a solo dance usually for temple worship, and its poses are based on the temple sculptures. Kathak, a fast-paced dance originated from North India, is based on the Radha-Krishna dances. Kathakali is a dance drama from Kerala (a State in India) which is performed by artists wearing elaborate masks and makeup. In some regions of India, there is a unique folk or tribal dance form which originates and thrives only in that particular region.

21. Indian fabric weaving and printing are renowned all over the world just as Indian silk, and muslin are prized all over the world. Fabrics range from fine muslin saris, earthy tribal shawls, silks embroidered with gold thread, hand-block-printed cotton, and intricately embroidered mirror work are a few of India's fabled and famous fabrics. Carpets of Kashmir, Agra and Bhadoi are famous all over the world. Similarly, metal-based works from Moradabad, silver-studded handicrafts from Hyderabad, and Gujarati wood carving and ivory works from Kerala are excellent and considered as prized possessions.

§5. Environmental Problems and Concerns

22. India is the world's second-most populous nation after China. Its population has exploded from 300 million in 1947 to 1,403 million. The growing population along with increased pressure on natural resources has put tremendous pressure on the environment. The main environmental problems are deforestation, soil erosion, air and water pollution, land degradation, etc. Industrial pollution is increasing public health risk and also consuming a significant portion of resources for its removal. Around 1.7 million Indians died due to air pollution in 2019, according to a report released on 21 December 2020 by Lancet Planetary Health titled 'The India State-Level Disease Burden Initiative' estimates. As per Report, the indoor, or household, air pollution caused 64% fewer deaths in the last two decades (1990–2019). It was the result of schemes such as the Pradhan Mantri Ujjwala Yojana and the Unnat Chulha Abhiyan which have aided in reducing household air pollution, the benefits of which have resulted in reducing death rate. However, the outdoor air pollution, or ambient air pollution, is not only increasing but also killing more. The death rate from outdoor ambient air pollution has increased during this period by 115%. India has lost 1.4% of GDP due to premature deaths and morbidity from air pollution. It is equivalent to INR 2,60,000 crore in monetary term – more than four times of the allocation for healthcare in the Union budget for 2020–2021. Lung diseases caused by air pollution accounted for the highest share of 36.6% in the total economic losses.

23. The growing population, high degree of mechanization and a steep rise in energy use has led to activities that directly or indirectly affect the sustainability of the environment. Reduction in forest cover has resulted in a reduction of sink for the carbon dioxide and soil degradation, contamination of surface and groundwater and pollution of the air with Suspended Particulate Matter (SPM), Respiratory Particulate Matter, hydrocarbons and acid gases, all of which are causing health problems. There is dumping of poisonous waste on ground. The water resources are polluted due to discharge of untreated or partially treated wastes from industry, domestic sewage and fertilizer or pesticide runoff from agricultural fields into water bodies.

24. Although India is the third most polluting country in terms of the amount of carbon dioxide emitted, but it does not appear in the ranking of the ten most polluting countries per capita. India is making considerable efforts to reduce its greenhouse gas emissions by investing in the development of renewable energies. There is also a need to shift to less energy-intensive modes of transport. This includes measures to improve the transport infrastructure, viz. roads, better design of vehicles, use of Compressed Natural Gas (CNG) and synthetic fuel, etc. Similarly, better urban planning is also necessary which will reduce the demand for energy use in the transport sector. A concerted effort is being made to move away from depletable to inexhaustible resources, viz. solar, wind, biomass energy, etc.

I. Nature and Extent of the Problem

25. The nature and extent of the problem of environmental pollution and conservation could be properly appreciated from the reports of the studies carried out on pollution by some agencies like World Health Organization (WHO).

A. Impact of Pollutants

26. In 2021, none of the cities in India met the prescribed WHO air quality standards of 5 micrograms per cubic meter, stated the World Air Quality Report 2021, prepared by Swiss organization IQAir. Delhi was found to be the most polluted capital in the world for the fourth consecutive year in 2021, and thirty-five of the fifty cities with the worst air quality were in India, according to a new report. The United Nations' Intergovernmental Panel on Climate Change (IPCC), in its periodic reports, has shown how climate change is impacting the world. For instance, monsoons in India have become uncertain; especially in the important kharif-sowing months of July and August 2021, and this has impacted the paddy harvest in several states of India. Again there was low yield of wheat because the weather was hot at the stage of growth of seeds which led to early ripening without full growth of and weight gain by seed.

B. State of India's Environment

27. Frequent unhealthy levels of pollution from sources ranging from vehicular emissions to the burning of coal and wood for cooking, increasing industrial activity, widespread construction activities, dust storms or forest fires affect most of the country. It is often not possible to compare pollution levels of cities from different regions, as northern India is landlocked, pollution build-up in the north is always higher. India's hills and mountains also act as basins that trap toxic air over vast swaths of the country, sometimes making the air too dangerous to breathe. In coastal cities of southern and western India, strong sea breezes lower this concentration. Many of the Particulate Matter (PM) found in the air of metro regions originate in rural areas, which are also badly affected by poor air.

28. Agricultural practices like burning crop stubble are also very widespread in northern India. This smoke then spreads to cities where it mixes with traffic exhaust, factory emissions, and construction dust making a hazardous mix. Contributing to nearly 30% of winter air pollution in Delhi, stubble burning across the nearby states of Punjab, Haryana, and Uttar Pradesh is attributed as one of the major factors for the amplification of air pollution in the region during the winter. Following a similar pattern as the last five-odd years, National Aeronautics and Space Administration recently spotted agricultural fires over the Indian states of Punjab and Haryana through its Visible Infrared Imaging Radiometer Suite satellite imagery.

29. Supreme Court has also taken cognizance of the issue and has given directions with respect to the menace of air pollution and stubble burning. Other than this, there are several other developments which repeat themselves every year around the same time. In fact, since 2016, Supreme Court and the National Green Tribunal (NGT) have been issuing judgments related to stubble burning and even use of firecrackers during Diwali in Delhi. The State Governments have taken actions including smog towers, odd-even policies, lockdown of schools, construction activities, and other day-to-day activities. The State Governments of Punjab and

Haryana have also banned the practice of stubble burning, imposed penalties, and also invoked the section 144 of Cr PC for arresting and putting offenders behind bars as well. There are national and state-level subsidy programmes for providing happy seeders at subsidized prices to farmers and farmer groups so that stubble burning is avoided.

30. India ranked 180th out of 180 countries in the Environment Protection Index, 2022 (EPI) by World Economic Forum. After being so ranked, the Ministry of Environment, Forests and Climate Change (MoEFCC) has proposed changes to the four key laws that govern environmental protection and pollution – the Environment (Protection) Act, 1986, Water (Prevention and Control of Pollution) Act, 1974, and Air (Prevention and Control of Pollution) Act, 1981, and the Public Liability Insurance Act, 1991. The changes, according to the government, are an attempt to 'decriminalize' minor infringements of environmental regulations. But there is fear that such changes will embolden violators to adopt a pollute-and-pay approach (The Hindu, 13 July 2022).

Chapter 2. Basic Principles of Environmental Law

§1. Definitions and Notions

31. The term 'environment' has been defined in different ways. Some of the definitions are as follows.

The declaration of the 1972 United Nations Conference on the Human Environment (UNCHE), Stockholm merely referred obliquely to man's environment, adding that, 'both aspects of man's environment, the natural and the man-made, are essential for his well-being and enjoyment of basic human rights'. The World Commission on Environment and Development relied on an ever more succinct approach; it remarks that, 'the environment is where we all live'. The 1992 Rio Declaration on Environment and Development refers at many points to environmental needs, environmental protection, environmental degradation and so on but nowhere identifies what these include; rather it avoids the term entirely in principle, declaring instead that human beings 'are entitled to a healthy and productive life in harmony with nature'.

The European Commission, while developing an Action Programme on the Environment, defined 'environment' as the combination of elements whose complex interrelationships make up the setting and conditions of life of individuals and of society as they are and as they are felt. The 1988 Convention on the Regulation of Antarctic Mineral Resource Activities defines damage to the Antarctic environment or dependent associated ecosystems as 'any impact on the living or non-living components of that environment or those ecosystems, including harm to atmospheric, marine or terrestrial life'. The Protocol on Environment Protection also adds the intrinsic value of Antarctica, including its wilderness and aesthetic values.

One of the broadest approaches is found in the 1992 Framework Convention on Climatic Change, which defines adverse effects on the environment to include the following:

> Changes in the Physical environment or biota, resulting from Climatic Change which have significant deleterious effects on the composition resilience and productivity of natural and managed eco-systems or on the operations of socio-economic systems or human health and welfare.

32. In this backdrop, the position under Indian law is that the terms 'environmental' and 'pollution' has been defined in different legislation. As per the Environment (Protection) Act of 1986, which contains the most comprehensive definition of 'environment', it includes 'water, air and land and the interrelationship which exists among and between water, air and land, and human beings, other living creatures, plants, micro-organism and property' (section 2a). The term 'environmental pollution' has been defined as 'the presence in the environment of any environmental pollutant' (section 2c). 'Environmental pollutant' means any solid, liquid or gaseous substance present in such concentration as may be, or tend to be injurious to environment (Clause 2b). According to the Air (Prevention and Control of Pollution) Act of 1981, 'air pollution means the presence in the atmosphere of any air pollutant' (section 2b). The term 'air pollutant means any solid, liquid or gaseous substance including noise present in the atmosphere in such concentration as may be or tend to be injurious to human beings or other living creatures or plants or property or environment' (section 2a).

The Water (Prevention and Control of Pollution) Act of 1974 defines the term 'water pollution' as such contamination of water or such alteration of the physical, chemical or biological properties of water or such discharge of any sewage or trade effluent or of any other liquid, gaseous or solid substance into water (whether directly or indirectly) as may, or is likely to, create a nuisance or render such water harmful or injurious to public health or safety, or to domestic, commercial, industrial, agricultural or other legitimate uses, or to the life and health of animals or plants or of aquatic organisms (section 2e).

§2. PROVISIONS IN THE CONSTITUTION

33. The Constitution of India is the fountainhead of all power and authority, and all laws derive their force from it. Part IV of the Constitution contains the Directive Principles of State Policy. Article 47 of this part provides that the State shall regard the raising of the level of nutrition and the standard of living of its people and the improvement of public health as among its primary duties. This general reference was considered as embodying the concept of environment protection until more particular provisions were brought in through amendments to the Constitution. As originally enforced, there was no explicit provision dealing with environmental protection in the Constitution.

34. In 1976, the Constitution (42nd Amendment) Act was passed which *inter alia* inserted Part IV A in the Constitution containing the fundamental duties and Article 48A containing provisions about the environment which read, 'The State shall endeavour to protect and improve the environment and to safeguard the forests and wildlife of the country. The protection and improvement of the natural environment including forests, lakes and wildlife, and to have compassion for living beings was included as fundamental duties of the citizens.' In addition, Article 51A (g) of the Constitution imposes a constitutional obligation and makes it a fundamental duty of every citizen of India 'to protect and improve the natural environment including forests, lakes and wildlife, and to have compassion for living creatures'. Further, Article 51A (h) calls upon Indian citizens 'to develop the scientific temper, humanism and the spirit of inquiry and reform'. The subject of forests and protection of wild animals and birds was moved from State List to Concurrent List so as to provide flexibility for Centre and States legislating on these items.

Article 37 of the Constitution lays down that it is the duty of the State to keep in view and apply directive principles in making the laws. The protection of the natural environment and compassion for living creatures were also made the positive fundamental duty of every citizen. Together, they highlight the importance of the protection and improvement of the environment. In case the environment is disturbed, the court can award damages not only for the restoration of the ecological balance but also for the victim who has suffered due to that disturbance.

35. Through the 73rd constitutional amendment in 1992, Panchayat Bodies (village-level representative bodies) were empowered (Article 243G) by inclusion in the Eleventh Schedule with responsibilities imposed on them for soil conservation, water management, watershed development, social and farm forestry, drinking water, fuel and fodder, non-conventional energy resources and maintenance of the community assets. Similarly for cities, municipalities were authorized to make rules for urban planning, regulation of land use, urban forestry, etc., as given in the Twelfth Schedule of the Constitution.

36. Environmental deterioration could ultimately endanger the life of present and future generations; therefore, the right to life (a fundamental right guaranteed under Article 21) has been interpreted by the courts in a broad and diversified manner in India. It includes, *inter alia*, the right to survive as a species, quality of life, the right to live with dignity and the right to livelihood and has been expressly recognized as a constitutional right. On the procedural side, the High Courts and Supreme Court have allowed individuals and non-governmental organizations (NGOs) to take up the issue of environment under Public Interest Litigation (PIL). The apex court through a series of judgments has laid down and evolved the basic notions of environmental law. In *M.C.Mehta v. Kamal Nath* (AIR 2000 SC 1997), the Supreme Court held that any disturbance of basic environment elements, namely air, water and soil which are necessary for 'life' would be hazardous to life within the meaning of Article 21 of the Constitution according to which 'No person shall be deprived of his life or personal liberty except according to procedure established by law.'

The Supreme Court of India has gone to the extent of asking the universities across the country to introduce environmental awareness courses and make them compulsory at undergraduate level. This direction came through a writ petition filed by M.C. Mehta, an environmental activist in 1991, to create awareness for protecting the environment.

37. Article 253 of the Constitution empowers the Parliament to make laws for the implementation of any treaty, agreement, convention or any decision made in any international conference, association or body. The Air (Prevention and Control of Pollution) Act of 1981 and Water (Prevention and Control of Pollution) Act 1974 were enacted in implementation of the (UNCHE) held at Stockholm in June 1972. Similarly, many other enactments have been brought into force in pursuance of international conventions.

Chapter 3. Historical Background

38. Through the ages, the people of India attach significance and have a special reverence for rivers, mountains, trees, birds, animals, etc., which reflects the general concern for preservation of nature and understanding of its importance.

§1. Ancient Scriptures

I. Vedas

39. The Vedas, the ancient scriptures of India, recommend and ask man to live in harmony with nature. Several items of the Rio Declaration of 1992 are found in Vedas. For instance, the first Rio Principle enunciates that human beings are at the centre of sustainable development in harmony with nature. The Vedas contain 'Maintaining well being in summer, winter, dew time, spring, autumn and rainy season. Grant us happiness in cattle and children. May we enjoy your wassailed protection.'

II. Arthashastra

40. Kautilya's *Arthashastra* (fourth century BC) enjoined the kings to protect forests and wildlife, particularly elephants. The cultural values in favour of protection of the environment were strong enough to give rise to the institution of the sacred groves or *Devara kadu* (literally forests reserved for God), where exploitation of forest produce including wildlife was severely restricted or prohibited. Some of these groves have survived even today. Several ancient hymns in Sanskrit were in praise of nature and specially prayed to God to bless the Earth with regular rainfall and greenery. Indian religions have emphasized non-violence (Ahimsa) and rights of animals to life and compassionate treatment.

§2. Bishnoi Movement

41. This enlightened attitude given in ancient scriptures drew attention towards environmental aspects and sometimes developed in the form of movements for protection of the environment. One such example was found in the Bishnoi Movement of Rajasthan, at least four hundred years ago. The people of this sect worship trees and resist any cutting or destruction. The Bishnoi Movement is believed to have been started by a sage called Sambaji four hundred years ago in Rajasthan and gave rise to emergence of the Bishnoi Sect.

§3. British Period

42. The environment protection in India had an early start and legislative efforts in the field of environment protection date back to the mid-nineteenth century. The

British Government in India took initial legislative steps in controlling pollution. The first legislation to protect the environment, viz., the Shore Nuisance (Bombay and Kolaba) Act was passed in 1853, thereafter came the Oriental Gas Company Act of 1857. The Indian Penal Code (IPC) of 1860 was a more comprehensive legislation containing several provisions for pollution control. Fines and even imprisonment were instituted for 'fouling of water of public springs and reservoirs' or for 'making atmosphere noxious to health' and for negligent conduct with respect to poisonous, combustible and explosive substances. The other notable and pioneering legislations of this period were the Indian Easement Act of 1882, the Bengal Smoke Nuisance Act of 1905, the Bombay Smoke Nuisance Act of 1912 and the Motor Vehicles Act of 1939.

The Motor Vehicles Act empowered State Governments to regulate emissions of smoke from vehicles. The Police Act of 1861 dealt with noise pollution in public places. The Indian Easement Act 1882 protected riparians against 'unreasonable' pollution of water by upstream users. The Indian Fisheries Act of 1887 penalized the killing of fish by poisoning or by explosives.

§4. Post-Independence

I. Piecemeal Approach

43. The initial approach to environment regulation was, however, piecemeal being a continuation of the colonial era. Action against a polluter was taken up by courts only upon complaints by affected people. When the affected people happened to be poor with no resources to approach the courts, the polluters went scot-free. Further, the penalty provided in law was not deterring enough, and legal action took a long time. Environment-related legislation was not accorded priority in implementation, and there were no institutions to prevent an adverse impact on the environment.

II. Development Versus Pollution Control

44. The main agenda of the country after independence was economic development – in agriculture, industry, infrastructure and building institutions to manage and promote development. This was the only way to end economic backwardness, poverty and under or unemployment. Even where environmental protection was concerned, reversing deforestation and soil erosion or land degradation was considered more important than preventing or controlling industrial pollution. The relative neglect of industrial pollution was partly because industrial development had not reached significant levels until the 1960s except in a few pockets here and there, and as such industrial pollution was not widespread and significant except in a few areas. It was also partly because an emphasis on pollution control was seen as conflicting with broader goals of economic development and poverty alleviation.

45. In the post-Independence period, initially, emphasis was on industrialization so that India could be ushered into the modern age that would help it catch up with the rest of the world. Therefore, no significant development took place in the area of pollution control. Some legislations were passed such as the Factories Act of 1948, the Industries Development and Regulation Act of 1951, the River Board Act of 1956, the Atomic Energy Act of 1962, the Insecticides Act of 1968, the Radiation Protection Rules of 1971 which dealt with pollution only incidentally but had no teeth and proved inadequate to control or prevent pollution.

III. The Stockholm Conference 1972

46. The Stockholm Conference of 1972 set a milestone and provided a breakthrough in the field of environment protection. The preparatory committee formed for this Conference became the precursor of the National Committee on Environmental Planning and Coordination (NCEPC) set up in 1972. It had the responsibility of reviewing policies and programmes for environment protection. It also undertook the appraisal of some development projects from the environmental angle and made suggestions for their modification so as to avoid adverse impact on the environment. This development led to a new surge of legislative activity and institution building for environmental monitoring and regulation. The Water (Prevention and Control of Pollution) Act of 1974 was enacted. Under this act, Pollution Control Boards (PCBs) were established for prevention and control of water pollution. A chain of water-testing laboratories was established to check water quality. To meet the expenses of the Boards, the Water Cess Act of 1977 was also brought into force requiring industries to pay a cess on water consumption. A separate Act of Air (Prevention and Control of Pollution) Act of 1981 was enacted. To enable an integrated approach to pollution control, the Water PCBs were authorized to deal with air pollution as well.

IV. The Bhopal Gas Tragedy

47. The Bhopal gas tragedy, which took place after midnight on 3 December 1984, proved to be a turning point and watershed in making environmental policy more stringent. Forty tonnes of highly toxic Methyl Isocyanate (MIC) gas stored in the pesticide plant of Union Carbide, located at Bhopal, leaked into the atmosphere killing around 3,500 people and seriously injuring 200,000, many of them permanently. This led to a spate of legislative activity and tightening up of the environmental law and its implementation. The legislative and judicial activism triggered by the Bhopal tragedy brought greater public awareness and resulted in the development of comprehensive legislation and the evolution of NGOs and individual environmental enthusiasts who continuously take up the cause of the environment on various forums including courts.

48. One of the first major steps taken by the Government after the Bhopal gas tragedy was to reconstitute and upgrade the Department of the Environment (DoE) into a Ministry of Environment and Forests, with greater powers in 1985. Later on, the Ministry was renamed as Ministry of Environment, Forest and Climate Change (MoEFCC). The States also constituted their own Ministries or Departments of Environment. The States had to abide by the standards of pollution treatment laid down by the Centre. However, they could make them more stringent if they wished. Therefore, comprehensive umbrella legislation – the Environment (Protection) Act of 1986 was passed, empowering the Central Government to take all necessary measures to protect the environment. Unlike the earlier acts which were piecemeal, this act covered water, air, land and the interrelationships that exist between them and human beings and other living creatures.

49. The MoEFCC was given powers to exercise the following main functions under this legislation:

(a) coordination of activities of various States and central authorities established under law;
(b) laying down minimum emission/effluent standards;
(c) obtaining information about industrial processes and inspect plant premises;
(d) giving directions for closure, prohibition or regulation of industrial processes;
(e) stoppage or regulation of the supply of water and electricity or any other services to industries violating pollution standards.

50. The MoEFCC exercises these functions through institutions like the Central and/or the State PCBs, with the overall control vested with MoEFCC. Necessary amendments to earlier acts were passed to enhance the powers of the PCBs. The Air Pollution (Amendment) Act of 1988 sought to control noise pollution subsequently full-fledged legislation for dealing with noise pollution was brought in.

51. Since the Bhopal gas tragedy involved handling hazardous substances, there was further tightening up of the law dealing with Hazardous Waste (HW). Rules were framed about handling hazardous substances, and a Public Liability Insurance Act of 1991 was enacted to provide immediate relief to persons affected by accidents occurring while handling such substances. To help early disposal of pollution-related cases, special Environmental Tribunals were also created. Environmental auditing of local municipal bodies was introduced. Statutory bodies and public limited companies were to evaluate the effect of their policies, operations and activities on the environment, particularly with respect to compliance with standards and generation and recycling of wastes. These annual reports (ARs) are helping in identifying and focusing attention on areas of concern and taking appropriate action.

V. Environmental Movements

52. The Bishnoi movement was the first common effort to save trees from being cut, thereafter a number of environmental movements started from time to time, either by individuals or by groups and thereafter by NGOs.

A. Chipko Movement

53. The people of Mandal village started their struggle, named as Chipko movement against deforestation in the Chamoli district of the State of UP in 1973. The movement received the leadership of Gaura Devi, Sunderlal Bahuguna and Chandi Prasad Bhatt.

B. Silent Valley Movement

54. This movement was against the construction of a 75 MW hydroelectric project on the Kuthipuzla (a tributary of the Periyar River) in the dense evergreen forest region of Western Ghats. It is home to many rare species of plants and fauna, which would otherwise have been destroyed by submergence.

C. Narmada Bachao Andolan (Movement)

55. A movement named Narmada Bachao Andolan (Save Narmada Movement) was started for proper rehabilitation of over 100,000 people being evicted for building multipurpose projects worth INR 10 billion over the Narmada River. Baba Amte and Medha Patkar led the movement. Arundhati Roy, the Booker prize winner, has also given support to this movement. The recent decision by the Supreme Court allowing the Gujarat Government to proceed with the construction was a heavy blow for this movement.

D. Baliyapal Movement

56. The Baliyapal Movement was against taking over of the thickly populated Baliyapal village's fertile land for testing of missiles.

57. Environmental concerns are now at the top of the agenda of the country, and the impact of pollution emanating from different sources has emerged as major and significant issues and concerns in policymaking and has also given rise to judicial activism. This concern is highlighted by and is evident from the ongoing debate about effects of pollution on health, environmental damage due to destruction of forests and lakes as a result of setting up of polluting industries, etc.

Chapter 4. The Role of Government Institutions in the Shaping and Administration of Environmental Law and Policy

58. The laws enacted by legislature are administered and implemented by the respective ministries. Some enactment bestows on them power to make rules, institutions and regulations and issue orders. There are also other institutions and bodies created either under some legislation or through executive order and which deal with matters related to the environment.

§1. The Government Institutions and Their Competencies

59. The State Governments and local bodies play a major role in the shaping and administration of environmental law and policy. In one case, the Supreme Court observed that the high concentration of pollution in certain cities, rivers and industrial areas is not due to lack of effort in building a sound environment regime, but rather because of lack of enforcement at local levels.

I. Establishment of the Ministry of Environment, Forests and Climate Change

60. The regulatory framework for pollution control and environmental management started taking shape around 1972, when the NCEPC was set up in the context of the Stockholm Conference. Acting on the recommendations of the Tiwari Committee Report, the DoE was created in 1980 and functions of the Ministry of Science and Technology were transferred to this newly created department. In 1985, the subjects of forests and wildlife were also brought under the Ministry of Environment and a separate ministry, that is, the MoEFCC was created. MoEFCC is the nodal agency in the administrative structure of the Central Government for the planning, promotion, coordination and overseeing the implementation of environmental and forest policies and programmes. The Ministry is the nodal agency for the United Nations Environment Programme (UNEP), South Asia Co-operative Environment Programme (SACEP), International Centre for Integrated Mountain Development (ICIMOD) and for the follow-up of the United Nations Conference on Environment and Development (UNCED). The Ministry is entrusted with the issues relating to multilateral bodies such as the Commission on Sustainable Development (CSD), Global Environment Facility (GEF) and regional bodies like Economic and Social Council for Asia and Pacific (ESCAP) and South Asian Association for Regional Cooperation (SAARC) on matters pertaining to the environment. It has overall administrative responsibilities for pollution monitoring, regulation and control.

61. The MoEFCC has four Divisions which are as follows:

(1) Establishment Divisions.
(2) Environment Divisions.

(3) Forest Divisions.
(4) Wildlife Divisions.

62. There are a number of autonomous agencies of the MoEFCC, some of which are:

- G.B. Pant Institute of Himalayan Environment and Development, Almora.
- Salim Ali Centre for Ornithology & Natural History, Coimbatore.
- Indian Institute of Forest Management, Bhopal (IIFM).
- Indian Plywood Industries Research and Training Institute (IPIRTI), Bangalore.
- Indian Council of Forestry Research and Education, Dehradun (ICFRE).
- Wildlife Institute of India, Dehradun (WII).

There are various other organizations, providing support to the MoEFCC in its functions. These are the Botanical Survey of India (BSI), Zoological Survey of India (ZSI), Indira Gandhi National Forest Academy, Directorate of Forest Education (DFE), National Zoological Park (NZP), National Museum of Natural History and the Forest Survey of India (FSI). These organizations help the ministry in the implementation of the Environment Protection Act (EPA) of 1986, and conduct primary research in areas and matters related to environmental conservation and protection. An NCEPC was set up in February 1972 in the Department of Science and Technology as an apex advisory body in all matters relating to environmental protection and improvement. Later replaced by the National Committee on Environmental Planning (NCEP) in April 1981, based on the recommendations of the Tiwari Committee. The NCEP was authorized to prepare an annual 'state of the environment' report, to arrange public hearings or conferences on significant environmental issues, establish a nationwide environmental information and communication system and propagate environmental awareness through the mass media. There are National Environmental Engineering Research Institutes (NEERI) under the Department of Science and Technology.

II. Central and State PCB

63. The Central Pollution Control Board (CPCB) was constituted by the Central Government and State Pollution Control Board (SPCB) by the State Governments to regulate and promote environmental protection and prevention of pollution under the Air, Water and Environment Acts. In UT, Pollution Control Committees (PCCs) have been constituted. All the States have, along with the SPCB, established departments with regional offices, which undertake pollution control and monitor the environmental protection programmes.

The CPCB at New Delhi is an autonomous national apex body of the ministry, set up in September 1974. It coordinates the activities of the SPCBs and PCCs. It is a nodal agency at the national level for pollution control. The CPCB has powers to take over the functions of the SPCB in specific cases, for example, in the event of inaction despite specific directions. The CPCB, being the authority for implementing policies formulated by the MoEFCC, also has the powers to frame implementation strategies for pollution control, the most important being the development of the minimal national standards. The CPCB, SPCBs and PCCs are responsible for implementing the legislation relating to prevention and control of pollution. It also publishes Rules and Notifications from time to time and advises the Central Government on all the matters concerning the prevention and control of environmental pollution.

64. There are various other authorities constituted under the EPA of 1976. These are the Taj Trapezium Zone (TTZ) Pollution (Prevention and Control) Authority for the Taj Mahal, the Environment Pollution (Prevention and Control) Authority created for the National Capital Region (NCR) of Delhi and the Dahanu Taluka Environment Protection Authority. The Genetic Engineering Approval Committee (GEAC) has been created under the Rules for the Manufacture, Use, Import, Export and Storage of Hazardous Micro-organisms, Genetically Engineered Organisms or Cells of 1989.

III. Functioning of PCBs

65. The Water (Prevention and Control of Pollution) Act of 1974 institutionalized the pollution control machinery by establishing the CPCB and SPCBs which were later on also authorized under the Air (Prevention and Control of Pollution) Act of 1981 to control air pollution. The PCBs achieve their objectives of pollution control and protection of the environment through the following instruments:

(a) consent to establish producing units, No Objection Certificate (NOC);
(b) consent to operate;
(c) setting standards for air and water pollution; and
(d) direct closure, prohibit or restrict the operation or process of industry.

A. *Organizational Structure of SPCBs*

66. SPCB is a statutory body established under the Water (Prevention and Control of Pollution) Act 1974 and Air (Prevention and Control of Pollution) Act, 1981, working under the supervision of the CPCB to implement the environmental laws and rules within the respective state for the protection of the environment. SPCB is comprised of a Chairman, and five members appointed by the State to represent the government. There is also a member secretary appointed with experience in dealing with the matters of environmental laws. Some members are appointed by the government who function as local authorities within the State. Persons representing the interest of fisheries, agriculture, trade and any other interest as the government may seem fit are also made part of the Board. Representatives from companies, corporations which are either controlled, owned or managed by the State are also appointed.

67. The SPCBs suffered from a number of problems like vacant posts, lack of technical staff and quality personnel with only a few legal professionals in the Boards, etc. In *Techi Tagi Tara v. Rajendra Singh Bhandari*,[2] the Supreme Court directed the Executives in all the States to frame appropriate guidelines or recruitment rules within six months, considering the institutional requirements of the SPCBs and the law laid down in the Statutes by the Supreme Court and as per the reports of various committees and authorities and ensure that suitable professionals and experts are appointed to the SPCBs.

B. *Finances of SPCBs*

68. The financial resources of a State Board consist of the following:

(1) Its own resources like consent fee collections, interest on investments, sample testing fees, consultancy receipts, receipts from sale of forms, fines and forfeitures.
(2) External assistance in the form of grants-in-aid from Central and State Governments, project-based grants from CPCB and other grants.

IV. Recombinant DNA Advisory Committee (RDAC)

69. The RDAC is constituted for the purpose of reviewing developments in biotechnology at the national and international levels and to recommend appropriate safety regulations in recombinant research, use and applications. This committee functions within the Department of Biotechnology of the Union Ministry of Science and Technology.

V. Review Committee on Genetic Manipulation (RCGM)

70. The RCGM committee has been constituted by the Department of Biotechnology to monitor the safety-related aspects of ongoing research projects and activities involving genetically engineered organisms/hazardous microorganisms. It also lays down procedures restricting or prohibiting production, sale, import and use of genetically engineered organisms mentioned in the schedule appended to the rules. The Institutional Biosafety Committee is constituted by an occupier or any person including research institutions handling microorganisms/genetically engineered organisms. India is signatory to the Cartagena Protocol on Bio-safety, the first international regulatory framework for safe transfer, handling and use of Living Modified Organisms which was negotiated under the aegis of the Convention on Biological Diversity (CBD). India acceded to this Protocol on 17 January 2003, and it came into force on 11 September 2003.

2. 2017 SCC OnLine SC 1165.

VI. Genetic Engineering Appraisal Committee

71. This committee formerly known as the GEAC had been formed under the Manufacture, Use, Import, Export and Storage of Hazardous Microorganisms /Genetically Engineered Organisms or Cells Rules, 1989. The Committee deals with the approval of activities involving large-scale use of hazardous microorganisms and recombinants in research and industrial production. This is also the agency for approval of proposals relating to release of genetically engineered organisms and products into the environment including field trials (Rule 4.4). The committee is to ensure that research, development and testing of Genetically Modified Organisms (GMOs) prior to environment release are conducted in a safe and scientific manner through appropriate implementation of Rules of 1989 and biosafety guidelines.

Besides, there can be a State Biotechnology Coordination Committee (SBCC) wherever necessary. This committee has powers to inspect, investigate and take punitive action and to review periodically the safety and control measures regarding GMOs and hazardous microorganisms (Rule 4.5). A District Level Biotechnology Committee monitors the safety regulations. The committee or any other person authorized by it may visit the installations and may formulate plans for meeting any emergency. This committee has to submit periodic reports to the SBCC and GEAC.

§2. The Actual Role of the Governmental Institutions

72. Environmental clearance of polluting or degrading development activities is done by the Central and/or the State Government, with the objective of optimal utilization of finite natural resources through use of better technologies and management packages and incorporating suitable remedial measures at the project formulation stage. The Environment Impact Assessment (EIA) Notification issued by the ministry in January 1994 reengineered and notified in the year 2006. Yet again, the Government is working on the revision of the EIA notification of 2006 which has since then been amended several times through notifications in 2014, 2015 and 2016. MoEFCC has published the draft EIA Notification 2020, with the intention of replacing the existing EIA Notification, 2006 under the Environment (Protection) Act, 1986. It classifies projects into A, B1 and B2. Category B2 projects do not require mandatory Environment Clearance (EC), unlike Category A and B1 projects.

73. The EIA Notification includes detailed procedures for obtaining environmental clearance and for public involvement besides setting time schedules. All the projects listed under Schedule A of the EIA Notification are required to obtain environmental clearance from the Central Government. Site-specific projects such as mining, pit head thermal power stations, hydropower, ports and harbours, will also have to obtain separate site clearance from the Central Government as specified in the EIA Notification. Over and above this, the Government of India (GOI) (MoEFCC) notifies certain areas as ecologically sensitive/fragile areas from time to time, and all development projects which are to be located in these notified areas need to obtain environmental clearance from the Central Government.

I. Notifications of Ecologically Sensitive Areas

74. Some of the identified ecologically sensitive/fragile areas notified under the Environment (Protection) Act of 1986 include Doon Valley, Murud-Janjira, Dahanu Taluka, Aravalli Ranges in the Gurgaon district of Haryana and Alwar district of Rajasthan, etc. Further, there are identified and notified coastal areas, forests, wildlife sanctuaries, national parks, wetlands, mangroves, biosphere reserves, hill and mountain areas, etc. There are also critically vulnerable coastal areas like Sunderbans region of West Bengal and other ecologically sensitive areas. The CRZ area of Greater Mumbai, Goa and Kerala including the backwaters and backwater islands are other such areas.

II. Environmental Statement

75. Submission of an Environmental Statement by polluting units seeking consent either under the Water (Prevention and Control of Pollution) Act of 1974 or the Air (Prevention and Control of Pollution) Act of 1981 or both and authorization under the Hazardous and Other Wastes (Management and Transboundary Movement) Rules, 2016 to the concerned SPCBs have been made mandatory. Though, those industries that do not require consent under Water (Prevention and Control of Pollution) Act 1974 and Air (Prevention and Control of Pollution) Act 1981 are now exempted by the amendment done in 2019 to the Rules of 2016[3] from requiring authorization under it, provided that hazardous and other wastes generated by such industries are handed over to the authorized actual users, waste collectors or disposal facilities. The Environmental Statement enables the units to take a comprehensive look at their industrial operations and facilitates understanding of material flows and focuses on the areas where waste reduction and consequently savings in input costs are possible.

III. Environment Information System

76. This system was set up by the MoEFCC in December 1982 and is implemented by its Economic Division. Since inception its focus has been on providing environmental information to decision-makers, policy planners, scientists and engineers, research workers, etc., all over the country. It has been designated as a focal point and Regional Service Centres for South Asia subregional countries by INFOTERRA (a global information system on the environment) of the UNEP in 1985. It also publishes the *Environment and Forests News Digest.*

77. Environmental information System plays a key role not only in formulating environmental management policies but also in the decision-making process aiming at environmental protection and improvement for sustaining good quality of life. Hence, management of the environment is a key component and plays an important

3. Vide Notification G.S.R. XX(E), dated 1 Mar. 2019.

role in effecting a balance between the demands and resources available for keeping the environmental quality at a satisfactory level. So Environment Information System (ENVIS) is a programme with a comprehensive network in environmental information collection, storage, retrieval, and dissemination to varying users, which include decision-makers, researchers, academicians, policy planners, and research scientists, etc. ENVIS is an information network with the subject-specific centres to carry out the mandates and to provide relevant and timely information to all concerned. Further, an association of the various State Governments/UTs was also felt necessary in promoting the ENVIS network to cover a wide range of subjects. The network was expanded with the involvement of thematic subject areas and State Government/UT departments to make it a more comprehensive environmental information network. ENVIS network at present consists of a chain of sixty-three network partners out of which thirty-four are subject specific and twenty-nine on State/UT-related issues. These network partners are called ENVIS Centres and are located in notable organizations/institutions/State/UT Government Departments/ Universities throughout the country. The focal point of ENVIS is located in the Ministry and assists the Environment Information (EI) Division in coordinating the activities of all the ENVIS network partners by making ENVIS a web-enabled information system.

IV. Establishment of Environmental Courts: NGT

78. The Supreme Court of India passed an order in December 2000 advising the Law Commission to consider the need for environmental courts with experts in environmental laws in addition to judicial members in the light of experience in other countries. Acting on this advice, the Law Commission reviewed the whole range of environmental law legislations including its objective, consolidation and codification. The Government brought into force on 18 October 2010 the National Green Tribunal Act, 2010. for establishment of NGT. NGT aims at effective and expeditious disposal of cases relating to environmental protection and conservation of forests and other natural resources including enforcement of any legal right relating to environment and giving relief and compensation for damages to persons and property.

Chapter 5. Sources of Environmental Law

79. The main sources of environmental law in India include the Constitution, legislation, judgments of the apex courts of the country, namely the Supreme Court, High Courts and NGTs being precedents, established industry practices and international conventions and treaties which have either been made part or otherwise ratified and made applicable. Out of all these, the most important source is legislation framed by the legislature from time to time. This includes general law, which only deals with the environment in certain respects, and there are specific laws dealing only with problems and issues of the environment. Since the law so formulated cannot contain technical, practical and procedural details, authority is vested and delegated by the Parliament to the Government to make rules, regulations and to issue orders. In pursuance thereof, a large number of such rules, regulations and orders have been framed, issued and are in force. These enacted laws are supplemented by judgments of the courts through interpretation and construction, which have binding force being precedents as per constitutional provisions.

80. In addition to legislation, there are a number of international treaties and conventions that have been adopted in the field of environmental law. Some international treaties and conventions have been the motivators and the basis of some legislation. For example, the International Convention on Civil Liability (CLC) for Oil Pollution Damages signed at Brussels dated 19 November 1969 and the International Convention for the Prevention of Pollution of the Sea by Oil of 1954 signed in London on 12 May 1954 have been referred to and made applicable for certain purposes in the Merchant Shipping Act of 1970 through an amendment in 1980.

§1. Provisions in the Criminal Procedure Code

81. Sections 133 and 144 of the Criminal Procedure Code (CrPC) prescribe the procedure for handling public nuisance by the executive authority. The District Magistrate or a Subdivisional Magistrate or any other Executive Magistrate on receiving the report of a police officer or other information can initiate action. An order duly made by a Magistrate shall not be questioned in any Civil Court.

§2. Indian Penal Code

82. Chapter XIV of the IPC deals with offences affecting public health, safety, etc. For example, a person is guilty of a public nuisance, who performs any act of commission or is guilty of an illegal omission, which causes any common injury, danger or annoyance to the public or to the people in general who dwell or occupy property in the vicinity or which must necessarily cause injury, obstruction, danger or annoyance to persons who may have occasion to use any public right (section 268 IPC).

§3. Preventive Powers under the Police Act

83. Section 30 of the Police Act of 1861 provides for preventive powers and prescribes that the District Superintendent of Police may set routes for a procession. Music may be regulated on the streets on the occasion of festivals and ceremonies.

The Indian Fisheries Act of 1897 also provides that if any person puts poison, etc., in water in order to catch fish, he shall be punished for two months or with a fine of INR 200. The Indian Ports Act of 1908 restricted the throwing of rubbish, etc.

§4. Enactment, Rules, Regulations and Other Notifications

84. The legislative history in the field of the environment dates back to the eighteenth century. The seeds of legal evolution for preservation of the environment were sown when in 1853 the Shore Nuisance (Bombay and Kolaba) Act of 1853 was enacted. Under this law, the Collector of Bombay was given power to remove nuisance, obstruction, etc., anywhere below the High Water Mark. This was followed by the Oriental Gas Company Act of 1857 (section 15), which provided that whenever the water is fouled by the gas of a company a fine of INR 100 per day shall be imposed while the offence continues. In 1860, the IPC 1860 was enacted (sections 268, 269, 277, 278 and 290). Section 277 of the IPC provides whosoever fouls or corrupts the water of a river or reservoir to make it less fit for the purpose for which the water is ordinarily used may be punished by imprisonment of three months or with a fine of up to INR 500. Section 284 dealing with negligent conduct with respect to poisonous substances prescribes imprisonment for six months or a fine of up to INR 1,000 or both. Next came the Sarai Act of 1867, the Northern India Canal and Drainage Act of 1881 and the Madras Forest (Validation) Act of 1882, which dealt with certain aspects of environment protection.

After independence, the Constitution of India was promulgated which laid down that it is the duty of the State to protect and improve the environment and to safeguard the forests and wildlife. The Constitution also imposes on every citizen a duty to protect and improve the natural environment including forests, lakes, rivers and wildlife. These constitutional provisions are backed by a number of laws, acts, rules, regulations and notifications. In addition to central enactments, there are several State enactments as well dealing with issues such as smoke, noise, pests, land utilization and improvement.

85. A list of enactments, rules, regulations and other notifications is given hereunder which deal with, in one way or other, the question of environmental protection and form the main sources of environmental laws in India.

I. Environment Protection: General

A. *Act*

86.

- The Environment (Protection) Act of 1986, amended 1991 (No. 29 of 1986) (23 May 1986).
- The National Green Tribunal Act, 2010.

B. *Rules*

87.

- Environment (Protection) Amendment Rules, 2022.
- The Environment (Protection) (Fifth Amendment) Rules, 2014 (G.S.R. 612(E)) on 25 August 2014, further amended in 2015 (S.O.3305(E)) (7 December 2015), 2016 (G.S.R. 978(E)) (10 October 2016) and in 2018 (G.S.R. 94(E)) (25 January 2018).
- The Environment (Protection) Fourth Amendment Rules of 2002 (G.S.R. 849(E)) (30 December 2002).
- The Environment (Protection) Third Amendment Rules of 2002 (G.S.R. 489(E)) (9 July 2002).
- The Environment (Protection) Second Amendment Rules of 2002 (Emission Standards for New Generator Sets) (G.S.R. 371(E)) (17 May 2002).
- The Environment (Siting for Industrial Projects) Rules of 1999 (S.O.470(E)) (21 June 1999).
- The Environment (Protection) Second Amendment Rules of 1999 (G.S.R. 682(E)) (5 October 1999).
- The Hazardous and Other Wastes (Management and Transboundary Movement) Rules, 2016 (Amended in 2016, 2018, 2019).
- The Prevention and Control of Pollution (Uniform Consent Procedure) Rules of 1999.
- The Environment (Protection) Rules of 1986 (S.O.844(E)) (19 November 1986).
- The NGT (Manner of Appointment of Judicial and Expert Members and Procedure for Enquiry) Rules, 2010.
- the NGT (Removal of Difficulties) Order, 2010.
- the NGT (Practice and Procedure) Rules, 2011.

C. *Notifications*

1. Coastal Regulation Zone

88.

- S.O.(2060) E – Constitution of Kerala Coastal Zone Management Authority.
- S.O.(936) E – Reconstitution of Odisha Coastal Zone Management Authority.

- S.O.(1054) E – Reconstitution of Maharashtra Coastal Zone Management Authority.
- S.O.(935) E – Reconstitution of Kerala Coastal Zone Management Authority.
- S.O.2264(E) (22 July 2013) – Reconstituting the Goa Coastal Zone Management Authority.
- S.O.2263(E) (9 July 2013) – Reconstituting the Karnataka Coastal Zone Management Authority.
- S.O.2262(E) (9 July 2013) – Reconstituting the Lakshadweep Coastal Zone Management Authority.
- S.O.2261(E) (9 July 2013) – Reconstituting the Daman & Diu Coastal Zone Management Authority.
- S.O.2260(E) (9 July 2013) – Reconstituting the Andhra Pradesh Coastal Zone Management Authority.
- S.O.20(E) (6 January 2011) – Island Protection Zone notification 2011.
- S.O.19(E) (6 January 2011) – Coastal Regulation Zone (CRZ) notification 2011.
- S.O.2507(E) (16 October 2012) – Gujarat Coastal Zone Management Authority.
- S.O.1449(E) (2 July 2012) – Reconstituting the Andaman and Nicobar Coastal Zone Management Authority.
- S.O.1300(E) (6 June 2012) – Constitution of West Bengal Coastal Zone Management Authority.
- S.O.956(E) (1 May 2012) – Puducherry Coastal Zone Management Authority.
- S.O.851(E) (19 April 2012) – National Coastal Zone Management Authority.
- S.O.490(E) (19 March 2012) – Reconstituting the Odisha Coastal Zone Management Authority.
- S.O.383(E) (6 March 2012) – Reconstituting the Maharashtra Coastal Zone Management Authority.
- S.O.91(E) (19 January 2012) – Reconstituting the Tamil Nadu Coastal Zone Management Authority.
- S.O.2843(E) (21 December 2011) – Reconstituting the Kerala Coastal Zone Management Authority.
- S.O.302(E) (8 February 2011) – Reconstituting the National Coastal Zone Management Authority.
- S.O.2058(E) (11 August 2008) – Andaman and Nicobar Coastal Zone Management Authority and Amendment.
- S.O.1759(E) (21 July 2008) – Orissa Coastal Zone Management Authority and Amendment.
- S.O.2057(E) (11 August 2008) – Puducherry Coastal Zone Management Authority and Amendment.
- S.O.1676(E) (9 July 2009) – Andhra Pradesh Coastal Zone Management Authority and Amendment.
- S.O.3250(E) (21 December 2009) – Daman & Diu Coastal Zone Management Authority.
- S.O.821(E) (9 April 2010) – Goa Coastal Zone Management Authority.
- S.O.1675(E) (9 July 2009) – Gujarat Coastal Zone Management Authority.
- S.O.2294(E) (7 September 2009) – Karnataka Coastal Zone Management Authority.
- S.O.1658(E) (21 July 2008) – Kerala Coastal Zone Management Authority.

- S.O.3251(E) (21 December 2009) – Lakshadweep Coastal Zone Management Authority.
- S.O.3011(E) (31 December 2008) – Maharashtra Coastal Zone Management Authority.
- S.O.1760(E) (21 July 2008) – Tamil Nadu Coastal Zone Management Authority.
- S.O.1757(E) (21 July 2008)– West Bengal Coastal Zone Management Authority.
- S.O.16(E) (4 January 2002) – Gujarat State Coastal Zone Management Authority.
- S.O.17(E) (4 January 2002) – Daman and Diu Coastal Zone Management Authority.
- S.O.18(E) (4 January 2002) – Maharashtra State Coastal Zone Management Authority.
- S.O.19(E) (4 January 2002) – Goa State Coastal Zone Management Authority.
- S.O.20(E) (4 January 2002) – Kerala State Coastal Zone Management Authority.
- S.O.21(E) (4 January 2002) – Karnataka State Coastal Zone Management Authority.
- S.O.22(E) (4 January 2002) – Pondicherry Coastal Zone Management Authority.
- S.O.23(E) (4 January 2002) – Tamil Nadu State Coastal Zone Management Authority.
- S.O.24(E) (4 January 2002) – Orissa State Coastal Zone Management Authority.
- S.O.25(E) (4 January 2002) – West Bengal State Coastal Zone Management Authority.
- S.O.26(E) (4 January 2002) – Lakshadweep Coastal Zone Management Authority.
- S.O.27(E) (4 January 2002) – Andhra Pradesh State Coastal Zone Management Authority.
- S.O.28(E) (4 January 2002) – Andaman and Nicobar Coastal Zone Management Authority.
- S.O.17(E) (8 January 2001) – Re-constitution of the National Coastal Zone Management Authority (NCZMA).
- S.O.991(E) (26 November 1998) – Constitution of the National Coastal Zone Management Authority.
- S.O.577(E) (13 July 1999) – Amendments to S.O.991(E) dated (26 November 1998).
- S.O.992(E) (26 November 1998) – Constitution of Andaman and Nicobar Islands Coastal Zone Management Authority.
- S.O.993(E) (26 November 1998) – Constitution of Andhra Pradesh Coastal Zone Management Authority.
- S.O.994(E) (26 November 1998) – Constitution of Tamil Nadu Coastal Zone Management Authority.
- S.O.996(E) (26 November 1998) – Constitution of Pondicherry Coastal Zone Management Authority.
- S.O.997(E) (26 November 1998) – Constitution of West Bengal Coastal Zone Management Authority.
- S.O.998(E) (26 November 1998) – Constitution of Daman and Diu Coastal Zone Management Authority.

- S.O.999(E) (26 November 1998) – Constitution of Gujarat Coastal Zone Management Authority.
- S.O.1000(E) (26 November 1998) – Constitution of Karnataka Coastal Zone Management Authority.
- S.O.1002(E) (26 November 1998) – Constitution of Lakshadweep Islands Coastal Zone Management Authority.
- S.O.1003(E) (26 November 1998) – Constitution of Maharashtra Coastal Zone Management Authority.
- S.O.995(E) (26 November 1998) – Constitution of Goa Coastal Zone Management Authority.
- S.O.518(E) (30 June 1999) – Amendments to S.O.995(E) dated 26 November 1998.
- S.O.1004(E) (26 November 1998) – Constitution of Orissa Coastal Zone Management Authority.
- S.O.399(E) (28 May 1999) – Amendments to S.O.1004(E) dated 26 November 1998.
- S.O.1001(E) (26 November 1998) – Constitution of Kerala Coastal Zone Management Authority.
- S.O.104(E) (12 February 1999) – Amendments to S.O.1001(E) dated 26 November 1998.
- S.O.88(E) (6 February 1997) – Constitution of Aquaculture Authority.
- S.O.623(E) (3 August 1999) – Amendments to S.O.88(E) dated 6 February 1997.
- S.O.80(E) (5 February 1999) – Amendments to S.O.88(E) dated 6 February 1997.
- S.O.99(E) (4 February 1998) – Amendments to S.O.88(E) dated 6 February 1997.
- S.O.774(E) (10 November 1997) – Amendments to S.O.88(E) dated 6 February 1997.
- S.O.493(E) (8 July 1997) – Amendments to S.O.88(E) dated 6 February 1997.
- S.O.421(E) (30 May 1997) – Amendments to S.O.88(E) dated 6 February 1997.
- S.O.173(E) (7 March 1997) – Amendments to S.O.88(E) dated 6 February 1997.
- S.O.19(E) (6 January 2011) – CRZ Notification as amended in 2015.

D. Policy

89. The National Environment Policy (NEP) 2006.

1. Delegation of Powers

90.

- S.O.1219(E) (26 July 2007) – Constitution of the Environment Pollution (Prevention and Control) Authority for the NCR.
- S.O.679(E) (27 April 2007) – Constitution of the Environment Pollution (Prevention and Control) Authority for the NCR.

- S.O.1207(E) (27 July 2006) – Constitution of the Environment Pollution (Prevention and Control) Authority for the NCR.
- S.O.281(E) (18 February 2005) – Delegation of powers to the Chairman, SPCBs as given in the table, to issue directions to any industry or any local or other authority for the violations of the standards and rules relating to biomedical waste, hazardous chemicals, industrial solid waste and municipal solid waste including plastic waste.
- S.O.1211(E) (2 November 2004) – Delegation of powers to the Chairman, SPCBs as given in the table, to issue directions to any industry or any local or other authorities for the violations of the standards and rules relating to notified HWs.
- S.O.727(E), S.O.728(E), S.O.729(E), S.O.730(E) (10 July 2002) – Amendments in the notification S.O.83(E), dated 16 February 1987 and delegation of powers – Delegation of Powers U/S 5 of E (P) Act of 1986 to CPCB.
- S.O.1189(E) (29 November 1999) – Composition of Expert and Monitoring Committees for Haryana and Rajasthan.
- S.O.93(E) (29 January 1998) – Constitution of the Environment Pollution (Prevention and Control) Authority for the NCR.
- S.O.319(E) (10 April 1997) – Delegation of Powers to State Governments for EIA of Thermal Power Projects.
- S.O.38(E) (14 January 1997) – Central Groundwater Board Authority, 1997, amended 2000.
- S.O.479(E) (25 July 1991) – Delegation of Powers to State Governments of Tripura.
- S.O.145(E) (21 February 1991) – Certain orders issued by Central Government.
- S.O.408(E) (6 June 1989) – Delegation of Powers to State Governments of West Bengal and Manipur.
- S.O.881(E) (22 September 1988) – Delegation of Powers to State Governments of Goa and Jammu and Kashmir.
- S.O.488(E) (17 May 1988) – Delegation of Powers to State Governments of Maharashtra.
- S.O.289(E) (14 April 1988) – Delegation of Powers to State Governments of Meghalaya, Punjab and Uttar Pradesh.
- S.O.152(E) (10 February 1988) – Delegation of Powers to State Governments of Andhra Pradesh, Assam, Bihar, Gujarat, Haryana, Himachal Pradesh, Karnataka, Kerala, Madhya Pradesh, Mizoram, Orissa, Rajasthan, Sikkim and Tamil Nadu.
- S.O.83(E) (16 February 1987) – Authorized Officers/Agencies to Enter the Premises for Inspection.
- S.O.727(E) (10 July 2002) – Amendments to S.O.83(E) dated 16 February 1987.
- S.O.84(E) (16 February 1987) – Officers/Agencies Authorized to Take Samples.
- S.O.728(E) (10 July 2002) – Amendments to S.O.84(E) dated 16 February 1987.
- S.O.394(E) (16 April 1987) – Officers Authorized for Taking Cognizance of Offences.

II. Eco-marks Scheme

A. *Notifications*

91.
- G.S.R. 85(E) (20 February 1991) – The Scheme on Labelling of Environment Friendly Products (ECOMARK).
- G.S.R. 768(E) (24 August 1992) – The Criteria for Labelling Cosmetics as Environment Friendly Products.

III. Eco-sensitive Zone

A. *Notifications*

92.
- S.O.2561(E) (22 August 2013) – Declaration of Marine National and Marine Sanctuary Eco-Sensitive Zone in the State of Gujarat, Notification.
- S.O.2930(E) (18 December 2012) – River Bhagirathi from Gaumukh to Uttarkashi as Eco-Sensitive Zone, Notification.
- S.O.2364(E) (4 October 2012) – Bandipur National Park as Eco-Sensitive Zone, Notification.
- S.O.1260(E) (31 May 2012) – Girnar Reserve Forest as Eco-Sensitive Zone, Notification.
- S.O.1259(E) (31 May 2012) – Purna Wildlife Sanctuary as Eco-Sensitive Zone, Notification.
- S.O.1258(E) (31 May 2012) – Vansda National Park as Eco-Sensitive Zone, Notification.
- S.O.1257(E) (31 May 2012) – Narayan Sarovar Wildlife Sanctuary as Eco-Sensitive Zone, Notification.
- S.O.191(E) (27 January 2010) – Sultanpur as Eco-Sensitive Zone, Notification.
- S.O.1545(E) (25 June 2009) – Mount Abu as Eco-Sensitive Zone, Notification.
- S.O.1400(E) (3 June 2009) – Khaparwas Wildlife Sanctuary as Eco-Sensitive Zone, Draft Notification for objections or suggestions.
- S.O.1399(E) (3 June 2009) – Bhindawas Wildlife Sanctuary as Eco-Sensitive Zone, Draft Notification for objections or suggestions.
- S.O.1398(E) (3 June 2009) – Abubshaher Wildlife Sanctuary as Eco-Sensitive Zone, Draft Notification for objections or suggestions.
- S.O.1397(E) (3 June 2009) – Chhilchhila Wildlife Sanctuary as Eco-Sensitive Zone, Draft Notification for objections or suggestions.
- S.O.1396(E) (3 June 2009) – Nahar Wildlife Sanctuary as Eco-Sensitive Zone, Draft Notification for objections or suggestions.
- S.O.1395(E) (3 June 2009) – Bir Shikargarh Wildlife Sanctuary as Eco-Sensitive Zone, Draft Notification for objections or suggestions.
- S.O.1394(E) (3 June 2009) – Khol hi Raitan Wildlife Sanctuary as Eco-Sensitive Zone, Draft Notification for objections or suggestions.

- S.O.1393(E) (3 June 2009) – Kalesar Wildlife Sanctuary as Eco-Sensitive Zone, Draft Notification for objections or suggestions.
- S.O.1392(E) (3 June 2009) – Kalesar National Park as Eco-Sensitive Zone, Draft Notification for objections or suggestions.
- S.O.133(E) (4 February 2003) – Matheran and Surrounding Region as an Eco-Sensitive Zone.
- S.O.52(E) (17 January 2001) – Mahabaleshwar Panchgani Region as an Eco-Sensitive region.
- S.O.825(E) (17 September 1998) – Pachmarhi Region as an Eco-Sensitive Zone.
- S.O.350(E) (13 May 1998) – Order Constituting the TTZ Pollution (Prevention and Control) Authority.
- S.O.884(E) (19 December 1996) – Dahanu Taluka Environment Protection Authority, 1996, amended 2001.
- S.O.481(E) (5 July 1996) – No Development Zone at Numaligarh, East of Kaziranga.
- S.O.319(E) (7 May 1992) – Restricting Certain Activities Causing Environmental Degradation at Aravalli Range.
- S.O.416(E) (20 June 1991) – Dahanu Taluka, District Thane (Maharashtra) to be Declared an Ecologically Fragile Area, amended 1999.
- S.O.102(E) (1 February 1989) – Restricting Location of Industries, Mining & Other Activities in the Doon Valley (UP).
- S.O.20(E) (6 January 1989) – Prohibiting Industries in Murud-Janjira, Raigarh District, Maharashtra.

IV. Environmental Clearance: General

93.

- S.O.60(E) (27 January 1994) – Restrictions & Prohibitions on the Expansion & Modernization of Any Activity or New Projects Unless Environmental Clearance has been Accorded, amended 2001.
- S.O.632(E) (13 June 2002) – Amendments to S.O.60(E) dated 27 January 1994.
- S.O.1148(E) (21 November 2001) – Amendments to S.O.60(E) dated 27 January 1994.
- S.O.648(E) (3 March 2016) – Preparation and presentation of EIA report and Environment Management Plan (EMP).

V. Environmental Labs

94.

- Guidelines for Recognition of Environmental Laboratories Under the Environment (Protection) Act, 1986.
- S.O.728(E) (21 July 1987) – Recognition of Environmental Laboratories and Analysts.
- S.O.97(E) (5 December 1994) – Reorganization of Environmental Laboratories and Analysts.

VI. Public Liability

A. Act

95.

- The Public Liability Insurance Act of 1991 (Act No. 6 of 1991) amended 1992 (No. 6 of 1991) (22 January 1991).
- The Civil Liability for Nuclear Damage Act, 2010.

B. Rules

96.

- The Public Liability Insurance Rules of 1991, amended 1993 (S.O.330(E)) (15 May 1991).
- G.S.R. 768(E) (4 November 2008) – Notification on Public Liability Insurance Act.
- S.O.1878(E) (13 July 2015) – Notification under Public Liability Insurance Act, 1991 – extension of the term of Fund Manager.

C. Notifications

97.

- G.S.R. 253 (27 March 1991) – Date on which the Public Liability Insurance Act of 1991 came into force.
- S.O.282 (19 March 1993) – List of Officers delegated powers by sections 13 and 18 of the PLI Act.
- S.O.779(E) (15 November 1991) – Delegation of powers to the State Governments.
- S.O.780(E) (15 November 1991) – Delegation of powers to the State Governments.
- S.O.227(E) (24 March 1992) – Hazardous substances and quantities to which the PLI is applicable.

VII. Authority and Tribunal

A. Act

98.

- National Green Tribunal Act, 2010, No. 19 of 2010 (Repealing the National Environment Appellate Authority (NEAA) Act of 1997, No. 22 of 1997 (26 March 1997) and the National Environment Tribunal Act of 1995, No. 27 of 1995 (17 June 1995)).

VIII. Water Pollution

A. Act

99.
- The Water (Prevention and Control of Pollution) Act of 1974, and Amendment Acts of 1977, 1978, 1988, 1992 (No. 6 of 1974) (23 March 1974).
- The Water (Prevention and Control of Pollution) Cess Act of 1977, amended in 1991, 1992, 1995 and 2003 (No. 36 of 1977) (7 December 1977).
- The River Boards Act, 1956.
- The Merchant Shipping (Amendment) Act, 1970.

B. Rules

100.
- The CPCB (Qualifications and other Terms and Conditions of Service of Chairman) (Amendment) Rules, 2012 (G.S.R. 860(E)) (30 November 2012).
- The CPCB (Member-Secretary, Terms and Conditions of Service and Recruitment) Rules, 2012 (G.S.R. 840(E)) (22 November 2012).
- The Water (Prevention and Control of Pollution) Cess Rules of 1978 (G.S.R. 378(E)) (24 July 1978).
- The Water (Prevention and Control of Pollution) Rules of 1975 (G.S.R. 58(E)) (27 February 1975) and Amendment Rules of 2011 (G.S.R. 830(E)) (24 November 2011).
- Central Board for the Prevention and Control of Water Pollution (Procedure for Transaction of Business) Rules of 1975 amended 1976.

C. Notifications

101.
- S.O.1621(E) (27 September 2006) – Date on which the Water (Prevention and Control of Pollution) Cess (Amendment) Act, 1974 (6 of 1974) came into force.
- S.O.498(E) (6 May 2003) – Date on which the Water (Prevention and Control of Pollution) Cess (Amendment) Act, 2003 (19 of 2003) came into force.
- S.O.499(E) (6 May 2003) – Rate of Cess notified under the Water (Prevention and Control of Pollution) Cess (Amendment) Act, 1977(36 of 1977).
- S.O.862(E) (26 November 1992) – CPCB constituted the PCC in the UT of Daman, Diu, Dadra & Nagar Haveli.
- S.O.698(E) (3 July 1998) – Amendment to S.O.284(E) dated 19 February 1995.
- S.O.787(E) (10 March 1992) – Delegation of Powers to the Union Territory of Pondicherry.
- S.O.777(E) (19 July 1995) – Amendment to S.O.787 dated 10 March 1992.
- S.O.198(E) (15 March 1991) – Delegation of Powers to the Union Territory of Delhi.

- S.O.199(E) (15 March 1991) – Delegation of Powers to the Union Territory of Chandigarh.
- S.O.842(E) (31 August 1988) – Delegation of Powers to the Union Territory of Lakshadweep.
- No. 8/1/-UTF I (4) – 88/4953 (11 April 1988) – Constitution of Appellate Authorities under the Water Act of 1974 for Chandigarh.
- G.O. Ms. No. 48/88/F6 (5 April 1988) – Constitution of Appellate Authorities under the Water Act of 1974 for Pondicherry.
- No. 1/2(71)/87.Plg. (7 April 1988) – Standards to prevent & control water pollution for small-scale Industries located in the Union Territories.
- S.O.247(E) (8 March 1988) – Delhi Zonal Laboratory of NEERI, Nagpur as a Central Water Laboratory.
- S.O.787(E) (19 November 1991) – CPCB, New Delhi as Central Water Laboratory.

IX. Other Related Enactments

102. Besides, there are certain other legislations which do not directly deal with water pollution but still are relevant while dealing with water pollution, and they are as follows:

- The Easement Act of 1882. This act allows private parties to use groundwater by viewing it as an attachment to the land. It declares that all surface water belongs to the State and is State property.
- Shore Nuisances (Bombay and Kolaba) Act of 1853 (Act No. 11 of 1853).
- The Indian Ports Act of 1908 (Act No. 15 of 1908) (section 6).
- The Inland Vessels Act of 1917 (Act No. 1 of 1917) and Amendment Act, 2007 (No. 35 of 2007) (providing for pollution control in inland waters).
- The Inland Steam Vessels Act of 1917.
- National Waterway (Allahabad-Haldia Stretch of the Ganga – 1982) (Act No. 49 of 1982).
- National Waterway (Kollam – Kottapuram Stretch of West Coast – 1992) (Act No. 25 of 1992).
- National Waterway (Sadia – Dhubri Stretch of the Brahmaputra – 1988) (Act No. 40 of 1988).
- Northern India Ferries Act of 1878 (Act No. 17 of 1978).
- The Inland Waterways Authority of India Act of 1985 (Act No. 82 of 1985).
- The Merchant Shipping (Amendment) Act of 1970, particularly the Merchant Shipping (Amendment) Act of 1983 (Part X B and Part XI A).
- Indian Carriage of Goods by Sea Act of 1925 (Act No. 26 of 1925).
- The River Boards Act of 1956 (Act No. 49 of 1956).
- Betwa River Board Act of 1976 (Act No. 63 of 1976).
- Brahmaputra Board Act of 1980 (Act No. 46 of 1980).
- The Indian Fisheries Act of 1897 (Act No. 4 of 1897).
- Major Port Trusts Act of 1963 (Act No. 38 of 1963).

- Territorial Waters, Continental Shelf, Exclusive Economic Zone (EEZ) Act of 1976 (Act No. 80 of 1976).
- Maritime Zones of India (Regulation of Fishing by Foreign Vessels) Act of 1981 (Act No. 42 of 1981).
- Marine Insurance Act of 1963 (Act No. 11 of 1963).
- Indian Boiler Act of 1923 (Act No. 5 of 1923).
- The Oil Fields (Regulation and Development) Act of 1948.

X. Legislation on Air

A. Act

103.

- The Air (Prevention and Control of Pollution) Act of 1981, amended in 1981, 1982, 1983, 1987 and 1988 (No. 14 of 1981) (29 March 1981).

B. Rules

104.

- The Air (Prevention and Control of Pollution) (Union Territories) Rules of 1983 (G.S.R. 6(E)) (21 December 1983).
- The Air (Prevention and Control of Pollution) Rules of 1982 (G.S.R. 712(E)) (18 November 1982).

C. Notifications

105.

- G.S.R. 714(E) (17 November 2006) – The 2-T Oil (Regulation of Supply and Distribution) Order.
- G.S.R. 489(E) (9 July 2002) – Emission Standards for New Generators.
- G.S.R. 371(E) (17 May 2002) – Emission Standards For New Generators.
- G.S.R. 935(E) (14 October 1998) – Ambient Air Quality (AAQ) Standard for Ammonia (NH3).
- G.S.R. 389(E) (23 September 1994) – CPCB re-established labs in Delhi, Calcutta, Vadodara and Kanpur.
- G.S.R. 384(E) (11 April 1994) – National AAQ Standards.
- S.O.1032(E) (12 December 1989) – Constitution of the Appellate Authority for the Union Territories.
- G.S.R. 429(E) (10 February 1989) – Declaring the UT of Dadra and Nagar Haveli as air pollution control area.
- G.S.R. 382(E) (28 March 1988) – The Date on which the Air Amendment Act of 1987 came into force.
- G.S.R. 71(E) (1 February 1988) – Declaring the UT of Chandigarh as air pollution control area.

- G.S.R. 54(E) (25 January 1998) – Declaring the UT of Pondicherry as air pollution control area.
- G.S.R. 106(E) (20 February 1987) – Declaring the UT of Delhi as air pollution control area.
- G.S.R. 351(E) (15 May 1981) – The date on which the Air Act of 1981 came into force.

XI. Some Other Enactments

106.

- The Factories Act of 1948 (63 of 1948) and Amendment Act of 1987.
- The Motor Vehicles Act of 1938, amended in 1986 and 1988.
- The Industries (Development & Regulations) Act of 1951.
- The Environment (Protection) Third Amendment Rules of 2016 – Emission and Noise Limits of Generator Sets.

XII. Radiation and Vibration (Nuclear and Non-nuclear)

A. Act

107.

- Atomic Energy Act of 1962 (Act No. 33 of 1962).
- The Civil Liability for Nuclear Damage Act, 2010.

B. Rules

108.

- The Atomic Energy (Radiation Protection) Rules, 2004 (G.S.R. 303) (25 August 2004).
- Atomic Energy (Safe Disposal of Radioactive Wastes) Rules, 1987 (G.S.R. 125) (3 February 1987).
- Atomic Energy (Working of the Mines, Minerals and Handling of Prescribed Substances) Rules, 1984 (April 1984).

XIII. Hazardous Chemicals/Waste/Pesticides

A. Rules

109.

- The Batteries (Management and Handling) Rules of 2001 (S.O.432(E)) (16 May 2001) as amended in 2010.
- The Municipal Solid Wastes (Management and Handling) Rules of 2000 (S.O.908(E)) (25 September 2000).

- The Recycled Plastics Manufacture and Usage Rules of 1999 (S.O.705(E)) (2 September 1999) and amendment Rules of 2002.
- Prohibition on the handling of Azodyes (S.O.243(E)) (26 March 1997).
- The Chemical Accidents (Emergency Planning, Preparedness and Response) (CAEPPR) Rules of 1996 (G.S.R. 347(E)) (1 August 1996).
- The Rules of 1989 for the Manufacture, Use, Import, Export and Storage of Hazardous Micro-organisms Genetically Engineered Organisms or Cells (G.S.R. 1037(E)) (5 December 1989).
- The Manufacture, Storage and Import of Hazardous Chemical Rules of 1989 (S.O.966(E)) (27 November 1989) as amended in 1994 and 2000.
- S.O.57(E) (19 January 2000) – The Manufacture, Storage and Import of Hazardous Chemical (Amendment) Rules of 2000.
- The Hazardous and Other Wastes (Management and Transboundary Movement) Rules of 2016 (G.S.R No. 395(E)) (4 April 2016) amended in 2019 (G.S.R. 178(E)) (1 March 2019).
- The Hazardous and Other Wastes (Management and Transboundary Movement) Amendment Rules, 2017 (G.S.R. 177(E)) (28 February 2017).
- The Bio-Medical Waste Management Rules of 2016 (G.S.R. 343(E)) (28 March 2016).

B. *Notifications*

110.
- S.O.843(E) (7 July 2000) – Recognition of the laboratories that are allowed to use pathogenic microorganisms or genetically engineered organisms or cells for the purposes of research.
- S.O.763(E) (14 September 1999) as amended vide S.O.979(E) of 27 August 2003 and S.O.2804(E) of 3 November 2009– Dumping and disposal of fly ash discharged from coal or lignite-based thermal power plants (TPP) on land.

XIV. Other Related Enactments

111.
- The Poisons Act of 1919 (Act No. 12 of 1919).
- The Insecticides Act of 1968 (to be replaced by Draft Pesticides Management Bill, 2017).
- Bhopal Gas Leak Processing of Claims Act of 1985 (Act No. 21 of 1985).
- Inflammable Substances Act of 1952 (Act No. 20 of 1952).
- Destructive Insects and Pests Act of 1914 (Act No. 2 of 1914).
- Drugs and Cosmetics Act of 1940 (Act 23 of 1940).
- Delhi Plastic Bag (Manufacture, Sales and Usage) and Non-Biodegradable Garbage (Control) Act, 2000 (Act No. 6 of 2001) (16 April 2001).
- Delhi Plastic Bag (Manufacture, Sale and Usage) and Non-Biodegradable Garbage (Control) Rules, 2002.

- Narcotic Drugs and Psychotropic Substances Act of 1985 (Act No. 61 of 1985) amended in 2014.
- The Ozone Depleting Substances (Regulation and Control) Rules of 2000 (S.O.670(E)) (19 July 2000) amended in 2014 (S.O.1033(E)) (13 March 2014).

XV. Noise Pollution

A. *Rules*

112.

- The Noise Pollution (Regulation and Control) (Amendment) Rules, 2010 (S.O.50(E)) (11 January 2010).
- The Noise Pollution (Regulation and Control) (Amendment) Rules of 2002 and 2006 (S.O.1088(E)) (11 October 2002) and (10 July 2006), respectively.
- Noise Pollution (Regulation and Control) Rules of 2000 (S.O.123(E)) (14 February 2000).

B. *Notification*

113.

- G.S.R. 176(E) (18 March 2013) – Noise Standards for firecrackers – amendments.
- G.S.R. 742(E) (25 September 2000) – Noise Limits for vehicles at manufacturing stage.

XVI. Legislation on Land Use

114.

- The Urban Land (Ceiling & Regulation) Act of 1976.
- The Model Regional and Town Planning and Development Law of 1985.
- The Industries (Development & Regulations) Act, 1951 and Amendment Act of 2016 (Act No. 27 of 2016).
- The Mines and Minerals (Regulation & Development Act of 1957) (Act No. 67 of 1957) (section 13-m).
- The Mineral Conservation and Development Rules of 2017 (G.S.R. 169(E)) (27 February 2017).
- The Coal Mines (Conservation & Development) Act of 1985.
- Environment (Siting for Industrial Projects) Rules of 1999.
- Provision in State Acts on Town and Country Planning.
- Northern India Canal and Drainage Act of 1873 (Act No. 8 of 1873).
- Damodar Valley Corporation Act of 1948 (Act 14 of 1948).
- The Ancient Monuments and Archaeological Sites and Remains Act of 1958 (Act No. 24 of 1958) and its Amendment and Validation Act of 2010 (Act No 10 of 2010).

- The Ancient Monuments Preservation Act of 1904 (Act No. 7 of 1904).
- Waste Lands Bio Diversity-Related (Claims) Act of 1863 (Act No. 23 of 1863).
- The Biological Diversity Act of 2002.

A. *Notifications*

115.
- The Eco-Sensitive Zone – Mahabaleshwar Panchgani Region 2001.
- The Eco-Sensitive Zone – Pachmarhi, Notification, 1998.
- TTZ Pollution (Prevention and Control) Authority order, 1998 (S.O.350(E)).

XVII. Forest Conservation

A. *Act*

116.
- Forest (Conservation) Act of 1980 (Act Number 69 of 1980) amended in 1988.
- The Indian Forest Act of 1927.
- The Damodar Valley Corporation Act of 1948.
- Criminal Procedure Code 1973 (section 133).
- Livestock Importation Act of 1898 (Act 9 of 1898).
- The Seeds Act of 1966.
- The Scheduled Tribes and Other Traditional Forest Dwellers (Recognition of Forest Rights) Act, 2006.

B. *Rules*

117.
- Forest (Conservation) Rules of 2003 (G.S.R. 23(E)).
- Forest (Conservation) Rules of 1981 amended 1992 (G.S.R. 719).

C. *Policy and Guidelines*

118.
- Guidelines for diversion of forest lands for non-forest purpose under the Forest (Conservation) Act of 1980 (No. 5-5/86-FC) (25 November 1994).
- National Forest Policy of 1988 (No. 3A/86-FP) (7 December 1988).
- The Indian Forest Act of 1927 (Act No. 16 of 1927) (sections 26(1) and 32(F)) and Amendment of 1984 and 2017.

XVIII. Wildlife

A. Act

119.
- The Wildlife (Protection) Act of 1972 (Act No. 53 of 1972), amended in 1983, 1986, 1991, 2002 (Act No. 16 of 2003) and 2006 (Act No. 39 of 2006).
- The Wild Birds and Animals Protection Act of 1912 (Act No. 8 of 1912).
- Elephants' Preservation Act of 1879 (Act No. 6 of 1879).
- Cattle Trespass Act of 1871 (Act 1 of 1871).

B. Rules

120.
- Recognition of Zoo Rules of 2009 (G.S.R. 807(E)) (11 November 2009) and amended in 2013 (G.S.R. 657(E)).
- The Declaration of Wildlife Stock Rules, 2003 (S.O.445(E)) (18 April 2003).
- The Wildlife (Specified Plant Stock Declaration) Central Rules of 1995 (G.S.R. 350(E)) (18 April 1995).
- The Wildlife (Specified Plants – Conditions for Possession by Licensee) Rules of 1995 (G.S.R. 349(E)) (18 April 1995).
- The Wildlife (Protection) Rules of 1995 (G.S.R. 348(E)) (18 April 1995).
- The Wildlife (Protection) Licensing (Additional Matters for Consideration) Rules of 1983 (G.S.R. 328(E)) (13 April 1983).
- The Wildlife (Stock Declaration) Central Rules of 1973 and Amendment of 1995 (G.S.R. 29(E)) (25 January 1973).
- The Wildlife (Transaction and Taxidermy) Rules of 1973 (G.S.R. 198(E)) (9 April 1973).
- The National Tiger Conservation Authority (Normative Standards for Tourism Activities and Project Tiger) Guidelines, 2012.

C. Guidelines and Policy Statements

121.
- National Zoo Policy.
- Guidelines for Appointment of Honorary Wildlife Warden.

D. Notifications, Orders & Circulars

122.
- S.O.665(E) Dated 21 May 2001, section 1(2) of the Wildlife (Protection) Act of 1972.
- S.O.574(E) Dated 11 June 2001, section 61(1) of the Wildlife (Protection) Amendment Act of 1991.

- Notification on Environmental Impact Assessment of Development Projects published *see* S.O.60(E) dated 27 January 1994, amended *see* S.O.356(E) dated 4 May 1994 and 10 April 1997.
- Environmental Delegation order *see* S.O.319(E) dated 10 April 1997.
- Circular No. 2 – 12013/14/98 1A – I dated 22 April 1998.
- Circular No. 2 – 12013/14/98 1A dated 27 October 1998.

XIX. Biodiversity

A. *Act*

123.
- The Biological Diversity Act of 2002 (Act No. 18 of 2003) (5 February 2003)

B. *Rule*

124.
- The Biological Diversity Rules of 2004.

C. *Coastal Zone-Related Notifications*

125.
- Notification No. 19(E) dated 6 January 2011 has been issued in supersession of Notification dated 19 February 1991, S.O.No. 114(E), under section 3(1) and section 3(2) (v) of the Environment (Protection) Act of 1986 and Rule 5(3)(d) of the Environment (Protection) Rules of 1986, declaring coastal stretches as CRZ and managing activities in the CRZ.
- CRZ – Notification dated 21 May 2002.
- Aquaculture Authority – Notification.
- Coastal Zone Management Authority – Notification.

XX. Animal Welfare

A. *Act*

126.
- The Prevention of Cruelty to Animals Act of 1960 (No. 59 of 1960).

B. *Rules*

127.

- The Performing Animals (Registration) Amendment Rules of 2001 (S.O.35(E)) (8 January 2002).
- The Animal Birth Control (Dogs) Rules of 2001 (S.O.1256(E)) (24 December 2001).
- The Performing Animals (Registration) Rules of 2001 (S.O.267(E)) (26 March 2001).
- The Prevention of Cruelty to Animals (Establishment and Regulation of Societies for Prevention of Cruelty to Animals) Rules of 2001 (S.O.271(E)) (26 March 2001).
- The Prevention of Cruelty to Animals (Slaughter House) Rules of 2001 (S.O.270(E)) (26 March 2001).
- The Transport of Animals (Amendment) Rules of 2001 (S.O.269(E)) (26 March 2001) and Amendment of 2009 (S.O.2465(E)) (22 September 2009).
- The Prevention of Cruelty to Animals (Transport of Animals on Foot) Rules of 2001 (S.O.268(E)) (26 March 2001).
- The Breeding of and Experiments on Animals (Control and Supervision) Amendment Rules of 2006 (S.O.1818(E)) (23 October 2006).
- The Breeding of and Experiments on Animals (Control and Supervision) Amendment Rules of 2001 (S.O.134(E)) (15 February 2001).
- The Breeding of and Experiments on Animals (Control and Supervision) Rules of 1998 (S.O.1074) (15 December 1998).
- The Experiments on Animals (Controls and Supervision) (Amendment) Rules of 1998 (S.O.732(E)) (26 August 1998).
- The Prevention of Cruelty (Capture of Animals) Rules of 1972 (S.O.No. 1056) (13 March 1979).
- The Prevention of Cruelty to Animals (Registration of Cattle Premises) Rules of 1978 (No. 14-20/76-LD.I) (30 November 1978).
- The Prevention of Cruelty to Animals (Application of Fines) Rules of 1978 (No. 14-21/76-LD.I) (15 February 1978).
- The Transport of Animals Rules of 1978 amended in 2009 (S.O.2465(E)) (22 September 2009).
- The Performing Animals Rules of 1973 (No. 35-4/72-LD.I) (22 May 1973).
- The Prevention of Cruelty to Animals (Licensing of Farriers) Rules of 1965 (No. 9-18/62-LD) (23 March 1965).
- The Prevention of Cruelty to Draught and Pack Animals Rules of 1965, amended in 1968 (No. 9-18/68-LD) (23 March 1965).

C. Notification

128.

- G.S.R. 619(E) (14 October 1998) – The Prevention of Cruelty to Animals (Restricted to the Exhibition of Animals Trained as Performers).

§5. International Conventions and Agreements

129. India is party to almost thirty-five International Conventions, Treaties and Protocols, some of them are as follows:

(1) Stockholm Declaration of the UN Conference on the Human Environment of 1972.
(2) International CLC for Oil Pollution, signed at Brussels on 19 November 1969 (refer section 352 N (3) of Merchant Shipping (Amendment) Act of 1970).
(3) International Convention for the Prevention of Pollution of the Sea by Oil of 1954 signed in London on 12 May 1954 (refer section 356 B (d) of Merchant Shipping (Amendment) Act of 1970).
(4) The Law of the Sea Convention of 1982, ratified by India in November 1994.
(5) The Montreal Protocol on Substances that Deplete the Ozone Layer adopted on 16 September 1987 (referred in Ozone Depleting Substances (Regulation and Control) Rules of 2000).
(6) Vienna Convention for the Protection of Ozone Layer of 1985.
(7) Framework Convention on Climate Change of 1992 (India has signed and ratified this convention as a non-Annexure 1 country and is therefore not obligated to reduce its emission of greenhouse gases).
(8) The International Tropical Timber Agreement (Geneva, 18 November 1983).
(9) Kyoto Protocol of 1997 on reduction of greenhouse gases.
(10) International Convention for the Regulation of Whaling of 1946.
(11) The Antarctic Treaty of 1959.
(12) The Convention on the Conservation of Antarctic Marine Living Resources of 1980.
(13) The Fund Convention of 1971.
(14) The International Convention for the Prevention of Pollution from Ships of 1973 and 1978 Protocol (MARPOL).
(15) The Ramsar Convention of 1971 (on wetlands).
(16) The Rotterdam Convention, 1998 (this Convention was ratified by India in 2005 and given effect in HWs (Management and Handling) Rules, 1989).
(17) The World Heritage Convention of 1972.
(18) The Convention on International Trade in Endangered Species (CITES) of 1973, Kyoto Modifications (1992) of CITES.
(19) The Convention on Migratory Species of 1979.
(20) Food and Agricultural Organization (FAO) International Undertaking on Plant Genetic Resources of 1983.
(21) The CBD of 1992 (this Convention has been given effect in India by the Biological Diversity Act).
(22) The Convention on Control of Transboundary Movement of HW and Their Disposal (Basel Convention) of 1989.

Part I. Pollution Control

Chapter 1. Introduction

130. The 1984 Bhopal gas tragedy was one of the world's worst industrial gas tragedies. It came as a warning, an eyeopener and turning point in the history of pollution control measures in India. It triggered judicial activism and process of review of existing legislation. For early disposal of cases pertaining to hazardous substances, special Environmental Tribunals were established. Environmental auditing of local municipal bodies was introduced. Statutory bodies and public limited companies were asked to evaluate the effect of their policies, operations and activities on the environment with respect to compliance with standards and generation and recycling of wastes so that areas of concern could be identified and focussed and appropriate remedial measures could be taken. As a result, at present, there is a whole body of general and specific legislation dealing with pollution control and conservation of the environment.

131. The honourable Supreme Court of India, in a case before it aptly remarked with respect to pollution control that, 'By destroying nature, environment, man is committing matricide, having in a way killed Mother Earth. Technological excellence, growth of industries, economical gains has led to depletion of natural resources irreversibly. Indifference to the grave consequences, lack of concern and foresight has contributed in large measures to the alarming position.' In this case, the victim was the flora and fauna in and around Kudremukh National Park, a part of the Western Ghats (West Coast of India). The forests in this area are among eighteen internationally recognized 'hot spots' for biodiversity conservation in the world.

§1. Tackling Pollution

I. Policy Statement on Abatement of Pollution

132. The MoEFCC 1992 Policy Statement on Abatement of Pollution and NEP 2006, which builds on earlier policies, provides instruments for dealing with pollution control and conservation of the environment in the form of stringent regulations, development of environmental standards, fiscal incentives, voluntary agreements, etc. The Policy Statement emphasizes integration of environmental considerations into decision-making at all levels. For achieving these objectives, the following steps have been recommended and initiated:

(a) prevention of pollution at source;
(b) encouragement, development and application of the best available practicable technical solutions;
(c) ensure that the polluter pays for the pollution and control arrangements;
(d) focus protection on heavily polluted areas and river stretches;
(e) involve the public in decision-making; and
(f) spatial environmental planning.

II. Impact Mitigation Measures

133. The best way of impact mitigation is preventing the occurrence of an event which has the potential of causing environmental pollution and devising ways and means so as to avoid and lessen the impact. To achieve this, efforts are made that developmental activities are located in areas outside agricultural lands and free of cyclones, earthquakes, ecologically sensitive areas, erosion, forests, flooding, human settlements, landslides, areas of natural scenic beauty, etc. In case this is not feasible or possible, the next step is selection and use of proper raw materials and clean technologies or processes or alternatives with least impact on the environment. The environment friendly processes or technologies are used which are efficient and produce recyclable wastes or minimum waste(s) that can be easily disposed of.

III. Waste Minimization and Cleaner Production Scheme

134. Industrial pollution can be avoided and controlled through use of waste minimization processes using cleaner technology. The objective of the scheme is to assist small- and medium-scale industries in adoption of cleaner production practices. The National Productivity Council (NPC) coordinates the activities related to establishment and running of Waste Minimization Circles (WMCs) through facilitators designated by it, training and awareness activities by NPC itself as well as through Development Commissioners.

IV. Green Rating Projects

135. The Green Rating Project (GRP) is a programme of the New Delhi-based non-profit Centre for Science and Environment (CSE) and is supported by United Nations Development Programme (UNDP) and the MoEFCC. It does not receive any financial support from any industry. The GRP assesses, and makes public, the environmental performance of companies within a sector. It aims to reduce the impact of industrial activity on the environment in the area of industrial activity. It helped stakeholders to understand environmental risk involved in a better way and enabled them to incorporate it in the process of decision-making and implementation. Now the ratings have become a feature of their balance sheet and ARs. The Green Leaves Award is given by CSE in recognition of the ratings achieved by industries on the basis of their environmental performance in various sectors covered under its GRP.

V. Life Cycle Assessment

136. Life Cycle Assessment (LCA) is a decision *cum* management tool providing information on the environmental effects of various products and processes so that necessary corrective measures can be taken to make the entire process efficient with optimal utilization of resources and minimal waste generation. The LCA studies have been initiated in various sectors, namely: steel, pulp and paper, and thermal power.

VI. Labelling of Environment Friendly Products

137. An environment friendly product is made, used or disposed of in such a fashion that the harm it would otherwise cause to the environment is significantly reduced. A scheme for labelling of environment friendly products such as ECOMARK has been instituted by the Government. It provides accreditation and labelling for household and other products on the basis of environmental criteria along with the quality requirements of the Indian Standard Institute (ISI). This scheme helps consumers to identify products, which are contributing to the protection of the environment. At least eighteen notifications have been issued defining ECOMARK criteria for various products.

VII. Policy Thrust

138. For proper environmental management, reliable information and database, and the mapping of areas are a necessary prerequisite. Under this programme, projects and pilot studies are carried on and have been initiated through various research institutions and organizations. The overall policy thrust has been towards pollution prevention and control through promotion of low waste technology, reuse and recycling, natural resource accounting, development of alternate energy resources, environmental audit, fixing standards and institutional and Human Resource Development (HRD). This is sought to be achieved through regulations, development of environmental standards, consent procedures, control of vehicular pollution, preparation of a zoning atlas for spatial environmental planning including industrial estates, etc.

139. The problem is that there is no independent regulatory body for environmental governance. It is looked after by the MoEFCC. Sometimes, excessive interference by government on the governance of the Ministry leads to poor implementation of environmental law. The MoEFCC had proposed a 'National Environmental Protection Authority' in its discussion paper which would act as a body for 'monitoring, regulation and enforcement' of environmental governance. It is important to have a general legislation for environmental protection.

VIII. Committee of Parties (COP-27)

140. COP-27 ended on 20 November 2022 in Sharamul Sheikh in Egypt reaffirmed commitment to the Paris Agreement of 2015 to ensure that the rise in temperatures does not exceed 2°C, and, as far as possible, stayed within a 1.5°C increase. It calls on countries to accelerate clean energy transitions, phase down 'unabated' coal use, and phase out 'inefficient fuel subsidies.' The Statement also calls for a 'roadmap' to double adaptation finance by 2025 to USD 40 billion. This is the money made available to developing countries and those most vulnerable to climate vagaries to build defences against future climate threats. A major demand from India and other developing countries is for the developed countries to make good on a 2009 commitment to allot USD 100 billion in climate finance every year from 2020. Costs have now increased, and so developed countries must come up with a 'New Collective Quantified Goal' by 2025. A lot of issues including mitigation work programme, the global goal on adaptation, loss and damage and climate finance are being negotiated as they remain contentious. The documents also expressed 'serious concern' that despite all the nationally determined contributions by countries – that lays out steps to curb emissions in the years ahead – net emissions are expected to be only 0.3% below the 2019 levels, which was 'not in line' with the need to keeping global temperature rise within 1.5°C–2°C.

Chapter 2. General Law

§1. Introduction

141. The efforts directed towards pollution control in India date back to the mid-nineteenth century. However, legislation brought from time to time did not comprehensively deal with the problem of pollution. Up to the eighties, the policy towards pollution control and protection of the environment was not proactive but reactive through managing the regulatory process, and the drivers of the policy were not intrinsic but external. For example, the Supreme Court had to intervene to keep the city of Delhi clean and to prescribe norms for regulating traffic. Thus the court had not only to intervene but also was forced to devise ways and means from time to time to deal with the problem of pollution.

§2. Statutory Structure and Legal Regime

142. There is a body of general and specific legislation dealing with the problem of pollution and conservation of the environment. A list of legislation and a brief description are given below.

I. Legislation

143.
- the Environment (Protection) Act of 1986;
- the Environment (Protection) Rules of 1986;
- the Environmental Audit Notification of 1992;
- the Environmental Standard Notification of 1993;
- the Environmental Clearance Notification of 1994;
- the Public Liability Insurance Act of 1991, Rules and Amendment Act of 1992;
- the Prevention and Control of Pollution (Uniform Consent Procedure) Rules of 1999; and
- the NGT Act of 2010.

II. Salient Features of Legislation

144. The salient features of some of the enactments and rules are described hereunder.

A. The Environment (Protection Act) of 1986

1. Umbrella Legislation

145. This act is a general umbrella legislation to control and regulate all types of pollution and provide for the protection and improvement of the environment and for other connected matters. Its scope is very wide, as is evident from definitions given in the act. For example, the definition of 'environment' includes water, air and land and the interrelationship which exists among and between water, air and land, human beings, other living creatures, plants, microorganisms and property. The 'environmental pollutants' have been defined as any solid, liquid or gaseous substance present in such concentration as may be, or tend to be injurious to the environment. The 'handling' has been defined in relation to any substance meaning: *inter alia*, manufacture, processing, treatment, package, storage, transportation, use, collection, destruction, conversion, sale, transfer or the like of such substance.

2. Hazardous Substances

146. The term 'hazardous substances' has been defined as any substance or preparation which, by reason of its chemical or physical-chemical properties or handling, is liable to cause injury to human beings, other living creatures, plant microorganisms and damage to property or the environment.

3. Role of the Central Government

147. The Central Government has been empowered to take all measures, as it deems necessary or expedient, for the purpose of protecting and improving the environment and preventing, controlling and abating environmental pollution. Samples for testing and analysis of air, water, soil or any other substance can be taken from any place, and appropriate action may be initiated if these are found to be unfit.

4. Directions by the Central Government

148. The Central Government has the power to take all those measures which are necessary for protecting and improving the quality of the environment and preventing, controlling and abating environmental pollution (section 3). It lays down the standard of quality of air, water or soil for various purposes and areas. The procedures and safeguards for handling hazardous substances are prescribed; restrictions on the location of industries and carrying on of operations in different areas are also prescribed by the Central Government.

One of the important features of this act is that section 5 gives power to the Central Government to issue directions to any person, officer or authority notwithstanding anything contained in any other law. The person or authority to which the direction is given is bound to comply with such directions. Similar power to issue instructions has been given to the Central Government under the Water (Prevention and Control of Pollution) Act of 1974 and Air (Prevention and Control of Pollution) Act of 1981.

While exercising powers of direction, the Central Government may order closure, prohibition or regulation of any industry, operation or process or may direct the stoppage or regulation of the supply of electricity or water or any other services to such industry. This power has been detailed in and regulated by the Environment (Protection) Rules of 1986. Rule 4 states the following:

- Any direction issued under section 5 of the act shall be in writing.
- The direction shall specify the nature of action to be taken and time within which it shall be complied with.
- The person to whom the direction has been issued shall have the right to file an objection.
- An opportunity to be heard shall be given to the affected party; however, it may be dispensed with if the Central Government is of the opinion that there is a likelihood of grave injury to the environment if action is not taken immediately.

B. The Environment (Protection) Rules of 1986

149. These rules have been framed by the Central Government under sections 6 and 25 of the Environment (Protection) Act of 1986. The rules provide for prohibition and restriction on the location of industries and their regulation, carrying on processes and operations in certain areas and matters to be taken into consideration while prohibiting or restricting any such location (Rule 5). The standards for emission or discharge of environmental pollutants from the industries, operations or processes have been prescribed in the schedules appended with the rules. The Central and SPCB can frame more specific standards for any specified industry, operation or process (Rule 3). Rules also provide for furnishing of information regarding discharge of any environmental pollutant in excess of the prescribed standard.

Any person carrying on an industry, operation or process which requires consent under the Water Act or Air Act or Hazardous Substances Rules of 1989 is required to submit an environment statement within a prescribed period to the concerned SPCB. These rules have been amended several times to accommodate the changing needs of the environment and to regulate the influx of new types of products affecting it.

C. The Public Liability Insurance Act of 1991

1. Immediate Relief

150. This act makes the owner of an industrial undertaking strictly liable for any injury or damage caused because of pollution and provides for immediate relief in respect of death or injury to any person or damage to any property resulting from an accident while handling hazardous substances. The payment made to the victim under the act is only meant for providing immediate relief and does not require establishing the claim on merits. The final compensation is, subsequently paid by the owner, arising out of any legal proceeding in due course.

2. Environment Relief Fund

151. The owner of an industrial undertaking is required to obtain insurance policies for an amount not less than the paid-up capital of such industrial undertaking, before handling hazardous substances so as to cover liability for any mishap. The act prescribes a simple and equitable procedure and empowers the District Collector on application by the victim to make payment, within thirty days of the award. The act enables the Government to create an Environmental Relief Fund (section 7A). It also contains a set of measures in broad terms, which are to be adhered to in handling hazardous substances. The negative aspect is that this act empowers the Government to exempt Central or State Government-owned corporations or local authorities from compulsory insurance required under the act (section 4(3)).

D. The NGT Act of 2010

152. The MoEFCC was directed by the Supreme Court to focus on environmental issues; the coming into force of the NGT Act from 18 October 2010 expressly repeals the two laws via section 38, i.e., the National Environment Tribunal Act 1995, and the NEAA Act, 1997, and, therefore, the closure of the NEAA – a quasi-judicial body empowered to hear appeals against the environmental approvals granted (or not) to projects. All the cases pending before the NEAA were transferred to NGT.

1. Objects Sought to Be Achieved

153. The object clause of the act states that the decisions have been taken at the UNCED held at Rio de Janeiro in June 1992 where India also participated. The conference called upon the States to develop national laws regarding liability and compensation for the victims of pollution and other environmental damages, and India decided to implement the decision of the conference, so far as they relate to protection of the environment and payment of compensation for damages to persons, property and the environment.

2. Procedure of Tribunal

154. This Tribunal is not bound by the procedure laid down under the CPC, 1908, but rather is guided by the principles of natural justice. The establishment of NGT has helped in the dedicated, effective and expeditious disposal of cases arising from accidents and provided relief and compensation for injury to persons, damage to property and the environment. It is mandated to make and endeavour for disposal of applications or appeals within six months of their filing. It has five places of sittings, with New Delhi as the principal place of sitting and the rest at Bhopal, Pune, Kolkata and Chennai.

E. Prevention and Control of Pollution (Uniform Consent Procedure) Rules of 1999

155. These rules have been framed by the Central Government in the exercise of the powers conferred by sections 3, 6, 8 and 25 of the EPA of 1986. The rules require that the industries listed in Schedule VIII have to obtain consent from the SPCB or Pollution Committees. The industries have been categorized as 'white, red', 'orange' and 'green'. The time period of consent accorded depends on this categorization. For consent relating to non-polluting industries such as cottage or small-scale industries, a simplified consent procedure has been prescribed.

§3. Fiscal Incentives to Encourage Prevention and Control of Pollution

156. The Government has offered a number of fiscal incentives to ensure that there is motivation to comply with the environmental standards prescribed under different acts and rules so as to prevent and control pollution. Some major fiscal incentives are described below.

I. Exemption from Income Tax

157. To ensure enthusiastic public involvement, particularly of the corporate sector and private individuals, a donation or contribution given by a taxpayer to any association or institution for programmes on conservation of nature and natural resources are eligible for 50% tax relief under income tax. The institutions and associations for this purpose are approved by the Secretary of the MoEFCC but not for more than three years at a time.

II. Depreciation Allowance

158. A depreciation allowance for Assessment Year 2021–2022 at the rate of 40% is allowed on devices and systems installed by industrial units for minimizing pollution or for conservation of natural resources.

III. Investment Allowance

159. In Jammu and Kashmir, a subsidy on Pollution Control Devices @ 60% of the cost of such devices is available subject to a maximum of INR 50 Lakhs. Green and Environment Protection Initiatives @ 50% is available with upper limits of INR 2 Lakhs to INR 6 Lakhs on the expenditure incurred on the equipment. In case of purchase and installation of Diesel Sets of 10 KW to 2,000 KW, subsidy @100% with a maximum limit of INR 40/45 Lakhs is available (http://jkindustriescom merce.nic.in/ips.html, accessed on 15 September 2022).

IV. Exemption from Tax on Capital Gains

160. This incentive is given to encourage industries to move from congested urban areas. Capital gains arising from the transfer of buildings or lands used for the purpose of business are exempt from tax if these are used for acquiring land or constructing buildings for the purpose of relocation of a business to a new place which is less polluted and crowded.

V. Custom Duty

161. Custom duty is levied at a reduced rate on equipment and spares meant for pollution control, and it is exempted on the import of equipment, machinery and capital goods required for the production of building materials such as bricks, lightweight aggregates, lightweight concrete elements using fly ash and phosphogypsum.

The Central Government has provided indirect fiscal incentives in the form of concessional customs duty (5% ad valorem) on the import of CNG kits and their parts. The Government of the National Capital Territory (NCT) of Delhi has given financial incentives in the form of exemption in sales tax and reduced interest on loans for replacement of old autos and taxis. The pollution level in Delhi and Mumbai in terms of sulphur dioxide (SO_2) and SPM has comparatively decreased, due to use of CNG as auto fuel.

VI. Easy Loans

162. There is provision for giving easy loans carrying concessional rates of interest for upgrading technology and modernization, leading to reduced pollution levels. In Delhi, loans were given to drivers when Phat-phat, an old model small public transport vehicle, was replaced by a more environment friendly vehicle on the direction of the Supreme Court. In other big cities also, schemes are being implemented for phasing out old passenger vehicles.

VII. Goods and Service Tax

163. The Goods and Services Tax on electric vehicles (EVs) has been lowered from 12%–5% and on chargers or charge stations from 18%–5%. Also to make them affordable to consumers, the government will provide additional income tax deduction of INR 1.5 lakh on the interest paid on the loans taken to purchase the EVs.

§4. Enforcement and Control-Environmental Clearance

I. Projects Requiring Clearance

A. *Optimal Utilization of Finite Resources*

164. Environmental clearance of polluting or degrading development activities is performed by the Central and/or the State Government, with the objective of optimal utilization of finite natural resources through use of better technologies and management packages and incorporating suitable remedial measures at the project formulation stage, so as to prevent the pollution at its very beginning and conserve the environment. The process of clearance has been made transparent as status of all pending cases is made available with relevant detail on the MoEFCC website

B. *Notification*

165. The EIA issued by the ministry in January 1994 has been replaced by a new notification in 2006, to simplify the clearance procedure. The Notification categorizes projects in A and B depending on likely pollution generation potential. A fresh EIA Notification 2020 is under process which will replace 2006 Notification.

166. The EIA 2006 as amended requires prior environmental clearance for certain projects before taking any other action. The Category A projects or activities have to obtain clearance from the MoEFCC on the recommendations of the Expert Appraisal Committee (EAC) constituted by the Central Government. The Category B projects and activities are required to take prior clearance from the State Environment Impact Assessment Authority (SEIAA) on the recommendations of State Expert Appraisal Committee (SEAC). These State authorities are constituted by Central Government as per laid down eligibility criteria. In case State authorities have not been constituted for a State, the category B project will be deemed to Category A project requiring central clearance.

C. *Prior Environmental Clearance*

167. The EIA notification requires a predetermined set of projects to obtain prior environmental clearance. The EIA notification schedule states the details of categories of projects or activities which require prior EC. It includes mining and extraction of natural resources and power generation projects, primary processing projects, material production projects, service sector projects, etc. The MoEFCC notifies certain areas as ecologically sensitive/fragile areas from time to time, and all developmental projects proposed to be located in these notified areas or within 10 km of proximity need to obtain prior environmental clearance. Some of the identified ecologically sensitive/fragile areas notified under the Environment (Protection) Act of 1986 include the Doon Valley, the Murud-Janjira, Dahanu Taluka,

Aravalli Ranges in the Gurgoan district of Haryana and the Alwar district of Rajasthan. Further, under the CRZ Notification, forests, wildlife sanctuaries, national parks, wetlands, mangroves, biosphere reserves, hill and mountain areas, etc., have been identified.

168. The EIA notification schedule contains 'specific conditions' for five categories of projects. The condition states that if any individual industry including proposed industrial housing operating or set up within those industrial estates, that have obtained prior environmental clearance, these new set up within those industrial estates do not require separate environmental clearance to operate. The condition is that the industrial estate must comply with the terms and conditions of prior environment clearance. If any proposed project or activity mentioned in the schedule is beyond the manner or limits set in the schedule, it would require prior environmental clearance as per the conditions mentioned in the EIA notification.

169. In the case of Project Director, *Project Implementation Unit v. P.V. Krishnamoorthy* (2020 SCC On Line SC 1005, decided on 8 December 2020), Supreme Court held that it is not necessary for the Central Government or National Highways Authority of India to apply for prior environmental /forest clearances or permissions before issuing notification under section 2(2) declaring the stretch/section to be a national highway or section 3A of the National Highways Act, 1956 to express intention to acquire land for the purpose of building, maintenance, management or operation of a national highway, as the case may be. Environmental/forest clearance is always site specific and, therefore, until the site is identified for national highways through section 3A notification, the question of making any application for permission under the environmental/forest laws would not arise.

D. Projects and Activities Requiring Clearance

170. The main projects and activities falling under Category A and requiring environmental clearance from the Union MoEFCC are as follows:

- nuclear power projects and processing of nuclear fuel – All projects;
- petroleum refineries – All projects;
- chemical fertilizers other than single superphosphate – All projects;
- petrochemical complexes – All projects;
- offshore and onshore exploration for oil and gas and their development and production;
- all projects (Seismic surveys which are part of Exploration Surveys are exempted provided the concession area has got previous clearance for physical surveys);
- synthetic rubber projects located outside the notified industrial area/estate;
- airports – All projects;
- TPP (with certain threshold on capacity, highway projects (national highways, pulp manufacturing and pulp and paper manufacturing industry)).

The following projects and activities are under category B where prior clearance is required from the State Environmental Impact Assessment Authority on the recommendation of SEAC:

- common Effluent Treatment Plants – All projects;
- integrated paint Industry – All projects;
- distilleries – All cane juice/non molasses-based distilleries;
- common Municipal Solid Waste Management (SWM) Facility – All projects;
- highways – All State highways projects and State highway expansion projects in hilly terrain or in ecologically sensitive areas;
- ports, harbours, breakwaters, dredging of 5 million TAP of cargo handling capacity and/or ports/harbours with less than 10,000 TPA of fish handling capacity.

Ministry of Petroleum and Natural Gas (MoP&NG) has issued the Petroleum (Safety in Offshore Operations) Rules, 2008 which require the conduct of operations in a safe manner and to immediately notify the government in case of an accident or release of hydrocarbon or other noxious substances whereby safety of marine environment is likely to be endangered.

II. Procedure for Clearance

171. The industrial licensing mechanism provides that the investor is to obtain a Letter of Intent (LOI) for manufacturing certain specific products. Therefore, the investor is to first approach the Ministry of Industry and obtain an LOI. With the LOI, the investor then approaches Central Government or concerned State Authorities (depending on whether it is Category A or B project) and the forest department of the State concerned if the location involves use of forest land. The SPCB evaluates and assesses the quantity and quality of effluents likely to be generated by the proposed unit as well as the efficacy of the control measures proposed by the investor to meet the prescribed standards. In case the SPCB is satisfied, it issues an NOC or permission, as the case may be, valid for fifteen years. Once an NOC is obtained, the LOI is converted into an industrial licence by the State Authorities themselves, provided that activity or project does not fall under Schedule I of the EIA Notification. If the activity or project is listed under Schedule I, then the investor is required to approach the relevant EIA authorities as required under Categories A and B of the Schedule of the EIA Notification 2006, for obtaining prior environmental clearance.

A. Environment Impact Assessment

172. Prior clearance is required for projects and activities listed in Schedule I. The clearance is given by designated EIA authorities at the central or state level based on prescribed dimensions of the project in the Notification. The activities and projects falling in Category A are dealt with at central level and B at state level. At the central and the state level, EAC provide recommendations for decision-making.

For category B, projects and activities application for prior clearance is scrutinized to assess whether EIA would be required or not. If it is required, then it is termed as B-1 and if not then B-2. For this categorization, MoEFCC issues guidelines from time to time. Public hearing is prescribed for all Category A and Category B1 projects.

B. De-licensed Industries

173. In case of de-licensed industries, all the procedural formalities are completed at the state level itself, except activities listed in Schedule I of the EIA Notification or if the proposed activity is to be located in any of the notified ecologically sensitive/fragile areas. Obtaining the necessary approvals is facilitated by following a set of 'Siting Guidelines' prepared by the MoEFCC. Separate guidelines for projects under various sectors such as river valley, TPP, mining, have been prepared and are available on the site of MoEFCC.

C. Documents Required for Clearance

174. The documents required for taking environmental clearances are as follows:

- prescribed Form with proposed Terms of Reference;
- pre-feasibility Project Report; or Conceptual Plan in case of construction project;
- terms of Reference determined by Environment Authorities;
- EIA Report/EMP;
- risk Analysis/Emergency Preparedness Plan in case of projects involving hazardous substances; and
- rehabilitation plans where the massive displacement of people is anticipated.

D. Environmental Appraisal

175. In an environmental appraisal, the documents submitted by an investor are examined and scrutinized by an EAC or State Level EAC as the case may be. The committee may conduct site visits in specific cases and interact with people affected and environmental groups if felt necessary. The committee also conducts a public hearing so as to ensure public participation in such development matters. After this, the Committee makes its recommendations for approval or rejection of a project. These recommendations are then processed in the MoEFCC for acceptance or rejection, for the purpose of environmental clearance.

For projects requiring both environmental clearance as well as approval under the Forest (Conservation) Act of 1980, proposals are submitted simultaneously to the concerned divisions of the MoEFCC and processing is also carried out simultaneously. The time period set by the MoEFCC for processing, after all the documents and data are received from the proposed investor, is ninety days from the receipt of the requisite documents and data and completion of the public hearing. The decision of the MoEFCC is to be conveyed within thirty days thereafter.

E. Rejection of the Report

176. In case of concealment of factual data or submission of false, misleading data/reports, decisions or recommendations, the project may be rejected and clearance may be denied. Even if approval is granted on the basis of false data, later on when it is detected, approval can be revoked. Misleading and wrong information covers false information, false data, engineered reports, concealing of factual data and false recommendations or decisions.

F. Appeal Against an Order

177. Any person aggrieved by any order granting environmental clearance in an area where industrial activity is restricted under the Environmental Protection Act can file an appeal before the NEAA.

III. Draft EIA Notification 2020

178. The MoEFCC has published the draft EIA Notification 2020, with the intention of replacing the existing EIA Notification, 2006 under the Environment (Protection) Act, 1986. The 2020 draft proposes to reduce the notice period for public hearings from thirty days to twenty days. The MoEFCC has claimed it to be 'in tune with the times', given the growth of internet and mobile telephony. By classifying a number of projects into A, B1 and B2, a host of projects are exempted from public scrutiny. Category B2 projects do not require mandatory Environment Clearance (EC), unlike the Category A and B1 projects. The projects under the exempted category include the following:

i. Offshore and onshore oil, gas and shale exploration.
ii. Hydroelectric projects up to 25 MW.
iii. Irrigation projects between 2,000 and 10,000 hectares of command area.
iv. Small and medium cement plants.
v. Acids other than phosphoric or ammonia, sulphuric acid.
vi. MSMEs in dye and dye intermediates, bulk drugs, synthetic rubbers, medium-sized paint units.
vii. All inland waterway projects and expansion or widening of highways between 25 km and 100 km with defined parameters. These include roads that cut through forests and dredging of major rivers.
viii. Aerial ropeways in ecologically sensitive areas.
ix. Specified building construction and area development projects; built-up area up to 1,50,000 sq. m.

179. Post-clearance compliance implies that once a project gets approved by the concerned authority, the proponent projects are required to adhere to certain rules laid down in the EIA report in order to ensure that no further environmental damages take place. The new draft EIA proposes the submission of compliance reports annually, whereas as per the 2006 notification, the compliance report was to be submitted every six months. Environmental experts are of the view that allowing a longer period for filling the compliance report will give an opportunity to project proponents to hide disastrous consequences, which could go unnoticed. Meanwhile, submission of the compliance report will be solely prepared by the project proponents itself, which, without oversight and review, may lead to inaccurate information submitted on the project. The EIA Notification 2020 excludes reporting of violations and non-compliance by the public. Instead, the government will take cognizance of reports only from the violator-promoter, government authority, Appraisal Committee or Regulatory Authority. The draft, by limiting public consultation, is not in consonance with protecting the rights of tribals, among others. While projects concerning national defence and security are naturally considered strategic, the government gets to decide on the 'strategic' tag for other projects. The 2020 draft says no information on 'such projects shall be placed in the public domain'. This opens a window for clearance for any project deemed strategic without having to explain why.

180. India has been an active participant in the United Nations (UN) Conference on Human, Environment and Development in Stockholm in 1972, the Rio Summit in 1992, the United Nations Framework Convention on Climate Change (UNFCCC) and the Paris Climate Accord which has significantly strengthened its environmental governance. After pledging allegiance to these international environmental instruments and now on the contrary proposing to weaken its EIA regime at the domestic level will weaken India's position as a global leader in environmental governance and climate politics.

§5. Evaluation of Efficiency of Legal Provisions

I. Environmental Monitoring

181. The environmental clearance may contain a set of recommendations and conditions to be complied with on the commissioning of the project. The investor submits a half-yearly compliance report to the MoEFCC after completion of the project. The MoEFCC is helped in post-project monitoring by regional offices. The cases of non-compliance are dealt with by the concerned SPCB that may initiate action against the defaulter. The MoEFCC proposes to establish a National Environment Assessment and Monitoring Authority (NEAMA). The idea of NEAMA was substituted by National Environment Management Authority. Such authority with domain expertise, technological finesse and field outreach may strengthen and professionalize the regimes of EIA and coastal zone management (CZM) under the Environment (Protection) Act 1986. However, as a matter of fact, the restructuring of environmental regulation process by creating a new set of authority as proposed by the Ministry of Environment and Forests may not serve the purpose. The problem is the lack of human, technical, financial resources and inability of SPCB staffs to adapt to the emerging environmental problems. The SPCBs also suffer from the lack of resources, and interference in their work creates hurdle in implementing environmental standards and norms effectively at the grassroots level.

II. Environmental Audits

182. The Environment (Protection) Rules of 1986 require that every person carrying on any industry, operation or process requiring consent under the Water or Air Act or authorization under the HW Rules have to submit an environmental audit report for each financial year to the PCBs. It is a self-regulating measure. Environmental auditing is used for checking whether a company is complying with environmental laws and regulations. It is used as a valuable tool for assessing a company's environmental management systems, policies compliance and equipment.

Chapter 3. Air Pollution

§1. Introduction

183. Air pollution is a serious and widespread problem in urban areas of India where automobile exhaust fumes and industrial areas are the major contributors. The other problem areas are those with a concentration of industries like TPP. The rural areas, which are not in close vicinity to major urban centres and industrial belts, are by and large free from air pollution but now certain parts of the country are facing problem because of stubble burning. Industrialization and urbanization are the two main contributors to the deterioration of air quality. The other sources of air pollution are vehicular emissions, untreated industrial smoke and toxic gases, PM such as fly ash, gases as a result of decay of organic matter. In addition to this, combustion of solid fuels (coal, lignite, wood, etc.) and liquid fuels (from petroleum sources) result in smoke and other harmful gases. Air pollution is a potential health risk and has led to an increase in respiratory and other diseases.

184. According to a report, called 'the Air Quality and Health in Cities', released by US-based Health Effects Institute in August 2022, New Delhi is the most polluted city in the entire world, with West Bengal's Kolkata bagging the second spot. But situation is changing with the intervention of the courts and actions of the government. For public transport, it has been made mandatory to use CNG-fitted buses only. Further expansion of Metro Rail has also brought a healthy change as these are run on electricity.

§2. Statutory Structure and Legal Regime

I. Constitutional Position

185. The Air (Prevention and Control of Pollution) Act of 1981 was brought into force after the UNCHE at Stockholm in 1972, as the Constitution of India empowers the making of law in pursuance of a treaty (Article 253). The Constitution also contains a division of power as to making of laws between the Centre and States through specifying subjects in three entries, namely the Union List containing subjects on which Centre has power to legislate; the State List containing subjects on which State can legislate and the Concurrent List with subjects on which both Centre and State can legislate. There is no specific entry with respect to air pollution. But other topics like public health and sanitation, regulations relating to mines and mineral development are in the State List, whereas motor vehicles find mention in the Concurrent List. The Supreme Court and High Courts have in various judgments held that the right to live in a pollution-free environment is a fundamental right, under Article 21 of the Constitution.

II. Legislation

186. The following legislations deal directly or indirectly with air pollution:

- the Air (Prevention and Control of Pollution) Act of 1981 (14 of 1981), Rules and Amendment Acts of 1981, 1982, 1983, 1987, 1988;
- the Factories Act of 1948 (63 of 1948) and the Amendment Act of 1987;
- the Motor Vehicles Act 1988; Amendment Act, 2019;
- the Indian Boiler Act of 1923; the Indian Boiler Regulations, 1950 as amended in 2017;
- the Industries (Development and Regulations) Act of 1951;
- the Environment (Siting for Industrial Project) Rules of 1999.

III. Salient Features of Legislation

A. The Air (Prevention and Control of Pollution) Act of 1981

187. This act deals with prevention and control of air pollution and prescribes standards for reduction in air pollution including noise pollution. The State Boards prescribe emission standards for industry and automobiles after consulting the Central Board and also take into account AAQ standards. The PCBs have power to close down a defaulting industrial unit, prohibit or restrain any industrial operation or process (section 31A).

The Board may approach courts for the issuance of restraint orders against polluters. The provisions of this act are similar to the Water (Prevention and Control of Pollution) Act of 1974. In order to maintain the AAQ at the desirable level under section 54 of the Air Act of 1981, the CPCB evolves emission regulations for air-polluting industries so as to control air pollution at source.

B. The Factories Act of 1948

188. The Factories Act provides for safety measures, health and welfare of the labour force working in a factory. It is the duty of the occupier to provide a safe environment in the factory premises and to take care of any health hazards. Effective arrangements are required to be made and mandatory to deal with the effluents and wastes (section 2) and render them innocuous. Similarly, accumulation and inhalation of any fumes, which may be injurious, is to be prevented. The threshold limits of exposure to chemical and toxic substances in the factory have also been prescribed under the act. The 'owner'/'occupier' along with the 'factory manager' are responsible for the safety of people living in areas adjacent to the factory and for protection of the environment during manufacture, storage and transportation of hazardous substances. The act identifies the hazardous substances, hazardous processes and permissible levels of certain chemical substances in the work environment. The State Government constitutes a Site Appraisal Committee. The occupier prepares a Site Emergency Plan dealing with disaster control. The occupier also constitutes a Safety Committee comprising representatives of workers and management. The occupier is bound to disclose all relevant information to the general public so that they are aware of the dangers from operations carried on in the factory.

C. Motor Vehicles Act of 1988 and Rules

189. Under this act, the Government specifies or fixes the life of a vehicle and prescribes the emission standards for vehicles. A fine amounting to INR 1,000 can be imposed for breach of prescribed air pollution or noise pollution standards. The rules lay down the general guidelines for exhaust gases and exhaust pipes. The Motor Vehicle (Amendment) Act, 2019 empowers the Central Government to recall old vehicle which may be harmful to the environment (sections 110A and 110B).

D. The Environment (Siting for Industrial Project) Rules of 1999

190. These rules prohibit the setting up of certain industries within the municipal limits of Municipal Corporations, Municipal Councils and Nagar Panchayats (Local City Bodies). These prohibitions also extend to a 25 km belt around the cities with a population of more than 1 million; the periphery of wetlands; around the periphery of national parks, sanctuaries and core zones of biosphere reserves, etc. The industries include hazardous industries like petroleum, chemical fertilizers, distilleries, cement, pesticides, etc.

191. The setting up of new units or expansion and modernization of existing units of industries around the Taj trapezium, i.e., in the 10,400 km^2 (approx.) area between 26°45'N and 77°15'E to 27°45'N and 77°15'E to the west of Taj Mahal and between 27°00'N and 78°30'N and 78°30'E to the East of Taj Mahal, is regulated by specific guidelines laid down by the CPCB and called the 'Inventory and Assessment of Pollution Emission in and around Agra Mathura Region'.

192. Other Archaeological Monuments are also safeguarded by these Rules as along with other rules that apply to them like Forest (Conservation) Act, 1980 and the rules made under it. The rules have Annexures which include and define industries that are covered and areas that are protected under them.

§3. INDUSTRIAL POLLUTION

193. Industrial development was considered as the means for the leap forward in the community of the nations of the world and as a tool for removal of poverty and for overall development of the country. These factors did not initially allow the policymakers to focus on the menace of industrial pollution, so there was neglect and lack of concern with respect to industrial pollution.

I. Bhopal Gas Tragedy

194. In the night of 23 December 1984, when the people of Bhopal city in the State of Madhya Pradesh were fast asleep, MIC leaked from a plant owned and operated by Union Carbide India Limited (UCIL). This plant manufactured the pesticides Sevin and Temik. MIC, a highly toxic gas, is an ingredient in the manufacture of these pesticides. UCIL was incorporated in India with 5.99% of its stock ownership held by the Union Carbide Corporation, a New York corporation. It led to a number of claims being filed in courts in New York as well as in India. The New York court dismissed the motion on the ground of forum non conveniens. The Government enacted the Bhopal Gas Leak Disaster (Processing of Claims) Act of 1985, which was upheld by the Supreme Court as constitutionally valid (*Charan Lal Sahu v. Union of India* AIR 1990 SC 1480). However, many cases related to this tragedy decided in June 2010 resulted in light punishment on technical grounds.

II. Industrial Pollution Abatement Through Preventive Strategies

195. The approach and action plan of abatement through preventive strategies is an amalgamation of a three-pronged approach, viz. Improve Audit Process, Revise Standard and Practices, Incentivize Law Enforcement, which have been laid down in the Action Plan for Combating Air Pollution in the Draft Paper of NITI Aayog named Breath India so as to revamp the regulatory framework around industrial air pollution.

III. Pollution Control in Highly Polluting Industries

196. In 2009, the CPCB classified industrial areas based on CEPI scores to prioritize for improving the environmental quality. CEPI is a rational number which ranges between 0–100. It captures overall quality of the environment covering air, water and land by following algorithm of pollution sources, pathways and receptors, is calculated using a formula (**CEPI = i_{max} + [(100 – i_{max}) × (i_2/100) × (i_3/100)]**

Where, i_{max} = maximum index (which may be Air EPI or Surface Water EPI or Groundwater EPI); and, i_2 and i_3 are indices for other media). Based on CEPI scores, Industrial Areas are classified in the following manner:

S. No.	*CEPI Scores*	*Categorization of Industrial Areas*
1	70 and above	Critically Polluted Areas (CPAs)
2	Between 60–70	Severely Polluted Areas (SPAs)
3	Less than 60	Other Polluted Areas (OPAs)

197. To assess the environmental quality in the Polluted Industrial Areas, monitoring is carried out by CPCB through recognized environmental laboratory periodically and CEPI is assessed based on the recorded monitoring data. The evaluated

CEPI reflects the environmental quality of the industrial areas and also serves as a yardstick to assess the progress achieved in the implementation of action plans.

198. CPCB in consultation with the MoEF&CC evaluated CEPI scores of eighty-eight industrial clusters across the country in 2009, and forty-three industrial clusters in seventeen states were identified as Critically Polluted Areas (CPAs). SPCBs/PCCs prepared and implemented time-bound action plans for improvement of environmental quality in CPAs. CPCB continued CEPI monitoring of forty-three CPAs during 2011 and 2013, also. In 2016 CEPI methodology was revised.

199. In CEPI evaluation during 2018, following the revised CEPI-2016 methodology, 100 Industrial Areas were monitored. Out of identified 88 prominent industrial clusters, 43 industrial clusters in 17 States having CEPI score of 70 and above were identified as CPAs. Further, 32 industrial clusters with CEPI scores between 60 and below 70 are categorized as Severely Polluted Areas (SPAs). The effective implementation of action plans prepared by SPCBs/PCCs for CPAs/SPAs is carried out by concerned stakeholders, and district/state level committees are constituted to review the progress of implementation of action plans (source: CPCB, Delhi).

200. CPCB has revised CEPI concept in concurrence with MoEFCC and subsequently issued directions on 26 April 2016 to all SPCBs/PCCs having CPAs for adoption of the revised CEPI concept, which includes: Environmental quality monitoring in all the CPAs, Installation of Continuous Ambient Air and water Quality Monitoring Stations, Application of Revised CEPI Version and Action Plan and Monitoring:

State	*Number of Industrial Clusters Identified as Critically/ Severely Polluted*	*Critically Polluted Air Quality CEPI 2018 (Air) Score >=60*	*Severally Polluted Air Quality CEPI 2018 (Air) Score: Between 50 and 60*
Uttar Pradesh	13	Mathura, Bulandshahr-Khurja, Ferozabad, Moradabad, Gajraula, Varanasi-Mirzapur, Kanpur, Agra	Noida, Ghaziabad, Aligarh, Meerut, Haridwar
Gujarat	8	Vadodara, Ankleshwar, Vapi, Bhavnagar	Vatva, Ahmedabad, Rajkot, Morbi

State	*Number of Industrial Clusters Identified as Critically/ Severely Polluted*	*Critically Polluted Air Quality CEPI 2018 (Air) Score >=60*	*Severally Polluted Air Quality CEPI 2018 (Air) Score: Between 50 and 60*
Maharashtra	7	Chandrapur, Tarapur, Dombivalli, Nashik, Navi-Mumbai, Chembur, Pimpri-Chinchwad	-
Rajasthan	5	Jodhpur, Bhiwadi, Pali, Sanganer Industrial Area, Jaipur	-
West Bengal	4	Howrah, Durgapur	Bandel, Asansol
Haryana	3	Gurugram, Panipat	Faridabad
Jharkhand	5	Hazaribagh	Saraikela, Ramgarh, Singhbum-Wet, Bada Jamtara

201. CPCB was also directed to undertake environmental quality monitoring in the CPAs through a third-party agency (laboratory) recognized under Environment (Protection) Act, 1986. The environmental quality data including CEPI score of the industrial area, as per revised concept, is to be placed in public domain by the concerned SPCBs/PCCs through website and published by the State Government periodically.

202. In March 2022, researchers at CSE analysed the 2018 Comprehensive Environmental Pollution Index (CEPI) air assessment score that depicts the air quality in industrial regions. As per the analysis of CSE, Uttar Pradesh and Maharashtra had the greatest number of 'critically polluted' industrial regions in India. CSE researchers found that as many as thirteen industrial areas in UP, seven in Maharashtra, eight in Gujarat and five in Rajasthan were still critically / severely polluted with respect to the 2009 air quality levels in these regions. Mathura, Bulandshahr, Firozabad, Moradabad in Uttar Pradesh; Chandrapur and Tarapur in Maharashtra; Vadodara and Ankleshwar in Gujarat; Jodhpur and Bhiwadi in Rajasthan were found to be the top critically polluted regions with a high CEPI air score. CSE also compared the latest 2018 assessment scores for air with the 2009 scores. They have found out that from the 2009 levels, air quality had worsened in several industrial clusters. The majority of these industrial regions belong to Uttar Pradesh. A drastic increase in CEPI air scores was observed in Mathura, Bulandshahr, Moradabad and Firozabad in Uttar Pradesh, Najafgarh drain basin in Delhi comprising Anand-Parvat, Naraina, Okhla and Wazirpur areas, Vadodara in Gujarat, Jodhpur and Pali in Rajasthan and Durgapur in West Bengal (Journals of India dated 31 March 2021; https://journalsofindia.com/cepi-index/; accessed on 16 September 2022).

IV. Development of Environmental Standards

203. Industry-specific as well as general effluent and emission standards for different pollutants and different categories of industries have been laid down under the Environment (Protection) Act and Rules of 1986. The MoE&F constituted an Expert Committee to evolve environmental standards. Based on the recommendation of the Committee, the standards have been notified for different industries and available on the website of the Ministry.

A. Sector-Wise Approach

204. The MoEFCC has initiated a sectoral approach for prevention and control of pollution in different sectors. Keeping this approach in view, the Action Plan finalized by the Working Group on Tanneries is being implemented. As regards distilleries, the industry has been advised to follow the protocol developed by the Indian Agricultural Research Institute and take the necessary measures to comply with the prescribed standards with respect to pollutants.

B. Industrial Pollution Control along the Rivers and Lakes

205. The programme for industrial pollution control along the rivers and lakes was started in August 1997. Under this programme, 851 defaulting grossly polluting industries (GPI) located along the rivers and lakes were identified for priority actions. The follow-up for the implementation was intensified which has resulted in reduction in the number of defaulting industries.

C. Environmental Surveillance Squad

206. The Environmental Surveillance Squad (ESS) is an important project undertaken by the CPCB under the direction of the honourable Supreme Court. The main objective of the squad is to identify the wilful defaulter through surprise visits. Action is also taken against the erring industries either directly by the CPCB or through the SPCB under environmental legislation. Under this project, industries are visited, and on the basis of the recommendations, the competent authority of the CPCB issues a closure notice to the defaulters.

§4. Global Warming and Climate Change

207. After the Industrial Revolution, the concentration of greenhouse gases in the atmosphere increased beyond their natural levels, which resulted in the enhanced greenhouse effect. This increase in global temperatures is known as global warming. The greenhouse gases in the atmosphere allow incoming ultraviolet solar radiation to pass through relatively unimpeded, but partially absorb and re-emit outgoing infrared radiation. This natural process raises the earth's average temperature, which has the potential of creating an imbalance with disastrous consequences.

208. As per the UNFCCC, India has promised to reduce the emissions intensity of its economy by 2030, compared to 2005 levels. It has also committed to having 40% of its energy from renewable sources by 2030. The Environmental Performance Index 2022 ranked India at the bottom of a list of 180 countries. The MoEFCC has refuted this Report with the plea that some of the indicators used in the Report are extrapolated and based on surmises and unscientific methods. This index has been published by the Yale Center for Environmental Law and Policy and the Center for International Earth Science Information Network, Columbia University. It used forty performance indicators across eleven categories to judge countries on climate change performance, environmental health and ecosystem vitality. In India, as per MoEFCC, a new indicator in the climate policy objective is 'projected GHG emissions levels in 2050'. This is computed based on the average rate of change in emission of the last ten years instead of modelling that takes into account a longer time period, extent of renewable energy capacity and use, additional carbon sinks, energy efficiency, etc., of respective countries. Forests and wetlands of the country are crucial carbon sinks but have not been factored in while computing the projected GHG emissions trajectory up to 2050 given by EPI 2022. Historical data on the lowest emission trajectory has been ignored in the computation.

I. The Stockholm Declaration of the UN Conference on Human Development of 1972

209. The Stockholm Declaration of the UN Conference on Human Development of 1972 emphasized the necessity to build a better environment, defend and improve it for future generations. This declaration also formed the basis for future conventions and agreements. It cautioned about global warming by laying down that the discharge of toxic and other substances and the release of heat should not exceed the capacity of the environment so that irreversible damage is not caused to the ecosystems. It requires the States to lay down environmental policies, regional planning, etc. The States are also under a duty to see that any activity within their jurisdiction or control should not cause damage to the environment of other States.

II. Kyoto Protocol and Framework Convention

210. India is a party to the UNFCCC and signed it on 10 June 1992 and was the thirty-eighth country to ratify it on 1 November 1993. Under the Kyoto Protocol, developed countries were required to make a definite commitment for reducing emission of Greenhouse Gases (GHG) during the first phase of the five years, that is, 2008–2012. Developing countries are not required to make any commitment during this phase; however, all countries are required to reduce emission of GHG by making mitigation efforts such as improving efficiency of energy conversion and utilization, stabilizing population growth, limiting methane emissions through proper waste management, afforestation, and phasing out subsidies.

In 1997, the Kyoto Protocol to the UNFCCC created three cooperative mechanisms namely Emissions Trading, Joint Implementation and Clean Development Mechanism (CDM) which allowed member countries flexibility in meeting their commitments with respect to reduction in emissions. The CDM is important from the Indian point of view as it allows developed countries to use certified emissions reduction credits from project activities in developing countries, and also assists them in achieving their development objectives.

211. Under existing international regimes, carbon markets have been established to facilitate reduction of carbon emissions at the global level through sale and purchase of carbon credits. India has been very proactive and has a good potential for CDM Projects.[4]

III. Sensitivity of India to Climate Change

212. India is highly vulnerable to climate change, as its economy is heavily reliant and dependent on climate-sensitive factors like agriculture and forestry. Further, its low-lying densely populated coastline is threatened by submergence because of a potential rise in sea level. India figures among the top ten contributors to greenhouse gas emissions. However, current per capita gross emissions are only one-sixth of the world's average. It is projected that by the end of twenty-first century, rainfall in India may increase by 15%–40% with high regional variability. The annual mean temperature may increase by 3%–6% over the century. India has committed to reducing the emission intensity of its Gross Domestic Product (GDP) by 33%–35% by 2030 against 2005 levels as promised under the Paris Climate Agreement. However, a report, 'Pathways For Meeting India's Climate Goals' released by the World Resources Institute, an international research organization, and the Open Climate Network said that India can reduce its greenhouse gas emissions intensity by 43% below 2005 levels by 2030 by effectively implementing and further enhancing certain climate and energy policies.

213. Extreme and unpredictable changes in the climate are a cause of serious concern throughout the world. In India, the adverse impacts of climate change are

4. UNEP-Risoe CDM Pipeline database.

already visible and have led to crop failure. The second part of the Sixth Assessment Report (Working Group II contribution) of the IPCC, released in early 2022, has referred to India as one of the countries to be most 'economically harmed' by climate change. The situation mandates urgent nationwide measures to build climate resilience by mitigating climate-related adversities and enabling adaptation. This report features the potential use cases of artificial intelligence-for-climate-action in the areas of transportation and water management and assesses their level or category of impact ('Down to Earth' dated 29 September 2022).

§5. Acid Rain

214. In the seventeenth century, scientists noted the ill effects of acidic pollution on animals, vegetation and people. However, the term 'acid rain' was coined two centuries later in 1872 when Angus Smith published a book called 'Acid Rain'. In the 1960s, the problems of acid deposition assumed international dimensions when fishermen noticed declines in fish numbers in many lakes throughout North America and Europe.

I. Acid Rain and Its Implications

A. Meaning and Incidence

215. The term 'acid rain' is used to describe the ways in which acids fall out of the atmosphere and affect the environment. A more precise term is acid deposition, which has two parts: wet and dry. Wet deposition refers to acidic rain, fog and snow. The strength of the effects depend on factors like how acidic the water is, the chemistry and buffering capacity of the soils involved, and the types of fish, trees, and other living things that rely on the water. According to scientists, SO_2 and Nitrogen Oxides (NOX) are the primary causes of acid rain. There have been many reports of acid rain in the past from different parts of the country.

B. Acid Deposition Formation

216. Acid deposition can form as a result of two processes. In some cases, hydrochloric acid can be released directly into the atmosphere. More commonly, it is due to secondary pollutants that form from the oxidation of Nitrogen Dioxide (NO_2) or SO_2 gases that are released into the atmosphere. The main sources of sulphur include coal burning, smelting of metal sulphide ores to obtain the pure metals, volcanic eruptions, and organic decay. After being released into the atmosphere, SO_2 either deposits on the Earth's surface in the form of dry deposition or undergoes reactions to produce acids that become part of the wet deposition. The major sources of nitrogen oxides include combustion of oil, coal, gas; bacterial action in soil; forest fires; volcanic action; lightning.

II. Effects of Acid Deposition

A. *Effects on the Ecosystem*

217. Acid deposition can have a variety of effects, including damage to forests and soil, fishes and other living things, materials, and human health thereby affecting the environment as a whole. Acid rain also reduces visibility, an effect called visibility reduction. In aquatic systems, with certain exceptions, acid deposition can affect these ecosystems by lowering their pH Streams, ponds or lakes that exist on bedrock or sediments rich in calcium and/or magnesium are naturally buffered from the effects of acid deposition.

B. *Decline in Fish Numbers*

218. One of the effects of aquatic acidification is the decline in fish numbers. In the middle latitudes, aquatic systems experience the phenomenon of acid shock. During the winter, the acidic deposits build up in the snowpack. With the arrival of spring, the snowpack begins to melt quickly, and the acids are released over a short period of time at concentrations five to ten times more acidic than rainfall. Most adult fish can survive this shock, but the eggs and small fry of many spring-spawning species are extremely sensitive to this acidification and perish.

C. *Effects on Soil*

219. The impact of acid deposition on vegetation depends on the type of soil in which plants have grown. In general, soils that have a lot of lime are better at neutralizing acids than those that are made up of siliceous sand or weathered acidic bedrock.

D. *Human Health and Livelihood*

220. Acid deposition also adversely affects the human health and economic livelihoods of people. Many lakes and streams became so acidic that the fish declined in numbers. The reduced fish numbers influence commercial fishermen and industries that rely on sport fishing tourism. Forestry and agriculture are also affected by the damage caused to vegetation.

E. *Effects on Heritage Sites and Buildings*

221. Acid deposition affects a number of inanimate features of building construction. Buildings and headstones that are constructed from limestone are easily attacked by acids, as are structures that are constructed of iron or steel. Paint on cars can react with acid deposition causing fading. The Taj Mahal at Agra in the State of UP and many other heritage buildings are under attack from the ill effects of acidic deposition.

§6. Traffic or Vehicular Pollution

222. Automobile exhaust fumes are one of the main contributors of pollutants in the ambient air. The MoEFCC plays a coordinating role in consultation with the Ministry of Road Transport and Highways, the MoP&NG and the Ministry of Industry, for upgrading of automobile technology, improvement in fuel contents and quality, expansion of urban public transport systems and promotion of integrated traffic management in controlling vehicular pollution.

I. Contribution of Vehicular Exhausts to AAQ

223. Air Quality in million Plus Cities of India under NAMP (Manual Stations) reveals that air quality has improved gradually since 2018 in most of the cities. Despite increased number of vehicles, growing population and increased industrial activity, India was able to achieve 13% reduction in PM10 and 9% in PM 2.5 in the 2021 w.r.t 2018 in Delhi, and there is also reduction in other parameters of air quality in most for other Million Plus Cities of India. India is the fifth-largest global car manufacturer with one of the highest compound annual growth rates (10%) of vehicle registration as of 2019. Due to various factors like economic growth, continued aspiration of vehicle ownership, etc., the annual car sales are projected to increase from the current 3.5 million to about 10.5 million (a three times increase) by 2030. Cars and two-wheelers will dominate the scene with a share of about 87%. This will further increase exposure to vehicular exhaust emissions which require improvement in emissions standards and in the measurement procedure for emissions testing of vehicles. The vehicle technology is changing rapidly with changes in fuel quality, exhaust treatment systems of the Internal Combustion Engines (ICE), electrification of vehicle segments and steps towards hydrogen-powered vehicles. But the current and future batches of ICE vehicles are likely to have a substantial share in on-road fleet till 2040.

224. The vehicular emission is a major cause of air pollution in urban areas and contributes 20%–30% of PM 2.5 (particles of size less than or equal to 2.5 micrometres) at the breathing level of air quality. This is more toxic because of the toxic constituents of its PM 2.5 emissions. According to studies, vehicles annually contribute about 290 gigagrams (Gg) of PM2.5. At the same time, around 8% of total greenhouse gas (GHG) emissions are from the transport sector, and in Delhi, it exceeds 30%. India has taken a major decision to abate vehicular emission by adopting BS-VI emissions standards for new vehicles. But the vehicles will have to remain low emitting in the real world when they are being driven which requires improvement in emissions measurement procedures in the laboratory as well as on roads.

225. The vehicle exhausts are the major cause of deterioration of urban AAQ. Considering CNG and Liquefied Petroleum Gas (LPG) as environment friendly alternate auto fuels, the Government is encouraging use of these fuels in automobiles. CNG has already become popular as an eco-friendly auto fuel. The Government has also permitted the use of LPG in automobiles. Ethanol (10%) blended with petrol is being used as an alternative auto fuel.

II. Mass Emission Standards

226. The Central Motor Vehicle Rules of 1989 provide for emission standards for both petrol and diesel vehicles. The rules require that vehicles must meet the smoke and co-emission standards. The mass vehicular emission norms for new vehicles were notified for the first time in India in 1991 for both the manufacturing stage as well as for in-use vehicles under the Environment (Protection) Act of 1986, the Air (Prevention and Control of Pollution) Act of 1981 and the Central Motor Vehicles Rules of 1989. Idle emission norms (pollution under control checks) for on-road vehicles also came into force in 1991. The emission norms are revised from time to time.

A. India 2000 to Bharat Stage VI

227. The Ministry of Surface Transport (*vide* G.S.R. 493(E) dated 8 August 1997) for the first time notified rules dealing with mass emission standards known as India 2000 akin to Euro I for all categories of vehicles manufactured on and after 1 April 2000 and were made effective from 1 April 2000 in the entire country. All vehicle manufacturers must sell only vehicles complying with the norms. With every revision, these standards aimed at tighter regulations by reducing the permissible level of tailpipe pollutants. For example, BS-IV – introduced in 2017, allowed fifty parts per million (ppm) of sulphur. The present BS-VI enforced from 2020 allows only 10 ppm of sulphur.

B. Old Technology

228. Even though there have been air quality gains achieved by the introduction of the new vehicle emission norms, the issue of pollution by the existing fleet of old technology vehicles and from old private vehicles still remains. Diesel vehicles emit inordinate amounts of PM, NO_2 and SO_2.

C. Fitness Certification

229. Vehicles pollute more as they become older; therefore, a solution has been found in mandatory and properly undertaken periodic fitness certification for all such vehicles. A rigorous maintenance schedule by the owner and genuine certification by authorized service stations can give good results out of these efforts. However, the problem remains that with the best of maintenance standards, the older vehicles may still cause an unacceptable level of pollution. In Delhi, a blanket ban has been imposed on petrol vehicle older than fifteen years and diesel vehicles older than ten years from plying on the roads or getting their papers reissued.

III. Auto Fuel

A. Auto Fuel Quality

230. As per the directions of the Honourable Supreme Court (Writ Petition Number 13029 of 1985 *M.C. Mehta v. Union of India and others*), the MoEFCC coordinated the preparation of action plans for control of vehicular pollution for compulsory switch over to CNG/LPG in the cities of Ahmedabad, Kolkata, Pune and Kanpur which were found to be equally or more polluted than Delhi. Nine cities, viz. Agra, Varanasi, Kanpur, Lucknow, Faridabad, Jharia, Jodhpur, Patna and Pune were also identified for improving air quality. Promotion of the Ethanol Blended Petrol and Biodiesel has also been taken up, and this petrol has been introduced in selective States as a first phase. An independent fuel-testing laboratory has been established at Noida in UP near Delhi. Oil companies have implemented major programmes for upgrading of petrol and diesel quality in the past few years.

B. Expert Committee on Auto Fuel Policy

231. The Auto Fuel Policy 2002 addressed the issue of vehicular emission, vehicular technologies and auto fuel quality in a cost-efficient manner while ensuring the security of fuel supply. The MoP&NG has again constituted an expert committee for preparation of a draft Auto Fuel Vision and Policy 2025. The Standing Committee on Petroleum & Natural Gas submitted its report on the National Auto Fuel Policy on 7 May 2015. The Auto Fuel Policy, 2003 addressed issues of vehicular emissions and vehicular technologies by applying fuel quality standards. This Committee was set up to review the Auto Fuel Policy, 2003 with the objective to draw a roadmap for the auto fuel quality till 2025. In order to achieve the unified fuel norm, the less polluting Bharat Stage (BS)-IV quality of fuel standard has been implemented across the country, and BS-VI quality of fuel standard was brought into force in 2020.

§7. Enforcement and Control

232. The following regulatory instruments are used in the process of enforcement as part of the pollution control mechanism:

– NOC.
– Consent.
– Standards.

I. No Objection Certificate

233. An NOC is required in the case of new industries. The concerned SPCB issues an NOC only after considering the impact of the proposed project on the environment.

II. Consent

234. Consent is obtained by the entrepreneur after the completion of the industrial project but before commissioning the industrial process. Running units and the units starting operation after establishing as per NOC issued by the Board also have to apply for consent to operate. The Board, considering compliance of environmental laws by the industry issues a letter of consent to the industry allowing it to continue its operation. The consent is normally granted lifetime for Green category, ten years for Orange category, five years for Red category and for the newly created White category, no consent is required. This is given, subject to the installation of all required pollution control equipment to abate pollution. A factory or industry cannot start its operation without such consent. The consent is reviewed every year. It is renewed only if pollution standards are complied with. Consent fees are a source of revenue for the PCBs. In addition to monitoring by the boards, Health Departments of Municipal Corporations also monitor industrial units to see if any of them cause health hazards to the public. Standards refer to specific parameters previously quantified with respect to measures for disposal, discharge and emission of solid, liquid and gaseous waste into the environment. These standards form the basis for the enforcement of any legislation for pollution abatement.

235. Submission of an Environmental Statement by polluting units seeking consent either under the Water (Prevention and Control of Pollution) Act of 1974 or the Air (Prevention and Control of Pollution) Act of 1981 or both and the authorization under the Hazardous and Other Wastes (Management and Transboundary Movement) Rules of 2016 to the concerned SPCBs have been made mandatory through a Gazette Notification under the Environment (Protection) Act of 1986. The Environmental Statement enables the industrial units to take a comprehensive look at their operations and facilitates understanding and focus on areas where waste reduction and consequently savings in input costs are possible.

III. Setting of Air Quality Standards

236. The CPCB had notified the National Ambient Air Quality Standards (NAAQS) for various pollutants in 1994 under the Air Act, 1981 for seven parameters. Thereafter in 1986, the Central Government notified standards for six parameters under the Environment (Protection) Act, 1986. The MoEFCC notified on 18 November 2009 'Revised National Ambient Air Quality Standards 2009' in the Official Gazette providing a legal framework for the control of air pollution and protection of public health.

237. The National Air Quality Index (AQI) was introduced in 2014 (ranging from good to severe). The NAAQS was more complex and difficult for the average person to understand as compared to the AQI. The AQI was developed for improving the general public's understanding of air quality conditions. The NAAQS 2009 took twelve contaminants into account, whereas the AQI only considered eight main pollutants. With the exception of benzene, benzopyrene, arsenic, and nickel, all NAAQS contaminants are included in AQI. The worst reading for each of the eight pollutants used to calculate the AQI which represents the city's AQI. These eight pollutants are the basis for the short-term (up to twenty-four hourly averaging period) National AAQ Standards.

238. The new NAAQS are expected to be brought in 2022. The revised guidelines would include more contaminants including ultra-fine constituents of PM which falls below PM2.5. Before making a decision, the WHO's guidelines and individual countries' requirements will be considered. When providing suggestions for updating NAAQS, the experts would also take geographical and meteorological conditions of the country into account. In addition to recalibrating places and times for long and short frequencies, the researchers will map the effects of air pollution on human health and flora. A team led by the Indian Institute of Technology (IIT) Kanpur including experts from National Physical Laboratory, NEERI, AIIMS and IIT Delhi has been awarded the task of updating NAAQS by the CBCP (Vide ET, 17 August 2021).

A. *Emission Standards for Generator Sets*

239. As generators run on various types of fuel, thus there are different sets of norms based on the type of fuel used. The norms for dedicated natural gas and LPG are as per the notifications vide G.S.R. 281(E) dated 7 March 2016, Serial Nos 95A, 95B and 95C under the Environment (Protection) Third Amendment Rules, 2016. These are effective from 1 July 2016 and apply to gensets above 400 cc up to 800 kW. These standards deal with dedicated natural gas or LPG gensets.

240. All engines up to 20 kW are to carry a (ISI) mark and meet the relevant Bureau of Indian Standards (BIS) specifications. Emissions from new diesel engines used in generator sets are regulated by MoEFCC, GOI. The regulations impose type approval testing, production conformity testing and labelling requirements. The regulations also include a list of authorized agencies for type approval testing. Emission limits for new diesel engines ≤ 800 kW used in gensets were set in the year

2002 (*see* G.S.R. 489(E)) and strengthened in 2013 (*see* G.S.R. 232(E)). The regulations also set noise limits for diesel generator sets up to 1,000 kVA. The strengthened emission standards became applicable from April 2014.

1. Draft Common Norms for DG Genset

241. As per government, the emission coming from the DG genset is one of the major contributors to air pollution in major urban centres in India. Fresh regulation on emission is imperative, considering the availability of cleaner fuels (BS-VI) and improved engine technology. On 18 December 2021, the NGT had directed the Uttar Pradesh PCB to take action to ensure the compliance of norms set to check air and noise pollution caused by diesel generators (DG). The case pertained to a petition filed against the Management of Windsor Park residents Welfare association in Ghaziabad, Uttar Pradesh. A study by the CSE has found that DG sets significantly contributed to air pollution in urban areas. The study reveals that DG consumes 60%–70% of the liquid fuel consumption of the studied region. The National Clean Air Programme (NCAP) suggest retrofitting of existing generators and replacing the DG sets with gas-operated generators.

242. On 19 February 2022, MoEFCC issued a draft notification for common emission norms for power generators, so there will be one standard pollution norm for all types of power generators. Until now, there are three different emission standards for Gasoline, Diesel and Dedicated CNG, LPG and Bi-fuel gensets. Hydrogen and green ammonia-powered generators have also been included in this notification. This will be a boost to the Hydrogen fuel sector in India. The Centre had already released green hydrogen and green ammonia policy to boost the large-scale indigenous production of green hydrogen to reduce the import of fossil and crude oil. This move will also help the country achieve its target of becoming a Carbon Neutral economy by 2070 as announced by the Government. The draft revised norms would be effective from July 2023 (Vide Deoxyribo Nucleic Acid (DNA), 19 February 2022).

B. Particulate Emission Limits for Thermal Power Stations

243. Major pollutants from coal-fired power plants are oxides of nitrogen (NOx), sulphur dioxide (SO_2) and PM. According to the CSE, TPPs account for more than 60% of total industrial emissions of PM; 45% of SO_2; 30% of NOx; and more than 80% of mercury. These are also responsible for 70% of the total freshwater withdrawal by all industries, according to an analysis by the green think tank. A recent compliance report by CSE showed that out of the twelve power plants located around Delhi, SO_2 control technology was available only in two plants. According to a study by the Centre for Research on Energy and Clean Air, 218 people die every year in Delhi from exposure to a toxic cocktail of fumes from the twelve TPP located in a 300 km radius of the national capital.

244. The MoEFCC (*see* Gazette Notification of 3 January 1989) issued the first amendment rules to the EPA of 1986 which stipulated the particulate emission limits for thermal power stations as Generation capacity 210 MW or more 150 mg/Nm^3, Generation capacity less than 210 MW 350 mg/Nm^3 and Units located in protected area 150 mg/Nm^3. Thereafter these were revised (*see* S.O.3305(E)) (dated 7 December 2015) and G.S.R.593(E) (dated 28 June 2018) with varying parameters of PM, SO_2, NOx and Mercury for Thermal Power Plant units.

245. The MoEFCC had revised emission norms for PM, sulphur dioxide and oxides of nitrogen for TPPs in December 2015, requiring them to instal emission control systems by December 2017. The deadline was pushed to December 2022 for all power stations in view of implementation issues and other challenges. However, power stations in the NCR were required to comply with the revised norms by December 2019. The Ministry of Power requested the MoEFCC to extend the deadline for meeting emission norms for all thermal plants from 2022 to 2024, citing delay due to various reasons, including the coronavirus pandemic and import restrictions.

246. The MoEFCC has amended rules vide notification dated 1 April 2022 allowing TPP within 10 km of the NCR and in cities with more than 1 million population to comply with new emission norms by the end of 2022. It also provides for constitution of a task force by the CPCB to categorize TPPs into three categories on the basis of their location. Also, TPP units in 'non-attainment cities' and those within 10 km of CPAs are required to meet the emission norms by 31 December 2023. Non-attainment cities are those which have consistently failed to meet the NAAQS. The CPCB has identified 124 such cities. TPPs in rest of the areas have to comply with the new standards by 31 December 2024. TPPs declared to retire before 31 December 2025 are 'not required to meet the specified norms in case such plants submit an undertaking to the CPCB and Central Electricity Authority (CEA) for exemption on ground of retirement', as per notification.

C. Air Quality Monitoring of Vehicular Pollution

247. The SPCB prescribe and enforce emission standards for automobiles after consulting the Central Board. The automobile emission standards are monitored and implemented by the Commissioners for Transport and their staff in the respective States. Monitoring of air quality directly by the CPCB and SPCB is undertaken only in a limited number of cities. In most cities, other institutions and agencies monitor AAQ.

D. Minimum National Standards

248. The BIS attended to the pollution problem by setting standards as early as the 1960s. The standards developed by the bureau have been adopted by the Government as the Minimum National Standards. The CPCB in pursuance of its mandate formulates national programmes for prevention and control of pollution. These include nationwide monitoring network, laying down national standards for ambient water and air quality, source-specific Minimal National Standards for effluents and emissions, and action plans for CPA and highly polluting industries. The pollutants regularly monitored are SO_2, Nitrogen Oxide (NOx) and PM, besides the meteorological parameters, like wind speed and direction, temperature and humidity.

IV. Air Quality Monitoring Network

249. At present AAQ is being monitored through a network of 1,208 manual and real-time monitoring stations in 460 towns and cities across the States and UTs which is being further strengthened under NCAP. The data thus generated is transmitted to the CPCB for scrutiny, analysis, compilation and publication in the form of a consolidated report (MoEF AR 2021–2022).

250. The air quality of different cities/towns for three critical pollutants has been compared with the respective National Air Monitoring System and has been classified into four broad categories based on an Exceedance Factor (EF) as calculated by the ratio between observed annual mean concentration of criteria pollutants and annual standard for the respective pollutant and area class.

The four air quality categories are as follows:

(1) Critical pollution (C): when EF is more than 1.5.
(2) High pollution (H): when the EF is between 1.0 and 1.5.
(3) Moderate pollution (M): with and EF between 0.5 and 1.0.
(4) Low pollution (L): where the EF is less than 0.5.

Based on the above indicators, a quarterly report is compiled by the CPCB in some of the major cities. For real-time data collection, automatic monitoring stations have also been established.

V. Online AAQ Monitoring Station

251. The continuous monitoring stations are operated and maintained by the CPCB and the SPCBs. All the data from these stations is available from CPCB website. Another source to download archived data is http://www.openaq.org, a portal with open access to monitoring data from stations across the globe. MoEFCC has launched 'PRANA', a portal for monitoring the implementation of NCAP on 7 September 2021. This portal for Regulation of Air pollution in Non-Attainment Cities (PRANA) has been developed for monitoring physical and financial progress of city action plan implementation for improvement of air quality made in 132 identified cities and disseminating the information to public (on www.prana.cpcb.gov.in). Source apportionment and emission inventory studies have been completed for 28 cities. Work is in progress in 60 cities, and it is at proposal stage in 44 cities. To tackle air pollution emergencies, Emergency Response System have been developed for 117 cities. It is in progress in 15 cities (MoEFCC Annual Report 2021–2022).

§8. Evaluation of Effectiveness of Legal Provisions

I. Air Quality Standards Developed under the Air Act

252. The compliance and enforcement structure was developed in the form of AAQ Standards under the Air Act of 1981. These standards have been developed as a policy guideline that regulates the effect of human activity on the environment so that pollutants emission into the air can be regulated. Standards specify a desired state or limit alterations. The programme is executed by CPCB.

253. MoEFCC has been implementing since 10 January 2019, an NCAP as a national-level strategy outlining the actions for reducing the levels of air pollution at city and regional scales in India. The NCAP targets to achieve 20%–30% reduction in PM concentrations by 2024 (base 2019) across the country. The long-term goal of NCAP is to meet the prescribed annual average AAQ standards at all locations in the country in a stipulated timeframe. Under NCAP, cities which are exceeding the NAAQS for five consecutive years are identified as non-attainment cities by CPCB.

II. Instrument of Enforcement

254. Direct regulation, inspection environment statements, auditing and economic incentives are the main enforcement mechanisms. But the process of taking action against polluters has not been very effective and can be termed as lax. This position was changed by amendments to the Air Act in 1987 which strengthened penal provisions and shifted focus from judicial to administrative enforcement and resulted in better compliance. The environment policy and legislation are now more integrated, focused, holistic and consequently more directed and effective.

A. Launching of Prosecution

255. The PCBs can launch prosecution on their own initiative and take administrative action. Third parties could also launch PIL against offenders. The power to initiate legal action by NGOs under PIL and the tendency to take administrative action against polluting industries has grown simultaneously.

B. Inspection

256. The PCBs carry out periodical inspections of factories. The frequency depends upon the type of industry and gravity of the pollution. CPCB has formulated a standard procedure to perform all inspections, report preparation and actions delineate the inspection procedure, steps to be followed before, during and post-inspection, and report submission.

257. An industrial unit in the Red Category is inspected at least once per three months (large- or medium-sized industry) or at least once per year (Small industry, i.e., capital investment below INR 10,000). For the large- or medium-sized industries in the Orange category, inspection is done at least once per year or once in three years for small industries. For the Green Category, the inspection is less frequent, only once in two years (large or medium-sized) or once in five years (small-sized). If persons or firms do not give information required by the PCBs, they are punishable with imprisonment of up to three months and/or fines of up to INR 10,000. Persons and/or firms causing pollution beyond the standards prescribed are also punishable with imprisonment of not less than one and a half years and up to six years with a fine.

C. Environmental Auditing

258. 'Environmental auditing' has forced industries to be more environment-conscious and has resulted in better compliance with environmental laws and regulations. Further, there is also a welcome trend towards adopting clean technologies instead of 'end-of-pipe' cleaning so that there could be better legal compliance. Technological competence of Indian industry to adopt clean technologies has considerably improved over the years. There are several companies specialized in producing pollution control equipment and in offering consultancy in the field. Where small plants cannot set up their own pollution abatement plants, collective treatment plants have been set up.

III. Problems in Enforcement

259. There are shortfalls and constraints in the enforcement mechanism, though policy and legislation look adequate on paper, but in practice, the situation can be very different. The implementation of pollution control laws now is certainly more effective. Even so, the position is not that all the pollution standards are followed by all the industries. The PCBs have the powers to close down offending industries, but the action is hesitant because of fear of causing unemployment and distress to the industry workers. Thus the problem of unemployment has also been linked with environmental issues.

260. Several industries, particularly small units, find it difficult to observe pollution standards prescribed by law. Some of these units were set up long ago, and pollution control is not process-integrated or a built-in device in their setup. On many occasions, they were ordered to close down, usually with the intervention of the Supreme Court in response to writ petitions by environmentalists. Tanneries in the city of Kanpur in the State of UP which were releasing very toxic pollutants into the River Ganga were similarly ordered to close down. In all such cases, thousands of low-paid workers lost their jobs and became almost destitute.

261. Despite all these problems in enforcement, the Supreme Court in *Municipal Council Ratlam v. Vardhichand and others* (AIR 1980 SC 1622) has clearly laid down that an authority entrusted with the task of pollution control cannot take the plea of paucity of funds. In this case, the inhabitants were disturbed because of stench and stink caused by open drains and other filth in the area.

Chapter 4. Water Pollution

§1. Introduction

262. Water being the base of every living being and essential for the existence and sustenance of the human race on earth is without any doubt the elixir of life. Therefore, demand for water resources is from multiple sources, and the impact takes diverse forms. The growth of urban areas, increased industrial activity and dependence of the agriculture sector on chemicals and fertilizers have led to a general deterioration in water quality and contamination of lakes, rivers and groundwater aquifers throughout the country. India has 17.7% of the world's population, but only 4% of its water resources, making it among the most water-stressed in the world. A large number of people face high to extreme water stress, according to a recent report by the NITI Aayog. India's dependence on an increasingly erratic monsoon for its water requirements increases this challenge. Climate change is likely to exacerbate this pressure on water resources, even as the frequency and intensity of floods and droughts in the country increase.

263. 'Water Pollution' has been defined in the Water Conservation (Prevention and Control of Pollution) Act of 1974 as such contamination of water or such alteration of the physical, chemical or biological properties of water or such discharge of any sewage or trade effluent or of any other liquid, gaseous or solid substance into water (whether directly or indirectly) as may, or is likely to, create a nuisance or render such water harmful or injurious to public health or safety, or to domestic, commercial, industrial, agricultural or other legitimate uses, or to the life and health of animals or plants or of aquatic organisms.

§2. Statutory Structure and Legal Regime

264. The Constitution does not contain any direct provision with respect to water pollution, but the Court has interpreted it under Article 21, a right to life guaranteed by it. Article 21 is to the effect that 'No person shall be deprived of his life or personal liberty except according to a procedure established by law.' In *Subash Kumar v. State of Bihar* (AIR 1991 SC 420), the Court has given a broad interpretation to include 'right to enjoyment of pollution free water environment' and further 'right to hygienic environment' in *Virendra Gaur & Others v. State of Haryana & Others* [(1995) 2 SCC 577]. Water, sanitation and health are enlisted in List II of the Seventh Schedule, which means that State Government exercises powers in this respect.

265. The Water (Prevention and Control of Pollution) Act, 1974 (the 'Water Act') was enacted by the Central Government in the exercise of the power vested in it by resolutions passed by two or more State Legislatures in accordance with Article 252 of the Constitution. The two main objectives of the Act are to prevent and control water pollution and maintain or restore the wholesomeness of water. The Water Act of 1974 was a milestone and a serious and coordinated attempt at controlling water pollution. Under this act, boards for prevention and control of pollution of water were established both at the central and state levels with the necessary technical competence and power to monitor the implementation of the law. Without waiting for the affected people to launch legal action, the boards were authorized to proceed on their own initiative against the violators. A chain of water-testing laboratories was also established to check water quality and pollution.

I. Legislation and International Conventions

A. Legislation

266. The legislations dealing with water pollution are given below:

- the Water (Prevention and Control of Pollution) Act of 1974 (6 of 1974) Rules and Amendment Acts of 1977, 1978, 1992;
- the Water (Prevention and Control of Pollution) Cess Act of 1977, Amendment Act of 1991, 1995, 2000 and 2003;
- the Indian Ports Act of 1908 (section 6);
- the Inland Steam Vessels Act of 1917;
- the Merchant Shipping (Amendment) Act of 1970; particularly the Merchant Shipping (Amendment) Act of 1983 (Part X B and Part XI A);
- the River Boards Act of 1956;
- the Inter-State Water Disputes Act, 1956;
- the Indian Fisheries Act of 1897;
- the Coastal Zone Regulation Notification of 2019 (G.S.R. 37(E) on 18 January 2019);
- the Oilfields (Regulation and Development) Act of 1948.

B. International Conventions and Treaties

267. There are a number of conventions and treaties dealing with water and water pollution; these are listed below:

- the International CLC for Oil Pollution, signed at Brussels on 19 November 1969 (referred in section 352 N (3) of the Merchant Shipping (Amendment) Act of 1970);
- the International Convention for the Prevention of Pollution of the Sea by Oil of 1954 signed in London on 12 May 1954 (referred in section 356 B (d) of the Merchant Shipping (Amendment) Act of 1970);
- the Law of the Sea Convention of 1982, ratified by India in November 1994;
- the Indus Water Treaty-India and Pakistan 1960;
- the Indo-Nepal Treaty on Integrated Development of Mahakali River 1996;
- the Ganga Water Sharing Treaty with Bangladesh – Sharing of Lean Season Flow of Ganga at Farakka Barrage in India 1996.

II. Salient Features of Legislation

A. *The Water (Prevention and Control of Pollution) Act of 1974*

268. This act provides for prevention and control of pollution of water and maintenance of water quality. The provision of this act has overriding effect notwithstanding anything inconsistent contained in any other enactment (section 60). Interference with any stream, well or sewer in a manner which may aggravate pollution is prohibited. The act enforces effluent standards for factories discharging pollutants into water bodies. The previous consent of the board is required before establishing or taking any step to establish any industry, operation or process or any treatment and disposal system or an extension or addition which is likely to discharge sewage or trade effluent into a stream or well or sewer or on land or bring into use any new or altered outlets for the discharge of sewage or begin to produce any new discharge of sewage.

The word 'stream' has been defined as including the following:

- river;
- watercourse (whether flowing or for the time being dry);
- inland water (whether natural or artificial);
- subterranean waters;
- sea or tidal waters to such extent or, as the case may be, to such point as the State Government may, by notification in the Official Gazette, specify.

In the case of *Punjab State Board v. M/s Vinod Paper Mills Ltd.* (1998 Criminal Law Journal 2235, Punjab and Haryana), it was held that the term 'stream' as defined in section 2(j) of the act covers water courses whether flowing or, for the time being, dry and inland water whether natural or artificial.

1. Functions of the Board

269. The board can constitute committees consisting of members and other persons. It can also associate persons for the purpose of assistance or advice in performing its functions (sections 9 and 10). A joint board can be formed by two or more Governments of neighbouring States or by the Central Government (section 13). The Government of the State for which the joint board is constituted is competent to give a direction under the provisions of the act only in those cases where such direction relates to a matter which is within exclusive territorial jurisdiction of such State. The Central Government alone can give directions in cases where such directions relate to a matter within the territorial jurisdiction of two or more States or related to a UT.

270. The functions of the Central Board as provided under section 16 are to promote cleanliness of streams and wells in different areas of the State and coordinate the activities of the State Board and settle disputes among them. It facilitates the State Board by its guidance and assistance and sponsors investigations and research relating to the problems of prevention and control of water pollution. It also organizes programmes through mass media and executes plans and schemes for prevention and control of water pollution.

271. According to section 17, some of the important functions of the State Board are as follows:

(a) Planning programme regarding prevention and control of water pollution.
(b) Advising the State Government on matters concerning the prevention and control of water pollution.
(c) Conducting and participating in investigation and research-related problems of water pollution and prevention, control or abatement of water pollution.
(d) Inspecting sewage or trade effluents.
(e) Reviewing plans, specifications or other data relating to plants set up for the treatment of effluents of water for purification.
(f) Evolving methods of utilization of sewage and suitable trade effluents in agriculture.
(g) Advising the State Government with respect to the location of any industry carrying on an activity which is likely to pollute a stream or well.

272. The Central Government has power to supersede the Central Board and Joint Boards in certain circumstances like default in the performance of the functions prescribed by the Central Government or under the act (section 61). Similarly, State Governments have power to supersede the respective State Boards.

2. Prevention and Control of Water Pollution under the Act

273. The State Government may restrict the application of the act to certain areas of the State and need not apply it to the entire State. A State Board or any officer empowered can take samples for the purpose of analysis from any stream or well or of any sewage or trade effluent. The result of the analysis is admissible in evidence subject to compliance with requirements as follows:

(a) Serve notice on the person in charge of, or having control over, the plant or vessel or occupying the place from where the samples have been taken.
(b) After collecting the sample, divide the samples into two parts in the presence of the occupier or the agent and each part should be placed in a sealed container and marked and signed both by the person taking the sample and the occupier or his agent and send one sample to a laboratory recognized by the Central Board in case the sample has been taken from an area situated in a UT and in case the sample has been taken from any other place, then to any other laboratory recognized by the State Board. The other sample on the request of the occupier or his agent may be sent to a Central Water Laboratory or a State Water Laboratory established under sections 51 and 52 of the act, respectively.

3. Action in an Emergency

274. The State Boards have power to take emergency measures in case of pollution of a stream or well and may take immediate action so as to remove the pollutant from the stream or well or on land as it may consider appropriate.

4. Power of the Central Government to Give Directions (Section 33)

275. The power of the board to issue directions is subject to any direction that the Central Government may issue under the provisions of the act. But this power is not unfettered. Rule 34 of the Rules of 1975 prescribes conditions and measures while giving directions so that this power is exercised with care and caution.

B. The Water (Prevention and Control of Pollution) Cess Act of 1977

276. This act empowers the SPCB to levy a cess on local authorities supplying water to consumers and water consumed by specified industries with a provision of incentives for conservation, reuse, lower discharge, etc. It augments the resources of the Central and SPCB and PCC for UT for the prevention and control of water pollution.

C. The Water (Prevention and Control of Pollution) Rules of 1975 (Water Rules of 1975)

277. Section 63 of the Water Act of 1974 empowers the Central Government to make rules. Similarly, under section 64, the State Government is bestowed with rule-making powers. The Water Rules of 1975 have been formulated by the Central Government after consultation with the CPCB. These rules prescribe terms and conditions of service of the members of the CPCB and the committee constituted by the CPCB. The rules also lay down the powers and duties of the chairman and secretary.

§3. Freshwater

278. The demand for freshwater has been identified as the quantity of water required to be supplied for specific use and includes consumptive as well as necessary non-consumptive water requirements for the user sector. The estimates for total national-level water requirements have been made for the years 2010, 2025 and 2050. The country's total water requirement by the year 2050 will become 1,450 billion m^3, which will be much in excess of the total utilizable average water resources of 1,121 billion m^3. At the national level, it would be a very difficult task to increase the availability of water for use from the 2006 level of approximately 1,121 km^3 to the desired level of 1,450 km^3 per year by the year 2050 as most of the undeveloped utilizable water resources are concentrated in a few river basins such as the Brahmaputra, Ganga, Godavari, and Mahanadi (India: State of the Environment Report 2009).

279. A provision concerning clean drinking water is included in the Constitution of India, conferring the duty of providing clean drinking water and improving public health standards to the State governments. The water quality monitoring (WQM) has been accorded a high priority, and institutional mechanisms have been developed at both national and state levels.

280. In *Ramji Patel v. Nagrik Upbhokta Marg Darshak Manch* [(2000) 3 SCC 29], the honourable Supreme Court held that the supply of pure drinking water is the statutory duty of the Municipal Corporation and the supply of such water has to be ensured to every citizen.

I. Surface Water Management

A. *Water Availability*

281. Water availability per capita is dependent on population of a country, and the per capita water availability in the country is reducing due to increase in population. The average annual per capita water availability in the years 2001 and 2011 was assessed as 1816 cubic meters and 1,545 cubic meters respectively which would have further reduced to 1,486 cubic meters in the year 2021 as per projected population projections. Further, the average annual water availability of any region or country largely depends on hydro-meteorological and geological factors and the availability of drinking water in rural areas is also affected by many factors which include, *inter alia*, depletion of groundwater level, contamination of surface water sources, drying up of ponds and wells, deficient rainfall leading to insufficient recharge of water bodies, etc.

B. *Rainfall*

282. The average rainfall in the country is 118 cm according to annual data from the Indian Meteorological Department (IMD). Some regions in India experience very high rainfall, and others receive very scanty rainfall. The difference between the recorded highest and lowest rainfall in India is approximately 1,178 cm. As per IMD, instances of heavy rainfall have increased by almost 85% in the country since 2012. 'India is highly dependent on the southwest monsoons and, in the last few decades, this is getting more erratic and abrupt due to climate change.'

C. Pollution of Water Bodies Including Rivers

283. The water bodies and rivers are most severely polluted around human settlements. The flow in rivers has progressively decreased due to upstream withdrawals/impounding and groundwater extraction along banks, uneven distribution denying the river the flushing dose required for ecological purposes. The problem of reduction in flow becomes acute when the river enters the plains and passes through cities because water is drawn for irrigation by farmers and for the drinking water supply in the cities. At the same time, rivers receive polluted discharge, the main pollutants being fertilizers and insecticides, untreated municipal sewage and industrial effluents.

284. The Supreme Court in the case of *Andhra Pradesh Pollution Control Board II v. Professor M.V. Nayudu* ((2001) 2 SCC 62) directed that the industries using hazardous substances cannot be permitted to be established near the water reservoirs. Since the chance of an accident within such close proximity of reservoirs cannot be ruled out, thus there is a very great risk that these highly hazardous materials could seep into the earth and reach the water bodies.

285. In the case of *A. Malliga v. The District Collector Cum The Chairman of the District Environment Impact Assessment Authority, Trichy & Others* (dated 23 September 2022), the Supreme Court held that once it is found that the land in question is a water body, nobody can be permitted to have mining activity in the water body and it is the duty of the state government to preserve and protect the water bodies ('Down to Earth' dated 23 September 2022).

II. Freshwater: An Exhaustible Resource

286. After independence, there has been a phenomenal development and tapping of water resources. India has successfully met water requirements for different usages. Preserving the quality and availability of freshwater resources, however, has become the most pressing of environmental challenges because of the increase in water use. The pollution of freshwater, being an exhaustible resource, has become a matter of grave concern.

287. India's total utilizable water resource is pegged at 1,123 billion cubic meters (BCM). In 2017, it was reported that approximately 946 BCM were consumed across all sectors, including agriculture (91.0%), industrial (2.0%), and domestic (7.0%). According to a 2019 NITI Aayog report on Water Management Index, India is facing the worst water crisis in its history. In a conservative scenario, water demand would grow to 1,100 BCM by 2025, assuming a population growth rate of 1.2% and an annual GDP growth rate of 7.0%. Compared to the estimated availability of 1,123 BCM of water, these projections for water demand indicate an overall net marginal positive balance of only 23 BCM of water by 2025.

§4. WATER SUPPLY MANAGEMENT

288. More than 6% of the population lack access to safe water, and about 15% population practises open defecation. A lack of household water connections and toilets contributes largely to water-borne illnesses, stunting, and death. However, there has been significant improvement in access to safe drinking water to urban and rural populations. Under the Jal Jeevan Mission over 8.45 crore or 44% of the total 19.22 crore rural households have been provided with piped water connections till 4 November 2021. Six states and Union Territories have already achieved 100% coverage to tap water connection for rural households. India is the third largest user of groundwater, and in Water Aid's 'Water Quality Index 2019' India ranked 120 among 122 nations. Depleting groundwater, contamination of resources and ageing supply infrastructure make the situation worse when it comes to access to safe drinking water. The rivers, one of the major sources of water, are also shrinking or getting contaminated due to rapidly surging population, industrialization and flow of other pollutants in it.

I. Jal Jevan Mission (JJM)

289. The Department of Drinking Water and Sanitation (DDWS) provides technical and financial assistance to the States to provide safe and adequate drinking water to rural India with focus on service delivery. The Department's Centrally Sponsored Scheme, the National Rural Drinking Water Programme, was renamed as Jal Jeevan Mission (JJM) to provide functional tap connection (FHTC) to every rural household, i.e., Har Ghar Jal, by 202. The kinds of works/schemes which are proposed to be taken up under JJM include in-village water supply (PWS) infrastructure for tap water connection to every household; reliable drinking water source development/ augmentation of existing sources; transfer of water (multi-village scheme; where quantity and quality issues are there in the local water sources); technological intervention for treatment to make water potable (where water quality is an issue, but quantity is sufficient).

290. The Jal Jeevan Mission aims to provide tap water connections to all rural households by 2024; however, the slow pace of the scheme in some states is a major concern. The largest state, Uttar Pradesh, has covered only 12.4% of its total rural household. Rajasthan, the State with water scarcity, has only 20.91% coverage of its over one crore total rural household. Similarly, the States including Assam (22%), Ladakh (16.62%), Jharkhand (15.16%), West Bengal (13.48%) and Chhattisgarh (13.23%) have lower coverage under the Jal Jeevan Scheme. The urban areas, specifically the slums and unauthorized colonies in cities, are also facing a serious threat of water crisis. A report by WWF released in 2020 predicted that around thirty Indian cities would face a grave water risk by 2050 due to rapid increase in population. A recent survey by the Delhi government showed that nearly 44% of residents of Delhi slums depend on bottled water for drinking.

II. Groundwater Supply

291. India is the largest user of groundwater with a fourth of the total global withdrawal. Indian cities cater to about 48% of its water supply from groundwater. The theme for 2022 World Water Day (22 March 2022) was also Groundwater, i.e., 'Making the invisible visible to bring attention to the invisible'. The unmanaged groundwater and increasing population may result in seasonal water shortages by 2050 for an estimated 3.1 billion people and perpetual water shortage for almost a billion. The groundwater level in 33% of the wells monitored by the Central Ground Water Board (CGWB) declined by 0–2 m in November 2020 as compared to the decadal water level average (2010–2019). There is also a decline of more than 4 m of the water table in a few pockets of Delhi, Chennai, Indore, Coimbatore, Madurai, Vijayawada, Dehradun, Jaipur, Allahabad, Ghaziabad, Kanpur, and Lucknow over the years.

A. Law on Groundwater

292. Groundwater falls under State List of the Constitution, so only States can make legislation on it. The Centre had come up with a Model Bill for guidance of States, namely the Groundwater (Sustainable Management) Bill, 2017. The Bill was drafted by the Ministry of Water Resources (MoWR), River Development & Ganga Rejuvenation (RD&GR) and provides a new template that states can use to adopt legislation capable of addressing the fast-increasing groundwater crisis faced by many states. This Bill follows an earlier model bill drafted in 1970 and updated several times until 2005 on which the dozen of existing groundwater acts are based. The 2017 Bill integrates legal developments having taking place since the 1970s, such as the decentralization reforms kick-started in the 1990s, the recognition of water as a fundamental right and its recognition as a public trust. In doing so, it provides new bases for regulating groundwater as a public resource and to take measures at aquifer level, something that is crucial to address ongoing overexploitation and falling water tables. States which have enacted the Ground Water (Control and Regulation) Act include Andhra Pradesh, Goa, Tamil Nadu, Kerala, West Bengal, Himachal Pradesh, Bihar and Union Territories of Chandigarh, Dadra and Nagar Haveli and Lakshadweep.

293. A Central Ground Water Authority has been constituted under section 3(3) of the Environment (Protection) Act, 1986 to regulate and control the development and management of groundwater resources in the country. The Authority has the following powers and functions:

i. Exercise of powers under section 5 of the Environment (Protection) Act, 1986 for issuing directions and taking such measures in respect of all the matters referred to in subsection (2) of section 3 of the said Act.
ii. To resort to penal provisions contained in sections 15–21 of the said Act.
iii. To regulate and control, management and development of groundwater in the country and to issue necessary regulatory directions for the purpose.

iv. Exercise of powers under section 4 of the Environment (Protection) Act, 1986 for the appointment of officers.

B. Groundwater Contamination

294. A large number of people are drinking toxic water as per the data released by Minister of Jal Shakti on 1 August 2022, in a reply to a question asked in the Parliament. Around 209 districts in 25 states and Union territories have arsenic in their groundwater and Uranium in parts of 152 districts across 18 states. According to the data, metals were found in the water sources: lead has been found in parts of 176 districts in 21 states; iron has been found in parts of 491 districts in 29 states and Union territories; cadmium in parts of 29 districts in 11 states; chromium in parts of 62 districts in 16 states. Further, the expanse of metal-infused water sources is also huge since there are 14,079 iron-affected, 671 fluoride-affected, 814 arsenic-affected, 9,930 salinity-affected, 517 nitrate-affected and 111 heavy metal-affected habitations in the country, the data showed. The amount of arsenic, iron, lead, cadmium, chromium and uranium in groundwater exceeding the prescribed standard has a direct effect on health. Excess arsenic means increased risk of skin diseases and cancer. Excess iron can mean diseases related to the nervous system like Alzheimer's and Parkinson's. Excess amount of lead in water can affect the nervous system. High levels of cadmium increase the risk of kidney diseases. High amounts of chromium can cause diffuse hyperplasia in the small intestine, which increases the risk of tumours. Excess amount of uranium in drinking water increases the risk of kidney diseases and cancer.

295. Water is a state subject, so it is the responsibility of the States to provide drinking water to the people. However, the central government is also running many schemes to provide clean drinking water. On 21 July 2022, the government informed the Parliament that under the Jal Jeevan Mission launched in August 2019, drinking water will be supplied to every rural household through taps by 2024. So far, out of 19.15 crore rural households in the country, 9.81 crore households are being supplied tap water. Apart from this, AMRUT 2.0 scheme has been started by the central government in October 2021. Under this scheme, a target has been set to supply tap water to all cities in the next five years, i.e., by 2026.

C. Central Ground Water Board

296. CGWB, a subordinate office of the MoWR, is the National Apex Agency entrusted with the responsibilities of providing scientific inputs for management, exploration, monitoring, assessment, augmentation and regulation of groundwater resources of the country. The CGWB has prepared a master plan for rainwater harvesting and recharging groundwater. An area of 4.5 lakh km^2 has been identified in the master plan for recharge with 36 billion m^3 of monsoon runoff. Groundwater recharge through rainwater harvesting has already been made compulsory in many states like Andhra Pradesh, Delhi and Uttarakhand.

III. Watershed Development

297. Integrated Watershed Management Programme (IWMP) was amalgamated as the Watershed Development Component (WDC) of the Pradhan Mantri Krishi Sinchayee Yojana (PMKSY) in 2015–2016. WDC-PMKSY is for the development of rainfed and degraded areas. As on 31 January 2021, end-line evaluation reports of 2,457 completed projects have been prepared. The evaluation reports reveal that there is a significant improvement in the availability of surface and groundwater, increase in productivity, vegetative cover, enhanced livelihood opportunities and household incomes in project areas. As per information from the States, since 2014–2015, 7.09 lakh water harvesting structures were created or rejuvenated, and an additional area of 15.17 lakh ha was brought under protective irrigation up to Q-3 of 2020–2021.

298. According to the National Commission for Integrated Water Resources Development, watershed development undertaken so far has shown mixed results. The projects undertaken by local communities, voluntary organizations and activists had much greater involvement by the people and were flexible and innovative. These projects have also evolved cost-effective techniques and use local traditional knowledge. The commission has emphasized the integration of rural area programmes into an umbrella programme and the inclusion of watershed development as an integral component.

§5. Wastewater and Other Pollutants

299. Discharge of untreated domestic wastewater is a major source of water pollution. Thirty-five metro-cities alone contribute more than 45% of the sewage generated in the country. Most of the cities lack adequate, organized wastewater collection and treatment facilities. Furthermore, the facilities constructed to treat wastewater do not function properly or remain closed most of the time due to improper design and poor maintenance, together with a non-technical and unskilled approach. Also, sewage is subjected to primary treatment and not to a subsequent secondary/tertiary treatment, which makes it unsuitable for artificial recharge. The smaller towns and rural areas do not contribute significantly to sewage due to the low per capita water supply. Wastewater generated in small towns and villages normally percolates into the soil or evaporates through cesspools.

300. The Indian water and wastewater treatment market is growing and gaining widespread attention. Government agencies are implementing regulatory and funding mechanisms to open up the water and wastewater treatment market for private investments. The governmental initiatives, such as the Atal Mission for Rejuvenation and Urban Transformation, National Mission for Clean Ganga (NMCG), Jal Jeevan Mission, and Community Drinking Water Schemes, contribute to the growth of the water and wastewater treatment market.

§6. SEA WATER

301. India has a vast marine ecosystem and biodiversity, which sustains a number of species. The coastal populace is dependent on the resources from this marine ecosystem. The need for protection of this ecosystem has been acknowledged worldwide, and the United Nations Convention on the Law of the Sea (UNCLOS) 1982 prescribes the responsibility of the Coastal States in preserving and protecting the marine environment and associated resources. The Maritime Zones of India Act 1976 enables the Government to take measures for protection of the marine environment. The Coast Guard Act 1978 states that the preservation and protection of marine environment and control of marine pollution is the function of the Indian Coast Guard (ICG). The ICG has been accordingly nominated in 1986 as the Central Coordinating Authority for oil-spill response in the Maritime Zones of India, and Coast Guard officers have been empowered under the Merchant Shipping Act 1958, for taking necessary actions against polluters.

I. Transportation and Marine Pollution

302. There is a serious and catastrophic probability of oil spills from ocean tankers. The threat to the marine ecosystem from these is so great that large colonies of fish and even coral reefs are completely wiped out. In view of marine pollution from oil, Part X B and Part XI A were added to the Merchant Shipping Act of 1958 through the Merchant Shipping (Amendment) Act of 1970 and 1983. These parts deal with marine pollution and civil liability for oil pollution and damages.

Part X B of the Merchant Shipping Act makes owners of an Indian ship and a foreign ship within the jurisdiction of India as per law liable for any pollution damage caused as a result of discharge of oil from the ship except in force majeure situations (section 352-I). Except in case of pollution damage as a result of actual fault of the owner, the liability in respect of any incident is limited to an aggregate amount of the following:

(a) 133 Special Drawing Rights for each ton of ship's tonnage; or
(b) 14 million Special Drawing Rights, whichever is lower. The value of Special Drawing Rights is determined by the Reserve Bank of India.

To meet the above liability, the owner may apply to the High Court for the constitution of a limitation fund (section 352K). The owner of every Indian ship which carries 2,000 tonnes or more oil in bulk has to maintain an insurance or other financial security of the amount specified in section 352 N, and the Director General shall issue a certificate that such security exists. The Indian ship is to possess this certificate for leaving or entering an Indian port. Similarly, a foreign ship must have a certificate issued in India or outside relating to maintenance of insurance or other financial security under the International CLC for Oil Pollution Damage signed at Brussels on 19 November 1969.

303. Part XI A of the Merchant Shipping Act deals with the prevention and containment of pollution of the sea by oil through tankers of 150 tonnes gross or more or other ships of 500 tonnes gross or more; and offshore installations (section 356 A). It prohibits the discharge of oil and oily mixture by tanker, ship or offshore installation except in certain circumstances (section 356 C&D). With respect to oil reception facilities in ports, the Government has been authorized to specify such ports by notification (section 356(4)). The Central Government has power to serve notice to the owner of a polluting ship (section 356 J) and to take measures for preventing or containing oil pollution (section 356 K). The Central Government may give directions to certain ships in case of pollution, to render specified services (section 356 L). The Government has also been given power to levy cess for the purpose of providing oil reception facilities, combating pollution, etc. (section 356 M).

§7. Enforcement and Control

I. Ambient Water Quality Standards

304. The quality standards of water are monitored by PCBs. These standards are to be met by stricter enforcement of source-oriented standards. Where water pollution is due to failure of municipalities and industries to treat water, institutions and mechanisms have been evolved for coordinated action for an area, an example of which is the Ganga Action Plan.

305. The PCBs promote collective treatment facilities in small-scale industrial units, which on their own, cannot afford to instal pollution abatement plants. In other cases, the intending investor is to apply in the prescribed form to the concerned SPCB for consent to establish and operate the industry. The consent contains the conditions with respect to temperature, volume, composition, rate and point of discharge of emissions, effluents, etc., and the period for which consent to operate an industry is granted. The owner of an industry may be required to construct a sewage and effluent treatment system.

306. In case directions of the board are not complied with, action may be initiated against the defaulting industry. Boards have power to initiate criminal prosecution and to move the courts for issuance of injunction so as to restrain polluters. Any person aggrieved by the order of the board may appeal to the Appellate Authority constituted by the appropriate State Government. The boards are empowered to close a defaulting unit and withdraw supply of power or water by their own administrative order, and concerned citizens are allowed to file suits in courts against polluters.

II. Monitoring Water Quality

307. The CPCB has carried out limited WQM of wells in different States and has found Dissolved Oxygen (DO) and total coliform (TC) levels far beyond the permissible limits in many cases. The studies of Central Water Commission on the chemical composition of groundwater in some places have revealed a high concentration of nitrates, potassium and even phosphates, while they are virtually absent or have low concentrations in other places. This is due to improper use of chemicals, fertilizers and poor water management. In the areas of intensive industrial activity, there is a high concentration of heavy and toxic metals in different proportions in groundwater.

308. The Water Pollution Act of 1987 was enacted to provide top priority to drinking water and proper management of water resources. The National River Conservation Plan (NRCP) was launched in 1995 to clean stretches of major rivers of the country. Further, the National Lake Conservation Plan (NLCP) has been in force since 1997 to clean and restore major lakes of the country.

III. The National WQM Programme

309. It was in 1976 that WQM was started by the CPCB starting with eighteen stations on the River Yamuna, and this programme was gradually extended. Now CPCB in collaboration with SPCBs in the States and PCCs in Union Territories has established a National Water Quality Monitoring Network (NWMP) in order to assess the status of water quality of water resources and to facilitate the prevention and control of pollution in water bodies. The WQM network under NWMP comprises 4,484 stations on surface and groundwater in twenty-eight States and eight Union Territories. Monitoring is carried out with a frequency on monthly, quarterly, half yearly and yearly basis. Water samples are analysed for nine core parameters, nineteen general parameters, nine trace metals and set of pesticides as per Guidelines on WQM, 2017 issued by MoEFCC. Analysed water quality parameters are compared with the designated best use water quality criteria recommended by CPCB or primary water quality criteria or outdoor bathing notified under The Environment (Protection) Rules, 1986 or BIS Drinking Water Specifications, i.e., ISO:10500-2012 or water quality standards for coastal water depending on the use of water bodies.

310. Water quality data is used for identification of polluted water bodies, identification of pollution sources in cities for formulation of River Action Plans including interception, diversion and treatment of municipal wastewater, waste management and stricter surveillance of industrial pollution sources. Water quality data is also used for dissemination of information, i.e., sharing of information with NGO, Students, and Researchers.

§8. Evaluation of the Efficiency of Legal Provisions

I. Implementation Failure

311. The environmental laws lay down the limits or standards for discharge of effluents into different water bodies and prescribe punishment in case of non-compliance. The main problem lies in the process of implementation and interaction within various authorities created for this purpose. There are two sources of water pollution, namely, point and non-point or diffuse sources. The point sources include disposal of untreated or partially treated industrial waste or effluents and domestic sewerage. The non-point sources include agricultural runoff. The non-point sources have been excluded from the Water Act. The Water Act requires 'knowledge' whereas other acts like Prevention of Food Adulteration Act, 1954 impose strict liability. So, manipulation is possible in this respect.

312. The EPA, 1986 is an umbrella legislation, equally applicable in case of water pollution, and prevails over the Water Act. The Central Government through MoEFCC lays down standards for maintaining quality of environment by restricting pollutants from various sources. The Act prohibits not only industries but also individuals from discharging effluents or pollutants in excess of the prescribed limits. However, this Act also suffers from various implementation failures due to inadequate infrastructure like monitoring stations to regulate and the frequency of monitoring. The problem of compliance with legal provisions with respect to water pollution is very acute and serious. The monitoring results indicate that water pollution continues to be the predominant source of pollution of aquatic resources.

II. Water Pollution: A Nuisance

313. Considering the criminal aspect, section 277 of IPC, 1860 highlights nuisance under criminal laws. This provision penalize voluntary corruption or fouling of the water of any public spring, reservoir or to render it less fit or unfit for the purpose for which it is ordinarily used. But the provision does not include rivers and private wells. The punishment prescribed is not harsh enough to have deterrence effect as it prescribes imprisonment of maximum three months and a fine of maximum INR 500. Section 133 of Code of Criminal Procedure, 1973 allows for speedy and summary remedy in case of unlawful obstruction or nuisance to be removed from public places or river or channel which may or is be used lawfully by the public. But, the injunctive relief given under the provision should not interfere with the orders of SPCB.

III. Multiplicity of Agencies

314. There has also been poor implementation by SPCB as they have not been successful to act against defaulters due to lack of financial, technical and human resources, leading to low rate of compliance. Further, multiple responsibilities on SPCB have caused problem in implementation as the Board is also to look after air pollution under Air (Prevention and Control of Pollution) Act, 1981.

315. The other major problem with the enforcement is the institutional setup. As many agencies are involved in collecting data, and this results in duplication of effort. A proper legal framework for regulating withdrawals of groundwater is not in place. Though efforts have been made to check overexploitation of groundwater through licensing, credit or electricity restrictions; however, these have not worked. In any case, the licences do not monitor or regulate the quantum of water extracted. Therefore, to effectively manage the country's water resources, an appropriate legal framework is required that clearly specifies the rights and responsibilities of the various stakeholders. The Centre had come up with a Model Bill for guidance of States, namely the Groundwater (Sustainable Management) Bill, 2017 which is still not made a law. The Bill was drafted by the MoWR, RD&GR, a template that states can use to adopt legislation capable of addressing the fast-increasing groundwater crisis faced by many states.

IV. Judicial Activism

316. The Supreme Court, various High Courts and NGT have adjudicated a number of cases and applied principles of polluters pay and precautionary principle to impose liability on defaulters. Few cases have given a chance to court to rectify the problems arising due to ineffective implementation or non-implementation of the existing provisions.

317. In *M.C. Mehta v. Union of India* (Kanpur Tanneries case) (AIR 1988 SC 1037) Court restrained the tanneries in Kanpur from discharging their untreated effluents into river Ganga. The Court held the financial condition of tanneries to set up treatment plant as irrelevant and asked them to either close or relocate. Again in another petition, *M.C. Mehta v. Union of India* (AIR 1988 SC 1115) Court held that SPCB has failed miserably to take into consideration the effluents being discharged by factories into river Ganga, thereby polluting it. The municipal authorities had the duty to avoid the public nuisance, but no step had been taken by them. Court further held that most of the provisions regarding water pollution in the Water Act and municipal laws have just remained on paperwork without any action being taken when it was needed.

318. The Court has successfully directed the authorities to reverse the environmental damage caused by tanneries in Tamil Nadu as it has polluted river Palar by discharging their effluents. This river was the major source of drinking water supply. The petition was filed by Vellore Citizens Welfare Forum (AIR 1996 SCC 2715) in order to suspend these factories from releasing their effluents into river or shut down completely.

319. In *Indian Council for Enviro-Legal Action v. Union of India and Others* (AIR 1996 SC 1446), there was a concern towards the quality of water that was affected in water bodies in Udaipur wherein the factories have released the sludge and toxic materials directly into water, thereby polluting it badly. The Court held the defaulters absolutely liable and levied costs.

320. The Court in *Andhra Pradesh Pollution Control Board v. Prof. M.V. Nayadu* (MANU/SC/0032/1999) held that it is a fundamental duty of citizen to access drinking water, and state has a duty to provide clean drinking water. Also, in *M.C. Mehta v. Union of India* (MANU/SC/0247/2004SC), the Supreme Court declared that groundwater is a public asset and citizens have right to access air, water or earth freely under Article 21. The Court in *Municipal Council, Ratlam v. Vardhichand* (AIR 1980 SC 1622) invoked section 133 of CrPC, to direct municipality to perform its duties.

321. The Court has not only accepted the principle of Sustainable Development through its judicial activism but also applied it in many cases. For example, in *U.P. Pollution Control Board v. Mohan Meakins Ltd.* [(2000) 3 SCC 569], the company was polluting river Gomati by discharging its effluents in river and thereby increasing pollution beyond permissible limits. The Court took managers and directors of company to task and prosecuted them by applying the principle of sustainable development for environment.

322. Supreme Court has held that courts cannot afford to deal lightly with cases involving pollution of air and water. It was observed that the message must go to all concerned. The courts will share the parliamentary concerns on the escalating pollution level of our environment. Those who discharge noxious polluting effluents into streams may be unconcerned about the enormity of the injury which it inflicts on the public health at large, the irreparable impairment it causes to the aquatic organisms, the damage it inflicts on the life and health of animals. So the courts should not deal with the prosecution for the offences under the act in a casual or routine manner. The court emphasized that Parliamentary concern in the matter is adequately reflected in strengthening the measures prescribed by the Water (Prevention and Control of Pollution) Act of 1974, and the courts should not ignore the seriousness of the matter.

323. So, despite various challenges in the implementation of the law, the courts through judicial activism and taking cognizance of petitions filed by public-spirited persons have been successful in controlling and preventing the water pollution caused by factories, industries, tanneries, individuals, etc.

Chapter 5. Waste

§1. Introduction

324. Every type of waste creates problems in the country whether it be municipal waste, industrial, biomedical or hazardous or e-waste. The problem of biomedical waste has also assumed disastrous proportions. India is the second-most populous country in the world and its population is increasing. This will definitely complicate the problem of municipal waste. Industrial waste is another huge problem which is being tackled through waste minimization methods and use of cleaner technology. Rather than taking an end of the pipe approach and then dealing with waste, prevention is the best approach.

§2. Statutory Structure and Legal Regime

I. Legislation

325. There are various legislation and rules that deal with handling and management of waste. A list is given below:

- the Insecticides Act of 1968;
- the Poisons Act of 1919;
- the Hazardous and Other Wastes (Management and Transboundary Movement) Rules of 2016;
- the MSIHCs, Rules of 1989 as amended in 1994 (Framed under the EPA);
- the SWM Rules, 2016;
- the Plastic Waste (Management and Handling) Use Rules of 2016;
- the Bio-medical Waste Management Rules of 2016;
- the CAEPPR Rules of 1996;
- E-Waste (Management and Handling) Rules, 2016.

II. Salient Features of Legislation

A. The SWM Rules of 2016

326. In 2016, the SWM Rules 2016 were introduced in supersession of Municipal Solid Waste Rules. These Rules broadened the scope of application by including places of pilgrims, airports, special economic zones, ports and harbours, defence establishments and every domestic, institutional, commercial and any other non-residential solid waste generator under its ambit. The Rules for the first time prescribed the duty of waste generator. A Central Monitoring Committee has been constituted to monitor the implementation. Criteria for landfilling and waste-to-energy plants are also provided. The Rules prescribe duties of Ministries and Departments other than MoEFCC.

B. The Hazardous and Other Wastes (Management and Transboundary Movement) Rules of 2016

327. In furtherance of the Convention on the Control of Transboundary Movement of HWs and their Disposal (Basel Convention) of 1989, the HW (Management and Handling) Rules 1989 were initially enacted. The rules were framed under sections 6, 8 and 25 of the Environmental Protection Act of 1986. These rules have been replaced by Hazardous and Other Waste (Management and Transboundary Movement) Rules 2016.

C. The Manufacture, Storage and Import of Hazardous Chemical Rules of 1989

328. These rules framed under sections 6, 8 and 25 of the Environmental (Protection) Act of 1986 prescribe the duties of the occupier of a site where hazardous chemicals are stored. The occupier is to notify major accidents (Rule 5) and furnish safety reports and to formulate on-site and off-site emergency plans. The rules are also applicable to the import of hazardous chemicals. The list of hazardous chemicals is given in Schedule 1, which, *inter alia*, includes LPG. For hazardous chemicals, the Government has specified certain threshold quantities within the framework of the EPA of 1986. If an industrial installation uses hazardous chemicals in an amount equal to or greater than the threshold quantity, it is to comply with these rules.

D. Bio-medical Waste Management Rules of 2016

329. On 28 March 2016, the GOI brought the Biomedical Waste Management Rules, 2016 replacing the Biomedical Waste (Management and Handling) Rules, 1998. Through Biomedical Waste Management Rules, 2016, several changes and additions have been made to further improve the collection, segregation, processing, treatment and disposal of the biomedical wastes in an environmentally sound manner. The existing biomedical waste treatment facilities are required to meet the revised standards of emissions and effluent also to instal the continuous monitoring equipment.

E. Plastic Waste (Management and Handling) Rules of 2011 as Amended in 2018

330. The Plastic Waste (Management and Handling) Rules 2011 as amended in 2018 lay down that the phasing out of Multilayered Plastic (MLP) is now applicable to MLP, which are 'non-recyclable, or non-energy recoverable, or with no alternate use'. The amended Rules also prescribe a central registration system for the registration of the producer/importer/brand owner. The Rules also lay down that any mechanism for the registration should be automated and should take into account ease of doing business for producers, recyclers and manufacturers. The centralized registration system will be evolved by CPCB for the registration of the producer/importer/brand owner. While a national registry has been prescribed for producers with presence in more than two states, a state-level registration has been prescribed for smaller producers/brand owners operating within one or two states.

F. Battery (Management and Handling) Rules of 2001

331. The Battery (Management and Handling) Rules of 2001 (as amended on May 2010) organize and streamline the collection and recycling of scrap lead batteries in an eco-friendly manner. These rules regulate the collection, channelization and recycling as well as import of used lead acid batteries in the country. The rules stipulate that used lead acid batteries can be auctioned or sold only to recyclers on the basis of their possessing environmentally sound facilities for recycling. Every manufacture, importer, assembler and re-conditioner is required that an equal number of batteries are collected against the new batteries sold. As per amended Rules, CPCB has been given the responsibility of registering the importers of new lead acid batteries. The CPCB has started a project for the development of web-based Battery (Importers) Registration Management System wherein the applicants for registration can apply online, view the status of their applications, give undertaking prior to import and also submit half yearly return on the same platform.

G. Rules Relating to Collections and Recycling of Used Oil and Waste Oil

332. The rules for ensuring proper collection and recycling of used oil and waste oil generated have been inserted in the Hazardous and Other Wastes (Management and Transboundary Movement) Rules, 2016.

H. E-waste (Management and Handling) Rules 2016

333. The E-Waste Management Rules, 2016 have been notified in supersession of the e-waste (Management & Handling) Rules, 2011. The new Rules are more stringent and reflect the government's commitment to environmental governance. The E-waste rules include Compact Fluorescent Lamp and other mercury containing lamps, as well as other such equipment. The Rules bring the producers under Extended Producer Responsibility (EPR), along with targets. The producers have been made responsible for collection of E-waste and for its exchange. The bulk consumers have to collect the items and hand them over to authorized recyclers. The different producers can have a separate Producer Responsibility Organization and ensure collection of E-waste, as well as its disposal in an environmentally safe and sound manner. The role of State Governments has been introduced to ensure safety, health and skill development of the workers involved in dismantling and recycling operations. E-waste recycling based on environmentally proper recycling principles is permitted under The Hazardous and Other Waste (Management and Transboundary Movement) Rules, 2016.

III. International Conventions and Protocols

A. *Basel Convention of 1989 on the Control of Transboundary Movement of HWs and Their Disposal*

334. India is a signatory to the Basel Convention, which aims at checking the illegal traffic in HW from one country to another and requires the countries to ensure that HWs and hazardous recyclable materials are managed in an environmentally sound manner. This convention aims at controlling improper treatment of HWs and takes care of the dangers arising out of the transboundary movement and disposal of HWs. The parties to the convention are required to initiate appropriate legal, administrative and other measures to implement and enforce the provisions of the convention.

The Regional Centre (RC) of the Basel Convention for SAARC countries started preliminary operations during 2000. The centre is being supported under the Canada-India Project. In a meeting of the convention countries held in Geneva in December 2002, the four major issues discussed were the strategic plan for implementation of the Basel Convention, the establishment of Basel Convention Regional Centres (RCs), mechanism for effective implementation of the convention and partnership with industry and multilateral environmental agreements. A Technical Working Group (TWG) and a Legal Working Group (LWG) have been set up under the Basel Convention. The TWG is preparing technical guidelines for environmentally sound management of ship breaking. India is actively participating in this effort along with Norway and the Netherlands.

B. *Rotterdam Convention on the PIC Procedure for Certain Hazardous Chemicals and Pesticides in International Trade*

335. The Rotterdam Convention on the Prior Informed Consent (PIC) Procedure for Certain Hazardous Chemicals and Pesticides in International Trade was adopted at a Conference at Rotterdam in 1998. The MoEFCC is the nodal ministry in the GOI for this Convention.

C. *Stockholm Convention on POPs*

336. India has signed the Stockholm Convention on Persistent Organic Pollutants (POPs) in May 2002. The convention aims to eliminate production, use, import and export of twelve POPs wherever techno-economically feasible and in the interim period restrict the production and use of these chemicals. A project entitled

'Preliminary assessment to identify the requirements for developing a National Implementation Plan in India as a first step to implement the Stockholm Convention on POPs' has been initiated.

§3. ORDINARY REFUSE/SWM

337. Under the 74th Constitutional Amendment, disposal and management of Municipal Solid Waste is one of the eighteen functional domains of the Municipal Corporations and Nagar Panchayats. The major rules and regulations for disposal of SWM are; the Bio-Medical Waste (Management And Handling) Rules, 2016; Municipal Solid Waste (Management And Handling) Rules 2000; The Plastic Waste (Management And Handling) Rules, 2011 as amended in 2018 and E-Waste (Management And Handling) Amendment Rules, 2016.

I. Collection and Disposal of Waste

338. SWM is a state subject, and it is the responsibility of the state governments to ensure that appropriate SWM practices are introduced in all the cities and towns in the State. However, SWM is a municipal function and Urban Local Bodies (ULBs) are directly responsible for it. The ULBs are required to plan, design, operate, and maintain the SWM in their respective cities/towns. India's 4,378 municipalities spend between 10%–50% of the municipal budget for SWM and between 30% and 50% of the total staff are typically engaged in SWM. This critical service, if performed poorly, results in deterioration of health, sanitation and environmental degradation. The SWM Rules, 2016 provide that only non-recyclable, non-biodegradable and non-combustible waste should go to a dumpsite. However, hundreds of tonnes of biodegradable and combustible waste are still dumped at the site every day. The towering mountain of garbage, as per government data, houses tonnes of mixed refuse. This has piled up over the years because of improper waste segregation and processing.

II. Efforts Made at Various Forums

339. The innovation and interventions are required across the waste cycle. For example, better packaging materials from the producers which must be biodegradable and channelize the same through 'Route to Recycle', community engagement for better waste segregation practices and proactive action by municipal authorities for effective collection and creating better Route to Recycle infrastructure. Waste management is still not very much organized.

340. The recycling industry is still within the informal sector. Ragpickers in every city go door-to-door to collect paper, glass, plastic, etc. More than 65% of recyclable and biodegradable waste ends up in landfills. The problem is the management of this vast amount of recyclable or biodegradable waste that is not collected by ragpickers. Further, the responsibility of the waste that is generated and its lifecycle is not the responsibility of Municipal authorities alone – this is a shared responsibility of waste producers and regulators. EPR addresses the waste disposal issue.

III. Guidelines on Fly Ash

341. Fly ash is the residue of coal combustion, which, if disposed of improperly, is hazardous for health and the environment due to the concentrated presence of heavy metals. The MoEFCC issuing mandates since 1999, prescribing targets for the use of fly ash with an aim to achieve 100% ash utilization in a phased manner. The notification dated 12 December 2021 issued by the MoEFCC, brings out a comprehensive framework for ash utilization including a system of environmental compensation based on polluter pays principle. This notification replaces the 1999 notification that had originally set up rules for fly ash utilization. It also supersedes the various amendments to the 1999 notification made in 2003, 2009 and 2016, which have all sought to manage the generation of fly ash.

342. As per Notification TPP are required to utilize 100% of their yearly fly ash output within a three-year cycle to avoid penalties and 'at no point' utilization fall below 80%. India has over 200 coal power plants that generate an enormous amount of fly ash. According to the CEA, India's coal plants generated 232.56 million tonnes of fly ash in 2020–2021. Although 93% was utilized, millions of tonnes accumulated over the years lie unused. A study by think tank CSE in March 2021 found that over half of India's power plants failed to fully utilize their fly ash and fell behind targets. The Notification also deals with 'legacy ash', or the build-up of fly ash by TPP over decades which is required to be utilized over a period of ten years from the time the notification is applicable, from 1 April 2022 onwards. Legacy ash must be dealt with 'over and above' the yearly ash output by power plants, as per the notification. The plants that fail to have 100% utilization levels within this period will have to pay the CPCB INR 1,000 per tonne of unutilized ash. The compensation money collected by the CPCB for ash that has not been utilized will be used 'towards the safe disposal of the unutilized ash' as well as research on ash-based products.

343. The Notification lists the ways in which the fly ash can be utilized, which include the manufacturing of bricks, tiles, cement, construction of roads, flyovers filling and export to other countries. It also allows for the 'filling of low-lying areas', filling of empty mines, and 'agriculture in a controlled manner based on soil testing'.

§4. HAZARDOUS CHEMICALS/WASTE/PESTICIDES

344. During 2020–2021, 10.92 MMT of HW (including quantity imported and previous stock) has been generated. This quantity of HW has been managed through recycling, utilization, co-processing and disposal in common /captive Treatment Storage and Disposal Facilities. For management of HW major contribution has been towards utilization (i.e., 4.18 MMT, including co-processing), followed by disposal (2.89 MMT) in secured landfill/incinerator and recycling (1.44 MMT). Further, of 4.18 MMT of HW utilized, 45% has been contributed by co-processing alone. There are 2,162 HW recycling units, 736 non-captive utilizers (under Rule 9 of HOWM Rules, 2016), 96 cement plants for co-processing of HW and 261 units involved in captive utilization of HW (National Inventory on Generation and Management of Hazardous and Other Wastes (2020–2021) CPCB, December 2021).

I. Legal Instruments

345. The legal instruments involved in the management of HWs are the Hazardous and Other Waste (Management and Transboundary Movement) Rules of 2016, E-waste (Management and Handling) Rules 2011, the Manufacture, Storage and Import of Hazardous Chemicals (MSIHCs) Rules of 1989 as amended in 1994, the Bio-medical Waste Management Rules of 2016, Regulation on Lead Contents in Household and Decorative Paints Rules, 2016, Regulation of Polychlorinated Biphenyls Order, 2016, Manufacture, Use, Import, Export and Storage of Hazardous Micro-organisms/Genetically Engineered Organisms and Cells of 1989, the Batteries (Management and Handling) Rules of 2001 and the Hazardous Substances (classification, packaging and labelling) Rules, 2011 to regulate and ensure proper classification and labelling of hazardous substances.

346. The Hazardous and Other Wastes (Management & Transboundary Movement) Rules, 2016 define any waste which by virtue of any of its physical, chemical, reactive, toxic, flammable, explosive or corrosive characteristics causes danger or is likely to cause danger to health or environment, whether alone or when in contact with other wastes or substances. The Rules also deal with 'Other Waste' and Waste Management in the sequence of priority of prevention, minimization, reuse, recycling, recovery, co-processing, and safe disposal.

II. Sources of HW

347. HW includes sludge contaminated by heavy metals, wastes from paints, dyes and organic chemical units and highly acidic and alkaline wastes. The relatively more industrialized States like Gujarat, Maharashtra, Tamil Nadu and Andhra Pradesh face problems relating to toxic and HW. The major hazard waste generating industries are petroleum and petrochemicals, pharmaceuticals, pesticides, paint and dyes, fertilizers, inorganic chemicals and general engineering industries, etc.

The presence of toxic chemicals in solid/liquid effluents from industries and other activities has led to groundwater contamination.

A. Import of HW

348. The import of HW containing toxic matter like beryllium, selenium, chromium, thallium, pesticides, e-waste, etc., has been restricted. The export and import of waste containing cyanide, mercury and arsenic have been prohibited since December 1996. The import of waste oil and metals such as brass, zinc and lead for processing to recover resources is fully regulated by the MoEFCC.

III. HW Management Guidelines

349. The guidelines for HW provide that the regulatory authorities should inform the occupier or generator of HW about certain aspects, some of which are given below:

- To keep a complete record of the types, quantities and characteristics of HW.
- To segregate HW at source from non-HW.
- To transport HW only through the specified and registered transporters.
- To fulfil the pre-transport requirements before transporting HW.
- To dispose of HW only at notified disposal facilities.
- The regulatory authority shall ask the occupier or generator to submit quarterly reports.
- The authorities should ensure that the occupier/generator sends a copy of the manifest to them as soon as the HW is transported or shipped for ultimate disposal.
- The regulatory authorities may allow the occupier/generator to store the HW on-site, provided that the waste is stored in specified containers and the occupier/generator follows the requirements for storing in the containers. The date upon which each period of storage begins is clearly marked and visible on each container. While being stored on-site each container is labelled or marked with the words 'HW', both in English and the respective local language.

IV. Guidelines for Owner or Operator of HWs Storage, Treatment and Disposal Facility

A. Licensing System

350. Every occupier/owner/manager of a site dealing with or generating HW must have a HW authorization or permit to handle, generate, dispose of, recycle, reuse or carry out any other activity involving HW. For the import and export of HW, prior approval is required to be obtained from the MoEFCC. The MoEFCC in its review of applications is assisted by a technical review committee. The regulatory authorities issue consent to an owner/operator of a facility who demonstrates his technical, financial and managerial competence, and that his staff are properly trained. The authorities specify in the consent the wastes which a facility can receive, the operational conditions which must be met, the monitoring and control procedures to be carried out and the records to be kept. Along with the application for consent, the following information is to be furnished by the owner/operator of the facility:

- Area required for the facility.
- Types of wastes to be handled, stored, treated, and/or disposed.
- Facilities available for managing these wastes.
- EIA of the area where the activity has been proposed.
- Contingency plan of the facility.

351. The regulatory authorities are to ensure that the owner or operator of a facility has all necessary equipment such as fire control equipment, decontamination equipment, water spray system and internal communication or alarm systems capable of meeting any emergency situation at the facility.

B. *Copy of the Manifest*

352. The owner or operator of a facility is to ensure that a copy of the manifest reaches the authorities after receiving the HW from the occupier/generator. The owner/operator should indicate the proposed treatment and disposal scheme to be followed for the HW.

V. Common Transport, Storage and Disposal Facility

353. According to the Hazardous and Other Wastes (Management and Transboundary Movement) Rules of 2016, all HWs are required to be treated and disposed of in the prescribed manner. In the absence of common disposal facilities in the country, permission has been granted to the HW generating units in the small-scale sector, for storing their waste temporarily in a secure, lined pit/facility within their premises. As a demonstration project, the MoEFCC has supported the setting up of a common Transport, Storage and Disposal Facility at Trans Thane Creak, State of Maharashtra.

VI. The Hazardous Substances Management Division

354. The Hazardous Substances Management Division (HSMD) is the nodal point within the ministry for management of chemical emergencies and hazardous substances. The main objective of the division is to promote safe management and use of hazardous substances including hazardous chemicals and HWs, in order to avoid damage to health and environment. The activities of the division can be grouped under three main thrust areas, viz. Chemical Safety; HWs Management and SWM. The division is also the nodal point for international conventions that is, the Basel Convention on the Control of Transboundary Movement of HWs and their Disposal; the Rotterdam Convention on the PIC Procedure for Certain Hazardous Chemicals and Pesticides in International Trade and the Stockholm Convention on POP.

355. To deal with the emergencies arising from hazardous chemicals, a control room and a Crisis Alert System have been established in the MoEFCC. A Red Book entitled 'Central Crisis Group Alert System' containing names, addresses and telephone numbers of central and state authorities and experts to be contacted in case of chemical emergencies has been published and is regularly updated.

§5. Nuclear Waste

356. Radioactive waste management in India is governed by the Atomic Energy (Safe Disposal of Radioactive Wastes) Rules, 1987, G.S.R.-125. It is mandatory for every user of radioactive material to obtain authorization from the AERB for the disposal of disused sources or waste. The Atomic Energy Regulatory Board (AERB) was constituted by the Central Government in November 1983 to exercise the regulatory and safety functions envisaged under sections 16, 17 and 23 of the Atomic Energy Act, 1962. The Board has five members including a full-time chairman, an ex officio member, three part-time members and a full-time secretary, HI India, the Chairman, of the AERB is the competent authority to enforce provisions of radiation safety. The AERB has powers to lay down safety standards and frame rules and regulations about regulatory and safety requirements envisaged under the Act. The regulatory control covers radiation safety and industrial safety of all the nuclear fuel cycle activities and radiation facilities under the Department of Atomic Energy (DAE) and of radiation installations in the medical, industrial and research institutions in India. Given the very small quantity of high-level waste generated post reprocessing and technologies for separation, partitioning and burning of waste being developed by the country, there is no need for a deep underground geological disposal facility in the near future. India is pursuing an indigenous three-stage nuclear power programme to provide the country with long-term energy security in a sustainable manner. In addition, Light Water Reactors based on foreign cooperation are also being set up.

357. Three types of wastes is generated from a nuclear power plant (NPP): Low, mid and high-level wastes. The very low-level wastes such as mops and gloves are disposed of in landfill-type sites. The low-level waste that includes low concentrations of long-lived radionuclides and high concentrations of short-lived radionuclides are buried within the exclusion zone in leak-proof reinforced cement concrete vaults/trenches/tile holes. It is the mid and high-level wastes that must be sequestered in DGRs. Heat-emitting and highly radioactive spent-fuel rods are kept in spent-fuel pools at the reactors for five operational years and cooled with borated water that absorbs neutrons and stops the chain reaction that had been going on inside the reactor. As the pool gets filled, the spent-fuel rods are moved and reprocessed.

§6. Recycling and Cleaner Technology

358. A Policy Statement for Abatement of Pollution has been adopted which provides several instruments in the form of regulations, legislation, agreements, fiscal incentives and various other measures to prevent and abate pollution. The issues pertaining to prevention and control of pollution are dealt with by adopting a multipronged approach. Importance is being given to promotion of clean and low waste technologies, reuse or recycling, improvement of water quality, natural resource accounting, institutional and HRD, control of pollution at source. The significant benefit of this approach is that when waste is reduced/eliminated or solvents are revived and reused, it leads to resource conservation during various industrial processes and minimizes the levels of pollutants.

I. Clean Technology

359. Under the clean technology, the focus has been sector specific, and there are separate programmes and schemes targeted at individual sectors such as solar, wind, energy efficiency. Each of the sectors is under the overall administrative jurisdiction of separate ministries at the central government level and their corresponding departments at the state government level. Thus, there is no single unified financing mechanism. The financing available under such schemes and programmes varies from support for technology development to capital subsidy for commercializing and rollout of projects.

II. Waste Minimization Circle in SSI

360. The WMC is a government-supported initiative that promotes waste minimization in India and sponsored by the MoEFCC. WMC assists Small and Medium-sized Enterprises (SME) in reducing waste in their manufacturing facilities. This project is being carried out by the NPC under the Ministry of Commerce and Industry and with partial support from the World Bank.

III. Waste Recycling

361. Waste from industrial, municipal, agricultural, construction and demolition (C&D) and other sources normally contain materials like ferrous metal, non-ferrous metals, plastics and glass. In India, recycling rates are below international benchmarks. It is estimated that waste management in India is potentially a USD 15 billion industry. Out of the entire waste produced, 25% are dry waste components that can be recycled. This recyclable waste, dumped into landfills due to a lack of proper collection and infrastructure, can be reused as raw material.

362. According to the Un-Plastic Collective study, India produces 9.46 million tonnes of plastic waste per year, with 40% of it remaining uncollected. India also generates about two million tonnes (MT) of e-waste annually, which makes plastics and electronics two key components of waste generation. However, these waste generation components, alongside solid waste, have a huge potential to be capitalized into channels of high revenue generation. Similarly, 81 billion worth of paper waste and paper pulp was imported to India in 2020. On the other hand, only 20% of paper waste is being collected, segregated, and recycled rest goes to landfills. The same applies to glass and metal waste. With more and more businesses aiming to find alternative and cost-cutting elements of production, recycled products are equally gaining the demand. A tonne of recycled paper saves 17 trees, 2.5 barrels of oil, 4100 kWh of electricity, 4 m^3 of landfill space, and 31,780 litres of water (TOI dated 9 June 2022).

§7. Evaluation of Efficiency of Legal Provision

363. The status of implementation of waste management is monitored by MoEFCC. With rapid urbanization, there is massive waste management challenge. India generates approximately 62 million tons of waste with an average annual growth rate of 4%. It is also found that currently, India generates 70 million metrics of municipal solid wastes. Out of it, only 20% is recycled, and the rest ends up in landfills and oceans affecting humans, and marine life, along with destroying the environment. The concept of common waste treatment facility is being widely promoted and accepted as it uses waste as a resource by either using it as a co-fuel or co-raw material in manufacturing processes. This has led to rise of Public-Private Partnership (PPP) models in waste management which has open doors for doing business in waste management. Bio-medical Waste (Management and Handling) Rules prescribe that there should be a Common Bio-medical Waste Treatment Facility at every 150 km in the country. CBWTFs have been set up and are functioning in cities and towns.

364. The failure to implement legislation to check environmental damage by industrial units led to PIL being filed. This resulted in orders for the closure/shifting of industrial units producing hazardous chemicals from Delhi, closure of 200 tanneries in Tamil Nadu and 35 foundries in Bengal. In *Indian Council for Environmental Legal Action v. Union of India* (AIR 1996 SC 103), the court focussed attention on the woes of the people living in a village. The sludge, a lethal waste, left out for years after the chemical industries were closed, caused heavy damage to the environment. Viewing the case as 'social action litigation' (SAL), the Supreme Court ordered that remedial action be taken and compensation be given for the silent tragedies in line with the '*Mehta* absolute liability' principle.

Chapter 6. Soil Pollution

§1. Introduction

365. Soil pollution is the presence of toxic chemicals (pollutants or contaminants) in soil, in high concentrations posing a risk to human health and/or the ecosystem. In the case of contaminants which occur naturally in soil, pollution occurs if the levels of the contaminants in soil exceed the levels naturally present. Besides, various compounds get into the soil from the atmosphere, for instance, with water, by wind activity or other types of soil disturbances, and from surface water bodies and shallow groundwater flowing through the soil. When the amounts of soil contaminants exceed natural levels, soil is said to be polluted.

366. Soil is used as the dumping ground of domestic, human, animal, industrial and agricultural waste material. A large number of hazardous chemicals and thousand tons of wastes are dumped on the land. These are leached by municipal and industrial wastes and are responsible for pollution of groundwater. The problem of soil pollution is compounded by the use of agrochemicals, e.g., pesticides, fungicides, insecticides, biocides, fertilizers and manure. Besides these, the soil is polluted by deadly pathogenic organisms. Soil pollution differs from air and water pollution in the sense that the pollutants in soil remain in direct contact with the soil for relatively longer periods. The soil has been heavily polluted as a result of industrial and green revolution.

§2. Statutory Structure and Legal Regime

I. Legislation

367. A great difficulty is faced in remediation of soil pollution in comparison with air and water; soil pollution as a threat to human life could not be dealt with properly due to lack of comprehensive legislation. The soil resources are facing threats from deliberate use of contaminated organics, materials and irrigation water or from atmospheric depositions, spillage of effluents, etc. (*Indian Council for Enviro-Legal Action v. uoi*, AIR 1996 SC 1446 and *Pravin Bhai Jashbhai and others v. State of Guj and others* (1995) 2GLR 1210).

368. There is no direct legislation dealing with soil pollution. This subject is dealt with indirectly in various legislation. In general, it is dealt with by EPA which deal with pollution. Some of the legislation are as follows:

- the Industries (Development and Regulations) Act and Amendment Act of 1987;
- the Mines and Minerals (Regulation and Development) Act of 1956 (section 13-qq);
- the Mineral Conservation and Development Rules of 1988;
- the Coal Mines (Conservation and Development) Amendment Act of 1985;
- the Environment (Siting for Industrial Projects) Rules of 1999;

– Provision in State Acts on Town and Country Planning;
– the Urban Land (Ceiling and Regulation) Act of 1976;
– the Model Regional and Town Planning and Development Law of 1985.

II. Global Soil Partnership – Action Framework 2022–2030 (GSP)

369. The commitment of many countries to the cause of soil health, security and function was confirmed at the Global Forum for Food and Agriculture's (GFFA) 14th Berlin Agriculture Ministers' Conference in January 2022. The agreed communiqué by the sixty-eight agriculture ministers stressed that healthy soils are key in addressing and combating the wide-ranging global challenges, in particular, the production of sufficient nutritious and safe food, adaptation to and mitigation of climate change, and the halting and reversal of biodiversity loss. The Communiqué adopted at the 14th GFFA calls for actions to restore soil health and for all nations to adopt SSM. The GSP's proposed new Action Framework is aligned to this call by translating it into concrete actions on the ground. The GSP may act as a global voice to give adequate recognition to healthy soils and promote their sustainable management, conservation, rehabilitation, and restoration. The GSP may fill the current gap in the assessment and monitoring of soil status and trends and develop specific measurable and harmonized targets and indicators.

§3. Causes of Soil Pollution

370. Soil is polluted when it is contaminated by different pollutants like toxic chemicals from man-made products or wind or precipitation. The chemicals within soil itself may also react with other chemicals and lead to soil contamination. If the chemical placed into the soil is unnatural and harmful, then the soil will be polluted or contaminated causing risk to the environment. In case contaminant is a natural component of the soil, still it could cause soil pollution if the concentration is already too high. The main sources and causes of soil pollution include industrial wastes, urban and domestic waste, radioactive pollutants, agrochemicals, chemical and metallic pollutants, biological agents, acid rain, etc. The causes of soil pollution are as follows.

I. Waste Disposal on Soil

371. A growing cause for concern is how waste is disposed of. Every person excretes a certain amount of personal waste in the form of urine and faeces. While much of it moves into the sewer system, there is also a large quantity that is dumped directly into landfills in the form of diapers. Even the sewer system ends at the landfill, where the biological waste pollutes the soil and water. This is because our bodies are full of toxins and chemicals that are now seeping into the land and causing pollution of the soil.

II. Acid Rain

372. Acid rain is caused when pollutants present in the air mix up with the rain and fall back on the ground. The polluted water could dissolve away some of the essential nutrients found in the soil and change the structure of the soil.

III. Agricultural Activities

373. The utilization of chemicals in agriculture has gone up tremendously since technology has provided modern pesticides and fertilizers. They are full of chemicals that are not produced in nature and are not broken down by it. As a result, they seep into the ground and after mixing with water, slowly reduce the fertility of the soil. Other chemicals damage the composition of the soil and make it more erodible by water and air. Plants absorb many of these pesticides, and when they decompose, they cause soil pollution since they become a part of the land. Pesticides enter the human body through inhalation, oral or dermal exposure, and the main cause of several diseases such as cancer, respiratory diseases, skin diseases, endocrine disruption, and reproduction disorders. Plants that are grown in polluted soil may accumulate high concentrations of soil pollutants through a process known as bioaccumulation. When these plants are consumed, all the accumulated pollutants are passed up the food chain. This can result in the loss/extinction of many desirable animal species. Also, these pollutants can eventually make their way to the top of the food chain and manifest as diseases in human beings.

374. Pesticides also affect non-target organisms, especially insect's natural enemies and pollinators which are very important. The destruction of natural enemies can trigger pest problems as they play an important role in regulating pest population levels. Along with natural enemies, populations of soil and aquatic arthropods are also considerably disturbed because of indiscriminate pesticide use in agriculture. Pesticides degenerate soil and harm invertebrates, including nematodes, microarthropods, earthworms, and other small organisms that play an important role in soil ecosystems.

IV. Construction Activity

375. Construction sites are the most important triggers of soil pollution in construction areas. Almost any chemical substance handled at construction sites may pollute the soil. However, the higher risk comes from those chemicals that can travel more easily through the air as fine PM. Further, construction dust may easily spread around through the air and is especially dangerous because of its lower particle size (less than ten microns). Such construction dust can trigger respiratory illnesses such as asthma and bronchitis, and even cancer. Moreover, the sites that involve the demolition of older buildings can release asbestos, a toxic mineral that can act as a poison in soil. Asbestos particles can be redistributed by the wind to a large area, thereby polluting soil around the site.

V. Industrialization

376. The rapid pace of industrialization, urbanization and infrastructural development has created immense problem of soil pollution and environmental disturbances. These activities have resulted in soil pollution directly through changed land use and also through the negative impacts of harmful gases, polluted water and waste disposal. Oil leaks can happen during the extraction, storage and transport of oil and chemicals. The chemicals present in the fuel deteriorate the quality of soil and make it unsuitable for cultivation. These chemicals can enter into the groundwater through the soil and make the water undrinkable. For example, foundry activities, tanning and manufacturing processes that involve release of pollutants may result in dispersion of contaminants in the environment.

VI. Mining Activities

377. Mining activity has been the biggest contributor to the problem, especially since the amount of mining for a variety of raw materials and manufacturing has increased. Most industries are dependent on minerals extracted from the earth. Whether it is iron ore, radioactive materials or coal, the by-products are contaminated, and they are not disposed of in a safe manner. As a result, the industrial waste lingers on the soil surface for a long time and makes it unsuitable for use.

§4. Enforcement and Control

378. The strategy to counter soil pollution includes treatment of catchment areas, comprehensive watershed management, low-cost measures for revegetation or reforestation, use of compost in place of chemical manures, etc. The problem areas are identified through remote sensing, and micro-level plans are made to reclaim and improve the affected lands to be implemented through local governments, NGOs and people's groups. The Government has also started many schemes so as to carry out objectives on soil conservation.

I. Use of Fertilizers, Pesticides and Insecticides

379. A balanced and integrated use of chemical fertilizers, pesticides and insecticides could enhance the crop yield, but an excess of it may poison the soil. The excess of chemical fertilizers could pollute the soil in several ways. It could mess with the pH levels and also destroy the good microorganisms in the soil. The runoff from such soils may cause water pollution. Thus, use of chemical fertilizers is to be avoided to the possible extent.

380. The emphasis is on using organic manure in agriculture by converting farm waste and municipal solid waste into good quality compost/manure/vermicompost and using them in place of chemical fertilizers. The Integrated Pest Management

(IPM) approach, being promoted since 1985, is an eco-friendly strategy of pest containment by exploiting the role of natural forces in harmony with other pest management tactics and with the sole aim to affect minimum disturbance to the environment and prevent soil pollution.

II. Recycle and Reuse

381. Recycle and reuse not only reduce waste generation but also ensure that soil pollution is reduced. At present, plastic forms a significant portion of the generated waste and this waste is buried in landfills. In these landfills, plastics and other materials decompose slowly and release toxic materials into the soil. These toxic substances are very harmful to the health of the soil and are a major source of soil pollution. By reusing and recycling things, it would be ensured that lesser wastes are dumped in these landfills, and this, in turn, would reduce soil pollution.

III. Promotion of Organic Method of Farming

382. Organic methods of farming are being supported, which do not use chemical-laden pesticides and fertilizers. The use of plants that can remove pollutants from the soil is being encouraged. Natural manure is one of the best sources of nutrients for the soil. It is not only harmless but also completely organic. It adds essential nutrients to the soil and restores the health of the soil. It has no harmful by-products that could harm the soil or the environment in any way. Similarly, organic pesticides, insecticides and herbicides are being increasingly used which do not cause soil pollution.

IV. Disposal of Pollutants by Industries

383. Industries are under duty to dispose industrial waste in accordance with the regulations, which aim at minimizing the area that becomes polluted. Several technologies have been developed to tackle soil remediation. There can be excavation and subsequent transportation of polluted soils from factory area to remote, uninhabited locations.

V. Involving Local Population

384. To deal with soil pollution, involvement of local people is very important as with their involvement things can work out better. Awareness programmes could be designed so that people understand soil pollution better. If people are aware, they will help, even subconsciously.

§5. Evaluation of the Efficiency of the Legal Provisions

385. A great difficulty is faced in the remediation of soil pollution in comparison with air and water. Soil pollution as a threat to human life is ignored due to lack of comprehensive information. The soil resources are facing threats from deliberate use of contaminated organics, materials and irrigation water or from atmospheric depositions, spillage of effluents, etc. There is no specific legislation dealing with soil pollution. In general, it is dealt with by EPA which deals with pollution (*Indian Council for Enviro-Legal Action v. uoi*, AIR 1996 SC 1446 AND *Pravin Bhai Jashbhai and others v. State of Guj and others* (1995) 2GLR 1210).

Chapter 7. Noise Pollution

386. The word 'noise' is derived and originated from the Latin word 'nausea' which means a feeling of sickness in the stomach with an urge to vomit. Noise is also defined as unwanted sound or disagreeable sound. Therefore, noise pollution can be termed as unwanted sound or noise emitted put into the environment without regard to its bad effect and which is harmful to health. It is an established fact that those who live in noisy environment suffer from physical, mental and nervous disorders. Even a child in the womb cannot only be affected by a noisy environment but also such noise may prove fatal. Noise interferes with the human system and causes stressful situations. Research at the University of California has shown that noise affects development of the brain (TOI, 19 April 2003). Whether a particular sound is noise is also a relative phenomenon. Music to one may be noise to another. For example, the younger generation likes the loud sound of music, whereas the same may cause annoyance to older people.

The Delhi High Court in *Free Legal Aid Cell v. Government of NCT of Delhi* [AIR 2001 Delhi 455] held that pollution is a wrongful contamination of the environment which causes material injury to the right of an individual; therefore, noise can well be regarded as a pollutant because it contaminates the environment, causes nuisance and affects the health of persons and would offend Article 21 of the Constitution if it exceeds a reasonable limit.

§1. Statutory Structure and Legal Regime

387. The noise pollution may fall either under the law of torts or under the Code of Criminal Procedure as a nuisance. A civil suit can be filed under the law of tort claiming damages for the nuisance which is an unlawful interference with a person's use or enjoyment of land, or some right over, or in connection with it. Besides, various legislations also contain provisions for noise abatement. The Motor Vehicles Act, 1988, The Industries Act, Specific Relief Act for redressal against health hazards, Environment (Protection) Act, 1986 etc., and the 1987 Amendments to the Air Act, 1981, specifically extend the provisions of the Act, including increased penalties, citizens' suits and the issuance of injunctions, to noise pollution. In *In Re: Noise Pollution* case, the Supreme Court held that 'no one can claim a right to create noise even in his own premises that would travel beyond his precincts and cause nuisance to neighbours or others'.

I. Legislation

388. The Motor Vehicles Act of 1939 and 1988, the Central Motor Vehicles Rules of 1989, the Indian Railways Act of 1890, the Factories Act of 1948 and the Environment (Protection) Act of 1986 contain certain provisions dealing with the regulation and legal control over noise pollution. Section 290 of the Indian Panel Code 1860 provides a fine merely extending up to INR 200. The other important legislation and norms relating to noise are contained in the Motor Vehicles Act of 1939 and 1988 and the Noise Pollution (Regulation and Control) Rules of 2000, as amended in 2010.

II. Salient Features of Legislation

A. *Motor Vehicles Act of 1939 and 1988*

389. Section 110(h) of the Motor Vehicles Act of 1939 and 1988 empowers the Central Government to make rules to regulate the construction, equipment and maintenance of motor vehicles. Rule 120 of Central Motor Vehicles Rules of 1989 provides as follows:

- Every motor vehicle shall be fitted with a device which by means of an expansion chamber or otherwise reduces as far as practicable the noise that would otherwise be made by the escape of exhaust gases from the engine.
- Every motor vehicle shall be constructed and maintained so as to confirm to noise standards as specified in Part E of Schedule VI to the Environment (Protection) Rules 1986 as amended from time to time.

The Motor Vehicles Rules of different States provide that the driver shall not blow his horn continuously except in the case of traffic safety. It also prohibits blowing the horn in silence zones, e.g., hospitals, schools, fitting or using ‘multitoned horn giving harsh, shrill or alarming noise’. Even vehicles creating undue noise while running or driving vehicles with ‘a muffler causing alarming sound’ are not allowed.

B. *The Noise Pollution (Regulation and Control) Rules of 2000*

390. In 1987, the CPCB notified the ambient noise standards acting under section 20 of the Air (Prevention and Control of Pollution) Act of 1981. The Government has made rules in exercise of powers conferred on the Government by clause (ii) of subsection (2) of section 3, subsection (1) and clause (b) of subsection (2) of section 6 and section 25 of the Environment (Protection) Act of 1986 (29 of 1986) read with Rule 5 of Environment (Protection) Rules of 1986. These Rules have been comprehensively amended in 2010. The rules deal with noise pollution emanating from sources like industrial activities, public address systems, generator sets, music systems, construction activities, pressure horns, firecrackers, etc. The rules were notified on 14 February 2000 through a notification (bearing number S.O.123(E)) according to which the increasing ambient noise levels in public places from sources like industrial activity, construction activity, generator sets, loudspeakers, public address systems, music systems, vehicular horns and other mechanical devices having deleterious effects on human health and the psychological well-being of the people. Therefore, it was considered necessary to regulate and control noise producing and generating sources with the objective of maintaining the AAQ standards in respect of noise. The ambient noise standards for various areas have been given in the schedule appended to the rules.

1. Categorizing the Area

391. The Central Government or authority designated by it categorizes areas into industrial, commercial, residential or silence zones for the implementation of noise zones for different areas. An area up to 100 m from hospitals, educational institutions and courts is declared as a silence zone. Further, the noise emanating from any source should not exceed the background level by ten decibels dB (A) or more when measured at a point outside the premises of the location of the source. If the noise level exceeds the background noise level by ten dB (A) or more, the Central Government or its designated authority shall direct such violators to remove the source of noise or take commensurate corrective measures to reduce the noise level.

The manufacture, sale and use of firecrackers, which may cause noise exceeding 125 dB (A1) or 145 dB(C) pk, measured at a distance of 4 m from the source of the noise, are prohibited. Loudspeakers and other public address systems can be used after obtaining permission from the District Magistrate or Police Commissioner or the officer designated as per local laws. The use of loudspeakers and public address systems has been prohibited at night between 10.00 p.m. and 6.00 a.m.

2. Definitions

392. Some important definitions given in Rule 2 are reproduced hereunder:

> 'Authority' means any authority or officer authorized by the Central Government, or as the case may be, the State Government in accordance with the laws in force and includes a District Magistrate, Police Commissioner, or any other officer designated for the maintenance of the ambient air quality standards in respect of noise under any law for the time being in force; (Rule 2 c).
> 'person' in relation to any factory or premises means a person or occupier or his agent, who has control over the affairs of the factory or premises (Rule 2 d).

3. AAQ Standards in Respect of Noise for Different Areas (Rule 3)

393. The AAQ standards in respect of noise for different areas/zones have been fixed as specified in the schedule given in Table 1.

Table 1 AAQ Standards in Respect of Noise
*(Referred to in Rule 3(1) and 4(1))**

Area Code	*Category of Area/Zone*	*Limits in dB(A) Leq*	
		Daytime	*Night Time*
(A)	Industrial Area	75	70
(B)	Commercial Area	65	55
(C)	Residential Area	55	45
(D)	Silence Zone	50	40

Note:
* Daytime shall mean from 6.00 a.m. to 9.00 p.m.
Night time shall mean from 9.00 p.m. to 6.00 a.m.

Silence zone is defined as an area comprising not less than 100 m around hospitals, educational institutions and courts. The silence zones are zones which are declared as such by the competent authority.

Mixed categories of areas may be declared as one of the four above-mentioned categories by the competent authority.

dB(A) Leq denotes the time weighted average of the level of sound in decibels on scale A which is relatable to human hearing.

A 'decibel' is a unit in which noise is measured.

'A', in dB(A) Leq, denotes the frequency weighting in the measurement of noise and corresponds to frequency response characteristics of the human ear.

Leq: Is an energy mean of the noise level, over a specified period.

The State Government may categorize the areas into industrial, commercial, residential or silence areas/zones for the purpose of implementation of noise standards. The State Government is to take measures for abatement of noise including noise emanating from vehicular movements and ensure that the existing noise levels do not exceed the AAQ standards specified under these rules.

394. All development authorities, local bodies and other concerned authorities while planning developmental activity or carrying out functions relating to town and country planning shall take into consideration all aspects of noise pollution as a parameter of quality of life to avoid noise menace and to achieve the objective of maintaining the AAQ standards.

4. Restrictions on the Use of Loudspeakers/Public Address Systems (Rule 5)

395. A loudspeaker or a public address system shall not be used except after obtaining written permission from the authority, and in any case these devices shall not be used at night (between 10.00 p.m. and 6.00 a.m.) except in closed premises for communication within, for example, auditoria, conference rooms, community halls and banquet halls.

5. Consequences of Violation in Silence Zones/Areas (Rule 6)

396. In case any person in any place covered under the silence zone/area commits any of the following offences, he shall be liable for a penalty under the provisions of the act:

- plays any music or uses any sound amplifiers;
- beats a drum or tom-tom or blows a horn either musical or pressure, or trumpet or beats or sounds any instrument; or
- exhibits any mimetic, musical or other performances.

6. Complaints to Be Made to the Authority (Rule 7)

397. Any person may make a complaint to the authority if the noise level exceeds the ambient noise standards by ten dB (A) or more given in the corresponding columns of the schedule against any area/zone. The authority shall act on the complaint and take action against the violator in accordance with the provisions of these rules and any other law in force.

7. Power to Prohibit (Rule 8)

398. If the authority (as defined in Rule 2 C) is satisfied from the report of an officer in charge of a police station or on the basis of other information received by him that it is necessary to do so in order to prevent annoyance, disturbance, discomfort or injury or risk of annoyance, disturbance, discomfort or injury to the public or to any persons who dwell or occupy property on the vicinity, he may, by a written order issue such directions as he may consider necessary to any person for preventing, prohibiting, controlling or regulating the following:

(a) the incidence or continuance in or upon any premises of the following:
  - any vocal or instrumental music;
  - sounds caused by playing, beating, clashing, blowing or use in any manner whatsoever of any instrument including loudspeakers, public address systems, appliance or apparatus or contrivance which is capable of producing or reproducing sound; or

(b) the carrying on in or upon, any premises of any trade, vocation or operation or process resulting in or attended with noise.

The authority empowered under sub-rule (i) may, either on its own motion, or on the application of any person aggrieved by an order made under sub-rule (i), either rescind, modify or alter any such order: provided that before any such application is disposed of, the said authority shall afford to the applicant an opportunity of appearing before it either in person or by a person representing him and showing cause against the order and shall, if it rejects any such application either wholly or in part, record its reasons for such rejection.

§2. Noise from Fixed Sites

I. Noise in Factories

399. Noise by machines in a factory may affect the health of the workers very badly. The Factories Act of 1948 provides (section 11) that the shop floor of the factory should be kept clean and free of nuisance, which includes noise. However, the maximum limit of noise has not been prescribed by the act.

II. Loudspeakers

A. Regulation for Use

400. Loudspeakers contribute a lot of noise especially during festivals which often occur at night. According to law, the loudspeaker can be used only after obtaining prior permission from the District Administration. Under the Noise Pollution (Regulation and Control) Rules of 2000, the use of loudspeakers and public address systems was restricted during the night between 10.00 p.m. and 6.00 a.m. except for the closed auditorium, banquet halls, etc. Owing to various representations received from State Governments, these rules were amended (*see* Notification S.O.1088(E) issued on 11 October 2002) to permit the use of loudspeakers or public address systems during night hours (between 10.00 p.m. and 12.00 midnight) on or during any cultural or religious festival for a limited duration not exceeding fifteen days in all during a calendar year. The amendment carried on in 2010 in the Rules requires that State Government should specify in advance the number and particulars of the days on which two-hour exemption would be operative.

B. The Court Cases

401. The noise created by loudspeakers has come up before the courts in many cases. In one case, the petitioner was a cardiac patient and had undergone coronary artery by-pass surgery. The house of the petitioner was situated near a Dharamshala (Community Guest House). This Dharamshala was used for religious functions and also rented out for religious and marriage functions during which loudspeakers were utilized and music played at a very high pitch. The petitioner petitioned to take action against the use of loudspeakers and other public address systems under the provisions of the Noise Pollution (Regulation and Control) Rules 2000 and not to permit the causing of such disturbances affecting public tranquillity. The court ruled that the use of loudspeakers and other public address systems should only be allowed after obtaining permission and directed the concerned authorities to see that there is no violation of the act and the rules (*Sayeed Maqsood Ali v. State of MP*, AIR 2001 MP 220).

402. The noise emanating from religious places is also subject to regulation, and plea cannot be made that there is already a lot of noise pollution. The noise in an area may exceed the permissible limit, but that would not be a ground for permitting others to increase it by beating drums or the use of voice amplifiers, loudspeakers or by such other musical instruments. The court felt that in a civilized society in the name of religion, activities which disturb old or infirm persons, students or children needing their sleep, or other persons carrying on other activities cannot be permitted (*Church of God v. K R Majestic Colony Welfare Association and others* 2000 (9) J T 575).

403. The public cannot be made a captive audience or listener even if permission is granted for using loudspeakers in public. The freedoms and fundamental rights granted under the Constitution do not mean that a citizen is coerced to hear anything which he does not like or which he does not require, ruled the Calcutta High Court. Certain guidelines were also laid down for the PCB for the grant of permission to use loudspeakers so as to maintain noise level in the State of West Bengal (*Om Birangana Religious Society v. State and others* C W N 1995–1996 (Vol. 100) 617). In *Madhvi v. Thilakan* (1988(2) Ker L T 730), the Kerala High Court held that 'We recognize every person's home to be his castle which cannot be invaded by toxic fumes, or tormenting sounds.'

III. Generator Sets

404. Noise Limit for Generator Sets run with Diesel were notified by Environment (Protection) Second Amendment Rules[5] and its amendments.[6] The maximum permissible sound pressure level for new diesel generator (DG) sets with rated capacity up to 1000 KVA, manufactured on or after 1 January 2005 shall be 75 dB (A) at 1 m from the enclosure surface. The diesel generator sets are to be provided with integral acoustic enclosure at the manufacturing stage itself. For diesel generator sets not covered as above, the following shall be applicable. Noise from DG set shall be controlled by providing an acoustic enclosure. The acoustic enclosure or acoustic treatment of the room shall be designed for minimum 25 dB (A) insertion loss or for meeting the ambient noise standards, whichever is on the higher side. The DG set shall be provided with proper exhaust muffler with insertion loss of minimum 25 dB (A). These limits shall be regulated by the SPCBs and the State PCCs. Every manufacturer or assembler or importer of DG set must have valid certificates

5. vide GSR 371(E), dated 17 May 2002.
6. vide G.S.R. 520(E), dated 1 Jul. 2003; G.S.R. 448(E), dated 12 Jul. 2004; G.S.R. 315(E), dated 16 May 2005; G.S.R. 464(E), dated 7 Aug. 2006; G.S.R. 566(E), dated 29 Aug. 2007 and G.S.R. 752(E), dated 24 Oct. 2008; G.S.R. 215(E), dated 15 Mar. 2011 under the Environment (Protection) Act, 1986.

of Type Approval and also valid certificates of Conformity of Production for each year, for all the product models being manufactured or assembled or imported from 1 January 2005 with the specified noise limit. Sale, import or use of DG sets not complying with the rules is prohibited.

§3. Traffic Noise

405. The Noise Limits for vehicles were notified by Environment (Protection) Amendment Rules, 2000, vide G.S.R. 742(E), dated 25 September 2000 and inserted as serial no. 93 of Schedule I of the Environment (Protection) Rules, 1986. Subsequently, these Rules were amended by the Environment (Protection) Amendment Rules, 2002, vide G.S.R. 849(E), dated 30 December 2002 and the Environment (Protection) Amendment Rules, 2005, vide G.S.R. 272(E), dated 5 May 2005, under the Environment (Protection) Act, 1986. To make these standards commensurate with the emission standards for vehicles, the notified rules have been revised and were phased out in two stages. In the first phase, two-wheelers, three-wheelers, and passenger cars have complied with the notified norms from 1 January 2003. A relaxation of three dB(A) was given to passenger and commercial vehicles of various categories and became effective from July 2003. In the second phase, noise limits for vehicles at the manufacturing stage were made applicable from 1 April 2005 which is at par with EC norms and based on engine power for various categories of vehicles.

§4. National Ambient Noise Monitoring Network

406. The National AAQ in respect of noise for day and night has been notified in Schedule III under Rule 3 of The Environment (Protection) Rules, 1986. The CPCB in association with SPCBs has established National Ambient Noise Monitoring Network in 7 metro-cities (Bengaluru, Chennai, Delhi, Hyderabad, Kolkata, Lucknow and Mumbai). A total of seventy Noise Monitoring Stations are operational in these metro-cities (ten Stations in each metro-city).

§5. Evaluation of Efficiency of Legal Provisions

407. Despite framing of the rules, the enforcement aspect is still wanting in the absence of full-fledged and separate enforcement machinery. The task has been assigned to authorities which are already overburdened. The CPCB and the SPCBs/PCCs carry out sporadic noise monitoring in urban areas, mainly during festivals such as Deepawali. A few SPCBs and PCCs have initiated regular noise monitoring since 2008–2009. As per available data, the prescribed noise norms for various areas are exceeded at many locations.

408. The honourable Supreme Court in September 2001 passed an interim order to comply with the notification of the ministry issued on 5 October 1999 to control noise from the bursting of firecrackers, which should not exceed 125 dB (AI) and 145 dB(C)pk. The manufacture, sale and use of firecrackers are restricted accordingly. While communicating this order to all State Governments and UT, they have been requested to conduct surveys to assess the noise pollution before and on Deepawali day. A monitoring protocol for noise level and ambient air monitoring especially during Deepawali festival was developed in 2008. Children have been made aware through schools about the harmful effects of firecrackers. As a result, there has been a decreasing trend of noise during the festive season. Now green firecrackers are available with about 30% reduction of particulate emissions.

409. The Calcutta High Court in *Burrabazar Fire Works Dealers Association and Others v. The Commissioner of Police Calcutta and Others* (AIR 1998 Calcutta 121) held that there is no inherent or fundamental right in a citizen to manufacture, sell and deal with fireworks which create sound beyond permissible limits and generate pollution which can endanger the health and the public order. That under Article 21 read with Article 19(1) g of the Constitution, citizens cannot be made captive listeners to bear the tremendous sound caused by fireworks or microphones.

410. Another problem related to enforcement is that the equipment for measuring the sound level is not easily available to the enforcement machinery so as to determine whether noise was above the specified decibel level. The equipment issues a printout indicating the decibel level of the noise. These printouts can be used as evidence before the court while prosecuting the offender. The officers of the rank of Assistant Commissioner of Police and above have been authorized to prosecute people. With the help of this equipment, the police can verify the noise level. If violation continues after the issue of notice, the person can be prosecuted. The penalty for each violation is a prison term of up to five years with a fine of up to INR 100,000 or both.

Chapter 8. Radiation and Vibrations (Nuclear and Non-nuclear)

411. As per Atomic Energy Ministry, there were no incidents of radioactive leakage to the environment from any NPP in the country in the last three years. The safety of NPPs is continuously monitored and reviewed by the AERB (ET, 1 December 2021). India has twenty-two nuclear reactors in operation in seven plants, with a total installed capacity of 6,780 MW(e), contributing about 3.3% of total power generation in India. An additional eight reactors are under construction.

412. The Atomic Energy Act, 1962 is the principle legislation dealing with radiation from nuclear sources. This Act also includes provisions which enable to exercise powers under other legislation. Section 23 of the Atomic Energy Act empowers the AERB with administration of Factories Act 1948, including enforcement of its provisions, appointment of inspection staff and making of rules in the installations of DAE. AERB is also empowered to perform the functions under sections 10(1) (powers of entry) and 11(1) (powers to take samples) of Environmental Protection Act, 1986 and Rule 12 (agency to which information on excess discharge of pollutants to be given) of the Environmental Protection (Amendment) Rules, 1987 with respect to radioactive substances. Section 52 of Air (Prevention and Control of Pollution) Act, 1981 states that in relation to the radioactive air pollution the provisions of Atomic Energy Act will apply.

413. The Atomic Energy Act of 1962 defines 'radiation' as meaning gamma rays, X-rays and rays consisting of alpha particles, beta particles, neutrons, protons and other nuclear and subatomic particles, but not sound or radio waves, or visible, infrared or ultraviolet light (section 2(h) of the Atomic Energy Act of 1962). 'Radioactive substance' or 'radioactive material' is defined in the act as any substance or material which spontaneously emits radiation in excess of the levels prescribed by notification by the Central Government (section 2(i)). The Shorter Oxford Dictionary defines it as an action or a condition of sending out rays of light.

§1. Statutory Structure and Legal Regime

I. Concerning Atomic Radiation

A. Atomic Energy Act of 1962 and Radiation Protection Rules of 1971

414. The main legislation dealing with radiation is the Atomic Energy Act of 1962 and rules framed under it. Under this act, the Central Government has been authorized to manufacture or otherwise produce and dispose of radioactive material or substances. This material can be disposed of either by the Government or through any other authority or corporation established by the Government (section 3(b) bb (ii)). The Central Government has also been vested with the power to provide for control over radioactive substances or radiation generating plants in order to ensure safe disposal of radioactive waste (section 3e (iii)). The AERB is the authority for granting, renewal, withdrawal and revocation of consents for Nuclear and Radiation

Facilities. AERB also exercises control over nuclear installations and the use of radioactive substances and radiation generating plants outside such installations. Sections 16 and 17 of the Atomic Energy Act refers to control over radioactive substance and special provisions for safety.

Any mineral, concentrate and other materials containing uranium in its natural state in excess of the proportion as prescribed by the Central Government shall be disposed of with the previous permission in writing and in accordance with the terms and conditions as imposed by the Central Government (section 6(I) of the Energy Act).

415. The Radiation Protection Rules were framed almost nine years after the Atomic Energy Act was brought into force. The rules extend to the whole of India. The rules define 'adequate protection' as protection against radiation provided that the prescribed operational limits on levels of radiation or contamination are not exceeded (Rule 2(b)). 'Contamination' means the presence of radioactivity that may be specified as excessive by the competent authority by notification for the purposes of these rules (Rule 2(e)).

The handling of radioactive material requires a licence (Rule 3) which is issued for a period of three years (Rule 7). The issuing authority can revoke or withdraw a licence. The licence holder is required to use radioactive material for the purpose specified in the licence at the specified location not exceeding the quantities allowed in the licence (Rule 110). The employer is to keep a personal, medical and occupational history of radiation workers. There is a provision for a specified medical examination prior to commencing radiation work and every year thereafter.

B. The Civil Liability for Nuclear Damage Act 2010

416. This Act provides for a civil liability for nuclear damage and prompt compensation to the victims of a nuclear incident through a no-default liability to the operator. It also contains provisions for appointment of claims commissioner, establishment of a Nuclear Damage Claims Commission and connected matters.

'Nuclear Damage' (Clause 2 f) has been defined as loss of life or personal injury to a person or loss or damage to property caused by or arising out of a nuclear incident and includes some other instances enumerated in the section to the extent notified by the Central Government.

'Nuclear Incident' (Clause 2 g) means any occurrence or series of occurrences having the same origin which causes nuclear damage or, but only with respect to preventive measures, creates a grave and imminent threat of causing such damage.

The Act fixes the maximum financial liability (Clause 6) and share of the operator (Clause 7) in case of accident in nuclear reactor. The amendments in Atomic Energy, Act 1962 have allowed private investment in the nuclear power.

II. Non-nuclear Radiation

417. The radiations from mobile towers have been a concern grown with the increasing network of mobile service providers. Mobile Tower Antennas being the source of radiation, the CPCB issued an awareness note on mobile tower radiation and their impact on human health. The provisions of various environmental laws, especially the Air (Prevention and Control of Pollution) Act, 1981 along with the Constitution of India have considered to be applicable, but there is no clarity as to whether the existing environmental statutes cover electromagnetic radiations. However, India has adopted the International Commission for Non Ionizing Radiation Protection Guidelines in 2008. The Department of Telecommunications framed advisory guidelines for state governments for issue of clearance for installation of mobile towers. In the case of *Arvind Gupta v. Union of India* (MANU/GT/0202/2015), the NGT observed that 'it is clear beyond doubt that the radiation from electromagnetic waves resulting from the mobile towers is not explicitly covered in any of the scheduled acts to the NGT Act, 2010. In fact, even under the NGT Act, 2010, relevant definition … do not refer to the radiation specifically', this judgment has been appealed in the Supreme Court of India.

418. The High courts have addressed the issue of electromagnetic radiations, and there have been orders which have either found electromagnetic radiations to be a health hazard or highlighted the uncertainty due to lack of evidence in this regard. The different High Courts have delivered different verdicts.

419. The Hon'ble High Court of Rajasthan in the case of *Justice I.S. Israni (Retd.) v. Union of India* (2013(4)CDR1973(Raj); MANU/RH/1496/2012) has held that towers on hospitals and school buildings, etc., should be avoided as children and patients may be more susceptible to possible harmful effects of electromagnetic radiation. The case related to the erection of mobile towers in certain high-risk areas like schools, hospitals and high-density residential areas and the validity of bylaws which prohibited the erection of mobile towers in such areas. The court declared the bylaws of the State Government valid which were made on the recommendation of the Central Government. In the case of the densely populated residential areas, the court directed the State Government and the local authorities to take decision on case-to-case basis in accordance with law.

420. In the case of *Vijay Verma v. State of Himachal Pradesh* (MANU/HP/1116/2015) petition was filed for prohibition from installing mobile towers on the roofs of the petitioners. In this case, the Hon'ble High Court of Himachal Pradesh held that the main issue was whether the radiations from the towers cause any health hazard or not. The Hon'ble High Court found out that radiation is something that is not new, and it was in existence since life began on earth. There was no alarm with regard to possible ill-effect of the Electromagnetic Field (EMF) from mobile phone towers or the mobile phones as the limit adopted by India will not have any biological effect on the life of the people. The Hon'ble High Court observed that there was no conclusive evidence or scientific backing that the mobile towers would cause health hazards. In 2016, in the case of *Asha Mishra v. State of UP* (MANU/UP/051/2016), it has been observed that 'all studies indicate that presently there appears to be no definitive scientific material or data which may warrant EMF radiation being classified as endangering health. However the state of the research can at present be best described as being still nebulous and tenuous. This is perhaps the reason for research in the field being continued and ongoing. The standards adopted in our country are stated to be more stringent than those suggested by the WHO'. In the case of *Reliance Infocom Ltd. v. Chemanchery Grama Panchayat* (AIR 2007 Ker 33), it was held that Right to Life enshrined under Article 21 includes all those aspects of life which make life meaningful and worth living. Development of technology has its own ill effects on human beings, but, at times, people will have to put up with that at the cost of their advantages.

III. International Conventions

A. *United Nations General Assembly Resolution 913 (X) Establishing the Scientific Committee on the Effects of Atomic Radiation (UNSCEAR) (3 December 1955)*

421. The basic objective of this resolution is to collect and interpret all the available scientific data on the effects of radiation on man and his environment, including assessment of radiation levels and exposures from both natural and man-made sources, and to report on these evaluations to the General Assembly and the world community.

B. *Convention on Early Notification of a Nuclear Accident (Hereinafter 'Notification Convention'), and Convention on Assistance in the Case of a Nuclear Accident or a Radiological Emergency, Vienna, 26 September 1986*

422. This convention enjoins upon the States to provide information as early as possible in order to minimize the transboundary environmental, health and economic consequences of a nuclear accident.

C. *The Convention Concerning the Protection of Workers Against Ionizing Radiation (ILO Convention 115, Geneva, 22 June 1960) – (Hereinafter 'Radiation Protection Convention, 1960')*

423. This convention contains fifteen substantive articles requiring, *inter alia*, that ratifying States make every effort to restrict the exposure of workers to ionizing radiation to the lowest practicable level, to fix maximum permissible doses of ionizing radiation which may be received from sources external or internal to the body, to provide appropriate warnings to indicate the presence of hazards from ionizing radiation, to monitor workers in order to measure their exposure to ionizing radiation, to provide appropriate medical examinations of workers and to provide appropriate inspection services for the purpose of supervising the application of its provisions.

§2. MINING OF RADIOACTIVE SUBSTANCES

424. There are a number of radioactive elements in the earth's crust. The moment this crust is removed and radioactive elements come into contact with oxygen in the air or water, they spread widespread contamination. Uranium-238 changes fourteen times before it becomes non-radioactive lead. After mining the uranium ore, uranium is extracted from it, and the other radioactive material is left behind at the mine site. These are highly dangerous from a health perspective. The half-life of some of these elements can be thousands of years; for example, Thorium-230 has a half-life of 80,000 years. So these elements have the potential of causing health problems to many generations.

I. Internal Radiation

425. Uranium mining releases both external and internal radiation. Internal radiation is of particular concern, as most of the chemical emissions in uranium mining are from Alpha particles. In internal radiation, Alpha particles like canon balls have less penetrating power, but more impact; that is, when they enter the human body, they settle in lungs, kidneys, and other delicate parts and continue to bombard the cells. Radioactive particles pose the greatest threat to human health when they are inhaled or ingested. They are so microscopic that they can enter into the skin via the sweat pores and hair follicles or through food, water and air.

II. Radium-226 and Radon-222

426. Radium is one isotope in uranium waste that is especially dangerous. This is because it is harmful to life forms at low concentrations, and it decays further into the even more dangerous radon gas. Besides this, as a chemical, radium is similar to calcium, so when ingested it migrates to the bones, teeth and breast milk and replaces the calcium. It is a bone seeker and is also readily taken up by vegetation.

§3. URANIUM MINES

427. The Jaduguda Mine uranium mine in the State of Jharkhand commenced operation in 1967 and was the first uranium mine in India. Subsequently, apart from other places, uranium was found in Tumalapalli village in Andhra Pradesh which is considered as one of the largest uranium reserves in the world. The continuous expedition in Tummalapalle in Kadapa and Koppunuru in Guntur led to the discovery of more uranium making this state the largest producer of uranium in India. These reserves were officially commissioned in 2012 as they were equipped in catering to 25% of the requirement of uranium in the NPP in India.

§4. Dumping of Nuclear Waste

428. AERB issues authorization for disposal of radioactive nuclear wastes under Atomic Energy (Safe Disposal of Radioactive Wastes) Rules, 1987. The evaluation of waste management aspects of the facilities under AERB regulation is carried out as per AERB Safety Code on Management of Radioactive Waste (AERB/NRF/SC/RW, 2007), AERB Safety Guide on Classification of Radioactive Waste (AERB/NRF/SG/RW-1, 2011) and Management of Radioactive Waste from Mining and Milling of Uranium and Thorium (AERB/NF/SG/RW-5, 2007). The waste management activities for both radioactive and chemical wastes generated from NPP and other nuclear fuel cycle facilities are within the power of the regulatory body. The waste management in industrial and research facilities of DAE is also under the purview of AERB. Radioactive wastes generated in the medical facilities using radioactive source for diagnostic and/or therapeutic applications also have to meet safety requirements stipulated by AERB.

429. For NPP involving reprocessing and recycling of the spent fuel, India has adopted closed fuel cycle option. During reprocessing, only about two to 3% of the spent fuel becomes waste and the rest is recycled. At the end, the high-level waste will be emplaced in geological disposal facilities. NPP are to submit 'return of waste disposed' to AERB. AERB reviews whether the wastes disposed by NPPs are within the limits specified in technical specification during regulatory inspections. Also, independent environmental survey is carried out by Environment Survey Labs instituted by Bhabha Atomic Research Centre to assess the actual impact on the environment.

§5. Vibrations

430. Regular and long-term exposure to vibrations causes complicated health problems faced by drivers, industrial workers, agricultural workers, etc. The vibrations may damage sensory nerves, muscles and joints in the hands and arms. Some occupations have an inherent risk to health from vibrations. The legislation which deals with the health aspects of the workers is the Factories Act of 1948. This act provides for fencing of rotating parts, provision of alarms and proper escape. The Mines Act, 1952 contains provisions for the medical examination of the workers so if vibrations are causing a health hazard then it can be taken care of. But these acts do not contain any provision for dealing with vibrations.

431. The Working Environment (Air Pollution, Noise and Vibration) Convention of 1977 provides that it should be the duty of the employer to arrange for equipment used to monitor, *inter alia*, vibrations in the working environment to be regularly inspected, maintained and calibrated. It also lays down that where continued assignment to work involving exposure to vibration is found to be medically inadvisable, every effort should be made, consistent with national practice and conditions, to provide the worker with suitable alternative employment and to maintain his income through social security measures or otherwise.

§6. ENFORCEMENT AND CONTROL

432. Under the Atomic Energy Act of 1962, the Central Government has powers to deal with radiation emanating in the process of using radioactive substances. The Central Government can provide for control over radioactive substances or radiation generating plants in order to prevent radiation hazards and secure public safety and safety of those handling radioactive substances or radiation generating plants (section 3 e (i) (ii)). AERB constituted under the Atomic Energy Act is the competent body to enforce the safety-related rules. AERB has also been empowered to perform the functions under sections 10(1) (Powers of entry) and 11(1) (Powers to take samples) of Environmental Protection Act, 1986 and Rule 12 (Agency to which information on excess discharge of pollutants to be given) under the Environmental Protection (Amendment) Rules 1987. Further, Rules 2(b) and 3 of the MSIHCs Rules 1989 under the Environmental Protection Act 1986 has notified AERB as the authority to enforce directions and procedures as per the Atomic Energy Act 1962. Under the Civil Liability for Nuclear Damage Act, 2010 and the Civil Liability for Nuclear Damage Rules, 2011, AERB also has the responsibility of notifying the occurrence of any nuclear incident. The constitution of AERB together with the Atomic Energy (Radiation Protection) Rules, 2004 requires it to develop and issue safety codes and standards and to develop safety policies in radiation and industrial safety areas. Therefore, AERB has issued a number of Safety Codes and Standards, wherein the policy objectives and the safety requirements applicable to the respective areas are established, e.g., Policies Governing Regulations of Nuclear and Radiation Safety – July 2014.

433. Dealing with radioactive substances has been prohibited except under a licence (section 14). The Central Government has made rules prescribing the conditions and criteria for location of any installation so as to protect against radiation and safe disposal of harmful by-products or wastes. Any contravention of the terms and conditions of the licence or consent granted under section 16 and rules made under section 17 of the Atomic Energy Act of 1962 is punishable with imprisonment for a term which may extend to five years, or with a fine, or both. AERB has issued a Code of Ethics (2008) which states its Mission and brings out the guiding principles and the core values to be upheld in its regulatory activities. The overall policy objectives for radiation safety and industrial safety in relation to the nuclear and radiation facilities in India are embedded in the Atomic Energy Act, 1962, the Atomic Energy (Radiation Protection) Rules, 2004, the Atomic Energy (Safe Disposal of Radioactive Wastes) Rules, 1987, the Atomic Energy (Factories), Rules, 1996, AERB's Mission Statement, the Safety Codes, Standards and the Code of Ethics issued by AERB. These policies and requirements for nuclear and radiation safety are generally in line with the requirements of the International Atomic Energy Agency's (IAEA) standards on 'Governmental, Legal and Regulatory Framework for Safety' (IAEA G.S.R. Part–1) and the IAEA standard 'Fundamental Safety Principles' (IAEA-SF-1).

§7. Evaluation of the Efficiency of the Legal Provisions

434. In India, radioactive substances are dealt with by the Government itself or by the Government Companies. The private players may now enter this area of activity as Atomic Energy Act, 1962 is amended by the Civil Liability for Nuclear Damage Act 2010. As is evident from the uranium mining and disposal of the radioactive waste in certain mines, the enforcement is not very strict. In Jadugora, the uranium is extracted from uranium mines leaving behind 85% of the other radioactive by-products which are mixed and made into slurry and pumped to a tailing dam. While the rice fields of the surrounding villages were acquired for the dams, their schools, vegetable gardens and water sources continue to be adjacent to these dams. Besides this, to 'save cost', the dams have been constructed with the radioactive tailings. These dams, each about 400 acres of land and about a 100 ft. deep, have been constructed in between villages, and the villagers continue to use them as thoroughfares, these being their traditional routes to the market, etc. As a result, they continually pose a threat to all the surrounding areas.

Chapter 9. Other Sectors

§1. Noxious Substances

435. The noxious substances are dealt with by the Manufacture, Storage and Import of Hazardous Chemical (MSIHC) Rules of 1989 and Chemical Accidents (Emergency Planning, Preparedness and Response (CAEPPR)) Rules of 1996. Under the Hazardous and Other Wastes (Management and Transboundary Movement) Rules, 2016, India banned the import of solid plastic waste, edible fats, animal oils and household waste.

I. Mercury Poisoning

436. India is exposed to high levels of mercury poisoning from companies producing caustic soda and chlorine according to a green rating undertaken by the CSE. The caustic-chlorine industry is regarded as the mother of all chemical industries. Caustic soda and chlorine are used extensively to make products such as plastics, bulbs, batteries and pesticides. The pollution results from the mercury cell process used in India. It has been suggested that the Government facilitate a switchover to membrane technology. Mercury poisoning can damage the nervous system which includes tremors, mood and personality changes. Mercury-based products such as electrical equipment, batteries and thermometers contribute to high levels of mercury emissions. The HWs (Management and Handling) Rules, 1989, prohibit the import and export of mercury-bearing waste and stipulate environmentally sound management. But mercury continues to make its way into the country in various forms.

II. Persistent Organic Pollutants

437. POPs are organic chemical substances which are toxic to both humans and wildlife. These substances once released into the environment remain intact for years on end, become widely distributed throughout the environment as a result of natural processes involving soil, water and air, and accumulate in the fatty tissues of living organisms including humans. POPs are recognized by the International Agency for Research on Cancer as Group 1 carcinogens or cancer-causing substances. Specific effects of POPs can include cancer, allergies and hypersensitivity, damage to the central and peripheral nervous systems, reproductive disorders, and disruption of the immune system.

438. Regulation of POPs Rules, 2018 have been notified vide G.S.R. 207(E), dated 5 March 2018 under section 3 and section 6 of the Environment (Protection) Act, 1986 (29 of 1986), read with Rule 13 of the Environment (Protection) Rules, 1986 which have come into force from 4 March 2019. These Rules prohibit 'manufacture, trade, use, import and export of certain chemicals – Chlordecone, Hexabromobiphenyl, Hexabromodiphenyl ether and heptabromodiphenyl ether,

Tetrabromodiphenyl ether and pentabromodiphenyl ether, Pentachlorobenzene, Hexabromocyclododecane and Hexachlorobutadine'. These toxic chemicals are listed under the Stockholm Convention. The Stockholm Convention aims to eliminate or restrict the production and use of all intentionally produced POPs found in industrial chemicals and pesticides. India signed the Convention in May 2002 and ratified it in January 2006. The waste containing these chemicals 'shall be disposed of as per the provisions of the Hazardous and Other Wastes (Management and Transboundary Movement) Rules, 2016'. However, these chemicals may be used, sold or imported in quantities as required for research and development activities in central universities, Council of Scientific and Industrial Research (CSIR) laboratories, government institutions or other research institutions or accredited laboratories in the government or private sector after the approval of MoEFCC.

439. As per Rules, the industrial units where these chemicals are handled or persons in possession of chemicals shall declare the total quantity which is in use and its stockpiles to the MoEFCC within six months. The industrial units or persons shall not drain or discharge or dispose of the chemicals directly or indirectly in effluent treatment plant, sewage treatment plant, onto any land, in public sewers, in inland surface water or in marine coastal areas.

§2. STATUTORY STRUCTURE AND LEGAL FRAMEWORK

I. Legislation

440. The MSIHC Rules of 1989, CAEPPR Rules of 1996; Ozone Depleting Substances (Regulation and Control) Rules of 2000 and the Hazardous and Other Wastes (Management and Transboundary Movement) Rules, 2016 deal with hazardous substances and chemicals.

II. Salient Features of Legislation

A. Ozone Depleting Substances (Regulation and Control) Rules of 2000

441. These rules have been issued by the Central Government (*see* notification number S.O.670(E) dated 19 July 2000) in exercise of the powers under sections 6, 8 and 25 of the Environment (Protection) Act of 1986. The dealers and users engaged in the manufacturing and use of ozone-depleting substances such as CFCs, HCFCs, carbon tetrachloride halon, methyl chloroform, methyl bromide are required to be registered. The Rules were amended in from time to time, last being in 2019 to facilitate implementation of ozone-depleting substances phaseout by the enterprise in various sectors.

1. Definitions (Rule 2)

442. Certain definitions which are necessary to understand the ambit and scope of these rules are as follows:

> 'Ozone depleting substance' means the ozone-depleting substances specified in column (2) of Schedule I, whether existing by themselves or in a mixture, excluding any such substance or mixture (blend) which is in a manufactured product other than a container used for the transportation or storage of such substance;
> 'Consumption' with respect to any ozone-depleting substance means the amount of that substance produced in India in addition to the amount imported less the amount exported;
> 'Calculated level of consumption' shall be determined by adding together calculated levels of production and imports and subtracting the calculated level of exports;
> 'Protocol' means the Montreal Protocol on Substances That Deplete the Ozone Layer, adopted on 16 September 1987.

2. Regulation of Production and Consumption (Rule 3)

443. The production or causing to produce of any ozone-depleting substance requires registration with the specified authority. A receiver of financial assistance from the Multilateral Fund in accordance with the protocol, to which the Central Government is a party for gradual reduction of production of ozone-depleting substances specified in the schedule, is required to limit the production of ozone-depleting substances.

3. Requirement of a Licence and Prohibition on Export to or Import from Certain Countries (Rules 4 and 5)

444. The import or causing of import from or export or causing export to any country not specified in the schedule of any ozone-depleting substance is prohibited. A licence is required for importing or causing to import from or for exporting or causing to export to, any country specified in the schedule, any ozone-depleting substance.

4. Regulation of the Sale, Purchase and Use of Ozone-Depleting Substances (Rules 6, 7 and 8)

445. Any ozone-depleting substance can be purchased, sold, stocked or exhibited for sale or distribution only by a person who is registered with the specified authority. Such person has to give a declaration in accordance with the rules. Any person shall not either himself or by any person on his behalf, or enterprise, sell, stock or exhibit for sale or distribute any ozone-depleting substance to any person or enterprise who has informed the Central Government that he or that enterprise shall not use the specified ozone-depleting substances in manufacturing or other activities after the date specified by such person or as the case may be, the enterprise.

5. Prohibition on New Investments (Rules 9, 10 and 12)

446. The expansion of any manufacturing facility for the production of any ozone-depleting substance after the specified date has been prohibited. The import, export and sale of products made with or containing ozone-depleting substances as well as manufacture, import and export of compressors are also regulated by the rules.

6. Procedure for Registration, Cancellation of Registration and Right of Appeal (Rule 13)

447. The procedures for registration and conditions of registration under various provisions of these rules have been provided in Schedule IX. The registering authority shall register if he is satisfied that the procedure for registration or conditions of registration is fulfilled. The registering authority shall give the concerned person an opportunity of being heard before passing such orders, and such orders shall be made in writing.

An appeal against an order of the registering authority can be filed within thirty days of communication of such order. The registration shall be valid for the period specified in Schedule IX and its renewal shall be necessary. The procedure for and conditions of renewal of registration are the same as applicable to registration.

7. Monitoring and Reporting Requirements (Rule 14)

448. The persons producing, importing, exporting or selling any ozone-depleting substance have to maintain records and file reports in the manner specified in Part I of Schedule X of the rules. Every person who has received technical or financial assistance from any international organization or any financial assistance, which includes concession or exemption from payment of duties, from the Central Government, is required to maintain records and file reports. The list of such persons is notified by the Central Government.

449. Every person who has the facility to reclaim an ozone-depleting substance shall maintain records and file reports in the manner specified in Part IV of Schedule X. Every person who has the facility to destroy any ozone-depleting substance shall maintain records and file reports in the manner specified in Part V of Schedule X. Every person who manufactures, imports, exports or sells compressors shall maintain records and file reports in the manner specified in Part VI of Schedule X. The records maintained in accordance with the above sub-rules shall be made available for inspection.

III. International Conventions

450. The stratospheric ozone layer is present from 10 to 50 km above the Earth's surface. The stratospheric ozone layer acts as a shield and protects from harmful ultraviolet-B (UV-B) radiation from the sun. Ozone-Depleting Substances (ODSs) such as Chlorofluorocarbons (CFCs), Hydrochlorofluorocarbons (HCFCs), Halon, Carbon Tetrachloride (CTC), Methyl Bromide, Bromofluoromethane (BFM), etc., deplete the ozone layer. This depletion has the potential to cause skin cancer, eye cataract, suppress body's immune system, decrease crop yield, etc.

451. It was in the early 1970s when global efforts to protect the ozone layer started. It culminated in the adoption of the Vienna Convention on Ozone Depleting Substances in 1985 (entry into force 22 September 1988) and the Montreal Protocol in 1987. India accepted the Montreal Protocol as amended by the London Amendment in 1992.

A. *The Vienna Convention for the Protection of the Ozone Layer (Vienna, 22 March 1985) and Montreal Protocol on Substances that Deplete the Ozone Layer (Montreal, 16 September 1987)*

452. These conventions protect the ozone layer by taking precautionary measures to control equitably total global emissions of substances that deplete it, with the ultimate objective of their elimination on the basis of developments in scientific knowledge, taking into account technical and economic considerations and bearing in mind the developmental needs of developing countries. India is a party to both the Convention and Protocol and all of the amendments. The Montreal Protocol has been recognized as the most successful international environmental treaty in history enjoying universal ratification from all the United Nations Member countries and has led to phaseout of 98% of ODSs globally.

453. The twenty-eighth Meeting of the Parties (MOP) to the Montreal Protocol on 15 October 2016 in Kigali, Rwanda, agreed to phase down Hydrofluorocarbons (HFCs) and approved a timeline for their gradual reduction by 80%–85% by the late 2040s. This agreement for phasedown of HFCs is called the Kigali Amendment to the Montreal Protocol. As per the Kigali Amendment, to the Montreal Protocol, India is to complete its phasedown of HFCs in four steps from 2032 onwards with cumulative reduction of 85% of production and consumption of HFCs by 2047. The Government on 18 August 2021 approved the proposal of MoEF&CC for ratification of Kigali Amendment to the Montreal Protocol on Substances that Deplete the Ozone Layer for phase-down of HFCs by India. It was also decided that a national strategy for phasedown of HFCs will be developed by 2023 after required consultation with all the industry stakeholders. The Kigali Amendment has entered into force on 27 December 2021.

B. *The Convention Concerning Protection Against Hazards of Poisoning Arising from Benzene (ILO Convention 136, Geneva, 23 June 1971) (Hereinafter 'Benzene Convention, 1971')*

454. This convention provides that whenever harmless or less harmful substitute products are available, ratifying States should use such substitutes instead of benzene.

§3. Enforcement and Control

455. In India, the major generator of HW are industries. The Hazardous and Other Wastes (Management and Transboundary Movement) Rules 2016 provide that owners of HW disposal facilities are liable to pay financial penalties if the rules of transportation, storage, and recycling of such waste are not complied with, and may even be imprisoned due to negligence. The rules also direct the state governments to identify locations for the construction of HW treatment facilities.

456. To deal with ozone-related matters, the MoEFCC has established an ozone cell which publishes a bimonthly newsletter on ozone issues. It conducts workshops, seminars and other programmes so as to create awareness with respect to ozone-depleting substances. The Ozone Cell acts as a National Ozone Unit (NOU) to render necessary services for effective and timely implementation of the provisions of the Montreal Protocol and its ODSs phaseout programme in India. The Ministry has also constituted an Empowered Steering Committee (ESC) under the Chairpersonship of the Secretary (MoEFCC) for overall implementation of the provisions of the Montreal Protocol in the country.

§4. Evaluation of the Efficiency of the Legal Provisions

457. The MoEFCC is the nodal agency for the management and control of hazardous substances, which include hazardous chemicals, waste and microorganisms. The responsibility for implementing the rules is with the SPCBs/PCCs and to some extent with the State Departments of the Environment. To deal with hazardous and noxious substances, the Government has formed the HSMD as a nodal point. Chemical safety is ensured by strict enforcement of the MSIHC Rules of 1989 and the CAEPPR Rules of 1996. These rules are implemented by the State/UT and constantly pursued and monitored by the MoEFCC. However, there is a general disregard and lack of proper attention and public awareness towards harmful effects of noxious substances. For example, cases of use of certain growth chemicals and hormones in vegetables have been reported like contaminated honey, growth hormones injections in vegetables, chemicals used for colouring of food items, etc., harmful effects of which are still to be studied.

458. In April 2016, the MoEFCC founded the National Coordination Committee for preparing a National Action Plan for Chemicals for preparation of a chemical inventory/database, taking into consideration the details of all chemicals used in India, including the total quantity produced each month, import and export figures, the types of chemicals manufactured and imported, and the gross national demand.

459. The Government has proposed to make vehicle tracking system must for all vehicles carrying hazardous goods as per Automotive Industry Standard (AIS) 140. In a draft notification issued on 16 February 2022, it is proposed that every goods carriage vehicle, carrying any dangerous or hazardous goods, shall be equipped with or fitted with a vehicle tracking system device. The decision has been taken in view of the fact that vehicles, which are not under the ambit of national permit, carrying various gases, mainly argon, nitrogen, oxygen, and other goods of dangerous or hazardous nature are not fitted with Vehicle Tracking System devices. Suggestions from all the stakeholders have been invited on the proposed changes so that the government could issue final notification in this regard.

In its draft notification, it is proposed to amend the existing Central Motor Vehicles Rules, 1989, in sub-rule (1) of Rule 129 seeking addition of a clause stating that 'every goods carriage carrying any dangerous or hazardous goods shall be equipped with or fitted with a vehicle tracking system device as per AIS 140' (The Statesman 16 February 2022).

Part II. Nature Conservation and Management

Chapter 1. Introduction

460. India is one of the twelve mega-diversity countries with a rich collection of all living organisms, viewing biodiversity as a whole. The biodiversity is estimated to be over 45,000 plant species representing about 7% of the world's flora, and its variety of animal life represents 6.5% of world's fauna. Fifteen thousand species of flowering plants, 53,430 species of insects; 5,050 species of molluscs, 6,500 species of other invertebrates; 2,546 species of fishes; 1,228 species of birds, 446 species of reptiles, 372 species of mammals and 204 species of amphibians have been identified. Further, 1,15,000 species of plants and animals have been identified and described. India stands tenth in the twenty-five most plant-rich countries of the world. To preserve the rich biodiversity, nine biosphere reserves have been set up in specific biogeographic zones: the biggest one being the Deccan Peninsula in the Nilgiris covering Tamil Nadu, Andhra Pradesh and Karnataka. Others are the Nanda Devi in Uttarakhand in the Western Himalayas, the Nokrek in Meghalaya, Manas and Dibru-Saikhowa in Assam, the Sunderbans in the Gangetic plain in West Bengal, Similarly in Orissa, the Great Nicobar and the Gulf of Mannar (GoM) in Tamil Nadu.

§1. Legislation on Conservation and Management

461. Articles 48 and 51 A of the Constitution of India describe the role of state and citizen's involvement in safeguarding and protecting the natural environment. As per Article 51(A) (g) of the Constitution, every citizen of India has a fundamental duty to protect and improve the natural environment including forest, lakes, rivers, and wildlife and should have compassion for living creatures. The National Forest Policy (NFP), 1988 (under revision by NFP of 2019) emphasized the need to restore the ecological balance and the conservation of the natural heritage. The National Conservation Strategy and Policy Statement, 1992 specifically include the conservation of the coastal ecosystem as a priority in its 'Agenda for Action'. The third National Wildlife Action Plan for 2017–2031 spells out the future road map for wildlife conservation. This Plan is unique as this is the first time India has recognized the concerns relating to climate change impact on wildlife and stressed on integrating actions that need to be taken for its mitigation and adaptation into wildlife management planning processes. The CRZ notification of 2011 issued under the Environment (Protection) Act of 1986 places restrictions on setting and expansion of industries, operations and processes in the CRZ areas except projects of atomic energy and industries which require waterfront like port, harbour, lighthouses, etc.

§2. Shortcomings

462. The ranking of India in the world is low in terms of nature conservation and management despite having specialized courts dealing with environmental cases. With rapid industrialization, deforestation, increase in population at a high rate and lack of knowledge among people about the environment and pollution, natural environment is deteriorating at a rapid pace. There are a number of shortcomings in legislation on natural conservation as well as its implementation.

463. In general, the laws related to natural conservation consider the superiority of human over ecosystem and nature. Industries take permission from the SPCB to discharge effluents and causing emissions, but there is laxity in compliance due to lack of strong penalty measures. There is also lack of independence given to the central and the state boards which have to depend on the State and the central government for many things. PCBs do not have legal authority, and their decisions may be overruled by the government. Further, the existing laws give importance to some specific types of pollution or specific categories of hazardous substances.

§3. Pressures on Natural Resources

464. The commercial, industrial and population pressures have taken a toll on rich forests and other natural resources. The local pressures for extension of cultivation are posing a threat to biodiversity. The people living in the forests or in its periphery are also dependent for their livelihood on forest produce and timber. No doubt, the flora and fauna are being protected through a wide network of national parks and sanctuaries covering its geographical area. But the threat is faced even by national parks and wildlife sanctuaries and other protected areas from the people living in and around these protected areas.

I. Direct Dependence on Natural Resources

465. In India, poor people mainly depend directly on the natural resource environment for their livelihood, and the bulk of GDP is generated out of the use of such natural resources. Agriculture, forestry, fisheries and mining contribute a fairly good share. For example, in 2020–2021 agriculture and allied activities contributed 19.9% GDP, which is higher than 17.8% in the previous year 2019–2020. But 41.49% people got employment in 2020–2021 from agriculture. Whereas GDP was

14% in 2018–2019 but 42% people got employment in agriculture sector. So declining share of the agriculture sector in GDP is not accompanied with a corresponding decline in its shares in the workforce. The non-agricultural sectors have generated more income, but not more employment. Therefore, pressure has not shifted and continues to remain on land, forests and fisheries and other natural resources.

II. Market Forces

466. In the nineteenth century and early twentieth century, deforestation took place on a massive scale resulting in depletion of timber due to pressure to meet the requirement of wood in urban areas for house construction, furniture, wooden poles for street lighting and expanding the railway network, etc. The Second World War put further pressure on the forests. The development of the iron and steel industry and paper and rayon industries accelerated this pressure. Even where forest areas stayed with the Forest Department, they became poorer in timber due to market forces. The same story is repeated in other areas as well. For example, in the case of fisheries, the mechanized trawlers resulted in the overexploitation of fisheries.

III. Development Versus Environment

467. It is considered that for eradication of poverty, development is the primary objective of developing countries and not preservation of the environment. At the time of the Stockholm Conference on Environment and Development in 1972, focus was on poverty and it was seen as the worst form of pollution. The policymakers considered that accelerating economic growth is necessary for eliminating poverty. An excessive concern with environment was feared, can dampen development effort and hence hinder the process of poverty alleviation. But the Bhopal gas tragedy changed the whole scenario, and India as a nation was convinced and public opinion developed that conservation of nature and control of pollution were as important goals as poverty alleviation and development.

IV. Using Natural Resources in a Sustainable Way

468. Those who are dependent on natural resources and do not use them in a sustainable way themselves threaten the sustainability of these resources. This is illustrated by the relationship of land and forest. The pressure on the grazing lands led to their depletion and the aggravation of land degradation. But there are examples of those who have a concern for the future and are conscious of their stake and responsibility. For example, the farmers put in a tremendous amount of planning and labour into building and maintaining terraced fields, controlling soil erosion, nurturing tree species for fuel, fodder and soil fixing, etc. The evolution and development of institutions of sacred groves and *Van Panchayats* to restrain indiscriminate use of forests, and also the *Pani Panchayats* (Panchayats for managing water distribution, for managing irrigation tanks and canals) are proof that the rural people had the vision and ingenuity to promote sustainable and equitable use of natural resources.

V. Natural Resource Management

469. National Natural Resources Management System (NNRMS), started in 1993, is an integrated natural resource management system aggregating the data about natural resources from the remote sensing satellites and other conventional techniques. One of the important elements of this system is the National Resource Information Systems which acts as feeder information system to the larger information system of the Government. NNRMS activities are coordinated at the national level by the Planning Committee of NNRMS which frames guidelines for implementation of the systems and oversees the progress of remote sensing applications for natural resources management.

A. The Natural Resource Management Division

470. Natural Resource Management Division of Indian Council of Agricultural Research is conducting basic research to develop technologies for conservation, management and sustainable utilization of the natural resources ensuring food, nutritional and environmental security through fifteen research institutes, ten All India Coordinated Research Projects, three network projects and two Consortia Research Platforms namely on Water and Conservation Agriculture with a wide network of the Cooperating Centres and State Agricultural Universities.

B. The National Museum of Natural History

471. This museum was set up in 1978 in Delhi. It promotes informal education in the areas of environment and conservation. It has permanent exhibit galleries on different facets of the environment and its conservation. There are three Regional Museums of Natural History located at Mysore in the State of Karnataka, Bhopal in the State of Madhya Pradesh and Bhubaneswar in the State of Odisha.

Chapter 2. Monuments and Landscapes

472. India is full of ancient historical sites and beautiful monuments and is facing the problem of their preservation and restoration. The Ajanta and Ellora caves, Khajuraho, Taj Mahal and many other heritage sites and buildings are under attack from the effects of air pollution resulting in acidic deposition and natural decay. The word 'monument' is generally understood as meaning any structure, erection or monument, or any tumulus or place of interment, or any cave, rock sculpture, inscription or monolith, which is of historical, archaeological or artistic interest.

473. Monuments are protected under the Ancient Monuments and Archaeological Sites and Remains Act of 1958 (as amended from time to time) and mining, quarrying, excavating, blasting, construction or any operation of a like nature are prohibited in protected areas and cannot be carried on by the owner or occupier or any other person. Therefore, not only the monument but also the ambience and landscape around it are protected by law. The Taj Heritage Corridor controversy is a good example of concern for preservation of ambience and landscape of a monument. The construction of the Heritage Corridor in the vicinity of the Taj Mahal is a case in point about which environmentalists felt that it will affect safety as well as the landscape around the Taj Mahal and consequently the project was shelved. Example of this concern is that the Supreme Court of India ordered the shutdown of polluting industries, regulated development within 500 m of heritage structures including a 100 m no-build zone and asked MoEFCC to plant a greenbelt around the Taj Mahal.

§1. Statutory Structure and Legal Regime

I. Legislation

474. The following are the main enactment and other policy documents dealing with monuments and landscapes:

- the Ancient Monuments Preservation Act of 1904;
- the Ancient and Historical Monuments and Archaeological Sites and Remains (Declaration of National Importance) Act of 1951;
- the Ancient Monuments and Archaeological Sites and Remains Act of 1958 (24 of 1958) as amended in 2010;
- Biological Diversity Act of 2002;
- the Rules for Setting of Industries around Taj Trapezium and other important archaeological monuments and other Areas (*see* S.O.470-E dated 21 June 1999);
- the National Lake Conservation Programme of 1993;
- the Coastal Zone Regulation Notification.

II. Salient Features of Legislation

A. *The Ancient Monuments and Archaeological Sites and Remains Act of 1958 (24 of 1958)*

475. This act is the main legislation providing for preservation of ancient and historical monuments and archaeological sites and remains of national importance. It regulates archaeological excavations and lays down norms for protection of sculptures, carvings and other like objects. The term 'ancient monument' has been defined as meaning any structure, erection or monument, or any tumulus or place of interment, or any cave, rock sculpture, inscription or monolith, which is of historical, archaeological or artistic interest and which has been in existence for not less than one hundred years, and includes the following:

(a) the remains of an ancient monument;
(b) the site as of an ancient monument;
(c) such portion of land adjoining the site of an ancient monument as may be required for fencing or covering in or otherwise preserving such monuments; and
(d) the means of access to, and convenient inspection of an ancient monument.

476. The 'archaeological site and remains' means any area which contains or is reasonably believed to contain ruins or relics of historical or archaeological importance which have been in existence for not less than one hundred years, and includes the following:

(a) such portion of land adjoining the area as may be required for fencing or covering in or otherwise preserving it; and
(b) the means of access to, and convenient inspection of, the area.

477. The 'protected area' means any archaeological site and remains, which is declared to be of national importance by or under the Monument Act. A 'protected monument' means an ancient monument which is declared to be of national importance by or under the Monument Act.

478. The Central Government may declare any ancient monument or archaeological site as of national importance by notification in the Official Gazette (section 4). Further, the Central Government has the right to acquire a protected monument if it apprehends that a monument is in danger of being destroyed, injured, misused or allowed to fall into decay (section 13). Activities like mining, quarrying, excavating, blasting or any other operation of a like nature cannot be carried out in the protected area by the owner or occupier or any other person. Construction is also prohibited in this area. In protected areas, cultivation is allowed if it does not involve the digging of more than one foot of soil from the surface. In case any building is constructed in violation of these provisions, then it can be removed by the district authorities and the cost of such removal shall be realized from the person who has committed the breach (section 19). The Central Government has been authorized to acquire any protected area containing an ancient monument or antiquities of national interest and value under the provisions of the Land Acquisition Act of 1894 (section 20). The Central Government can also carry out archaeological excavation in protected or unprotected areas, and where as a result of such excavation any antiquities are discovered, the Central Government can compulsorily acquire such antiquities.

479. The Ancient Monuments and Archaeological Sites and Remains (Amendment) Bill, 2022, listed for passage during the next session of Parliament, aims to rationalize prohibited areas around protected monuments, addresses blanket ban on construction around them and give more powers to the Archaeological Survey of India to decide on encroachments. The Amasr Act, 1958, was amended in 2010 which prohibited construction of 100 m around a protected monument. The next 300-m radius is also regulated. The changes propose to do away with the ban on construction within 100 m of an ASI-protected monument and regulate construction within 100–200 m under the Act that protects monuments and sites over 100 years old. Bill also gives powers to expert committees to examine cases. The amendment will change section 20A, which refers to the prohibited area, to 'rationalise' the prohibited and regulated areas. Many critics and urban planners have objected to the suggestions in the past, saying it will pave the way for more people seeking concessions around a protected monument. ASI too is expected to get powers similar to those mentioned in the Forest Act. Right now, ASI is dependent on law enforcement authorities for removing encroachments (E.T, 18 July 2022).

B. Guidelines Framed for the Protection of Monuments

480. Guidelines have been framed under the Environment (Protection) Act of 1986 and Environment (Protection) Rules of 1986 relating to the establishing of industries around national parks, sanctuaries, and core zones of biosphere reserves, wetlands, Taj Trapezium and other important archaeological monuments (S.O.470(E) dated 21 June 1999). New units like refineries, chemical fertilizers, tanneries, etc., are not allowed to be set up within 7 km periphery of those monuments which have been listed in the Annexure appended with the notification. These monuments *inter alia* include the Rani Jhansi Mahal in Jhansi, UP, the Red Fort Delhi, the Fatehpur Sikri near Agra, etc.

481. The National Monuments Authority (NMA) has engaged heritage expert agencies and universities to prepare the draft regulations mandated by the Ancient Monuments and Archaeological Sites and Remains (Amendment and Validation) Act, 2010. In the last ten years, bylaws have been framed only for seven monuments/sites and presented to Parliament. The ASI's regional directors (defined as competent authority), were entrusted with the responsibility of preparing the draft. However, only 101 could be prepared till January 2020. Apart from Indian National Trust for Art and Cultural Heritage which was already mentioned in the Act, more than thirty expert heritage bodies like Reach Foundation, Chennai, Aga

Khan Trust for Culture and School of Planning and Architecture, Bhopal, were added to the list of experts agencies to prepare the bylaws. There are 3,691 protected sites under ASI's jurisdiction with the highest, 745, in Uttar Pradesh (Indian Express, E-Paper, 2 May 2022).

C. Draft Model Regulations for Conservation of Natural and Man-Made Heritage, 1995

482. These regulations deal with development or construction activity at or around natural and man-made heritage sites.

D. Biological Diversity Act of 2002

483. Acting under section 37 of this act, the State Government in consultation with the local bodies may notify in the Official Gazette areas of biodiversity importance as biodiversity heritage sites. The State Government, in consultation with the Central Government is to frame rules for the management and conservation of the entire heritage sites. The State Government is also to frame schemes for compensating or rehabilitating any person or section of people economically affected by such notification.

To map biological diversity, botanical and zoological surveys have been carried out through launching All India Coordinated Project on Capacity Building in Taxonomy. So far, around 91,000 species of animals and 45,500 species of plants have been identified and described, but still a large number of animals and plants are to be explored, identified and described.

§2. International Conventions and Concerns

484. The international community has been conscious of the need to protect the world heritage as a duty towards future generations. In this endeavour, ways and means have been devised to protect the cultural and historical heritage.

I. Convention Concerning the Protection of the World Cultural and Natural Heritage 1972 (Paris, 12 November 1972)

485. This convention protects cultural monuments and natural sites within the territory of a State that are recognized to be of such outstanding universal value that safeguarding them concerns humanity as a whole. Besides, habitats of threatened species of animals and plants of universal value from the point of view of science and conservation are regarded as natural heritage under the convention. A World Heritage Committee has been established under the convention. The State parties to the convention are required to take proper legal, scientific, technical, administrative and financial measures which are required for the purpose of identification, protection, conservation and rehabilitation of the heritage.

II. Archaeological Park and World Heritage Complex

486. The areas where a number of monuments are situated are being developed as Archaeological Park or World Heritage Complex. The Qutab-Mehruali area in Delhi with many monuments dating back to the twelfth century is proposed to be developed as an Archaeological Park. It will be accomplished by integrating the numerous small but important monuments around Qutub Minar into one large World Heritage Complex. Efforts are being made to convince United Nations Educational, Scientific and Cultural Organization (UNESCO) to grant World Heritage Status to the Red Fort. This seventeenth-century monument has been on the UNESCO deferred list for many years. Massive restoration work is being undertaken in the Fort so as to restore it to its original glory.

§3. Taj Protection Mission

I. Protection of the Taj Mahal

487. In consequence of the Supreme Court orders (dated 4 September 1996 in Writ Petition No. 13381/84), the Planning Commission estimated (in consultation with the State Government) an amount of INR 60 billion on a 50%:50% (Centre-State) matching basis to implement various schemes relating to protection of the Taj Mahal. A Mission Management Board has been constituted for overseeing the implementation, monitoring and reviewing of the various programmes and schemes formulated for the protection of the Taj Mahal. Schemes were submitted relating to uninterrupted power supply, augmentation of water supply, improvement of drainage and sanitation, city tree plantation in the context of environmental protection of the Taj Mahal.

488. The TTZ Pollution (Prevention and Control) Authority has been established (S.O.350(E) dated 13 May 1998) under the Environment (Protection) Act of 1986. The authority *inter alia* includes the chairman of the UP SPCB, a representative of the MoP&NG and the MoEFCC; and a representative of the Archaeological Survey of India as its members. The authority has been given power to monitor progress of the implementation of various schemes for protection of the Taj Mahal and programmes for protection and improvement of the environment in the TTZ and take all necessary steps to ensure compliance of specified emission standard and fuel quality standards by motor vehicles. The authority functions under the overall supervision and control of the Central Government and furnishes a report about its activities once every two months to the MoEFCC. The headquarters of the authority are at Agra. Taking a tough stand on the non-functional TTZ Authority, a Supreme Court Bench scolded the Agra Divisional Commissioner and demanded to know how the TTZ Authority was allowing polluting units to operate in Agra despite a ban since 1996 (TOI 27 June 2018).

489. The Government of the State of UP has prepared an additional five projects covering construction of sewerage in Agra, afforestation in the Taj Trapezium, Agra by-pass – Part II (Northern Park), improvement of twenty-one Agra city roads, construction of a parking site near the western gate of the Taj Mahal and construction of Agra Barrage under the Taj Protection Mission.

II. Taj Heritage Corridor Controversy

490. The construction around the regulated area is prohibited by the Ancient Monuments and Archaeological Sites and Remains Act of 1958. The proposed construction will disturb the ambience required to maintain the status of these World Heritage Sites. The Heritage Corridor Plan was brought into focus by a newspaper report highlighting the possible damage to the landscape of the Taj Mahal. The plan could have ruined the view forever. It is reported that it was in violation of World Heritage Monument Conservation and Protection Norms which require an NOC to be obtained from the Archaeological Survey of India for any construction in the vicinity of a World Heritage site. Both the Taj Mahal and the Agra Fort are World Heritage sites.

491. The controversial Taj Heritage Corridor plan of 2003 has now been resurrected in a new ‘green’ area along the Yamuna river bank. In 2017, the foundation was laid for the new Taj View Garden, sandwiched between the Taj Mahal and the Agra Fort. The Supreme Court had asked the Archaeological Survey of India to clean up the debris from the corridor site and develop the eighty acres of reclaimed land as a green buffer to insulate the Taj Mahal from air pollution. The original corridor project was to begin from Khan-e-Alam, close to the Taj Mahal, and end 2 km towards the city behind Agra Fort. It was to be extended later to allow tourists to reach Etmaddaula and Ram Bagh on the other side of the river. Later on persuasive efforts of environmentalists and local politicians succeeded to get work started on clearing the debris and developing the green stretches.

III. Present Status

492. Almost three decades after the Supreme Court announced measures (in 1993) to insulate the Taj Mahal from environmental degradation, not much seems to have changed. There has been no fundamental change in the environmental conditions in Agra, Mathura, Firozabad districts that come under the TTZ. The water, air and noise pollution levels continue to remain alarming, as high as they were in 1993, when the judgment came. The Supreme Court had ordered that several rows of trees be planted on the western periphery of the city to filter the dust-laden westerlies that blow from Rajasthan. That has not happened, and greenery has all but vanished as tall buildings now stand where community ponds once existed. The shifting orders for dairies, dhobi ghats, cremation sites and petha units have been shelved. Transport companies emitting pollutants on the Yamuna riverbed Road have not been shifted either. The NGT has been struggling with its orders on clearing encroachments on Yamuna flood plains. After years of dilly-dallying even the boundaries of the flood plains have not been clearly demarcated. A dry and polluted Yamuna remains a constant threat to the safety of the Taj Mahal. Water in the Yamuna was required for the good health of historical monuments along Yamuna's banks because the foundations need continuous moisture and a pollution-free ambience.

§4. Biosphere Reserves

493. Biosphere reserves are rich in biological and cultural diversity. The goal of setting these reserves is, *inter alia*, to facilitate conservation of representative landscapes and cultural heritage and to provide support for research, monitoring, education and information exchange. So far, eighteen reserves have been set up and designated as Biosphere Reserves in India. Out of these, eight biosphere reserves are part of the World Network of Biosphere Reserves based on UNESCO Man and Biosphere (MAB) Programme List. These reserves protect representative landscapes. Protection is granted not only to flora and fauna of the reserve but also to the human communities who inhibit these regions and their ways of life. The MoEFCC provides financial assistance to the respective State Governments for conservation and management of these biosphere reserves (*see also infra* Part II, Chapter 4).

Chapter 3. Protected Areas

494. Protected areas are those in which human occupation or the exploitation of resources is limited. There are several kinds of protected areas, which vary by level of protection depending on the enabling laws of the country or the regulations of the international organizations involved. The term 'protected area' also includes Marine Protected Areas (MAPs), the boundaries of which will include some area of ocean, and Transboundary Protected Areas that overlap multiple countries which remove the borders inside the area for conservation and economic purposes. Following are generally considered as protected areas: National Parks; Wildlife Sanctuaries; Conservation Reserves; Community Reserves; and MAPs. PAs in India comprise National Parks, Sanctuaries, Conservation / Community Reserves and Tiger Reserves (Table 2). It does not include Reserved Forests. Protected Area (PA) has been defined in the Wildlife (Protection) Act, 1972 (WLPA). Section 2(24A) says: 'Protected Area' means a National Park, Sanctuary, Conservation / Community Reserve. These are notified under Chapter IV of the WLPA titled 'Protected Areas'. A Tiger Reserve on the other hand is notified under Chapter IV B of the WLPA titled 'National Tiger Conservation Authority'. Since, all notified Core or Critical Tiger Habitats of Tiger Reserves are either Sanctuaries or National Parks with tiger populations they get considered as PAs. This is as mandated by the Explanatory clause in section 38V(4)(i) on Core or Critical Tiger Habitats. However, Buffer or Peripheral Areas notified under section 38V(4) (ii) typically contain Reserved Forests which are not included in Sanctuaries or National Parks and hence they will not have the status of a PA.

Table 2 Protected Areas of India (As on December 2021)

National Parks	106	44,372.42	1.35
Wildlife Sanctuaries	564	1,22,509.33	3.73
Conservation Reserves	99	4,726.24	0.14
Community Reserves	218	1,445.71	0.04
Protected Areas (PAs)	987	1,73,053.69	5.26

Geographical Area of India (http://knowindia.gov.in/)	=	32,87,263 km^2
Forest cover of India (FSI, 2021)		
Forest + Tree Cover Area 7,13,789 + 95,748	=	8,09,537 km^2
Forest + Tree Cover Percentage 21.71% + 2.91%	=	24.62% of the geographical area of India

Source: ENVIS Centre on Wildlife and Protected Areas.

§1. DESIGNATION AND PROTECTION

I. National Parks and Sanctuaries

495. The Jim Corbett National Park formed in 1936 was India's first wildlife park. There are 106 national parks covering an area of 44,372.42 km2, which is 1.35% of the geographical area of the country. The number of wildlife sanctuaries is 565 covering an area of 122560.85 km2, which is 3.73% of the geographical area of the country. Another 218 sanctuaries are proposed in the Protected Area Network Report covering an area of 16,829 km^2 (National Wildlife Database, 31 May 2022). These parks and sanctuaries are committed to maintaining the delicate ecosystems necessary to ensure the survival of flora and fauna and team with an astounding variety of animals and plant life. As for fauna, India's parks play an enormously significant role in the protection of wild animals, including its tiger population. The parks provide a safe haven for tigers, which outside the parks are forced to compete with about 100 million humans who make their livelihood from forests and reside in or around the forest. The tigers in the past were threatened by the shooting safaris of the Maharajas, Nawabs and British colonists, but today an even greater threat is posed by the demand for tiger bones and other body parts by the practitioners of 'traditional' medicine in certain regions of Asia.

II. Conservation Reserve

496. Conservation Reserves and community reserves denote protected areas of India which act as buffer zones to or connectors and migration corridors between established national parks, wildlife sanctuaries and reserved and protected forests of India. There are 100 existing Conservation Reserves in India covering an area of 4927.28 km^2, which is 0.15% of the geographical area of the country (National Wildlife Database, May. 2022). Section 36 A of Wildlife (Protection) Act 1972 deals with the declaration and the management of the Conservation Reserve. The State Government after consultation with the local community declares that any area owned by the government adjacent to the national parks and sanctuaries is connected with one protected area to another. Section 36B provides for establishment of a committee for management of conservation reserve. Such Committee advises the Chief Wildlife Warden to conserve, manage and maintain the conservation reserve. There should be one representative of each village panchayat in whose jurisdiction the reserve is located and the three representatives of NGOs working in the field of wildlife conservation and one representative each from the Department of Agriculture and Animal Husbandry.

III. Community Reserve

497. There are 219 Community Reserves in India covering an area of 1446.28 km^2, which is 0.04% of the geographical area of the country (National Wildlife Database, May. 2022). Section 36C and section 36D deal with the community reserve. Section 36C provides for the declaration and management of community reserve. According to this provision the state government may declare any private or community land not within a national park, sanctuary, or conservation reserve, as a community reserve for protecting fauna, flora and traditional or cultural conservation. After issuing of the notification, no change in the land use pattern can be made within the community reserve. Section 36D provides for constitution of management committee for a Community Reserve. The State Government has been given right to constitute a Community Reserve management committee which shall be the authority responsible for maintaining and managing the Community Reserve.

IV. Marine Protected Area

498. A Marine Protected Area (MPA) is a space in the ocean where human activities are more strictly regulated than the surrounding waters. These places are given special protections for natural or historic marine resources by local, state, territorial, native, regional, or national authorities. India's coastline stretches for 8118 km, covering an EEZ of 2.02 million km^2. The continental shelf of India extends to 372,424 km^2 across nine states and seven union territories. As one of the seventeen mega-bio diverse countries of the world, it faces unique challenges in protecting its biodiversity. MAPs in India are the area defined under IUCN Guidelines. They limit anthropogenic activities and exploitation of resources in these areas.

499. Several steps have been taken to achieve the National Biodiversity and to conserve coastal and marine areas in the country. Towards achieving these targets, 106 coastal and marine sites have been identified and prioritized as Important Coastal and Marine Areas (ICMBAs) by the WII. Sixty-two ICMBAs have been identified along the west coast of India, and forty-four have been identified along the east coast. Of these, twenty-two ICMBAs have been prioritized for immediate conservation actions and proposed to be upgraded as Protected Areas under categories such as Conservation or Communities Reserve to increase participation of the local communities in governance.

§2. Statutory Structure and Legal Regime

500. The parks and reserves are dealt with under the Wildlife (Protection) Act of 1972. The salient features of this act relating to parks and reserves and its latest proposed amendment are discussed hereunder.

I. The Wildlife (Protection) Act of 1972

A. Declaration

501. The State Government through notification can declare its intention to constitute an area as a National Park which it considers of adequate ecological, faunal, floral, geo-morphological or zoological importance and which serves the purpose of protecting, propagating and developing wildlife (section 35). The State Government may constitute an area comprised within any reserve forest or the territorial waters as a sanctuary (section 18). This area must be of adequate ecological, faunal, geomorphologic, natural or zoological significance for the purpose of protecting, propagating or developing wildlife or its environment to be included in a sanctuary. A declaration of any area or property as a sanctuary cannot be challenged by the owner of such area or property (*Nagar Palika Parishad, Mussorie v. State of UP*, AIR 1998 All 232).

B. Regulation with Respect to Entry

502. There are restrictions on entry to a sanctuary or a national park for persons other than a public servant (section 27). Only after obtaining a permit from the Chief Wildlife Warden, any person may enter or reside in a sanctuary or a national park for all or any of the following purposes (section 28):

(a) investigation or study of wildlife;
(b) photography;
(c) scientific research;
(d) tourism;
(e) transaction of lawful business with any person residing in the sanctuary.

C. Grant of a Permit

503. Destruction, exploitation, etc., in a sanctuary is prohibited. No person shall destroy, exploit or remove any wildlife from a sanctuary or destroy or damage the habitat of any wild animal or deprive any wild animal of its habitat within the sanctuary except under and in accordance with a permit granted by the Chief Wildlife Warden. The permit is not granted unless the State Government is satisfied that such destruction, exploitation or removal of wildlife from the sanctuary is necessary for the improvement and better management of wildlife (section 29). The use of injurious substances, chemicals and explosives, which may cause danger to wildlife, is banned in a sanctuary and national park (section 32). Before laying any refinery pipeline through a forest area, permission under section 29 of the act must be obtained by the person who intends to lay such a pipeline (*Gujarat Narodaya Mandal v. State of Guj*. AIR 1998 Guj 141).

D. The Wild Life (Protection) Amendment Bill, 2021

504. The Wild Life (Protection) Amendment Bill, 2021 has been approved by the Lok Sabha (Lower House of the Parliament) on 3 August 2022. The proposed amendment will implement the CITES of Wild Fauna and Flora.

II. Human Dwellings

505. In some protected areas, people live both within the forest and on its periphery. The forest dwellers are mostly tribal, and their economy and livelihood to a large extent are dependent on the forests. The tribal groups also cultivate lands surrounding their hamlets and sometime have to kill animals attracted by crops which disturbs the natural ambiance and creates environmental problems. The Wildlife Act of 1972 makes settlements within a national park illegal. The official approach to conservation in parks and sanctuaries is to relocate the forest dwellers on the periphery of these protected areas, by constructing colonies or settlements for them. There is provision for the construction of houses, which are invariably better than those in which they lived in the forests, and also for allotment of land for cultivation. In these colonies, primary education for children, family health care, drinking water, and sanitation are taken care of. Still, there is reluctance on the part of forest dwellers to settle in these dwellings as for generations they have been used to forest life.

506. The Schedule Tribes and Other Traditional Forest Dwellers (Recognition of Forest Rights) Act, 2006 and Rules of 2008 recognizes and vests the forest rights and occupation in forest land in Scheduled Tribes and other traditional forest dwellers who are living in the forest for generations but their rights were not recorded. It provides for a framework for recording the forest rights.

III. Institutions and Bodies

A. Central Zoo Authority

507. The Central Zoo Authority (CZA) with its headquarter in New Delhi was established in 1992 under the provisions of the Wildlife (Protection) Act of 1972 to upgrade the management of zoos in the country with a view to enhance their role in conservation. The CZA consists of twelve members and one full-time Member Secretary and is chaired by the Minister, MOEFCC. Two committees namely the 'Administrative Committee' under the Chairmanship of the Director General of Forests and the Technical Committee under the Chairmanship of the Additional Director General of Forests (Wildlife) carry out the functions of the CZA.

508. The following are the main functions of the CZA:

- Specify minimum standards for housing, upkeep and veterinary care of the animals in the zoos.
- Recognize zoos on the basis of evaluation of their functioning.
- Identify endangered species of wild animals for the purpose of captive breeding and assigning responsibility in this regard to the zoo.
- Coordinate the acquisition, exchange and loaning of animals for breeding.
- Ensure maintenance of a studbook of endangered species of animals in captivity.
- Coordinate training of zoo personnel in India and outside.

– Provide technical and other assistance to zoos for management and development on scientific lines.

509. The CZA has prepared a national policy on zoos, which provides appropriate direction to the Government and other zoo operators. The CZA hosts an interactive website (www.cza.nic.in). The complete inventory of animals of all the large, medium and small zoos is on the website. The zoos can access their respective inventory on this website and enter deaths, births and other details directly. The CZA is also responsible for the creation of rescue centres, for rehabilitation of circus animals, consequent upon a ban on performance of wild animals in circuses. Six rescue centres were identified and are functional at Chennai, Visakhapatnam, Tirupati, Bannerghatta (Bangalore), Bhopal and Nahargarh (Jaipur). The CZA has revised the evaluation format of the zoos in terms of the Recognition of Zoo Rules, 2009 as amended in 2013.

B. Botanical Survey of India

510. The BSI established in 1890 is responsible for the survey and identification of the plant resources of the country. It is headquartered in Kolkata with nine circle offices located in different parts of the country. The scientists from the BSI carry on survey and exploration tours of the country, and data with respect to flora so collected is published.

§3. Parks, Sanctuaries and Gardens

I. Corbett National Park

511. This park, situated 186 miles northeast of Delhi in the Himalayan foothills was a popular hunting ground of the British before Independence. This 201 mi^2 park was named in honour of the late Jim Corbett, the legendary hunter-naturalist turned author and photographer who helped in demarcating the park's boundaries. With the help of the World Wildlife Fund, Project Tiger was launched in Corbett National Park in 1973, and this park was one of the first such tiger reserves in the country.

The varied topography of the park comprises hilly and riverine areas, temporary marshy depressions, plateaus and ravines. The lower areas are full of Sal trees. There are 110 tree species, fifty mammals species, 580 bird species and twenty-five reptile species in the park. Corbett is a heaven for tigers with its plentiful prey – four kinds of deer, wild boar and other animals. Leopards are found in the hilly areas of the park but often do not cross paths with tigers in their territories. The sloth bear is found in the lower regions of the park, while the Himalayan black bear is seen in the higher hills only. Elephants (solitary bulls and breeding herds) are one of the main attractions of Corbett. Along the Ramganga River shores, one can spot the long-snouted, fish-eating gharial crocodile and the mugger crocodile. Also seen on the rocky hillsides is the ghoral (goat-antelopes). The langur and rhesus monkeys are well distributed throughout the park.

II. NZP, New Delhi

512. Inaugurated on 1 November 1959, this park is spread over an area of 176 acre and houses about 1,257 animals and birds of 136 species. It plays a major role in *ex-situ* conservation, fostering understanding, knowledge and appreciation for wildlife through education, research and caring of animals in simulated conditions.

III. Bandhavgarh National Park

513. Set among the Vindhya Hills of Madhya Pradesh with an area of 168 mi^2, this national park contains a wide variety of inhabitants including a large number of tigers. Over half of the area of the park is covered by sal forests, and there are stretches of bamboo and grassland. Animals found in the park include chousingha (small four-horned) antelope, chinkara (Indian gazelle), nilgai (blue bull) antelope, wild boar, jackal, muntjak (barking) deer, sambar deer, chital (spotted deer), jungle cat, striped hyena, porcupine, ratel, rhesus macaque, black-faced langur monkey and more. In March and April, gaur (Indian bison) move down from the higher hills to the southeast of the park and make their way to the central meadows. There are also around 150 species of birds in this park.

This park is also rich in history because of the existence of caves dug into the sandstone of an ancient fort with inscriptions dating from the first century. In the recent past, the fort was last occupied by the Maharaja of Rewa until it was designated as a National Park in 1968. In fact, Madhya Pradesh's forests were immortalized by Rudyard Kipling in his *Jungle Books*.

IV. Gir Forest National Park

514. This 116 m^2 sanctuary lies in the southwest of the State of Gujarat. This sanctuary was created to protect the last wild population of lion outside Africa. The Gir is a mixed deciduous forest with teak, flame of the forest, some acacia and banyan trees. It is a hilly tract with many rivers. In the year 1913, merely twenty lions were there in India, the significant drop was due to encroachment and hunting. The Government putt conservation efforts very seriously and things started changing. As per the 2020 census, the lion population there had been registered an increase of 25% in the previous five years and now presently stood at 674 (https://www.thehansindia.com/life-style/world-lion-day-2022-why-asiatic-lion-need-other-home-apart-from-gujarats-gir-757042). Other animals in the park are leopard, sambar deer, chital, spotted deer, nilgai antelope, chousingha (four-horned antelope), chinkara gazelle, wild boar, langur monkey, jackal, and hyena.

V. Keoladeo Ghana (Bharatpur) National Park

515. While many of India's parks have been developed from the hunting preserves of princely India, Keoladeo Ghana was created by the Maharaja of

Bharatpur. By diverting water from a nearby irrigation canal, a fabulous ecosystem that sustains a wealth of bird life was created. Over 350 species of birds find refuge in Bharatpur's 11 mi^2 of shallow lakes and woodland. It is considered to be unique in the total number of bird species as well as the quantity of bird life. It has an impressive assortment of land and arboreal birds, but the grand spectacle is provided by the aquatic species. There are four species of cormorants, eight species of egrets, three ibises, seventeen species of duck and geese, and two species of crane. The Siberian Crane is one of the rarest species in the world, and Bharatpur is its only known wintering ground in India.

VI. Little Rann of Kutch

516. Little Rann of Kutch, situated in the Thar Desert of the State of Gujarat was established in January 1972 as a sanctuary for the last population of Indian wild ass (khar). This area becomes partly inundated by about two feet of water in the monsoon months (July–September). Once below sea level, this area was raised by earth movements which cut it off from the Gulf of Kutch, and was broken up by later earth movements into the flat saline areas (where people make salt), and higher grounds with sandy, salt-free soil. The wild ass depends on the thorny scrub of the higher ground area for its food. Also found in this park are chinkara gazelle, nilgai antelope, wolf, blackbuck antelope, hyena, desert fox, jackal, desert cat and caracal.

VII. Nagarhole National Park

517. This 247 mi^2 park in Karnataka has an astonishing abundance of wildlife including large mammals such as tiger, leopard, wild elephant, dhole (Indian wild dog), and gaur (Indian bison) Other species present are chital spotted deer, muntjak (barking deer), mouse deer, four-horned antelope, wild boar, sloth bear, hyena, mongoose, civet, otter, and more. The landscape is one of the gentle slopes and shallow valleys. Dry deciduous forest trees are leafless in the summer rather than in the winter. There are grassy swamps where the soil consists mainly of clay, perennially moist, and which support a luxuriant growth of green grass all year. The change in terrain throughout the park is refreshing and the river system provides a unique wildlife viewing experience.

VIII. Ranthambore National Park

518. Ranthambore encompasses nearly 152 mi^2 of dry deciduous forest in southwestern Rajasthan and, in the heart of this forest, the Aravali and Vindhya mountain ranges meet. The park derives its name from the fort of Ranthambore which sits on a rocky outcrop in the forest. The fort dates back to the eleventh century when it was a vital citadel for the control of central India. In 1981, Ranthambore was awarded national park status and though overrun by vegetation, remnants of the summer palaces, temples and guard stones within the fort still remain. Ranthambore is famous for its tigers and is a favourite with photographers.

The landscape is dotted with ancient banyan trees, dhok and pipal trees, and clusters of mango trees and crisscrossed with evergreen belts. The terrain is made up of massive rock formations, steep scarps, perennial lakes and streams, and forest. The park has a rich diversity of fauna and flora species. There are a total of 40 species of mammals, 35 species of reptiles and 320 species of birds, migratory as well as residential of the natural habitat. It is due to this reason the national park is also a haven for bird watchers in the wild. The Park has 300 plant species.

IX. The National Botanic Garden at Noida-Delhi

519. A National Botanic Garden at Noida in UP near Delhi has been set up by the MoEFCC to facilitate *ex-situ* conservation and propagation of threatened or endangered plants of the country to serve as a 'centre of excellence' for research and training, to cater to the conservation needs of the endangered species in the region and to build public awareness on conservation needs through education on conservation of plant diversity. The scheme has been identified as a 'Green Channel' project under the National Jai Vigyan Science and Technology Mission of the Ministry of Science and Technology for expeditious processing. The rationale for development of a Botanic Garden at Noida-Delhi stems from the urgent need for a conservation-oriented garden in the country. Setting up of this National Botanic Garden aims at consolidating India's plant conservation efforts in a major way as well as help India to fulfil its obligations as a signatory to the CBD (June 1992). Apart from normal indigenous plants, medicinal plants are also being grown in this Park.

§4. Special Projects

520. Some special reserves have been created like biosphere reserves, reserves for tigers and elephants.

I. Biosphere Reserves

521. Biosphere reserves are terrestrial and coastal ecosystems, which are internationally recognized within the framework of UNESCO's MAB Programme. These reserves are rich in biological and cultural diversity. The goal of setting these reserves is to facilitate conservation of immense biological diversity and cultural heritage, foster economic and human development that is culturally and ecologically sustainable and to provide support for research, monitoring, education and information exchange.

A. World Network of Biosphere Reserves

522. For inclusion in the World Network of Biosphere Reserves designated by UNESCO, a reserve is required to meet a minimal set of criteria and adhere to a minimal set of conditions. The world's major ecosystem types and landscapes are represented in this Network, which is devoted to conserving biological diversity, promoting research and monitoring as well as seeking to provide models of sustainable development in the service of humankind. So far, eighteen reserves have been set up in India. These reserves protect representative ecosystems and also serve as laboratories for evolving alternative models of development. The MoEFCC provided financial assistance to the respective State Governments for conservation and management of these reserves. Eleven biosphere reserves from India are now included in the World Network. Inclusion in World Network facilitates international recognition and attracts additional funding for these sites. The Secretariat for GEF has approved funding a special project for long-term conservation and sustainable utilization of the resources of the GoM Biosphere Reserve.

B. Details of Biosphere Reserves

523. A list of biosphere reserves set up so far along with their area and location is given in Table 3.

Table 3 Biosphere Reserves

Sl. No.	*Name of the Site and Area (km ^{2})*	*Date of Notification*	*Location (State) and Biogeographic Zones*
1.	Nilgiri (5,520)	1 September 1986	Part of Wayanad, Nagarhole, Bandipur and Mudumalai, Nilambur, Silent Valley and Siruvani Hills (Tamil Nadu, Kerala and Karnataka) – Western Ghats
2.	Nanda Devi (5,860.69)	18 January 1988	Part of Chamoli, Pithoragarh & Almora Districts (Uttaranchal) – West Himalayas
3.	Nokrek (820)	1 September 1988	Part of Garo Hills (Meghalaya) – East Himalayas
4.	Manas (2,837)	14 March 1989	Part of Kokrajhar, Bongaigaon, Barpeta, Nalbari, Kamrup and Darrang Districts (Assam) – East Himalayas

Sl. No.	*Name of the Site and Area (km ^{2})*	*Date of Notification*	*Location (State) and Biogeographic Zones*
5.	Sunderbans (9,630)	29 March 1989	Part of delta of Ganges and Brahmaputra river system (West Bengal) – Gigantic Delta
6.	Gulf of Mannar (10,500)	18 February 1989	Indian part of GoM between India and Sri Lanka (Tamil Nadu) – Coasts
7.	Great Nicobar (885)	6 January 1989	Southern most islands of Andaman and Nicobar (A&N Islands) – Islands
8.	Similipal (4,374)	21 June 1994	Part of Mayurbhanj district (Odisha) – Deccan Peninsula
9.	Dibru-Saikhowa (765)	28 July 1997	Part of Dibrugarh and Tinsukia districts (Assam) – East Himalayas
10.	Dehang Debang (5,112)	2 September 1998	Part of Siang and Debang valley in Arunachal Pradesh – East Himalayas
11.	Pachmarhi (4,926.28)	3 March 1999	Part of Betul, Hoshangabad and Chhindwara districts of Madhya Pradesh – SemiArid-Gujarat Rajputana
12.	Kanchanjunga (2,619.92)	7 February 2000	Parts of Kanchenjunga Hills in Sikkim – East Himalayas
13.	Agasthyamalai (1701)	12 November 2001	Neyyar, Peppara and Shenduruny Wildlife Sanctuaries and their adjoining areas in Kerala
14	Achanakamar-Amarkaulak	2005	Amapur and Didori Districts of Madhya Pradesh and parts of Bilaspur in Chhattisgarh
15	Kachch	29 January 2008	Parts of Kachchh, Rajkot, Surendranagar and Pattan Districts of Gujarat
16.	Cold Desert (7770)	28 August 2009	Pin Valley National Park and surroundings, Chandratal and Kibber Wildlife Sanctuary in Himachal Pradesh
17.	Seshachalam (4755.997)	20 September 2010	Seshachalam in Eastern Ghats comprising parts of Chittoor and Kadapa

Sl. No.	*Name of the Site and Area (km²)*	*Date of Notification*	*Location (State) and Biogeographic Zones*
18.	Panna (2998.98)	25 August 2011	Part of Panna and Chhatarpur District in Madhya Pradesh

II. Biodiversity Conservation

524. Biodiversity is defined as the variability among living organisms and the ecological complexes of which they are part, including diversity within and between species and ecosystems. Biodiversity manifests at species, genetic and ecosystem levels. The indirect ecosystem services provided through biodiversity are photosynthesis, pollination, transpiration, chemical cycling, nutrient cycling, soil maintenance, climate regulation, air, water system management, waste treatment and pest control. The scheme on CBD was initiated during 1991–1992 to ensure coordination among various agencies dealing with issues relating to the conservation of biodiversity and to review, monitor and evolve adequate policy instruments for the same. The main implementation measures for the CBD are through national strategies, legislation and administrative instruments to be developed in accordance with each country's particular conditions and capabilities.

A. Convention on Biological Diversity

525. India became a party to the International CBD in May 1994. The three objectives of the convention are as follows:

- conservation of biological diversity;
- sustainable use of components of biological diversity; and
- fair and equitable sharing of benefits arising out of the utilization of genetic resources.

B. National Biodiversity Strategy and Action Plan Project

526. The National Biodiversity Strategy and Action Plan is meant for implementation of the CBD at the country level. A National Biodiversity Action Plan (NBAP) was prepared in 2008. Five years later, it was considered necessary to align the existing NBAP in accordance with the Strategic Plan for Biodiversity 2011–2020 and the Aichi Biodiversity Targets. This was achieved by formulating India's National Biodiversity Targets and developing a monitoring framework using indicators, and through an evaluation of funding support for biodiversity conservation. The draft document was prepared and reviewed through a series of national stakeholder consultations and technical review meetings, based on which the 'National Biodiversity Action Plan: Addendum 2014 to NBAP 2008' has been finalized.

C. Steps Initiated to Conserve Biodiversity

527. The following steps have been taken to conserve biodiversity:

- Establishment of a protected area network of national parks and wildlife sanctuaries.
- A programme of eco-development involving local communities is being implemented.
- A specific programme for the conservation of wetlands, mangroves and coral reefs is also being implemented.
- Six internationally significant wetlands of India have been declared as Ramsar sites under the Ramsar Convention.
- A centrally sponsored programme of National Lake Conservation was launched in 1994 which is now being funded on certain percentage sharing basis between Centre and concerned State.
- Under the World Heritage Convention, five natural sites have been declared as World Heritage Sites.

§5. Compensation

I. Compensation for Acquisition

528. When an area is notified as a sanctuary, the collector enquires and determines the existence, nature and extent of the rights of any person in or over the land comprised within the limits of the sanctuary (section 19, Wildlife (Protection) Act of 1972). The collector enquires into the claims with respect to the existence of any right and ascertains from the records of the State Government and may also take evidence from any person who is acquainted with the matter (section 22, the Wildlife Act).

A. Claim

529. After considering all the aspects of the case, the collector passes an order either admitting or rejecting the claim in whole or part. In doing so, the collector may exclude such land from the limits of proposed sanctuary or may proceed to acquire such land or right except where by an agreement between the owner of such land or holder of rights and the government, the owner or holder of such rights has agreed to surrender his rights to the Government, in or over such land, on a payment of compensation as provided in the Right to Fair Compensation and Transparency in Land Acquisition, Rehabilitation and Resettlement Act of 2013 (30 of

2013). The collector may also allow, in consultation with the Chief Wildlife Warden, the continuance of any rights of any person in or over any land within the limits of the sanctuary.

B. Award for Compensation

530. In the event that the collector proceeds with the acquisition of land or over the right of such land. he makes an award for compensation. Such compensation can be in land or money or partly in land or partly in money.

II. Financial Assistance

531. The protected area network includes 104 (one hundred four) national parks, 551 wildlife sanctuaries, 88 Conservation Reserves and 127 Community Reserves. The scheme for financial assistance has been modified in 2008 and renamed as Integrated Development of Wildlife Habitat. Under this scheme, 100% central assistance is provided for non-recurring items of expenditure, and 50% assistance is provided for recurring items of expenditure. Protected Areas in mountains, deserts and coastal regions supporting large populations of endangered species like snow leopard, red panda, rhino, Sangai deer, Phary's leaf monkey, musk deer, Hangul, Great Indian Bustard, Chinkara and black buck are eligible for 100% central assistance for recurring and non-recurring items of expenditure. Apart from assistance to protected areas, the modified scheme also covers protection of wildlife outside the protected area and recovery programme for critically endangered species.

532. The scheme on assistance to botanical gardens and centres for *ex-situ* conservation was started in 1992 to augment *ex-situ* conservation of rare endemic plants. One-time financial assistance is provided to the existing botanical gardens for improvement of their infrastructural facilities to augment *ex-situ* conservation of rare endemic plants. The MoEFCC has reconstituted the Expert Group on the Scheme in December 2008 which identifies and recommends proposals received for financial assistance and also monitors and review progress of the sanctioned projects.

III. Balance Between Protection and Economic Development

533. The need for environment protection with respect to forests, parks and sanctuaries has to be balanced with economic development. In the case of *Consumer Education and Research Society v. Union of India* (AIR 2000 SC 975), the Supreme Court laid down that if an attempt is made by the State Legislature and State Government to balance the needs of the environment and needs of economic development, it would not be proper to apply the principle of prohibition in such a case. In this case, the State of Gujarat reduced the size of a sanctuary in order to economically develop the backward area of Kutch by exploiting its mineral wealth. The Supreme Court allowed a reduction in size of the sanctuary and controlled mining of the minerals in the area.

IV. Resettlement

A. *Financial Help*

534. Financial help for resettlement is available, at least to some extent, in the form of the Eco-Development Project, supported by an International Development Agency credit and also a grant under the GEF. The project is being implemented through the MoEFCC, the GOI and Forest Departments of seven States including Karnataka. Though the direct purpose of the project is to help conservation of biodiversity in protected areas by improving their management, it also covers tribal development and village eco-development to minimize or compensate for the adverse impact of conservation efforts on tribals and other villagers.

B. *Joint Forest Management of the Protected Areas*

535. The forest dwellers who were seen as a threat to conservation will be agents of conservation as they are now involved in the process of its management. Collecting forest produce like firewood, fodder and wood required for housing or construction is being permitted in community forests with some conditions. The forest dwellers could be employed as forest guards or watchers. Employing them can enable park authorities to benefit from the knowledge of tribal groups about wildlife and forests.

C. *Eco-development Scheme in and Around National Parks and Sanctuaries Including Tiger Reserves*

536. The scheme was launched to provide alternate sources of sustenance to the communities living on the fringes of national parks and sanctuaries including tiger reserves, to improve the ecological productivity of the buffer zones of protected areas through the involvement of these communities in protecting these sanctuaries and national parks and their wildlife; through a well-designed package of activities aimed at providing sustenance to the forest communities and ameliorating their hardships to minimize conflicts between those communities and the forest protection staff.

The activities undertaken under the scheme are as follows:

- Habitat improvement.
- Alternate sources of energy.
- Infrastructure building/roads, etc.
- Small welfare measures.

D. India Eco-development Project

537. The India Eco-development project is implemented in seven protected areas in seven different States as the externally aided Centrally Sponsored Plan Scheme under 'Eco-development Around Protected Areas Including Tiger Reserves'. It covers two national parks and five tiger reserves. The main aim of the project is to conserve biodiversity through eco-development, effective and extensive support for eco-development and preparation of future biodiversity projects. The project is implemented in seven areas namely Buxa, Palamau, Nagarhole, Periyar, Pench, Ranthambore Tiger Reserves and Gir National Park.

Chapter 4. Protection and Management of Species

538. The country's animal and plant species face a variety of threats, ranging from habitat destruction and illegal wildlife trade to reduction in forest cover outside protected areas. Significant populations of these species exist outside Protected Areas moving for dispersal from their natal habitats or for seasonal migrations. Pollution like air pollution, water pollution, and waste pollution, especially in the form of plastic plays a very dominant role in the endangerment of species. Pollution not only causes health hazards for humans, but it affects animals also.

539. The MoEFCC, in consultation with Wildlife Institute and other scientific institutions/ organizations, identified sixteen terrestrial and six aquatic species with the objective of saving critically endangered species/ecosystems that to ensure their protection outside Protected Areas, across the wider landscape/seascape. Species Recovery Plans were prepared for several of these species. The Lion and Rhinoceros populations are showing an increasing trend, and the Sangai and Hangul populations are stable, but the populations of the Great Indian bustard and the Nicobar megapode have recorded declines. Vulture populations, in particular Gyps bengalensis, that had declined substantially in recent times have registered a small upward trend, indicating that conservation measures taken for the species are showing a positive outcome. Efforts are underway for developing protocols for monitoring the status and trends of the remaining species.

540. In ancient times, King Ashoka enforced certain norms in the nature of preservation of wildlife. He prohibited the killing of parrot, ruddy, geese, rhinoceros, etc. These were engraved as edicts. The wildlife in India is facing two-pronged attacks because of fragmentation and destruction of their habitats for reasons like industrial development, mining of minerals, land cleared for agriculture, etc. The ecosystem of India otherwise is endowed with rich biodiversity, including plant and animal forms and their produce that is critical for human sustenance. With mounting agricultural, industrial and demographic pressures, wilderness areas, which are the repositories of wildlife and biodiversity have either shrunk or disappeared. There is a need to realign development priorities to take into account ecological imperatives, including the protection of wild species, which sustain and enhance natural habitats.

§1. Problem Areas

I. Illegal Trade in Wildlife

541. Because of the demand for wildlife and its products on the market, illegal trade has become a lucrative business and resulted in depletion of many endangered animal species. The illegal trade in tiger skin, bones, claws, etc., is well known because of its demand in some countries where these items are used for making medicines.

II. National Wildlife Crime Control Bureau

542. A National Wildlife Crime Control Bureau under the MoEFCC, to combat organized illegal trade in wildlife and their derivatives has been created as a statutory authority. The Wildlife Protection Act, 1972 was amended by the Wildlife (Protection) Amendment Act, 2006, which containing enabling provisions for constituting the Bureau. The Act received the assent of the President on 3 September 2006, and its provisions came into force on 4 September 2006. The GOI notified the constitution of the Tiger and Other Endangered Species Crime Control Bureau to be known as the Wildlife Crime Control Bureau vide Order No. S.O.918(E) dated 6 June 2007. It became operational in the year 2008.

§2. Legislative Structure and Legal Regime

I. Legislation

543. There are a number of enactments and bodies for the implementation of policies concerning preservation of animal and plant species. The first legislative effort in the field of wildlife was the enactment of the Elephant Preservation Act of 1873 (Madras). Thereafter came the Wild Birds Protection Act of 1887 which was subsequently enacted as the Wild Birds Protection Act of 1912 and 1935. The killing and capturing of wild animals and birds were prohibited for the first time by the Act of 1912. Subsequently, other legislations were brought into force such as the Wildlife (Protection) Act of 1972 and the Biological Diversity Act of 2002.

II. Salient Features of Legislation

A. The Wildlife (Protection) Act of 1972

544. For the protection of wild animals, birds and plants and for other connected matters, the Wildlife (Protection) Act of 1972 was enacted. This Act has been adopted by all States except the State of Jammu and Kashmir, which has its own law. Under this Act, the Central Government appoints a Director, Assistant Director, and a few other officers and employees as may be required for the preservation of wildlife. Apart from this, the State Government also appoints a Chief Wildlife Warden, other wardens, one Honorary Wildlife Warden in each district and other officers and employees. This Act has brought uniformity with respect to wildlife which was earlier governed by numerous states' Acts.

1. The Wild Life (Protection) Amendment Bill, 2021

545. The Wild Life (Protection) Amendment Bill, 2021 has been approved by the Lok Sabha (Lower House of the Parliament) on 3 August 2022. The Wild Life (Protection) Act of 1972 protects a number of species, but the proposed amendment will implement the CITES of Wild Fauna and Flora. The Bill provides for the central government to designate a Management Authority for granting export or import permits for trade of specimens. As per CITES, the Management Authority may use an identification mark for a specimen. The Bill prohibits any person from modifying or removing the identification mark of the specimen. Additionally, every person possessing live specimens of scheduled animals must obtain a registration certificate from the Management Authority.

546. The Bill empowers the central government to regulate or prohibit the import, trade, possession or proliferation of invasive alien species. Invasive alien species refers to plant or animal species which are not native to India and whose introduction may adversely impact wildlife or its habitat. The central government may authorize an officer to seize and dispose of the invasive species. For sanctuaries falling under special areas, the management plan must be prepared after due consultation with the Gram Sabha (Village Council) concerned. Special areas include a Scheduled Area or areas where the Scheduled Tribes and Other Traditional Forest Dwellers (Recognition of Forest Rights) Act, 2006 is applicable. The Bill empowers the central government to notify a conservation reserve. The Bill provides for any person to voluntarily surrender any captive animals or animal products to the Chief Wild Life Warden.

2. Wildlife Advisory Board

547. A Wildlife Advisory Board is constituted for the State consisting of the following members (section 6):

- the Minister in charge of Forests in the State or UT;
- two members of the State Legislature;
- secretary of the State Government;
- the Forest Officer in charge of the State Forest Department;
- chief wildlife warden; and
- five officers of the State Government.

The functions and duties of Wildlife Advisory Board *inter alia* include the following:

(a) the selection of areas to be declared as sanctuaries, national parks and closed areas;
(b) to formulate policies regarding the protection and conservation of wildlife and specified plants;
(c) to take measures in connection with the needs of the tribal groups and other dwellers of the forest regarding the protection and conservation of wildlife.

The Board is to follow orders of the State Government on any matter related to wildlife protection (section 8).

3. Prohibition on Hunting of Animals and Uprooting of Plants

548. In general, the hunting of animals is prohibited except in certain cases and circumstances (sections 9 and 10). The picking, uprooting, etc., of plants of specified categories has also been prohibited. But the State Government may direct the Chief Wildlife Warden to grant a permit to pick, uproot, acquire or collect plants from a forestland (section 17A). Schedules I and II of the Act contain a list of endangered species requiring the highest protection. There is a prohibition on trade in rare and endangered species.

B. The Biological Diversity Act of 2002 (No. 18 of 2003)

549. This Act provides for protection and conservation of biological diversity, sustainable use of its components and fair and equitable sharing of the benefits arising out of the use of biological resources, knowledge and for matters connected therewith or incidental thereto. The Act also prevents bio-piracy and exploitation of knowledge of rich biodiversity by foreign individuals and organizations without sharing the benefits. India is a party to the United Nations CBD signed at Rio de Janeiro on 5 June 1992 which came into force on 29 December 1993. Therefore, it was considered necessary to provide for conservation, sustainable utilization and equitable sharing of the benefits arising out of utilization of genetic resources and also to give effect to the said convention; thus, the present legislation was brought. The provisions of the act are in addition to, and not in derogation of the provisions in any other law relating to forests or wildlife (section 59). To facilitate the implementation of the Act, National Biodiversity Authority (NBA) has been set up on 1 October 2003. The Biological Diversity Rules of 2004 framed under the Act have also been enforced.

1. Definitions

550. Some definitions given in the act and necessary to understand the concept of biodiversity are as follows:

> 'Biological diversity' means the variability among living organisms from all sources and the ecological complexes of which they are part, and includes diversity within species or between species and of eco-systems (Section 2 b);
> 'Biological resources' means plants, animals and micro-organisms or parts thereof, their genetic material and by-products (excluding value added products) with actual or potential use or value, but does not include human genetic material (Section 2 c).

2. Biodiversity-Related Activities only with the Approval of the NBA

551. Any person (as this term is defined in the act) can, with the previous approval of the NBA, obtain any biological resource occurring in India or knowledge associated therewith for research or for commercial utilization or for bio-survey and bio-utilization (section 3).

The following persons are required to obtain the approval of the NBA:

(a) a person who is not a citizen of India;
(b) a citizen of India, who is a non-resident as defined in clause (30) of section 2 of the Income Tax Act of 1961;
(c) a body corporate, association or organization which comes under the following categories:
  - not incorporated or registered in India; or
  - incorporated or registered in India under any law for the time being in force which has any non-Indian participation in its share capital or management.

3. Transfer of Results of Research with the Approval of the NBA

552. No person shall transfer the results of any research relating to any biological resources occurring in, or obtained from, India for monetary consideration or otherwise to any person without the previous approval of the NBA (section 4).

4. Constitution of the National, State and Local Biodiversity Funds (Sections 27, 32, 42, 43)

553. The National, State and Local Biodiversity Funds are constituted under this act. The National Fund will be applied for channelling benefits to the benefit claimers, conservation and promotion of biological resources and development of areas from where such biological resources or knowledge associated therewith have been accessed, etc. The State Biodiversity Fund shall be applied for the management and conservation of heritage sites, compensating or rehabilitating any section of the people economically affected by notification of biodiversity heritage sites, etc.

5. The Central Government to Develop National Strategies Plans (Section 36)

554. The Central Government shall develop national strategies, plans and programmes for the conservation and promotion and sustainable use of biological diversity including measures for identification and monitoring of areas rich in biological resources, promotion of *in situ*, and *ex situ*, conservation of biological resources, incentives for research, training and public education to increase awareness with respect to biodiversity.

6. Protection of Local Knowledge

555. The Central Government is required to respect and protect the knowledge of local people relating to biological diversity, as recommended by the NBA through registration of such knowledge at the local, State or national levels, and take other measures for protection.

7. Central Government Notifies Threatened Species (Section 36)

556. The Central Government, in consultation with the concerned State Government provides notice of any species which is on the verge of extinction or likely to become extinct in the near future as a threatened species and prohibits or regulates collection thereof for any purpose and takes appropriate steps to rehabilitate and preserve such species.

8. The NBA is Bound by the Directions Given by the Central Government (Section 48)

557. The NBA in the discharge of its functions and duties is bound by directions on questions of policy as the Central Government may give in writing to it from time to time. However, the NBA shall be given the opportunity to express its views before any direction is given under this subsection. The decision of the Central Government whether a question is one of policy or not will be final.

III. International Conventions

A. CITES in Wild Fauna and Flora (Washington, 3 March 1973)

558. This convention ensures, through international cooperation, that the international trade in specimens of species of wild fauna and flora does not threaten the conservation status of the species concerned.

B. Bonn Convention on the Conservation of Migratory Species of Wild Animals (Bonn, 23 June 1979)

559. This convention aims at conserving migratory species by the signatory parties, through restricting harvests, conserving habitat and controlling other adverse factors. Sustainable utilization is an implicit goal of this convention.

IV. Institutions and Bodies

A. *Department of Endangered Species Management*

560. The Department of Endangered Species Management (ESM) has the mandate to work for the conservation of rare and endangered species of India through status surveys, research, monitoring, development of conservation action plans and advocacy. The conservation projects include research on olive Ridley turtles; monitoring endangered carnivores, mountain ungulates and pheasants in the Himalaya; assessment of the impacts of the tsunami on the Nicobar megapode; development of a conservation action plan for the hangul or Kashmir stag; carrying out status surveys of the Indian peafowl, Himalayan brown bear and Asiatic black bear; and listing of species in the IUCN red lists and reviewing the listing in the schedules of the Indian Wildlife (Protection) Act.

561. ESM is involved in many research projects dealing with the ecology and monitoring of endangered species in a wide range of study areas from the high Himalaya to the coasts and islands and the southern Indian Ocean and Antarctica. A few projects also involve working with managers and local indigenous communities to resolve human–wildlife interface issues.

B. *Wildlife Institute of India, Dehradun (WII)*

562. The WII was initially established in 1982 under the Ministry of Agriculture and subsequently in 1986 brought under the MoEFCC as an autonomous institute. This institute imparts training to government and non-government personnel, carries out research and training activities and advises on matter of conservation and management of wildlife resources. The institute became an autonomous institute of the ministry, with a forty-six-member Wildlife Society headed by the Union Minister for Environment and Forests, with the GOI as its apex body. Research is conducted on ecological, biological, socioeconomic and managerial aspects of wildlife conservation in various parts of the country. The research projects generate valuable scientific data, help evolve study techniques relevant to the Indian ground conditions and also create a group of trained field biologists, socioeconomists and wildlife managers. The scientific information generated is utilized for the management of protected areas. The Salim Ali Centre for Ornithology and Natural History, Coimbatore also carries on research programmes in the above-stated areas as performed by the Wildlife Institute.

C. *The Indian Board for Wildlife*

563. Set up in 1952, the Indian Board for Wildlife is the apex advisory body in the field of wildlife conservation and is headed by the Honourable Prime Minister of India. The Board oversees and guides the implementation of schemes for wildlife conservation.

D. The Zoological Survey of India

564. The ZSI is a premier institute under the MoEFCC. The ZSI undertakes survey, exploration and research leading to the advancement of knowledge on the exceptionally rich faunal diversity of the country since its inception in 1916. With its headquarters at Kolkata and sixteen regional stations located in different parts of the country, the ZSI in recent years has reoriented its plan of work by grouping the survey and studies under the following five major programmes:

- Fauna of States.
- Fauna of Conservation Areas.
- Fauna of Important Ecosystems.
- Status Survey of Endangered Species.
- Ecological Studies.

E. The National Biodiversity Authority

565. As per section 8 of the Biological Diversity Act of 2002, the NBA is a body corporate with perpetual succession and a common seal, with power to acquire, hold and dispose of property, and to contract, and shall by the said name sue and be sued. The head office of the NBA is in Chennai, and the NBA may, with the previous approval of the Central Government, establish offices at other places in India.

The NBA consists of a Chairperson appointed by the Central Government and fifteen other members.

It is the duty of the NBA to regulate activities relating to approval, transfer of results of research and approval relating to the grant of intellectual property rights and by regulations issue guidelines for access to biological resources. For a UT, the NBA exercises the powers and performs the functions of a State Biodiversity Board (SBB).

F. The SBB (Section 22)

566. A Board may be constituted for the State under section 22 of the Biological Diversity Act of 2002. The Board will be a body corporate with perpetual succession and a common seal, with power to acquire, hold and dispose of property, both movable and immovable, and to contract, and shall by the said name sue and be sued. The Board consists of a Chairperson appointed by the State Government, not more than five ex officio members and not more than five members appointed from among experts in matters relating to conservation of biological diversity.

G. Biodiversity Management Committees (Section 41)

567. Every local body is required to constitute a Biodiversity Management Committee within its area for promoting conservation, sustainable use and documentation of biological diversity including preservation of habitats, conservation of land races, domesticated stocks and breeds of animals and microorganisms and chronicling of knowledge relating to biological diversity.

568. The NBA and the SBBs are to consult the Biodiversity Management Committees while taking any decision relating to the use of biological resources and knowledge associated with such resources occurring within the territorial jurisdiction of the Biodiversity Management Committee. The Biodiversity Management Committees may levy charges by way of collection fees from any person for accessing or collecting any biological resource for commercial purposes from areas falling within their territorial jurisdiction.

H. The National Institute of Animal Welfare

569. This institute has been established in Ballabhgarh, Faridabad district, Haryana, for providing various courses on animal welfare. The institute offers intensive specialized diplomas in specific streams. This institute is working as a teaching, research and extension centre. It imparts teaching in disciplines like history of animal welfare movement, psychology of animal behaviour, animal diversity, animal laws, animal nursing, animal breeding, zoo management, park management, aquatic management, animal stress and pain, etc.

I. The Animal Welfare Board of India

570. The Animal Welfare Board of India (AWBI) is a statutory body constituted under section 4 of the Prevention of Cruelty to Animals Act 1960, with headquarters in Chennai. Its basic mandate is to create awareness and advise the Government on animal welfare issues. The AWBI gives financial assistance to eligible animal welfare organizations for shelter houses, model *gaushalas* (cow sheds) for setting up of biogas plants, famine/drought relief, earthquake relief, etc. It also deals with stray animals and prevention of cruelty to animals. Its functions include rescue of cattle from illegal smuggling and transportation, rehabilitation of rescued circus animals, lab animals, inspections and incurs legal expenses in connection with court cases pertaining to animal welfare.

J. The Committee for Control and Supervision of Experiments on Animals

571. This is also a statutory body under section 15 of the Prevention of Cruelty to Animals Act of 1960 with headquarters in Chennai. This committee registers and monitors animal breeders and institutions conducting experiments on animals. So far, 731 units have been registered with this committee.

§3. NATIONAL WILDLIFE ACTION PLAN

572. The first Wildlife Action Plan was released for 1983–2001 and the second for 2002–2016. The MoEFCC has announced the third National Wildlife Action Plan for 2017–2031. These Plans are envisaged to conserve and protect wildlife through the protected-area centric approach. Protected areas are well-defined geographical spaces, recognized through legal and other means, to achieve long-term conservation of nature with its associated ecosystem. The third Action Plan contains detailed recommendations to be practised in the protected areas. The key focus areas of this plan are wildlife health, conservation of marine ecosystem, reduction of human–wildlife conflict, conservation of coastal ecosystem and integration of climate change into wildlife planning. This is the first time that an action plan on wildlife is recognizing the impact of climate change on wildlife.

I. Project Tiger

573. The total tiger population as per the Tiger Census 2018 is 2,967 tigers, which was 33% more than the 2014 Census and more than double, than the 2006 Tiger Census. At present, Project Tiger looks after fifty-three tiger reserves spread across 75,000 km^2 of green cover in an effort to conserve the population of the Royal Bengal Tiger. Project Tiger was launched in April 1973 on the recommendations of a special task force of the Indian Board of Wildlife with the following objectives:

- to ensure maintenance of a viable population of tiger in India for scientific, economic, aesthetic, cultural and ecological values;
- to preserve the areas of such biological importance as a national heritage for the benefit, education and enjoyment of the people.

574. The Wildlife (Protection) Act, 1972 was amended in 2006, and a separate chapter has been provided for strengthening tiger conservation. The effective protection and concerted conservation measures inside the reserves have brought about considerable achievements also, viz. arresting erosion, enrichment of water regimes and thereby improving the water table and overall habitat resurrection. Financial assistance is provided to tribal families for voluntary relocation from the protected tiger reserves. In general, the project has been instrumental in mustering local support for conservation programmes.

The National Tiger Conservation Authority (Normative Standards for Tourism Activities and Project Tiger) Guidelines, 2012 have been framed under clause (c) of subsection (1) of section 38 O of the Wildlife (Protection) Act, 1972 by the National Tiger Conservation Authority. These Guidelines have been framed for the purpose of tiger conservation in the buffer and core area of tiger reserves and lay down standards for tourism activities in tiger reserves.

575. At present, there are fifty-three tiger reserves spread over different States. Covering an area of 75,000 km^2. Details of some tiger reserves along with the location are given in Table 4.

Table 4 Name of the Tiger Reserves in Tiger Range States with the Year of Creation and Area

Sl. No.	*Year of Creation*	*Name of Tiger Reserve*	*State*	*Total Area (km^2)*
1.	1973–1974	Bandipur	Karnataka	866
	1999–2000	Nagarhole	(extension)	643
2.	1973–1974	Corbett	UP	1,316
3.	1973–1974	Kanha	Madhya Pradesh	1,945
4.	1973–1974	Manas	Assam	2,840
5.	1973–1974	Melghat	Maharashtra	1,677
6.	1973–1974	Palamau	Bihar	1,026
7.	1973–1974	Ranthambore	Rajasthan	1,334
8.	1973–1974	Similipal	Odisha	2,750
9.	1973–1974	Sundarbans	West Bengal	2,585
10.	1978–1979	Periyar	Kerala	777
11.	1978–1979	Sariska	Rajasthan	866
12.	1982–1983	Buxa	West Bengal	759
13.	1982–1983	Indravati	Madhya Pradesh	2,799
14.	1982–1983	Nagarjunsagar	Andhra Pradesh	3,568
15.	1982–1983	Namdapha	Arunachal Pradesh	1,985
16.	1987–1988	Dudhwa	UP	811
17.	1999–2000	Katerniaghat	(extension)	551
18.	1988–1989	Kalakad-Mundanthurai	Tamil Nadu	800
19.	1989–1990	Valmiki	Bihar	840
20.	1992–1993	Pench	Madhya Pradesh	758
21.	1993–1994	Tadoba-Andheri	Maharashtra	620
22.	1993–1994	Bandhavgarh	Madhya Pradesh	1,162
23.	1994–1995	Panna	Madhya Pradesh	542
24.	1994–1995	Dampha	Mizoram	500
25.	1998–1999	Bhadra	Karnataka	492
26.	1998–1999	Pench	Maharashtra	257

Sl. No.	*Year of Creation*	*Name of Tiger Reserve*	*State*	*Total Area (km^2)*
27.	1999–2000	Pakhui-Nameri	Arunachal Pradesh Assam	1,206
28.	1999–2000	Bori, Satpura, Pachmarhi	Madhya Pradesh	1,486
Total				**37,761**

Project Tiger is a centrally sponsored scheme. The States receive 100% financial assistance for non-recurring items and 50% for approved recurring items.

A. *Core-Buffer Strategy*

576. The tiger reserves are constituted on a 'core-buffer strategy'. The core area is kept free of biotic disturbances and forestry operations and collection of minor forest produce, grazing, human disturbances are not allowed. However, the buffer zone is managed as a 'multiple use area' with twin objectives of providing habitat supplement to the spill-over population of wild animals from the core conservation unit, and to provide site-specific eco-developmental inputs to surrounding villages for relieving the impact on the core. No relocation is visualized in the buffer area, and forestry operations, Non-timber Forest Produce (NTFP) collection and other rights and concessions to the indigenous communities are permitted in a regulated manner to complement the initiatives in the core unit.

Project Tiger is trying to put the tiger on a course of recovery from the brink of extinction, and has successfully resurrected the floral and faunal genetic diversity in some of India's unique and endangered wilderness ecosystems.

II. Project Elephant

577. The Project Elephant was launched in the year 1992 as a Centrally Sponsored Scheme with objectives to protect elephants, their habitat and corridors; to address issues of man-animal conflict; and for welfare of captive elephants. The MoEFCC provides the financial and technical support to major elephant range states through Project Elephant. There are thirty Elephant Reserves in the country. The latest addition to this list is the Singphan Wildlife Sanctuary as the Singphan Elephant Reserve which got approved by the Government on 16 August 2018. The Indian subcontinent is considered to be the last remaining stronghold of the Asian elephants. With more than 26,000 elephants, it is home to more than half the global Asian elephant population in the wild. Considering the sociocultural importance elephants hold in India, they also have been given the tag of National Heritage Animal.

III. Holding Last Surviving Population

578. The Gir Forest holds the last surviving population of Asiatic lion in the world, and Kaziranga National Park in Assam is home to a large population of one-horned rhinoceroses and wild buffalo. Bandipur is one of the finest habitats of the Asian elephant. The parks protect other species of wildlife as well. For example, Little Rann of Kutch in the State of Gujarat situated in the Thar Desert, is a sanctuary for the last population of Indian wild ass. India's largest bird sanctuary is located in Keoladeo Ghana National Park, more commonly known by its old name, Bharatpur. In the past, it was the shooting preserve of the Maharaja of Bharatpur, where in 1938 the Viceroy of India's party shot 4,273 birds in one day. Now the park protects 375 species of birds. Some of the rarest wildlife is found in India's national parks, such as the golden langur, the world's rarest monkey. Golden langurs are found in a small patch of forest on the Manas River, which forms the border between the Manas Wildlife Sanctuary in Bhutan and the Manas National Park in India.

§4. Conservation Initiative

579. A schemes has been initiated to protect the biodiversity and minimize the mortality of critically endangered and threatened animals. The Wetland (Conservation and Management) Rules 2010 have been brought to protect wetlands in India. The Government has also initiated the scheme, namely National Plan for Conservation of Aquatic Eco-System that lends assistance to the States for the sound management of all wetlands. In order to curb the illegal trade of wildlife and that of endangered species, Wildlife Crime Control Bureau has been established. Special organizations like WII, Bombay Natural History society and Salim Ali Centre for Ornithology and Natural History are formed to conduct research on conservation of wildlife. For restocking of the endangered species, the Central Government first initiated Integrated Development of Wildlife Habitat Scheme and later modified it by including a new component, Recovery of Endangered Species which included animals like Hangul/stag deer in Jammu & Kashmir, Vultures in Punjab, Haryana and Gujarat, Snow Leopard in Jammu & Kashmir, Himachal Pradesh, Uttarakhand and Arunachal Pradesh, Swiftlet in Andaman & Nicobar Islands, Nilgiri tahr in Tamil Nadu, Sangai Deer in Manipur. intensified Anti-poaching activities initiated and special patrolling strategy adopted for monsoon season.

§5. Enforcements and Control

I. Enforcement Agencies

580. The Wildlife (Protection) Act of 1972, the Biological Diversity Act, 2002, the provisions of the CITES and the export and import policy of India with respect to wildlife are enforced by a number of agencies namely the Regional Deputy Directors of Wildlife Preservation located at Delhi, Mumbai, Kolkata and Chennai with the help of the State Wildlife Department, the State Police Departments, the Customs Departments, Border Security Force and Coastguards.

II. Ban on Import and Export

581. Section 5 of the Foreign Trade (Development and Regulation) Act of 1992 requires notification of the Export-Import Policy (Exim Policy). This policy contains a negative list of imports and the negative list of exports. Both these lists contain certain items which pertain to animals and their products. Similarly all items of plants are included in Appendix I and II of the CITES.

III. Penalty for Wildlife Offences

582. Section 39 of the Wildlife Protection Act of 1972 provides that any weapon, tool, vehicle which is used or suspected to have been used in any wildlife offence and seized shall become the property of the Government. The Wildlife (Protection) Amendment Act of 2003 enhanced penalties for violation of the provisions of the Act (The Penalties have been further enhanced in Wildlife (Protection) Amendment Bill, 2022). Chapter IV A provides for forfeiture of property derived from illegal hunting and trade. There is prohibition of holding illegally acquired property (section 58C). The illegally acquired property means property attributable to be acquired through illegal hunting and trade of wildlife and its products and derivatives. Such property can be identified (section 58E) and can be seized or freezed (section 58F).

IV. List of Endangered Species

583. The list of endangered species has been appended to the act as schedules. Schedule V contains species which are not threatened. The species of animals which are listed in Part I of Schedule II, Schedule III and Schedule IV are granted importance. The highest protection is accorded to animals listed in Schedule I and Part II of Schedule II, which are called scheduled animals.

584. India has ratified the CITES of Wild Fauna and Flora on 18 October 1976. The provisions of the convention find support from Article 253 of the Constitution.

V. Special Coordination and Enforcement Committee

585. A 'Special Coordination and Enforcement Committee for strengthening measures for control of poaching and illegal trade in wildlife' has been constituted under the Chairmanship of the Secretary (MoEFCC), and Special Secretary (Ministry of Home Affairs), Chairman (Central Board of Excise and Customs, Ministry of Finance), Director, Central Bureau of Investigation as members and the Additional Director General Wildlife as the Member Secretary. As per the decision of this committee, the State and UT Governments were to set up state level/district level Coordination Committees to control poaching and illegal trade in wildlife.

VI. Disclosure of Wildlife Stock

586. A scheme of voluntary disclosure has been initiated for possession of animal skins, tusks and other wildlife stock. The purpose of this scheme is certification of ownership of wildlife stock by individuals and institutions. The data is kept by the Chief Wildlife Warden (HT 31 July 2003). It is now being introduced through Wildlife (Protection) Amendment Bill, 2021. The Bill provides for any person to voluntarily surrender any captive animals or animal products to the Chief Wild Life Warden.

VII. Captive Breeding Farms

587. The MoEFCC is exploring the possibility of allowing private persons to breed wild animals and extract medicinal products from them. This captive breeding will satisfy the demand for body parts of wild animals. At present, this demand is being met illegally and in the process wild animals are being brutally killed. For example, deer are killed for their musk and antlers. These animals could be reared commercially. They can then complete their entire life span and continue yielding musk and antlers for many years.

VIII. Protection and Enforcement of Biological Diversity Norms

A. Powers of the Civil Court

588. The NBA for the purposes of discharging its functions shall exercise the same powers as are vested in a civil court under the CPC, 1908 in respect of the following matters:

(a) summoning and enforcing the attendance of any person and examining him on oath;
(b) requiring the discovery and production of documents;
(c) receiving evidence on affidavits;
(d) issuing commissions for the examination of witnesses or documents;
(e) reviewing its decisions; dismissing an application for default or deciding it ex parte;
(f) setting aside any order of dismissal of any application for default or any order passed by it ex parte;
(g) any other matter which may be prescribed.

The proceedings before the NBA are deemed to be judicial proceedings within the meaning of sections 193 and 228 and for the purpose of section 196 of the IPC; the NBA is deemed to be a civil court for the purposes of section 195 and Chapter XXV1 of the Code of Criminal Procedure, 1973.

B. Appeal (Section 52)

589. Any person, aggrieved by any determination of benefit sharing or order of the NBA or an SBB is allowed an appeal in the High Court within thirty days from the date of communication to him, of the determination or order of the NBA or the SBB, as the case may be. However the High Court may, on showing a sufficient cause allows it to be filed within a further period not exceeding sixty days.

C. Execution of Determination or Order (Section 53)

590. The order made by the NBA or an SBB under this act or the order made by the High Court in any appeal against any determination or order of the NBA or an SBB shall, on a certificate issued by any officer of the NBA or an SBB or the Registrar of the High Court, as the case be, be deemed a decree of the civil court and is executable in the same manner as a decree of that court.

D. Penalties (Section 55)

591. Any person contravening or abetting the contravention of the provisions of section 3 or 4 or 6 which deal with approval to undertake biodiversity-related activities, prohibition on transfer of results of research and matters relating to application for intellectual property rights shall be punishable with imprisonment for a term which may extend to five years, or with fine which may extend to INR 1 million, and where the damage caused exceeds INR 1 million, such fine may be commensurate with the damage caused, or with both.

E. Penalty for Contravention of Directions or Orders (Section 56)

592. If any person contravenes any direction given or order made by the Central Government, the State Government, the NBA or the SBB for which no punishment has been separately provided under this act, he shall be punished with a fine which may extend to INR 0.1 million and in case of a second or subsequent offence, with fine which may extend to INR 0.2 million and in the case of continuous contravention with an additional fine which may extend to INR 0.2 million for every day during which the default continues.

F. Offences (Sections 59 and 61)

593. The offences committed under the Biodiversity Act are cognizable and non-bailable (section 59).

A court can take cognizance of any offence on a complaint made by the following authorities:

(a) the Central Government or any authority or officer authorized to do so;
(b) any benefit claimer who has given notice of not less than thirty days in the prescribed manner, of such offence and of his intention to make a complaint, to the Central Government or the authority or officer authorized as aforesaid.

Chapter 5. Agricultural Resources

594. India is the second-largest food producing country in the world and ranks first in the production of milk, pulses, rice, fish, vegetables and wheat. The production of food grains in the country in 2021–2022 is estimated at a record 314.51 million tonnes which is higher by 3.77 million tonnes than the production of food grain during 2020–2021. The production during 2021–2022 is higher by 23.80 million tonnes than the previous five years' average production of food grains. However, a large population of the country suffers from hunger and malnutrition. According to the United Nations' 'The State of Food Security and Nutrition in the World 2022' Report, the struggle of poor for survival has increased sharply after the 2019 Corona period. In 2021, 224 million (29%) people in the India were undernourished. There has certainly been slow progress in India on the anti-hunger front. About 80 crores, i.e., about 60% people are dependent on subsidized ration provided by the government under the Pradhan Mantri Garib Kalyan Anna Yojana, apart from the special epidemic assistance of free five kg of food grains, the beneficiaries are given five kg of food grains per month at only INR 2–3 per kg per person.

595. India's position in the Global Hunger Index has fallen further. India was ranked 94th out of 116 countries in 2020, while in 2021 it has slipped to 101st. According to the United Nations Report, there are 97.33 crore people in India who do not have a healthy diet. According to this, 70% of Indians do not get healthy food. India is the second-largest producer of wheat and rice in the world, it is unfortunate that such a vast population does not have access to a healthy diet. However, the report also said that the situation in India was improving, but the Corona epidemic put a brake on it. In 2017, 75% of Indians did not have access to a healthy diet. The number dropped to 71.5% in 2018 and 69.4% in 2019, but in 2020 the figure rose again to over 70%.

596. With the diversification and growth of economy, agriculture's contribution to GDP has steadily declined. While agriculture has achieved grain self-sufficiency but the production is resource intensive, cereal centric and regionally biased. The resource intensive ways of Indian agriculture has also raised serious sustainability issues. Increasing stress on water resources of the country need a realignment and rethinking of policies. Desertification and land degradation also pose major threats to agriculture in the country. Agriculture is said to have been started in India at least 5,000 years ago, that is, around 3,000 BC. With such a long history of cultivation, it is remarkable that agriculture continues to produce the yields even at the current levels using less chemical fertilizers and pesticides than many advanced countries. Most of India's agriculture even today is based on rainfed areas and irrigation accounts only for approximately one-third of the net sown area.

§1. Agriculture: The Main Occupation

597. Agriculture, with its allied sectors, is the largest source of livelihood in India and 70% of its rural households still depend primarily on agriculture for their livelihood. The recently published Center for Monitoring Indian Economy report showed that the country's unemployment rate rose by 0.68%–7.80% on a monthly basis, as against the level of 7.12% in May 2022. This increase in the unemployment rate is mainly due to the increase in the rural unemployment rate which has increased by 1.41%–8.03% on a monthly basis.

§2. Methods Employed for Sustainable Use

I. Crop Rotation

598. In India, in ancient times, a complex and ingenious system was developed to make sustainable use of soil which has maintained productivity over centuries through a system of crop rotation, crop diversification, and regular replenishment of soils through the use of organic manure. The choice of crops was such that in some areas nitrogen fixing crops like pigeon pea and Bengal gram were grown along with other varieties. In the process, farmers nurtured a wide variety of millets and pulses – a variety and diversity which is not so easy to come across in any other country in food grains. One of the rituals in India insist on giving '*Daan*' (charity) which should include among other things, *Navadhanyas*, or not less than nine varieties of pulses to earn *punya* or merit for entry to heaven. This ritual has also contributed indirectly to the growing of varied crops from ancient times.

II. Maintaining Cattle

599. Maintaining cattle is an important part of the strategy of taking care of soils, which give farmers milk, a rich diet and a base for many other food products. Cow dung is collected carefully from cowsheds and from grazing lands, and deposited in compost pits. Organic leaves and cow urine channelled from animal sheds is mixed with dung in compost pits. The compost manure is spread on the fields and ploughed into the soil. The humus from the compost helps the soils to retain moisture. Despite an increase in the use of chemical manure, the old methods are still in use side by side.

§3. Green Revolution

600. The impetus for the Green Revolution came from harvest failures and famine conditions in the mid-1960s. Its main goal was to ensure India's national food security and self-reliance in food grain production. India has achieved self-reliance in food grain production and has become the world's second-largest producer of both wheat and rice and the largest exporter of rice. Despite the large increases in total production, per capita availability of all food grains has increased only modestly because of rapid increase in population.

601. Initially the Green Revolution through the adoption of High Yielding Varieties on a widespread basis, together with fertilizers, was confined to irrigated areas and to wheat and rice crops but with the passage of time, it spread to rainfed areas and other crops before the end of the 1970s. From a net importer of food grains, India has now emerged as a net exporter because of advancement in the field of agriculture. Per capita availability of food grains for fiscal year 2021 amounted to about 185 Kgs per annum which was barely 144 Kg in 1951.

§4. Desertification

602. Desertification is one of the major environmental problems which has a direct impact on soil, vegetation and other aspects of the life of the inhabitants of the affected areas in terms of decreased agricultural and hence food output, depletion of natural resources and deterioration of the environment.

I. Desert Development Programme

603. The basic object of the Desert Development Programme (DDP) was to minimize the adverse effect of drought and control desertification through rejuvenation of natural resource base of the identified desert areas. The programme strives to achieve ecological balance in the long run; aims at promoting overall economic development and improving the socioeconomic conditions of the resource poor and disadvantaged sections inhabiting the programme areas. DDP initiated in 1977–1978, covers both the hot desert regions of Gujarat, Rajasthan and Haryana and the cold desert areas in Jammu, Kashmir, and Himachal Pradesh. It is functional in 131 blocks of 21 districts in 5 States covering an area of about 0.362 million km^2 and a population of 15 million.

II. UN Convention to Combat Desertification

A. Aims and Objects

604. Desertification is one of the major environmental problems which has direct impact on soil, vegetation and results in deterioration of the environment. India is a signatory to the UN Convention to Combat Desertification (UNCCD) since 14 October 1994, and it came into effect in India on 17 March 1997. The MoEFCC is the coordinating body for this programme and National Afforestation and Eco-development Board (NAEB) is the nodal point within the Ministry to coordinate all matters pertaining to the Convention. The convention's main objective is to take appropriate measures for combating desertification and to mitigate the effects of drought in an integrated manner to achieve sustainable development. It also aims at enhancing food security, eliminating poverty, and improving socioeconomic development with a focus on sustainable development.

B. Implementation of the Convention at the National Level

605. The focus of the convention is on initiation of long-term integrated strategies promoting the objective of conservation and protection of the environment, in terms of afforestation, improved productivity of land, conservation and sustainable management of land and water resources leading to improved living conditions, particularly at the community level. Under the convention, all affected country parties including India have prepared a National Action Programme for combating desertification and drought in their respective countries.

606. Out of India's total geographical area of 328.73 mha, 304.89 mha comprise the reporting area and 264.5 mha only is under agriculture, forestry, pasture and other biomass production. Soil degradation in India is estimated to be occurring on 147 mha of land, including 94 mha from water erosion, 16 mha from acidification, 14 mha from flooding, 9 mha from wind erosion, 6 mha from salinity, and 7 mha from a combination of factors.

C. Implementation of the Convention at the Regional Level

607. Under the Regional Action Programme for Asia, six Thematic Programme Network (TPN) areas have been identified for regional cooperation among member parties and to help the member parties strengthen their existing infrastructure for tackling the problems related to these areas. India is the nodal country for hosting the TPN-2 namely, 'Agro-forestry and Soil Conservation in Arid, Semi-arid and Dry Sub-humid Regions in Asia.' The network's focal areas are given in Table 5.

Table 5 Focal Area of TPN Programme Paragraph 490

TPN-1 Desertification monitoring and assessment	Host country – China
TPN-2 'Agro-forestry and soil conservation in the arid, semi-arid and dry sub-humid regions in Asia'	Host country – India
TPN-3 Range and pasture management in arid areas with particular emphasis in controlling, shifting sand dunes	Host country – Iran
TPN-4 Water resources management for agriculture in arid, semiarid and dry sub-humid areas	Host country – Syria
TPN-5 Drought preparedness and mitigation in the context of climate	Host country – Mongolia
TPN-6 Strengthening planning capacities for drought management & controlling desertification	Host country – Pakistan

D. Network on Agro-forestry and Soil Conservation in Arid, Semiarid and Dry Sub-humid Regions in Asia

608. India is host to the TPN-2 and the Central Arid Zone Research Institute (CAZRI) Jodhpur in the State of Rajasthan is the nodal institution for its implementation in Asia. India launched the TPN-2 on 14–15 March 2000 at New Delhi followed by a field visit to Rajasthan organized by the CAZRI from 16–18 March 2000. The network has strengthened partnerships between the countries of Asia to address issues of land degradation. India participated in the conference of the parties to UNCCD which was held in Buenos Aires, Argentina from 21 September to 2 October 2009 to review the implementation of the Convention. The Agenda *inter alia* included arrangement for Regional Coordination Mechanism, four-year work plans and two-year work programmes, etc.

§5. Land Degradation

I. Extent of the Problem

609. According to 'Desertification and Land Degradation of Selected Districts of India', an atlas published in 2021 by the ISRO's Space Application Centre, Ahmedabad, 96.40 million ha, or about 29.32% of the Total Geographic Area of the country is undergoing degradation whereas it was 29.3% during 2011–2013. Therefore, the legal provisions and government actions have brought some results. A few states were afflicted with more than 50% of their area under desertification. The States of Jharkhand, Rajasthan, Delhi, Gujarat and Goa have more than 50% area under desertification/land degradation. Kerala, Assam, Mizoram, Haryana, Bihar, Uttar Pradesh, Punjab and Arunachal Pradesh had less than 10% area under desertification/land degradation. Around 23.95% of desertification/land degradation was contributed by nine states namely Rajasthan, Maharashtra, Gujarat, Jammu & Kashmir, Karnataka, Jharkhand, Odisha, Madhya Pradesh and Telangana.

A. Wastelands

610. Wastelands are degraded lands which can be brought under vegetative cover currently lying as unutilized and which are deteriorating for lack of appropriate water and soil management or on account of natural causes. Estimates of wastelands differ considerably due to definitional and coverage inconsistencies. The estimates of cultivable wastelands are 1.2 mha in blocks of 100 ha. India's total land area is around 329 mha. Out of this, the government classifies 90 mha as 'wasteland' meaning non-productive land. These occur in different agro-climate and soil zones. These wastelands form the core of degraded lands in India.

1. National Wasteland Development Board

611. The strategy adopted by the National Wasteland Development Board (NWDB) emphasized more on tree planting activities through Community Participation for wasteland development. In the year 1992, the new Department under the Ministry of Rural Development (now Ministry of Rural Areas and Employment) was created and the NWDB was placed under it. The Board was reconstituted in August 1992 and was made responsible for development of wastelands in non-forest areas in totality by involving local people. It aims at creating a scenario where the Government acts as a facilitator and the people at the grass root level become the real executioner of the programme. Integrated Wasteland Development Programme (IWDP) has been implemented for improving the productivity of waste and degraded lands keeping in view the poverty, backwardness, gender and equity.

2. Integrated Wasteland Development Programme

612. The IWDP started in 1989–1990, seeks to develop Government wastelands. The IWDP is aimed at overall economic development and improving the economic conditions of the resource poor population. The new guidelines for watershed development have changed the role of the Government from that of governance to facilitation. The arrangements envisaged in the Guidelines can be seen as a true reflections of the Agenda 21 where the sustainability is achieved the involvement of local people and the local bodies.

II. Causes of Land Degradation

613. Land degradation in India has been brought about mainly through: (i) displacement of soil materials and their deposition and (ii) *in situ* degradation. Top soil loss and terrain deformation through water and wind erosion and also overblowing through wind erosion are manifestations of the first category and chemical degradation involving loss of nutrients and/or organic matter, salinization and pollution, and physical degradation in the form of waterlogging, mass movement, landslides, compaction, crusting and sealing, of the second.

A. Soil Erosion

614. Soil erosion results in the loss of topsoil and terrain deformation. It is a function of geological formation, rainfall, susceptibility to erosion, length and steepness of slopes, agricultural practices, vegetative cover, etc. Soil erosion accounts for 60% of the total degraded land in India. Erosion due to water is greater in regions, which receive heavy rainfall over short periods than in places with low intensity rainfall. Water erosion across the country is also a major cause of topsoil loss (93.68

mha) and terrain deformati. The principal reasons for this state of affairs are non-adoption of proper soil and water conservation measures, improper crop rotation and extension of cultivation onto lands of low potential or high natural hazards.

615. The loss of topsoil due to erosion depletes the productive upper surface since essential plant nutrients are present there. Soils over much of the subcontinent are also highly deficient in Soil Organic Matter. The problem is widespread in the cultivated areas of the subtropical belt, including areas under shifting cultivation or *Jhumming* in the northeastern States. India loses nearly 5,334 million tonnes of soil due to erosion annually.

B. Intensive Cultivation

616. The quest for increased agricultural productivity has led to intensive cultivation of marginal lands causing their degradation. The extension of cultivation to land of lower potential and fertility, with greater natural degradation hazards such as steep slope areas of shallow or sandy soil, or with laterite crusts, arid or semiarid land bordering on deserts, which are called fragile or marginal lands, in many parts of the country has resulted in their degradation.

C. Use of Agrochemicals and Pesticides

617. The agrochemicals are being used extensively in modern agriculture. In addition, sewage sludge and composted municipal wastes which also contain other chemicals including detergents are used improperly and indiscriminately, leading to the contamination of soil and water with toxic substances and heavy metals. This problem is widespread all over the country. Pesticide residues are being found increasingly in farm produce posing a threat to human health.

D. Waterlogging and Salinity

618. Intensive agricultural practices that rely heavily on water, chemical fertilizers and pesticides have caused waterlogging and salinity in many parts of the country. The expansion of the irrigation system without adequate steps for treatment of the catchment areas has further exacerbated this problem. Canal irrigation has also resulted in widespread waterlogging and salinity problems. Disturbances of the hydrological equilibrium resulting from excessive recharge because of inefficient use of irrigation water, poor land development, seepage from unlined watercourses, and poor drainage have all resulted in a rise of the water table in most canal command areas. This has occurred on a large scale in several parts of canal command areas such as the Indo-Gangetic plains and the Indira Gandhi Nahar Project. In arid, semiarid and sub-humid tracts of the country, large areas have been rendered barren due to the development of saline–sodic soils because of unhealthy land management in respect of irrigation, drainage and crop husbandry.

E. Overexploitation of Common Property Resources

619. The Common Property Resources (CPR) are resources on which all the people have an equal right of use. These resources include community pastures, community forests, wastelands, and common dumping and threshing grounds. Pastures, fallow lands, cultivable waste lands and parts of forest lands which are available for use by the locals have long been used as CPR. They have sustained the livelihood of local people, especially the poor, meeting their needs without their having to resort to the market. There has been a decline in the quality and quantity of these lands due to overexploitation and encroachments. This has been tried to be corrected by regenerating lands, involving the local people in their management. However the fact remains that some of the most degraded lands in the country are the CPR.

F. Industrialization

620. An increase in industrialization, urbanization and infrastructural development has progressively taken away considerable areas of land from agriculture, forestry, grasslands and pastures, and unused lands with wild vegetation, resulting in land degradation and environmental disturbances. This process has resulted in the degradation of land directly through changed land use and also through the negative impacts of waste disposal.

G. Mining Activities

621. Land degradation is the inevitable result of any form of mining, particularly open cast mining, which thoroughly disturbs the physical, chemical and biological features of the soil. The Mining Lease (ML) area is approximately 0.8 mha, which may be taken as degraded directly due to mining activities in addition to the areas affected indirectly.

§6. ENFORCEMENT AND CONTROL

622. The strategy to counter land degradation includes treatment of catchment areas, comprehensive watershed management, low-cost measures for revegetation or reforestation. The emphasis is on implementing these measures through people's participation at grass root level. The problem areas are identified through remote sensing, and micro-level plans are made to reclaim and improve the affected lands implemented through local governments, NGOs and people's groups.

I. Marginal Farmers and Landless Labourers

623. Marginal farmers and landless households in the rural areas have composite livelihood support systems, comprising deriving fuel wood and fodder for the livestock particularly and also collect raw material for biomass-based cottage industries like basket and mat weaving, broom binding, rope making, etc. In addition, they also collect wood for selling in the nearby towns exercising a tremendous impact on the green cover. Unless their basic needs are satisfied, the ecological management will continue to be vulnerable, as the poor exploit natural resources for their livelihood needs. Thus, the basic biomass survival needs of the poor and landless for fuel wood, for self-consumption and for the market, fodder for their livestock and raw materials for the cottage industry for the village wastelands and nearby forests are to be ensured.

II. Balanced and Integrated Use of Fertilizers and Organic Farm Waste and Municipal Solid Waste in Agriculture

624. India, the second-largest agro-based economy, generates a large amount of agricultural waste, including crop residues. In the absence of adequate sustainable management practices, approximately 92 metric tons of crop waste is burned every year, causing excessive PM emissions and air pollution. Crop residue burning has become a major environmental problem causing health issues as well as contributing to global warming. There is a centrally sponsored scheme on balanced and integrated use of fertilizers so as to popularize soil test based application of fertilizers. The soil testing laboratories have been set up for this purpose. The waste can be used as compost which improves the health of soil by providing organic matter for the required biological activities in addition to improving the physical condition of the soil.

III. Integrated Pest Management

625. The IPM approach, being promoted since 1985, is an eco-friendly strategy of pest containment by exploiting the role of natural agents/forces in harmony with other pest management tactics and with the aim to cause minimum disturbance to the environment. Cultural control, use of natural enemies and plant resistance are basically compatible and supportive tactics in the IPM strategy. There is a need to provide new, safer and efficacious quality pesticide products to the farmers and encourage the use of biopesticides and biocontrol agents.

IV. Plant Quarantine

626. Plant quarantine is a regulatory function under the Destructive Insect Pests Act of 1914 and 1992 amendment and the Plants, Fruits and Seeds (Regulation of Imports into India) Order of 1989. India being a signatory to the World Trade

Organization-Sanitary and Phyto-Sanitary Measures (SPS Agreement), it is obligatory to provide quarantine services. Plant quarantine is of great significance as this plays an important role in regulating import and export.

V. Committees on Agro-biodiversity

627. The NBA may constitute a committee to deal with agro-biodiversity. Here 'agro-biodiversity' means biological diversity, of agriculture-related species and their wild relatives. Besides, the NBA may constitute such number of committees as it deems fit for the efficient discharge of its duties and performance of its functions under the Biological Diversity Act of 2002. The subcommittee can co-opt such number of persons, who are not the members of the NBA, as it may think fit and the persons so co-opted shall have the right to attend the meetings of the committee and take part in its proceedings but shall not have the right to vote (section 13).

VI. International Undertaking on Plant Genetic Resources (Rome, 23 November 1983) as supplemented

628. The basic purpose of this convention is to ensure that plant genetic resources are preserved, particularly cultivated varieties of plants, plants or varieties which have been in cultivation in the past, primitive versions of cultivated plants, wild relatives of such plants and certain special genetic stocks and restricts the destructive impact of development activities to conserve plant varieties which are threatened with extinction as a result of deforestation (especially in tropical areas) or changes in agricultural practices.

VII. Programmes

629. The prevention of land degradation and the augmentation of the carrying capacity of land to provide food, fuel and fodder requirements have been a primary concern. Special Development Programmes have been funded to mitigate the harsh living conditions of people through better land management, water harvesting and conservation practices on a watershed basis. Some of such schemes and programmes are being described hereunder.

A. *Soil Conservation for Enhancing Productivity of Degraded Lands in the Catchments of River Valley Projects and Flood Prone Rivers*

630. Two centrally sponsored schemes for soil conservation and integrated watershed management in the catchments of flood prone regions are being implemented. During the Ninth Plan, both schemes were merged into a new one – 'Soil Conservation for Enhancing Productivity of Degraded Lands in the Catchments of River Valley Projects and Flood Prone Rivers'. The Scheme is meant for improving land and crop productivity by promoting production of crops suitable to the soil conditions, with farmers being encouraged to take up horticulture, fuel wood plantation and fodder species.

B. Development of Degraded/Rainfed Land

631. The UN has adopted 2030 Agenda for Sustainable Development in 2015 with its seventeen Sustainable Development Goals (SDG). 'The UNCCD is to develop a ten-year strategy to implement the SDG target by the year 2030, combat desertification, restore degraded land and soil, including land affected by desertification, drought and floods, and strive to achieve a land degradation-neutral world' – creates a new urgency to address the issue of land degradation in a systematic manner. There are also existing policies relating to land use which require to be kept in mind. These include the National Water Policy 2012, National Land Use Policy Outline 1988, NFP, National Agricultural Policy 2000, National Policy for Farmers 2007, National Policy on Biodiversity 1999, NBAP 2008, and NEP 2006. Clearly, there is a need to harmonize these policies at the central and state levels, and a mechanism is required that can take a composite view of the land resource base and the competing and conflicting demands on it. Further, without the participation of local and community institutions, the sustainability of interventions to reverse land degradation, particularly of common pool resources including forestlands, is limited.

C. Integrated Watershed Programme

632. The Department of Land Resources, Ministry of Rural Development is implementing the Integrated Watershed Development Programme (IWMP) from 2009–2010 with an objective to cover 55 mha of rain fed land by 2027. The programme is being implemented in all the States of the country and financed by central and state government in the ratio of 90:10. The IWMP is the second-largest watershed programme in the world after China. The programme aims at restoring the ecological balance by harnessing, conserving and developing degraded natural resources such a soil, vegetative cover and water through watershed management initiatives. The outcome of IWMP is prevention of soil runoff, regeneration of natural vegetation, rainwater harvesting and recharging of the groundwater table This enables multi-cropping and the introduction of diverse agro-based activities. These help in providing sustainable livelihoods to the people residing in the watershed area. In 2015, the IWMP along with On-Farm Water Management scheme and Accelerated Irrigation Benefit Programme was subsumed into PMKSY.

§7. Water Resource Management in Agriculture

633. The net area sown works out to be 43% of the total geographical area. The net irrigated area is 68.4 million hectares and the rest is dependent on the monsoon which adversely affects the adoption of improved production technologies and results in poor productivity in the agricultural field.

I. Canal Water

634. Canal irrigation is the most important form of irrigation in the country. About 159.40 lakh hectare land was under irrigation by canals during 2018–2019. The environmental problem such as waterlogging and salinization in the vicinity of irrigation canals are widespread. The poor drainage system results when soil having less permeable substratum below pervious soil is not able to drain water deep into ground which causes high water table. If proper drainage is not provided then the storm water constantly percolates and level of water table rises. Providing intercepting drains along canals prevent seeping canal water from reaching the waterlogged areas. To keep from salting out the soil, there must be proper drainage system. When the drainage is insufficient to counter this salt influx, the zone becomes salinized.

II. Groundwater

635. The overexploitation of groundwater has resulted in many white areas being converted into black and grey. The Green Revolution has also affected the quality of groundwater in some places due to leaching of excess fertilizers and chemicals. Besides, there are several areas where there is a natural arsenic in groundwater beyond tolerance levels, for example, West Bengal. The overexploitation of underground water has also led to depletion of aquifers in many areas and in a decline in the groundwater table. Groundwater account for 60% of all irrigation water and over 80% of the rural and urban domestic water supplies. To check overexploitation, there is a need to enact legislation so as to regulate groundwater use. In some areas like Delhi, the boring of wells has been banned.

III. Rainwater Harvesting

636. There is now emphasis on rainwater harvesting. Rainwater harvesting for recharging the groundwater and efficient utilization of water for crop production is an important method in watershed development programmes. Rainwater harvesting has been taken up in some major cities like Delhi in a big way and in certain areas it has been made mandatory to instal water harvesting devices in homes and society flats.

§8. Thrust Areas Identified by NITI Aayog

637. The NITI Aayog is the premier policy Think Tank of the Government providing both direction and policy inputs. The Agriculture vertical at NITI Aayog works to make plans and policies for the development of agriculture, animal husbandry, dairy, fisheries, agricultural land policies and food processing for famers' welfare. It works in close coordination with the line departments of Central Ministries as well as States. Agriculture has been considered as a key for promoting inclusive growth. NITI Aayog has identified 117 Aspirational districts for transformation through development of education, heath & nutrition, agriculture and water resources, skill development, financial inclusion and basic infrastructure. NITI Aayog has finalized the Operation Greens programme of Ministry of Food Processing Industries. Emphasis was given to focus more on 'operations' than infrastructure and also on strong market intelligence. Facilitation of operations like aggregation, transport, storage and professional management along with post-harvest facilities like storage at farm level, collection centres/ pack house, value addition infrastructure, storage facilities at aggregation, sorting, grading, packing facilities, etc., are included under Operation Greens.

638. GOI has also launched Soil Health Card scheme on 19 February 2015. The scheme aims to issue soil card to farmers with crop-wise recommendations for nutrients and fertilizers use at individual farms to help farmers to improve farms productivity through judicious use of inputs and to avoid fertilizers and other chemical which are not required.

Chapter 6. Forests

639. India's biological diversity is reflected in the heterogeneity of its forest cover. India is at the meeting point of three major biogeographic realms, namely the Indo-Malayan (the richest in the world), the Eurasian and Afro-tropical. India also has the two richest biodiversity areas, one in the northeast and the other in the Western Ghats (shore).

§1. Benefits to the Economy

640. The total forest cover in India (2022) is 7,13,789 km^2 which is 21.71% of the total geographical area. India has added 1,540 km^2 of forest cover from 2019 to 2021 whereas it is trying to achieve a target of keeping 33% of its geographical area under forest cover for decades. There has been rapid deforestation in recent years, primarily due to its focus on economic development. Nearly 275 million poor people in India (more than a fifth of the population), especially tribal communities, depend on forests for subsistence and livelihoods. Almost 50% of the food requirements of forest dwellers are met by the forests itself. Several important pieces of legislation have been brought to recognize the tribal population's right to self-determination and to guarantee tenurial rights to forest-dwelling communities, such as Panchayats (Extension to the Scheduled Areas) Act of 1996 and Scheduled Tribes and Other Traditional Forest Dwellers (the Forest Rights) Act of 2006.

§2. Historical Background

I. Ancient India

641. The tradition of sanctity and importance of certain trees and plants such as the peepal, banyan, neem and tulsi dates back to the Vedic Period. The tulsi plant (basil) was grown, a practice which still continues, in every household in the centre of the courtyard and regularly watered. It was used in medicine and believed that its presence in the house will keep away diseases. For thousands of years, the neem tree was considered as a gift of nature and purifier of the environment and thus a powerful pollution fighter. This revered tree of ancient Indians is now being hailed as the most promising of all plants by modern science. The tradition of sacred groves and forests in India are as ancient as the civilization itself. Still there are some sacred groves in India particularly among tribal people.

Gautam Buddha gave a very apt definition of forests as 'a peculiar organism of unlimited kindness and benevolence that makes no demand for its sustenance and extends generously the products of its life activity; it affords protection to all beings, offering shade even to the axe man who destroys it'.

II. Pre-independence Period

A. Control over Forests

642. Before Independence, the British Government systematically established control over forests on the pretext of public use and isolated local people and loosened their control over forests as far as possible. This was meant to serve two purposes. Having depleted their oak resources in Britain, the British Government had eyes on the rich timber resources of India to meet the needs of ship building and railway expansion. Teak, black wood, sandalwood and other such trees were promptly declared Government property to prevent local people from using them. The second purpose was conservation of forests and to protect the forests from practices like slash-and-burn cultivation and also to reduce the pressure of grazing on forests both of which were considered as destructive practices. As early as 1807, a proclamation was issued in the Bombay Presidency asserting the East India Company's right of sovereignty or eminent domain over the forests and forbidding the fetching of timber by private individuals as reported by Dietrich Brandis.

B. Forest Department

643. The Forest Department was created at the Centre in 1864 with Dietrich Brandis, a German, as the first Inspector General of Forests. The Government Forest Act of 1865 empowered the Government to declare any forest as government property. There was a tradition of State ownership of forests and the act formalized this fact. The forest legislation was made more comprehensive and stringent through the Indian Forest Act of 1878, classifying forests into three categories of Reserved, Protected and Village Forests. The Government held absolute rights of ownership in the Reserved Forests, and their products could not be used by local people unless specifically permitted as a privilege and not as a matter of right of locals. Protected Forests were those which were yet to be surveyed and settled, but the local peoples' access and privilege were permitted for the time being except in those cases where they were specifically prohibited (e.g., cutting valuable timber). With respect to Village Forests, the rights of locals were conceded in respect of grazing.

C. Categories of Forests

644. The Indian Forest Act of 1927 continued the earlier classification of forests, and gave more powers to the Government in the Reserved Forests, increased the number of listed offences and enhanced the punishment for some of the offences. In the case of 'Protected Forests', rights and privileges of 'persons' was recorded and the Government had no powers to reduce them. The emphasis in the act was more on the rights and privileges of individuals rather than local communities. Though local people had full access to Village Forests and limited access to Protected Forests, the area under both was very limited. The bulk of forest area was placed under the reserved category. This meant extreme pressure on Village Forests leading to overexploitation and alienation of local people from forests which led to serious discontent and protest movements as it adversely affected the local economy. Since locals did not have any responsibility in the management of forests, especially the Reserved Forests and thus became disinterested in their protection and preservation.

D. Commercial Use

645. The use of forest produce for the development of the economy had started during the British rule mainly for the expansion of the railway network which took a large toll of timber resources and consequently forests. Modern saw mills were set up during the nineteenth century itself. The Second World War further accelerated the exhaustion of forest resources.

III. Post-Independence

646. The first forest policy of independent India was enunciated in 1952, which viewed forests as national assets. After Independence, the emphasis shifted from timber to pulpwood used by paper and rayon mills. State governments encouraged these industries as they created employment and met the needs of paper and clothing. But the prices paid for raw materials were so low that the industries had no interest in regenerating the forest even in lands earmarked for them to meet their needs. When industries exhausted raw material sources allotted earlier, they could obtain new areas for similar exploitation.

A. Extending Cultivation to Forests

647. Once a forest was exhausted, encroachers were tempted to extend cultivation into the cleared forests. Even where forests were replanted, it was at the cost of natural forests. Huge areas of natural forests were cleared to plant trees like eucalyptus needed by industry, destroying in the process biodiversity in the concerned areas and also depriving the local communities of sources of their biomass supply. Rehabilitation of people displaced by development projects, roads, mining, and above all extension of cultivation by people in search of a livelihood made large demands on areas which were rich in forests.

B. Social Forestry

648. In the early 1980s, a new movement was started to launch social forestry projects in almost all the States. The objective was to meet people's needs for fuel wood, fodder, small wood for fencing and other agricultural purposes, and wood needed for housing construction of local communities. Land, which was neither under Reserved Forests nor under cultivation, was identified for this purpose, and planted with trees enlisting people's cooperation in protecting them. The Forest Department took tremendous pains to make a success of this so that the pressure on Reserved Forests could be eased and green areas extended.

C. Joint Forest Management with Local People

649. The Forest Department in order to extend tree cover preferred quick growing trees like eucalyptus, acacia auriculiformis and pine. These trees met the needs of the pulpwood industry too. Large stretches of uncultivated lands were taken up for mono-species plantations to meet the needs of industry and biomass needs of local people were neglected. Though owned by the Government, these lands had been traditionally used by people as CPR for grazing and meeting their biomass needs. But in many social forestry projects, such lands were closed to grazing to prevent tree saplings being browsed or trampled upon and destroyed. The grazing pressure was diverted to Reserved Forests in the neighbourhood. The Forest Department realized its mistakes and started consulting people. Soon this process of consultation transformed itself into joint forest management. The concept that forests have to be managed jointly by the Forest Department and local people together caught on. This prompted the development of new legislation relating to right of the people on forest produce including forest dwellers, e.g., the Scheduled Tribe and Other Forest Dwellers (Recognition of Forest Rights) Act.

D. Development Versus Conservation

650. It has been accepted that there must be complete harmony between development and preservation. Development should not be at the cost of environmental degradation. The apex courts have observed that there should be both development and proper environment and a balance has to be found (*People United for Better Living v. Union of India* AIR 1993 cal 215).

In *Banwasi Seva Ashram v. State of U.P.* (AIR 1987 SC 374), the Honourable Supreme Court observed that there is no doubt that forests are a much wanted national asset. The depletion of forests has given rise to scanty rains and other ecological disturbances. But at the same time for industrial growth and the provision of improved living facilities, electricity is a basic requirement. Therefore, a scheme for electric generation cannot be deferred.

§3. Types of Forests

651. The forests in India range from tropical wet evergreen forests to Alpine. Most of these forests are natural, and their distribution is controlled by climatic conditions like rainfall, soil and relief.

I. The Evergreen Forests

652. The evergreen forests are found on the eastern hills, the foothills of the Himalayas, the Meghalaya, the western slopes of the Western Ghats and Andaman and Nicobar Island. The principal varieties of trees found in these forests are chaplash, bishopwood, toon, rosewood, gurjan, etc.

II. Monsoon Deciduous Forests

653. These forests are found on the eastern slopes of the Western Ghats, some areas of the Eastern Ghats, the Chota Nagpur plateau region, the Upper Mahanadi valley, the hills of Madhya Pradesh and the foothills of the Himalayas. The varieties of trees found in this type of forest include teak, sal and sandalwood, which are the most important commercial timbers. Besides, various forest products like lac, resin, turpentine are also extracted.

III. The Savanna Grasslands

654. These are found in Punjab, Haryana, UP, Rajasthan and the central part of the Deccan, South India. These forests are used as a grazing ground for cattle. Some of the grasses are used for thatching, mat making, rope making, pulp making, etc.

IV. Thorn Forests

655. These forests are found in Rajasthan, some parts of UP, Punjab and the southern part of the country. The main trees which are found are of babool, acacia and thor.

V. Himalayan Forests

656. The Eastern Himalayas are wetter than the Western Himalayas, and this factor has influenced the vegetation and species of forests in these two areas. In the Western Himalayas chir-pine, fir, cedar, etc., are found. In the eastern Himalayas oak, magnolias, laurels, maples, etc., are the main trees.

VI. Mangrove Forests

657. These forests are found in the river deltas of the Ganga, the Mahanadi, the Godavari, the Krishna and the Kaveri. These forests contain evergreen trees of sundari, passur, bain, keora, garan, gewo, garjan, hental, etc., and a large variety of creepers.

§4. PRESSURE ON FORESTS

658. The country's forest resources are under tremendous pressure. Intensified shifting cultivation, indiscriminate removal of timber, fuel wood, fodder and other forest produce, forest fires and encroachment has led to forest degradation and deforestation. The problems and constraints in forestry development include lack of awareness about multiple roles and benefits of forests; no linkage between management and livelihood security of the people; low level of technology; inadequate research, weak planning capability, wastage in harvesting and processing, low levels of people's participation and NGO's involvement and lack of private sector participation, sometimes unwanted restrictions on felling, transport and marketing of forest produce grown by the people, etc.

I. Deforestation

659. The overexploitation of forests (deforestation) has been done in the past in the name of human welfare and development. Because of massive deforestation, many wild animals and birds have become rare species. Forests are nature's protective shield, but this shield is being eroded by human greed. Mahatma Gandhi once said, 'Nature has enough for everybody's need but not for everybody's greed.' Indiscriminate felling of trees is destructive and contra-productive and urgent steps are called for to put down this evil. Indiscriminate cutting of trees disturbs the ecological balance, causes environmental pollution, soil erosion and landslides, floods, water sources may get dried, climatic changes. Due to deforestation, the forest cover of India has fallen below the minimum recommended level. Satellite pictures show that India has gained in forest area but it is not uniform throughout the country. The forests land also being diverted for non-forest purposes like dams, industries, roads and agriculture.

II. Cultivation in Forests

660. There has been a substantial increase in yields of crop per hectare achieved during the Green Revolution. So, there is now enough food to feed the increasing population, but poverty is still a source of pressure on land. This is reflected in the form of encroachments into forests and other common lands for an extending cultivated area, and overexploitation of forests.

§5. STATUTORY STRUCTURE AND LEGAL REGIME

661. Through the 42nd Amendment Act of the Constitution, the subject of forests which was earlier on the State List was included in the Concurrent List of the Constitution of India. This enabled both the Centre and States to enact legislation dealing with the regulation and development of forests. In pursuance thereof, the Central Government enacted the Forest Conservation Act of 1980 and Rules in 1981.

I. Legislation

662. The main enactments dealing with protection of the environment of the forest are listed below:

- the Indian Forest Act of 1927 (sections 26(1) and 32(F));
- the Forest Conservation Act of 1980 as amended in 1988;
- the Forest (Conservation) Rules, 2022;
- the National Fire Prevention and Control Guidelines of 1999;
- the Scheduled Tribes and Other Traditional Forest Dwellers (Recognition of Forest Rights) Act, 2006;
- the Scheduled Tribes and Other Traditional Forest Dwellers (Recognition of Forest Rights) Rules, 2008;
- the Compensatory Afforestation Fund Act, 2016.

Besides, some States have their own forests legislation, but all these are based on the Forest Act of 1878 or 1927.

II. Salient Features of Legislation

663. The salient features of some of the enactments are given below:

A. *The Indian Forest Act of 1927*

664. This act consolidated the law relating to forests, the transit of forest produce, the duty payable on timber and other forest produce. It regulates the management of forests by State Governments. In some States, this act has been adopted in its totality, whereas some States have implemented an amended version in harmony with their requirements. Under this act, the State Government has power to declare any forest land or waste land which is the property of the Government or over which the Government has proprietary rights as a reserve forest or protected forest through notification in the Official Gazette (sections 3 and 29 of the act). This act is not a mere taxing legislation but aims at preserving, protecting and promoting the forest wealth of the country and to achieve this, the act vests in the government control over forests and other areas (*State of Tripura v. Sudhir*, AIR 1997 SC 1168).

665. The act prohibits certain acts in the forest such as lighting fires, trespassing or allowing cattle to graze, quarrying stone, burning lime or charcoal, clearing or breaking up any land for cultivation or for any other purpose. The act prescribes penalties for forest offences. The offences of a trivial nature are covered under section 68 and can be disposed of by compounding. The act gives powers to any forest officer or police officer to arrest any person against whom a reasonable suspicion exists of commission of any serious forest offence punishable with imprisonment for one month or upwards. Such arrest can be made without orders from a magistrate and without a warrant (section 64).

666. In the event of commission of a forest offence in respect of any forest produce, such produce together with all tools, boats, carts or cattle used in committing such offence can be seized by any forest officer or police officer (section 52). But it has to be proved that the owner of boats, tools or other property used for committing a forest offence knew of such use. Therefore, in cases where the owner is not directly charged or captured for the commission of a forest offence, the prosecution fails (*Asst. Forest Conservation v. Sharad Ramchandra Kale*, AIR 1998 SC 2927).

An officer may be invested with powers to issue a search warrant under the Code of Criminal Procedure (section 72(C)). This power is used for searching for stolen forest produce.

667. The States have made amendments in this Act notable being West Bengal and Karnataka. The Central Government has introduced the Indian Forest (Amendment) Act, 2017 amending the Indian Forest Act, 1927. Through this amendment, the word 'Bamboo' has been omitted from the definition of a tree. It opens the growing and use of bamboo for commercial purposes and as an additional income to growers as no permit is required.

B. The Forest (Conservation) Act of 1980 as Amended in 1988

668. This act provides for the conservation of forests and for matters connected therewith and checks indiscriminate diversion of forest land for non-forest purposes. The act extends to the whole of India except the State of Jammu and Kashmir, which has its own law on the subject. The State Governments and UT are required to submit formal proposals to the MoEFCC for use of forest land for non-forest purposes in the prescribed *pro forma* along with details such as flora, fauna and a map of the area. Despite continuous pressure on forests, the regulatory mechanism has stabilized the forest cover in the last decade of the millennium.

The contravention or abatement of the contravention of the provision of section 2, which is to the effect that forest land shall not be used for non-forest purposes, is punishable with simple imprisonment for a period which may extend to fifteen days (section 3a). The Central Government may constitute a committee for the purpose of researching the question and advising the Government whether permission can be granted for the use of forest land for non-forest purposes and any other matter connected with the conservation of forests. The Central Government has been empowered to make rules for carrying out the provisions of the act. The rules made under this provision are required to be placed before each House of Parliament (section 4).

C. Forest (Conservation) Rules of 2003

669. Acting under powers given in section 4 of the act, the Central Government made the Forest (Conservation) Rules of 2003. These rules contain details with respect to the composition of the committee, conduct of business of the committee and other aspects dealing with the functioning of the committee (Rules 2A and 3). When an application seeking permission for use of forest land for non-forest purposes is made, the Central Government acquires advise of the committee and after such further enquiry as it may consider necessary, grants approval to the proposal with or without conditions or reject the same (Rule 6). A time limit of ninety days at the level of the State Government and sixty days at the level of the Central Government has been provided for taking decisions with respect to permission.

1. Forest Conservation Rules of 2022

670. MoEFCC has notified new rules called the '2022 Forest Conservation Rules (FRA)' in the last week of June 2022. The new rules will replace the 2003 FRA and its subsequent amendments in 2004, 20014 and 2017. One of the major changes in the new Rules is that they make no mention of the Gram Sabha's consent before stage II clearance, which was made mandatory in the Forest Conservation Act in 2017 through an amendment. The MoEFCC had delinked its processing of forest diversion applications from the requirement of Gram Sabha consent. The MoEFCC had delinked its processing of forest diversion applications from the requirement of Gram Sabha consent. The new FRA 2022 have totally done away with the clause of complying with FRA and have made it into a whimsical feature according to the discretion of the state governments. The 2022 FRA will be placed for approval before the Lok Sabha and the Rajya Sabha for thirty working days.

671. A notification issued by MoEFCC is to the effect that the Forest (Conservation) Rules, 2022 on 28 June 2022 wherein new provisions and procedures have been introduced for the processing of the proposals received from various user agencies for prior approval under the Forest (Conservation) Act, 1980. In the above context, the following is clarified:

i. Provisions of Forest (Conservation) Rules, 2022 shall apply to the proposals submitted online through Parivesh portal and which have not been accepted by the Nodal officer before 28 June 2022. The Guidelines issued by the Ministry in the Handbook of Forest (Conservation) Act, 1980 dated 28 March 2019 and the Guidelines issued thereafter separately, from time to time, after 28 March 2019 shall apply to such proposals to the extent they are not inconsistent or contrary to the Forest (Conservation) Rules, 2022.
ii. Provisions of Forest (Conservation) Rules, 2003 shall apply to the proposals submitted online through Parivesh Portal and which have been accepted by the Nodal Officer before 28 June 2022 (File No. FC-11/118/2021-FC, dated 18 July 2022).

§6. Enforcement and Control

I. Regional Offices of the Ministry of Environment, Forests and Climate Change

672. The Regional Offices of the MoEFCC monitor and evaluate the ongoing forestry projects and schemes with specific emphasis on conservation of forests and follows up action on the implementation of conditions and safeguards laid down by the MoEFCC and Supreme Court while granting clearance to development projects. The Regional Chief Conservator of Forests decides cases for diversion of forest land for non-forestry purposes up to the extent of five ha except mining and regulation of encroachment. They have also been empowered to examine cases involving forest land from five ha to twenty ha in consultation with the State Advisory Group. The MoEFCC has six Regional Offices located in Bangalore, Bhopal, Bhubaneswar, Lucknow, Shillong and Chandigarh with its headquarter unit at the MoEFCC in New Delhi.

II. The National Compensatory Afforestation Fund Management and Planning Authority

673. The National Compensatory Afforestation Fund Management and Planning Authority (CAMPA) (National Authority) came into existence in place of the Ad-hoc CAMPA with effect from 30 September 2018; the day the Compensatory Afforestation Fund (CAF) Act, 2016 and Compensatory Afforestation Rules (CAF) Rules, 2018 have come into force. Hon'ble Minister, Environment, Forest and Climate Change, GOI is the Chairperson of the Governing Body of the National Authority. The Governing Body is assisted by an Executive Committee and Monitoring Group and an administrative support mechanism. The CAF Act led to the establishment of two special interest-bearing funds, namely the 'National Compensatory Afforestation Fund (National Fund)' and 'State Compensatory Afforestation Fund (Name of the State)' under the Public Account of India and under the Public Accounts of such States/ UTs, respectively. The CAF realized against approvals under the Forest (Conservation) Act, 1980 and/ or under sections 18, 26A or 35 of the Wildlife (Protection) Act, 1972 is distributed in the National Fund and the State Fund in the ratio of 10:90 and is made available to the National Authority and to respective State Authorities through budgetary process.

III. Institutes and Other Bodies

A. Central Board of Forestry

674. This board was constituted in 1950. It provides guidance to the government in the formulation of policy and programmes in the field of forestry.

B. Forest Survey of India

675. The FSI was established on 1 June 1981 as the successor to the Pre-investment Survey of Forest Resources (PISFR), a project initiated in 1965 by the GOI and sponsored by the FAO and UNDP. The main objective of the PISFR was to ascertain the availability of raw material for establishment of wood-based industries in selected areas of the country. Further, the National Commission on Agriculture, in its report in 1976, recommended the creation of a National Forest Survey Organization for the collection of data on scientific lines through a countrywide comprehensive forest resources survey at regular intervals. Consequently, the PISFR was reorganized as the FSI. In 1986 after a critical review of activities undertaken by the FSI, the GOI redefined its mandate in order to make it more purposeful and relevant to the needs of the country. The FSI, an organization of the ministry, is engaged in generating information and a database on forest cover and forest resources. It also provides training and has facilities for research in the field of forests.

1. Objectives of the FSI

676. The main objectives of the FSI are as follows:

- to prepare a Comprehensive State of Forest Report with the generation of Digital Forest Cover maps;
- to undertake work in regard to the preparation of a Forest Inventory for trees outside the forest areas;
- to collect, store and retrieve necessary forestry and forestry-related data needed for national and state level planning and to create a National Basic Forestry Inventory System;
- to design methodologies related to forest surveys and subsequent processing and updating;
- to undertake special studies.

2. Organization

677. A Director heads the FSI. Dehradun is the headquarters of the organization. The FSI has four zones, each headed by a Regional Director, located at Shimla (North Zone), Kolkata (East Zone), Nagpur (Central Zone) and Bangalore (Southern Zone). The total strength of the organization is 436. Zonal officers largely carry out an inventory of forest resources inside and outside forest areas.

3. Forest Cover Mapping

678. The forest cover of the entire country has been assessed by employing a digital interpretation of satellite data on a 1:50,000 scale. In addition, the FSI has assessed minimum mappable area of 1 ha which can be discerned through satellite imageries by using appropriate stratification, sampling and field inventory methods.

4. Forest Inventory

679. A methodology has been developed for a comprehensive assessment of forest resources inside and outside forest areas at national level by stratifying the country into physiographic zones and to take a sample of 10% of ha districts for detailed inventory during a cycle of two years. The FSI was conducting the field inventory both on forest and tree outside forest areas until 2007–2008. The FSI is now carrying out a new study on production and consumption of wood.

C. Indian Institute of Forest Management

680. This institute was established in 1982 as an autonomous organization with the main objective of research, forest management education, training for capacity building, etc. The IIFM contributes to the process of policy formulation in the area of natural resource management. Some of the new initiatives to be taken up in the Tenth Plan are as follows:

- establishment of a National Forest Data Centre;
- establishment of a policy cell for undertaking policy research to provide inputs to policymaking; and
- establishment of a Centre for Excellence in Medicinal Plants.

D. Indira Gandhi National Forest Academy

681. This academy was constituted in the year 1987 by renaming the Indian Forest College. The academy imparts induction training to Indian Forest Service probationers and in-service training to serving officers. The academy has also started professional skills upgrading of training for officers promoted to the Indian Forest Service from the State Forest Service (SFS).

E. ICFRE, Dehradun

682. The ICFRE is the main forestry research organization with the mandate to formulate, organize, direct and manage forestry research, transfer the technologies developed to States and other user agencies and impart forestry education. There are ten Research Institutes of the ICFRE located at Dehradun, Coimbatore, Bangalore, Jabalpur, Jorhat, Jodhpur, Shimla, Ranchi, Chhindwara and Allahabad.

F. Directorate of Forest Education

683. The DFE was delinked in 1991 from the Forest Research Institute and colleges and now functions directly under the MoEFCC. The Directorate is responsible for controlling, coordinating and managing the entire regular training courses of the SFS and Forest Range Officers in the country. This Directorate also organizes diploma and certificate courses, short-term special refresher/capacity building courses, promotion-linked skill upgrading and basic training skill courses for in-service officers.

There are three SFS Colleges situated in Dehradun (Uttarakhand), Coimbatore (Tamil Nadu) and Burnihat (Assam) and one Rangers College, namely the Eastern Forest Rangers College, Kurseong (West Bengal) under the control of the GOI. Besides, there are five State-run rangers colleges under the technical control of the DFE.

G. IPIRTI, Bhopal

684. With a modest beginning in 1962 as a cooperative research laboratory under the CSIR, the institute is now the main research and training organization in the field of panel materials from renewable fibres, including plantation timbers, wood and bamboo and forest/agro residues. Since 1990, it is an autonomous institute under the MoEFCC and carries out applied research and training on all aspects of technology for manufacturing plywood, panels and other engineered/reconstituted products from lingo-cellulosic materials.

H. G. B. Pant Institute of Himalayan Environment and Development, Almora (Uttranchal)

685. Established in 1988, this institute is an autonomous organization of the MoEFCC. It develops strategies, technologies and knowledge base for ecologically sound development of the Himalayan region. Three weather-monitoring stations have been installed by the institute in Sikkim, Himachal Pradesh and Nagaland for collecting and analysing climatic data of the Himalayan region.

I. National Afforestation and Eco-development Board

686. The NAEB was set up in August 1992 for promoting afforestation, tree planting, ecological restoration and eco-development activities. Special attention is given to the regeneration of degraded forest areas and lands adjoining forest areas, national parks, sanctuaries and other protected areas as well as ecologically fragile areas such as the Western Himalayas, Aravallis, Western Ghats.

1. Regional Centres

687. The board has seven RCs located in universities/national level institutions. These centres help the NAEB in promoting the extension of replicable technologies and for the dissemination of research findings. They provide technical and extension support to the State Forest Department in preparing projects for regeneration of degraded forests and adjoining lands with people's participation, and also act as a forum for the exchange of ideas and experiences among the States of the region as well as across the regions.

2. Professional and Special Services

688. The board takes up special studies of important issues relating to policy formulation, programme implementation, etc. The board also engages special consultants for a variety of assignments. The studies are conducted on areas like eco-development, joint forest management, employment generation, reorientation of existing programmes, etc. It has evolved schemes for the promotion of afforestation and management strategies so as to help States in developing specific afforestation and eco-development packages.

J. Eco Task Forces

689. The Eco Task Force is an ongoing scheme. Ecological Task Forces of ex-servicemen are employed in remote and difficult areas to undertake restoration of degraded ecosystems through afforestation, soil conservation and water resource management techniques. Under the Eco Task Force Scheme, six battalions are being supported in the State of Uttarakhand, Rajasthan, Jammu and Kashmir and Assam.

§7. The NFP, 1988 and Draft Policy 2018

690. The first NFP was formulated in 1894. After independence, the Forest Policy of 1952 came into force. Realizing the importance of forests to the ecological stability of the country, the Forest Policy was re-examined and emphasis was given to conservation and ecological aspects. The 1988 policy states that the principal aim of the Forest Policy must be to ensure environment suitability and maintenance of ecological balance, including atmospheric equilibrium, which is vital for the sustenance of all life forms, human, animal and plant. The policy also mentions among its basic objectives (paragraph 2.1) the need for meeting the requirement of fuel wood, fodder, minor forest produce and small timber for rural and tribal populations.

691. The NFP enjoins that land laws should be modified so as to facilitate and motivate individuals and institutions to undertake plantation on their own land. The land can also be given on lease, and there must be appropriate regulations governing the felling of trees on private landholders (paragraph 4.2.4).

With respect to the diversion of forest land for non-forest purposes, the policy lays down that forest land or land with tree cover should be considered as a national asset which requires to be carefully safeguarded for providing sustained benefits to the entire community.

692. After almost twenty-nine years of Forest Policy of 1988, the Central Government has come up with a draft NFP, 2018, which takes into account the issue of climate change as well. The previous NFP 1988 was focused on environmental stability and maintenance of ecological balance. NFP, 2018 takes care of climate change mitigation through sustainable forest management. The overall objective is to safeguard the ecological and livelihood security of people, of the present and future generations, based on sustainable management of the forests for the flow of ecosystem services. The draft policy document also talks about degraded land and how it can be improved by undertaking afforestation activities using PPP models. The degraded lands available with the forest corporations which are underutilized will be managed to produce quality timber with scientific interventions. Public-private participation models will be developed for undertaking afforestation and reforestation activities in degraded forest areas. The document proposes creation of a community forest management mission for the community resource management under Forests Rights Act.

693. The Forest Policy Division of MoEFCC by its order dated 31 March 2022 decided to constitute a task force led by Director General of Forest to study and analyse the NFP, 1988, the proposed NFP, 2018, proposed amendments in the Forest (Conservation) Act, 1980 and the current regulatory regimes on agro-forestry/tree outside forests across the country.

§8. Afforestation

I. National Afforestation Programme Through Community Participation

694. Keeping in view the objective of achieving 33% tree/forest cover as part of the target to be monitored, a very ambitious afforestation programme has been launched with people's involvement for the sustainable management of the country's forests. Under this programme, all forestation schemes of the MoEFCC have been brought under a single National Afforestation Programme being implemented through decentralized Forest Development Agencies (FDAs) set up at the forest division level. The FDAs are a confederation of Joint Forest Management Committee (JFMC) at the village level to provide a link between the forest departments and the grass root level communities. Achieving 33% target is considered by some critics as unrealistic given growing population and its pressure on forest land.

II. Watershed Programme

695. The watershed programmes are important for bringing land areas under tree cover. The main objectives of the Watershed Management Programme are to restore the ecological balance by harnessing, conserving and developing degraded natural resources such as soil, vegetative cover and water. The outcomes are prevention of soil runoff, regeneration of natural vegetation, rainwater harvesting and recharging of the groundwater table.

III. National Forestry Action Programme

696. A National Forestry Action Programme (NFAP) has been formulated which is a comprehensive strategic long-term plan for the next twenty years to address the issues underlying the major problems of the forestry sector in line with the NFP, 1988. The objective of the NFAP is to bring one-third of the area of the country under tree/forest cover and to arrest deforestation for achieving sustainable development of forests.

IV. Joint Forests Management

697. The MoEFCC issued guidelines named as Joint Forests Management (JFM) on joint management of forests. The FDA can be registered under the Societies Registration Act, 1860. The Panchayat (Extension to the Scheduled Area) Act, 1996 legally recognized the traditional entitlement of the forest-dependent communities and aims at reducing the conflict and provide long-term incentives to conserve the forests. Further, these rights have been consolidated by the Scheduled Tribes and Other Traditional Forest Dwellers (Recognition of Forest Rights) Act, 2006 and the Scheduled Tribes and Other Traditional Forest Dwellers (Recognition of Forest Rights) Rules, 2008. In view of coming into force of the Act and Rules, some critics argue that JFM Guidelines are no longer relevant.

§9. FOREST FIRE CONTROL METHODS

I. National Fire Prevention and Control Guidelines of 1999

698. The MoEFCC has issued the National Fire Prevention and Control Guidelines of 1999. It is proposed that the JFMC shall be assigned specific roles for fire prevention and control.

II. Integrated Forest Protection Scheme

699. Forest fire danger rating systems and fire forecasting systems have been evolved through the FSI. With the help of the ICFRE and other research organizations, losses on forest fires are estimated. A national master plan for prevention and control of forest fires has been prepared by the MoEFCC after consultation with State Governments. With these changes, the scheme has been modified and renamed as 'Forest Fire Control and Management'. Guidelines for prevention and control of forest fires have been issued to the States and measures have been suggested for creating an efficient fire prevention and control mechanism in the States. The guidelines include proposals for efficient implementation of sections 33 and 79 of the Indian Forest Act of 1927.

III. Village Forest Protection Committees

700. So far twenty-seven States have issued resolutions for JFM. As on 1 December 2002, 14.26 mha of forest lands in the country are being managed and protected by 64,000 Village Forest Protection Committees. The activities under the JFM programme are monitored by the JFM Cell of the MoEFCC. The ministry reviews this programme after consulting all the stakeholders and issues further guidelines to the States for strengthening the programme. The guidelines *inter alia* include providing legal backup to the JFM Committees, extension of JFM in good forest areas with sharper focus on activities concentrated on NTFP management, integration of a micro plan with working plan, contribution for regeneration of resources and monitoring and evaluation, etc.

§10. Conservation of Medicinal Plants

701. The MoEFCC has identified over 9,500 plant species with medicinal property. Out of these about sixty-five species have large and consistent demand in world trade. India produces only a small quantity of 7% with sixth place in the world. In the Southern States of Kerala, Tamil Nadu and Karnataka, Medicinal Plants Conservation Area and Medicinal Plants Conservation Network established for *in situ* conservation carry on the activities of conservation of medicinal plants. The Foundation for Revitalization of Local Health Traditions and the State Forest Departments are also involved in these efforts. The UNDP-CCF-I assisted sub-programme on Medicinal Plants is being executed in the States of Andhra Pradesh and Maharashtra. The MPCAs (thirteen in Maharashtra and eight in Andhra Pradesh) have been established in the forest areas.

§11. Diversion of Forest Land for Non-forest Purposes

702. The Compensatory Afforestation Fund Act was passed in 2016 and the related rules were notified in 2018. This Act was enacted under the direction of the Supreme Court so as to manage the funds collected for compensatory afforestation. Compensatory afforestation as per Act means that every time forest land is diverted for non-forest purposes such as mining or industry, the user agency pays for planting forests over an equal area of non-forest land, or when such land is not available, twice the area of degraded forest land. As per the Compensatory Afforestation Rules 2018, 90% of the money is to be given to the States while 10% is to be retained by the Centre. The funds are used for treatment of catchment areas, assisted natural generation, forest management, wildlife protection and management, relocation of villages from protected areas, managing human-wildlife conflicts, training and awareness generation, supply of wood saving devices, etc. A CAF Authority has also been established under this Act.

703. For the diversion of forest land between five and forty hectares, the application is processed and recommendations are made by the Regional Offices located at Lucknow, Shillong, Bhopal, Chandigarh, Bhubaneswar and Bangalore to the Ministry in consultation with the State Advisory Committee. The proposals above forty hectare are forwarded by the State Government to the MoEFCC and these are examined by Forest Advisory Committee (FAC) constituted under the Forest Conservation Act, 1980. In cases where area is more than 100 hectares, a site inspection is carried out by the officers of Regional office and then proposal is examined by FAC. On the basis of recommendations of FAC, MoEFCC takes final decision stipulating appropriate mitigation measures. The Regional Offices of the MoEFCC have been empowered to clear the proposal up to 5 hectares, except in respect of proposals for regularization of encroachment and mining. Detailed guidelines including *pro forma* applications for forest clearance have been laid down. Proposals which are complete in all respects are disposed of within the stipulated time limit of ninety days from the date of receipt of the proposal.

I. Industrial Project under EIA

704. For Clearance in Respect of Industrial Projects under EIA Notification 2006, the proposals for seeking the environmental clearance as contained in Category A, except under the CRZ Notification and mining cases are to be sent directly to the MoEFCC. In case a project falls in category B, it will require prior environmental clearance from UT/SEIAA which will base its decision on the recommendations of SEAC. Specific guidelines and a questionnaire are available for various sectors such as industry, thermal power, mining, river valley, hotels and beach resorts, ports and harbours and roads. The proposals for environmental clearance which are complete in all respects are considered and decisions taken within ninety days of receipt of the requisite information.

A. Prior Environmental Clearance

705. In June 2021, the NGT in the case of Peshwa Plastics held that industrial units that manufacture synthetic organic chemicals – specifically, formaldehyde in the State of Haryana – were required by law to obtain environmental clearance from the Union environment ministry before commencing operations. The units were also required to prepare an EIA report and conduct a public hearing before the approval is granted (or not). Since none of the units in question had a prior environmental clearance, the NGT found to be operating in violation of the law. Subsequently, the aggrieved industrial units approached the Supreme Court to challenge the tribunal's decision. They argued that they were 'bona fide under the impression' that they were not required to obtain environmental clearance to manufacture formaldehyde and further that 'it was thought that Environmental Clearance was not required for (the) units'.

B. Ex Post Facto Clearance

706. In *Pahwa Plastics Pvt Ltd. v. Dastak Ngo* (25 March 2022), the question law before the Supreme Court was whether an establishment employing around 8,000 workers and set up after receiving the 'consent to establish' and the 'consent to operate' from the competent authority and which has applied for ex post facto environmental clearance can be closed pending issuance of the clearance – even though it may not release pollutants and/or may be found to comply with the required norms. In Pahwa Plastics, the Supreme Court invoked the doctrine of proportionality to hold that closing an industrial unit would be disproportionate to the offence committed. That is, administrative action should not be more drastic than it ought to be to obtain the desired result. In other words, the court says, 'don't use a cannon to shoot down a sparrow'.

707. The Supreme Court bench concluded that 'the manufacturing units of the Appellants appoint about 8,000 employees and have a huge annual turnover. An establishment contributing to the economy and providing livelihood ought not to be closed down only on the ground of the technical irregularity of not obtaining prior environmental clearance irrespective of whether or not the unit actually causes pollution. … Ex post facto environmental clearance should not be granted routinely, but in exceptional circumstances taking into account all relevant environmental factors. … The 1986 Act (Environment Protection Act 1986) does not prohibit ex post facto [Environmental Clearance]. Some relaxations and even grant of ex post facto EC in accordance with law, in strict compliance with Rules, Regulations, Notifications and/or applicable orders, in appropriate cases, where the projects are in compliance with environment norms, is not impermissible.'

708. The term post facto clearances does not exist either in the Environment (Protection) Act 1986 nor in the EIA Notification 2006. It is a term that the executive introduced through 'office memorandum' – i.e., an order to regulate the working of the office. What exists in law is 'prior environmental clearance' – i.e., an approval from authorities before the commencement of work. A unit not obtaining prior approval as required amounts to a 'technical irregularity' – but according to the court, it is a 'technical irregularity' even if the unit pollutes the environment. This conclusion will have serious consequences on the environmental rule of law as well as on the right to life of the citizens, guaranteed under Article 21 of the Constitution. This is not the first time the court legalized 'post facto approvals'. Pahwa Plastics itself draws from the Supreme Court's judgment in Electrosteels.

709. In *Electrosteel Steels Limited v. Union of India* (decided on 9 December, 2021) a unit that had obtained environmental clearance had shifted its premises by nearly 5.3 km from the site for which it had obtained the clearance. Since these clearances are site specific, and based on each site's ecological parameters, the shift required a fresh clearance. But the court held that 'the question is whether an establishment contributing to the economy of the country and providing livelihood to hundreds of people should be closed down for the technical irregularity of shifting its site without prior environmental clearance, without opportunity to the establishment to regularize its operation by obtaining the requisite clearances and permissions, even though the establishment may not otherwise be violating pollution laws, or the pollution, if any, can conveniently and effectively be checked. The answer has to be in the negative'. The court concluded that '… ex post facto environmental clearance should not ordinarily be granted, and certainly not for the asking. At the same time ex post facto clearances and/or approvals and/or removal of technical irregularities in terms of Notifications under the 1986 Act cannot be declined with rigidity, oblivious of the consequences of stopping the operation of a running steel plant'.

710. The 'post facto approval' was stated to be permitted under the Environment (Protection) Act 1986. However, the Act contains no reference to 'post facto approvals'. In the EIA Notification of 2006 also, there is no reference to 'post facto' clearances. Thus the court allowed decision-makers unfettered discretion. Specifically, while 'ex post facto environmental clearance should not be granted routinely,' according to Pahwa Plastics, it can be granted in 'exceptional circumstances'. These 'circumstances' have not been defined, however. Finally, the court provided a window within which the government could grant a 'post facto approval' – 'where the adverse consequences of denial of ex post facto approval outweigh the consequences of regularization of operations by grant of ex post facto approval'.

II. Single Window Clearance

711. When a project requires environmental clearance as well as approval under the Forest (Conservation) Act of 1980, proposals for both are processed independent of each other except where prior environmental clearance is required. However, environmental clearance is accorded only after forest clearance is granted in applicable cases by the division concerned of the MoEFCC.

§12. Conservation Versus Development

712. A major problem while executing an infrastructure project is that it may involve the destruction of forests. For example, electric power is seen as crucial for stepping up industrialization and employment generation, and to improve the quality of life of people in general. The benefits from conserving forests do not look so conspicuous and immediate. The dilemma becomes acute when micro hydropower units which have a minimal adverse impact on the environment are assessed as uneconomical, unstable and undependable, and when forests facing submergence through major power projects are rich in biodiversity. The loss of such forests cannot be made good by raising compensatory man-made forests elsewhere since they cannot be as rich in biodiversity as natural forests.

Chapter 7. Fish Resources

713. The fishery sector has been growing continuously with improvement in productivity and utilization of untapped resources. The State Legislatures are competent to legislate on fish and fish-related matters as per distribution of power between Centre and State as enshrined in the Constitution. For the people of coastal areas and certain States like Assam and West Bengal, fish is not only an important element but also the main diet. Through the ages, traditional conservation of inland fisheries in India has been practised, though not on a wide scale. One example is the observation of fishing seasons. In West Bengal, for instance, consumption of prized hilsa fish has been religiously prohibited after the *Durga Pooja* until *Saraswathi Pooja*, which period corresponds with the breeding season of the fish. Even otherwise, during the breeding season, people avoid the consumption of fish.

§1. Distribution of Fish

714. On the basis of areas in which the fish are found in India, the fish can be classified into: (a) deep-sea fisheries, (b) coastal and estuarine fisheries, and (c) inland freshwater fisheries.

I. Deep-Sea Fisheries

715. The deep-sea fisheries lie in the Bay of Bengal and the Arabian Sea at a distance of about 13 km–16 km from the coastline. The principal varieties of fish found in this area are herring, mackerel, catfish, mullets, pomfrets, salmon, halibut, etc. In the deep sea, there are sharks and whales. A subsidy is provided to the fishermen by the Government for motorizing their boats. This increases the fishing areas and the frequency of operation which results in an increase in the catch and a consequent increase in earnings.

II. Coastal and Estuarine Fisheries

716. The coastal and estuarine fisheries have been developed in the estuaries of the Ganga, Brahmaputra, Mahanadi, Godavari, Krishna and the continental shelf of West Bengal, Odisha, Andhra, Tamil Nadu, Kerala and Maharashtra. The main fish found in this area are hilsa, lobster, vetki, chanda, bhangur, etc.

A. Brackish Water Aquaculture

717. Through the shrimp culture, vast brackish water areas of the country have been utilized. The shrimp farmers are provided with technical, financial and extension support by the Brackish Water Fish Farmers Development Agencies (BFDAs).

At present there are thirty-nine BFDAs functioning in the coastal areas of the country. The Central Aquaculture Authority Act, 2005 and Rules of 2005 deal with aquaculture.

B. Control

718. Guidelines have been prepared for the development and management of brackish water aquaculture and circulated to all maritime States and UT and other agencies. These guidelines contain directions as to measures to be taken for mitigating and preventing the adverse impact of shrimp farming on the coastal ecosystem.

III. The Inland Fisheries

719. The inland fisheries are found in the rivers, canals, lakes, tanks, ponds, etc. The Ganga in the State of UP, Bihar and West Bengal, the Brahmaputra in Assam, the Mahanadi in Odisha, the Kaveri in Tamil Nadu are the main sources of freshwater fish. West Bengal, Assam and Bihar produce about 70% of the total production of freshwater fish in India.

In view of the important role of inland fisheries in overall production of fish, the Government is implementing a programme namely 'Development of Fresh Water Aqua Culture through the Fish Farmers Development Agencies (FFDA)'. A package of technical, financial and extension support is provided to the fish farmers by these agencies. At present, FFDAs numbering 429 are functioning covering all the main districts of the country.

§2. Statutory Structure and Legal Regime

I. Legislation

A. The Indian Fisheries Act of 1897 and the Fishing Regulation Act of 1981

720. The Indian Fisheries Act of 1897 was originally enacted in 1897 and later on amended in 1927 and in 1980. It prohibits the use of dynamite for fishing in all waters and regulates the use of fixed engines for the capture of fish. The prohibition or regulation of the use of nets with a mesh below a minimum size is also dealt with in the Act. During the close season the capture of or sale of all or any kinds of fish is prohibited. There must be total cessation of fishing for a period not exceeding two seasons.

B. Zones of India (Regulation of Fishing by Foreign Vessels) Act, 1981

721. The Maritime Zones of India (Regulation of Fishing by Foreign Vessels) Act, 1981, was enacted to put an end to poaching activities conducted by foreign fishing vessels within the EEZ. It also safeguards the resources of the EEZs from Indians and foreign vessels working within the territorial waters of without permission and licence. The violations of permits and licences granted as per sections 4 and 5 of the Act within the territorial waters, result in punishment. This Act authorizes Government officials, navy, and police to implement the provisions of the Act, specifically the power of apprehending and arresting that is vested in the local police of the coastal states. According to this Act, prior approval of the Government does not need to be taken for carrying out prosecutions of offences. The Maritime Zones of India (Regulation of Fishing by Foreign Vessels) Rules, 1982, were formulated under section 25 of the Maritime Zones of India (Regulation of Fishing by Foreign Vessels) Act, 1981 by the Government.

722. Further, the Central Aquaculture Authority Act, 2005 and Rules of 2005 have created a central authority to deal with aquaculture.

II. International Conventions

A. Third United Nations Conference on the Law of the Sea (1982)

723. The present capture fisheries regime covering the resources of the world's oceans, as unfolded by the Third United Nations Conference on the Law of the Sea (1982), has provided the opportunity for all coastal countries to participate more fully in the utilization of their resources and to increase the contributions they make to national economic, social and nutritional objectives. At the same time, attention has also been drawn to the potential roles of inland water fisheries and aquaculture as food suppliers, within the overall socioeconomic context of rural development. These new opportunities and challenges have called for reappraisal of national policies for fisheries development and management.

B. The FAO Kyoto Conference, December 1995

724. The FAO Kyoto Declaration addressed the following major issues:

(a) need to increase efforts relating to estimation of quantity of fish, marine mammals, sea birds, sea turtles and other forms of life which are incidentally caught and discarded in fishing operations;
(b) determination of the effects of such actions on the fish species and stocks;
(c) initiation of urgent action necessary to minimize waste and discards by using selective, environmentally safe and cost-effective fishing gear and techniques;
(d) the discussions during the conference focussed on conflicts between traditional community based and other small-scale fisheries, and modern industrial fisheries. The issues applicable to traditional fisheries were identified as sustainability, food security, economic welfare and cultural existence.

Other important items highlighted were the role of genetically improved aquatic organisms to global food security and conservation of biological diversity. Two recent regulatory actions at international level relate to the reduction of an incidental catch of sea birds in long-line fisheries and conservation and management of sharks.

III. Fishery Institutes and Bodies

725. There are a number of institutes and bodies working for betterment of fisheries sector and providing training and research in the field of fisheries. The main institutes are the Central Marine Fish Research Institute, the Central Institute of Fish Technology at Cochin, the Central Inland Fisheries Institute Barrackpore (West Bengal). These institutes conduct research on issues and problems related to marine and inland fisheries.

A. National Fisheries Development Board

726. The National Fisheries Development Board (NFDB) was established in 2006 as an autonomous body under the Department of Animal Husbandry, Dairying & Fisheries, Ministry of Agriculture and Farmers Welfare to enhance fish production and productivity in the country and to coordinate fishery development in an integrated and holistic manner. A number of fishery development activities viz., intensive aquaculture in ponds and tanks, culture based capture fisheries in reservoirs, establishment of fish landing centres, fishing dressing centres and solar drying of fish, domestic marketing, ornamental fisheries and upgradation and capacity building of fishermen and fish farmers are being supported through the State Governments and other Implementing agencies. This body aims at enhancement of fish production and productivity; to supplement nutritious protein for the growing population and to accelerate the overall economy of the country.

§3. Capture and Aquaculture Fisheries

I. Fisheries Scenario

727. India is the second-largest fish producing country in the world accounting for 7.56% of global production. It contributes about 1.24% to the country's GVA and over 7.28% to the agricultural GVA. Indian Fisheries and Aquaculture sector is considered as a sunrise sector and is poised to play a significant role in the Indian economy. The sector has shown impressive growth with fish production registering an average annual growth of 7.53% during last five years. Besides the domestic market, fisheries and aquaculture sectors contribute greatly to India's export earnings as well. The country exported 12.89 lakh metric tons of fisheries products valued at INR 46,662 crores (USD 6.68 billion) during 2019–2020, largely mitigating the adverse impact of Covid-19 pandemic. Realizing the sector's potential, the Government has committed to a national target to increase fish production to 22 million metric tons by 2024–2025, which will have a positive impact on 28 million fishers and fish farmers and almost twice that number along fish-related value chains.

II. Problems Posed by Capture Fisheries

728. The major problems posed in India with respect to capture fisheries are overexploitation of fishery resources, destructive fishing practices, damage to natural habitats, fishing in non-traditional areas, misuse and wastage of surplus catches, etc. In addition, some ethical issues are also involved. These are: water quality maintenance and protection, abatement of pollution, protection of natural biodiversity, protection of traditional fishing areas, customs and habitats, sustainability of fishing practices, ensuring social, ecological and technical stability, protection, restoration and recovery of endangered species and stocks, balancing population pressure in neighbouring areas, and conflicts with other developmental activities.

729. The important social, legal and management issues vis-à-vis the environment and specifically related to capture fisheries are as follows:

(a) Reduction of excess fishing capacity, multi-species management of resources, control of discarded incidental catches including marine mammals, sea birds, sea turtles, etc.
(b) Development and use of selective, environmentally safe and cost-effective fishing gear and techniques, sustainable development of unexploited or underexploited species, protection of endangered species and strict compliance of fishing area norms.

A. *Overfishing and Discard*

730. Overfishing is the most important problem facing capture fisheries. A high rate of discard fish is another issue, which requires urgent action. Therefore, the main challenges for maintaining and enhancing inland fish production and prevent associated degradation of aquatic resources and environment, the need is to focus attention towards evolution of ways so that the percentage of discard can be reduced.

B. *Coastal Fisheries*

731. Coastal fisheries become drastically affected by environmental degradation of the adjacent land, which can affect life cycles of fish stocks, migration of fish from freshwater systems to the sea and by population pressures leading to increased coastal subsistence fishing.

C. *Problems of Inland Fisheries*

732. The status of inland waters and their species are of broad concern, yet threats to freshwater fisheries and associated biodiversity have received proper attention from conservation groups and the media. This imbalance is particularly dangerous considering evidence that freshwater ecosystems and the species they support are more threatened than marine ecosystems. Inland waters and their species experience many direct and indirect stresses in addition to overfishing, including altered flows and habitat fragmentation due to dams and other infrastructure, pollution, non-native species introductions. Although the importance of other anthropogenic stressors in relation to fishing may appear greater for inland waters than for the seas, the contributions of pollution, species introductions, and other human impacts in the collapse of coastal ecosystems has resulted in irreparable damage.

733. The negative human actions which have affected fisheries of Indian reservoirs, lakes and estuaries are drastic water abstraction, pollution by domestic, municipal and industrial sources, disruption of fish breeding grounds, habitat destruction, overexploitation, use of explosives, flood control measures, silting, artificial barriers affecting fish migration, large-scale destruction of fish seed incidentally caught with prized cultured species like shrimps and prawns, and the introduction of exotic species.

D. *Issues Related to Deep-Sea Fishing*

734. Technological lag and financial constraints are the major bottlenecks in the delayed take off of the deep-sea fishing industry in India. The maritime states of Gujarat, Kerala and Tamil Nadu have already demonstrated their ability to harvest deep-sea fisheries resources in the Indian EEZ. Nevertheless the major contribution in fish production still continues to be from coastal water.

III. Sustainability Concept for Capture Fisheries

735. The sustainable development of fisheries must be such that the management and conservation of the natural resources base and the orientation of technological and institutional change is brought in such a fashion so that the attainment and continued satisfaction of human needs for the present and future generations is ensured without creating any imbalance. Such development in the fisheries sector conserves land, water, plant and animal genetic resources; is environmentally non-degrading, and socially acceptable. Thus, considerations on the sustainability issue in capture fisheries development involve *inter alia*, ecological, environmental, social, economic, legal and institutional parameters.

A. Introduction of New Breeds

736. Some of the exotic fish introduced into the country for increasing production from confined waters have established themselves in some of the natural water systems, mainly reservoirs. Specific examples are: silver carp replacing major carps and contributing to more than 80% of catches in Govindsagar, tilapia contributing to a major share in catches from the Amaravathi reservoir, and common carp overtaking native fish in Kashmir and Manipur. Experts have opined that out of more than 300 species of fish introduced in the country for cultural, ornamental and biological purposes, only the trout has been found to positively contribute to local capture fishery system, both ecologically as well as productively. Such a scenario calls for extreme caution and strict analyses before introducing any more fish into Indian waters.

§4. Conservation and Control

737. The Indian Fisheries Act of 1897 formed the basis for the States and UT to introduce fishery laws and rules to suit local demands and conditions. Since every State has made its own law, this has resulted in a lack of uniformity.

I. Regulatory Measures

738. Regulatory measures have been adopted in many States, particularly regarding mesh size, dynamiting, destruction of fish seed, destruction of brood stock, etc. Some examples of regulatory measures adopted are as follows:

- The Government of Kerala introduced in 1980 a ban on trawler fishing for a period of forty-five days during monsoon months. The spawning of shrimps, sardines and mackerel, which are the main components of Kerala major fishery resources, takes place during this period. Very recently a committee has recommend sixty-five days of ban during the monsoon season every alternate year.
- Strong protest demonstrations and strikes organized in 1994 by fishers and entrepreneurs associated with all activities of the marine fisheries sector, demanding that the Government should abandon its policy of giving licences to joint ventures for deep-sea fishing.

II. Environment Impact Assessment

739. It is only in recent years that action has been taken in India to study EIA in relation to capture fisheries. This has been mainly due to a lack of appreciation as well as a scarcity of environment based on technological competence. Investigations carried out by the Central Inland Capture Fisheries Research Institute on EIA in riverine ecosystems are particularly noteworthy.

Chapter 8. Subsoil and Minerals

740. Like any other development activity, mineral exploration and exploitation give rise to pollution and affect the environment in some instances drastically. The exploitation of mineral resources has to be managed in such a fashion so that there is optimal utilization without disturbing the ecological balance and containment of natural hazards through taking preventive action and resorting to environment friendly technology. But sometimes there is a conflict situation between mining, a development activity and preservation of the environment. For example, notifying new national parks or extending the existing ones has created problems for some of the existing mines such as the Kudremukh Iron Ore Company Ltd. in Karnataka. Since many mineral deposits which are considered commercially exploitable are located in and around these parks, it has become necessary to consider this issue in a broader context. Any mining zone around national parks/zoos/sanctuaries will have to be decided after due consideration to the adverse impact of the technologies likely to be used for the extraction of minerals.

§1. Mining of Coal and Other Ores

741. Coal mining and mining for ores give rise to various problems of pollution. The Supreme Court considered the ecological imbalance caused by limestone quarries in Dehradun as a serious threat to the life of human beings (*Rural Litigation and Entitlement Kendra, Dehradun and Others v. State of U.P. and Others*, AIR 1985 SC 652). The court considering the right to a pollution-free environment an integral part of the right to life as enshrined in Article 21 of the Constitution directed the closure of these quarries.

I. Coal Mines

742. Earlier most of the coal mines in India were underground mines, restricted to the Jharia and Raniganj coalfields. However, in the last two decades, open cast mining has been increasingly resorted to. Open cast mining pollutes the environment much more severely than underground mining through degradation of the land and displacement of the population from the mining areas. As per the guidelines on rehabilitation, the project design should minimize the need for involuntary resettlement and ensure that those who have to move from their land benefit from the project that displaces them.

II. Coal Washeries

743. The amount of washed, mediocre and rejected coal which is discharged with the effluent is assessed. Therefore the more coal is recovered the less the pollution. The treatment efficiency of the settling tank in a coal washery is evaluated to justify the claim of zero discharge. Though adequate settling tanks are available for treating the effluent, their maintenance is not properly done. During the dry season, it is possible to contain the effluent, but during the wet season, it is difficult. It cannot be ruled out that during the rainy season, surface runoff may carry huge quantities of fine coal, which ultimately join the river and pollute it.

III. Legislation Dealing with Control and Prevention of Pollution in Mines

744. The environmental concerns of mining are taken care of directly and indirectly by the Mines Act of 1952, the Mines and Mineral (Regulation and Development) Act of 1955, the Mineral (Conservation and Development) Rules of 1988 and the Forest Conservation Act of 1980.

A. *Prospecting Licence*

745. Acting under section 4A of the Mines and Minerals (Regulation and Development) Act of 1956, the Central Government after consultation with the State Government, may request the State Government to resort to premature termination of a prospecting licence or lease in the interest of preservation of the natural environment, control of floods and prevention of pollution so as to avoid danger to public health.

The Forest Conservation Act of 1980 requires that for exploring and mining on forest land, the prior permission of the Government should be obtained since mining operations use forest land for non-forestry purposes.

B. *Responsibilities of the Licensee*

746. Chapter V of the Mineral Conservation and Development Rules of 1988, framed under section 18 of the Mines and Minerals (Regulation and Development) Act of 1957 contains provisions for the protection of the environment and control of pollution by a holder of a prospecting licence or ML. The rules also provide for reclamation and rehabilitation of land affected by mining operations (Rule 34). Air pollution, discharge of toxic liquid and noise are required to be controlled and kept within permissible limits (Rules 37, 38 and 39). The holder of a licence or lease is required to take action so that the least damage is caused and the flora is restored in case of any damage to it (Rule 41).

C. *Rule-Making Power*

747. Section 13(qq) of the Mines and Minerals (Regulation and Development) Act of 1957 gives power to the Central Government to make rules in respect of the manner in which rehabilitation of flora and other vegetation such as trees, shrubs and the like, destroyed by reason of any prospecting or mining operations, shall be made in the same area or in any other area selected by the Central Government (whether by way of reimbursement of the cost of rehabilitation or otherwise) by the person holding the prospecting licence or ML. Further, under section 18, the Central Government is required to take all steps for the protection of the environment by preventing or controlling any pollution caused by prospecting or mining operations. The Central Government can frame rules by which directions may be issued for the protection of the environment by preventing or controlling pollution caused by mining operations.

§2. Hydrocarbon Sector

748. The hydrocarbon sector can be divided into upstream and downstream. Each of them has its peculiar pollution-related problems.

I. Legislation

749. The specific legislation dealing with the oil sector also contains provisions regarding the problem of pollution. A list of such enactments is given below:

– the Petroleum Act of 1934;
– the Oil Fields (Regulation and Development) Act of 1948;
– the Petroleum and Natural Gas Rules of 1959;
– the Oil Mines Regulations of 1981;
– the Merchant Shipping Act of 1956;
– the Territorial Waters, Continental Shelf, EEZ and Maritime Zones Act of 1976.

II. Brief Description of the Legislation

750. The Government can lay down norms to be followed for preventing the escape of water and oil from an oilfield and for other measures for the prevention of pollution under the Oilfield (Regulation and Development) Act of 1948. Acting under the Territorial Water Act, the Central Government can declare an area a designated area and make provision for the protection of the marine environment of such designated area (section 5). The Central Government has also been authorized to make rules for the preservation and protection of the marine environment and prevention and control of marine pollution for the purposes of the act (section 15).

§3. Upstream Petroleum Sector

751. In the upstream hydrocarbon sector, there can be two situations with respect to protection of the environment and pollution control. First, the areas where national oil companies are carrying on work are governed by a Petroleum Exploration Licence (PEL) or ML as the case may be and the relevant legislation on the subject as described above. Second, for the blocks which are under a Production

Sharing Contract (PSC) (Contract) regime and now under Revenue Sharing Contract, provisions of the Contract are also applicable in addition to the terms and conditions of the PEL or ML and relevant legislation.

I. Provisions in the Contract for the Environment

752. Article 14 of the Contract dealing with protection of the environment, acknowledges and recognizes that petroleum operations will cause some impact on the environment in the contract area. Therefore, in the performance of the Contract, the contractor is required to conduct operations with due regard to concerns with respect to protection of the environment and conservation of natural resources.

A. Contractor to Minimize Damage

753. The contractor is required to: (a) employ Modern Oilfield and Petroleum Industry Practices (MOPIP) and standards and advanced techniques, practices and methods of operation for the prevention of environmental damage in conducting its petroleum operations; (b) take necessary and adequate steps to: (i) prevent environmental damage and, where some adverse impact on the environment is unavoidable, to minimize such damage and the consequential effects thereof on property and people; (ii) ensure adequate compensation for injury to persons or damage to property caused by the effect of the petroleum operations.

B. Contractor to Remedy the Failure

754. The contractor in the conduct of operations is to comply with the requirements of applicable laws and the reasonable requirements of the Government from time to time. In case the contractor fails to comply with the requirements or contravenes any relevant law, and such failure or contravention results in any environmental damage, the contractor has to take all necessary and reasonable measures to remedy the failure and the effects of pollution.

C. Right of the Government to Direct

755. If the Government has reason to believe that any works or installations erected by the contractor are causing or may cause pollution, or are harming or may harm fauna or flora or the environment to a degree which the Government deems unacceptable, the Government may require the contractor to take remedial measures and to repair any damage to the environment or to discontinue petroleum operations until the remedial measures are taken or damage is repaired.

D. Environmental Impact Studies

756. The contractor is required (under Article 14.5 of the Contract) to carry out two environmental impact studies in order to determine, at the time of the studies, the prevailing situation relating to the environment, human beings and local communities, the flora and fauna in the contract area and in the adjoining or neighbouring areas, and to establish the likely effect on the environment, human beings and local communities, the flora and fauna in the contract area and in the adjoining or neighbouring areas in consequence of the petroleum operations to be conducted under the Contract, and to submit methods and measures for minimizing environmental damage and carrying out site restoration activities.

757. The studies so conducted contain proposed environmental guidelines to be followed in order to minimize environmental damage and shall also include proposed access cutting; clearing and timber salvage; wildlife and habitat protection; fuel storage and handling; use of explosives; camps and staging; liquid and solid waste disposal; cultural and archaeological sites; selection of drilling sites; terrain stabilization; protection of freshwater horizons; blowout prevention plan; flaring during completion and testing of gas and oil wells; abandonment of wells; reclamation of abandonment; noise control; debris disposal; protection of natural drainage and water flow, etc.

E. Environment Clearance by the Government

758. Subject to applicable laws and notifications, the Government is to convey its decision regarding any proposal for environmental clearances submitted by the contractor within 120 days from the date of submission of the application by the contractor seeking such clearance. Any clarification/additional information required by the Government shall be asked by it within ninety days from the date of submission of the application by contractor. The final decision by the Government should be conveyed within thirty days thereafter. In case forest clearance is also required, the contractor shall have to obtain approval of the Central Government through the State Government concerned. The decision of the Central Government will be taken within sixty days from the date of receipt of the proposal from the State Government (Article 14.5.4).

In the Article 14, reference to Government includes the State Governments as well (Article 14.12).

F. Responsibility of the Contractor

759. The contractor is to ensure that the operations are conducted in an environmentally acceptable and safe manner consistent with MOPIP and properly monitored. The pertinent completed environment impact studies are made available to its employees and to subcontractors so as to develop adequate and proper awareness of the measures and methods of environmental protection. The contracts entered into between the contractor and subcontractors relating to operations shall also include the provisions stipulated in Article 14 of the Contract and any established measures and methods for the implementation of the contractor's obligations in relation to the environmental protection under the Contract.

G. Contingency Plan

760. The contractor, prior to conducting any drilling activities, is required to prepare and submit for review by the Government a contingency plan for dealing with oil spills, fires, accidents and emergencies. The plan must be designed to achieve rapid and effective emergency response. The plan is discussed with the Government and concerns expressed are to be taken into account.

H. Emergency

761. In the event of an emergency, accident, oil spill or fire arising from a petroleum operation affecting the environment, the contractor is to notify the Government and shall promptly implement the relevant contingency plan and perform such site restoration as may be necessary in accordance with Good International Petroleum Industry Practice (GIPIP). In the event of any other emergency or accident arising from the petroleum operations affecting the environment, the contractor is required to take such action as may be prudent and necessary in accordance with MOPIP.

I. Removal of Equipment and Site Restoration

762. On expiry or termination of the Contract or relinquishment, the contractor is to remove all equipment and installations from the relinquished area or former contract area in a manner agreed with the Government, and perform all necessary site restoration in accordance with MOPIP and take all other action necessary to prevent hazards to human life or to the property of others or the environment.

The contractor is required to prepare a proposal for the restoration of the site including an abandonment plan and requirement of funds for this and any annual contribution in accordance with the scheme framed by the Government to the site restoration fund. Any and all costs incurred by the contractor for environmental pollution are costs recoverable from the oil/gas produced from the block.

The obligations and liability of the contractor for the environment are limited to damage to the environment which:

(a) occurs after the effective date of the Contract which is the date of issuance of PEL; and
(b) results from an act or omission of the contractor.

J. National Parks, Mangroves, Etc.

763. Where the contract area is partly located in areas forming a part of certain national parks, sanctuaries, mangroves, wetlands of national importance, biosphere reserves and other biologically sensitive areas, passage through these areas shall generally not be permitted. However, if there is no passage, other than through these areas to reach a particular point beyond these areas, permission of the appropriate authorities shall be obtained (Article 14.13 of the Contract).

K. Terms Used in the Provision

764. The meanings of some of the terms used in the above provision of the Contract as defined therein are reproduced for a clear understanding and better appreciation of the scope of the provision:

> 'Effective Date' means the later of the date on which this Contract is executed by the Parties or the date of issue of licence or date from which licence has been made effective by the Central Government or State Government(s) as the case may be (Article 1.40).
> 'License' means a petroleum exploration licence referred to in the Rules (Article 1.59).
> 'Rules' mean the Petroleum and Natural Gas Rules, 1959 and any amendment made thereto from time to time (Article 1.81).
> 'Petroleum Operations' means, as the context may require, Exploration Operations Development Operations or Production Operations or any combination of two or more of such operations, including construction, operation and maintenance of all necessary facilities, plugging and abandonment of wells, safety, environmental protection, transportation, storage, sale or disposition of petroleum to the delivery point, site restoration and any or all other incidental operations or activities as may be necessary (Article 1.74).
> 'Site Restoration' as defined in Article 1.84 of the Contract means all activities required to return a site to its state as of the effective date pursuant to the contractors environmental impact study and approved by the Government or to render a site compatible with its intended after-use (to the extent reasonable) after cessation of petroleum operations in relation thereto and shall include, where appropriate, proper abandonment of wells or other facilities, removal of equipment, structures and debris, establishment of compatible contours and drainage, replacement of top soil, revegetation, slope stabilization, infilling of excavations or any other appropriate actions in the circumstances.
> 'Environmental Damage' means soil erosion, removal of vegetation, destruction of wildlife, pollution of groundwater or surface water, land contamination, air pollution, noise pollution, bush fire, disruption to water supplies, to natural drainage or natural flow of rivers or streams, damage to archaeological, palaeontological and cultural sites and shall include any damage or injury to, or destruction of, soil or water in their physical aspects

together with vegetation associated therewith, aquatic or terrestrial mammals, fish, avifauna or any plant or animal life whether in the sea or in any other water or on, in or under land (Article 1.41 of the Contract).

II. Abandonment and Site Restoration Fund Scheme 1999

765. A Site Restoration Fund Scheme has been introduced under subsection (1) of section 33 ABA of the Income Tax Act of 1961. But this scheme is more concerned with funding rather than the environmental aspect. The scheme made effective from 1 April 1999 applies to acreage for which the GOI has entered into PSCs. The assessee is required to make a deposit out of profits derived from the business consisting of prospecting for, or extraction or production of, petroleum or natural gas or both (paragraph 3(3)) in a designated branch of the State Bank of India. The withdrawal of deposit and/or interest accrued on it, can only be made to the extent necessary to meet any expenditure to be incurred on the expiry or termination of the agreement or relinquishment of part of the contract area towards removal of equipment and the installation, in a manner agreed with the Central Government pursuant to an abandonment plan or towards necessary site restoration activities in accordance with GIPIPs. Withdrawal can also be made for meeting expenses necessary to prevent hazards to life, property or the environment consequent on expiry, termination or relinquishment of the area under the contract.

III. Production Operations and Pollution

766. During development and production operations, the principal wastes arise from drilling operations and sometimes accidental spills of oil and blowout. The former includes drilling mud, additives, cements, well-treating fluids, and flow enhancers applied for stimulating production. Another main waste from production is the brine associated with the oil/gas in the crude-bearing formation or reservoir. It is mostly water with dissolved mineral salts, which also contains dissolved petroleum in small concentrations.

767. When production of gas associated with oil is not within the commercial quantity, it is flared and such flaring has adverse impacts on air in the form of emissions of oxides of sulphur and nitrogen, and carbon dioxide, which is an important greenhouse gas. Rule 25 of the Petroleum and Natural Gas Rules, 1959, authorizes the Government to issue directions to a lessee with respect to use of petroleum or natural gas which leads to the creation of unnecessary fire hazards, or permits gas produced from a gas well to escape into the open air.

§4. DOWNSTREAM

I. Refining and Pollution

768. The pollutants given out in the refining process are sulphur oxides, nitrogen oxides, carbon oxides, etc. The gases are mixed in the air and create air pollution in the vicinity of the refinery. A refinery, by itself may not significantly adversely affect air quality. However, a refinery located in an already polluted area can have a major environmental impact. Discharge of refinery effluents also has an adverse impact on the receiving water body.

II. Storage

769. Vapours are emitted when storage tanks breathe as well as when vapours are displaced during filling, and when liquids evaporate. Floating roof tanks are provided for the storage of high vapour-pressure hydrocarbons to minimize evaporation loss from the liquid surface. This can bring about nearly 95% reduction in emissions.

III. Oil Spills

770. There can be oil spills or seepage of oil in and around the producing field. While transporting crude oil by truck, rail, barge, tanker or pipeline there is a build-up of Bottom Sediment Waste, which is to be discharged and such discharge may entail pollution. There is also the probability of spills from pipelines and ocean tankers which can wipe out entire colonies of fish and even coral reefs. The oil pollution in sea is tackled by International Convention, Merchant Shipping Act, 1958 and M.S. (Prevention of Pollution of the Sea by Oil) Rules, 1974.

A. Merchant Shipping Act, 1958

771. In view of marine pollution from oil, Part X B and Part XI A were added to the Merchant Shipping Act of 1958 through the Merchant Shipping (Amendment) Act of 1970 and 1983. These parts deal with marine pollution from oil and civil liability for oil pollution and damages (for details *see supra* Part I, Chapter 4).

B. M.S. (Prevention of Pollution of the Sea by Oil) Rules, 1974

772. These rules are applicable to all tankers of 150 tons gross or more and all other ships of 400 tons gross or more. The rules specify the limits of the prohibited zones, the equipment to be carried on board the ship and general precautions to be taken for prevention of leakage and accidental discharges as well as precautions to be taken while loading, transferring and unloading oil by tankers. The rules also require all vessels to maintain oil records book to indicate any operations carried out on board with respect to oil.

C. *International Conventions*

1. International Convention for the Prevention of Pollution from Ships (London, 2 November 1973)

773. This convention aims at preventing pollution of the marine environment by the operation and discharge of oil and other harmful substances and the minimization of accidental discharge of such substances.

2. The International CLC for Oil Pollution Damage, Brussels 1969

774. This convention apportions the liability of oil pollution on the owner of the oil tanker.

3. The International Convention on Establishment of an International Fund for Compensation of Oil Pollution Damage, Brussels 1971 (Fund Convention)

775. This convention provides for a compensation system in order to ensure full compensation to victims and to distribute the economic burden between shipping and cargo interests.

Chapter 9. Other Sectors

776. India being a vast country has a network of rivers, areas with sand dunes in the desert as well as coastal areas, wetlands, lakes and coral reefs. The Central Government has declared that the coastal stretches, seas, bays, estuaries, creeks, rivers and backwaters which are influenced by tidal action have been classified as different CRZ zones by CRZ notification 2011 and has imposed restrictions on setting up and establishing industries, operations or processes in these areas with certain exceptions.

§1. Dunes

777. Sand dunes are common features of shoreline and desert environments in India. Dunes provide habitat for highly specialized plants and animals, including rare and endangered species. They protect beaches from erosion and provide sand to eroded beaches. As per the 2011 CRZ Notification, the sand dunes in coastal zones are classified as CRZ-I (B) where most activities are prohibited except some like laying of conveying system and projects relating to the DAE.

§2. Rivers

778. The rivers play an important part in influencing the economic development of the country. In fact, India is a land of rivers and the earliest civilization of India is associated with the Ganga, Yamuna and the Indus rivers. But slowly and gradually, these great rivers have been polluted and in fact in some stretches these rivers are not more than a drain.

I. Sources of Rivers

779. On the basis of their source, the rivers of India are classified into the rivers emerging from the Himalayas and flowing through northern India, the rivers of the inland drainage basin and the rivers of south India. There are three main rivers, which emerge from the Himalayas namely the Indus, the Ganga and the Brahmaputra. These rivers originate from the Himalayas and flow from west to east. The source of the Indus River lies in Tibet, and it flows through Kashmir and thereafter Pakistan and finally discharges its water into the Arabian Sea. The main tributaries of the Indus are the Sutlej, the Beas, the Chenab and the Jhelum. Out of these, the Sutlej is the main river on which the Bhakra Nangal Project has been developed.

780. The Ganga is the longest river in India. The main source of the Ganga is the Bhagirathi which rises from the Gangotri glacier, and the other source is the Alakananda which rises from the Alakapuri glacier. Both these rivers join at Debaprayag and thereafter are known as the Ganga. It flows through UP, Bihar and Bangladesh and finally falls into the Bay of Bengal. The delta formed by the Ganga is the largest delta in the world. The Brahmaputra river originates from the Chema-yungdung glacier which lies 100 km southeast of Manasarovar. Near its source, the Brahmaputra is called Tachhog, Khabab. In Tibet, it is called Tsangpo. The river finally flows through the Assam valley, and in Bangladesh, it joins the Padma River.

781. On the basis of the direction of their flow, the rivers of south India are categorized into three groups: as rivers flowing towards the east into the Bay of Bengal, rivers flowing towards the west into the Arabian Sea and rivers flowing towards the north into other rivers. The rivers of south India originate from the Western Ghats, the Satpura ranges, the Mahadeo and Vindhya ranges of mountains. The main east flowing rivers are the Mahanadi, the Godavari, the Krishna, the Kaveri, etc. The principal west flowing rivers are the Narmada and the Tapti and the north flowing rivers are the Chambal, the Betwa, the Dhasan, the Sone, etc.

II. Water Quality Profile of Major Rivers

A. River Brahmaputra

782. The Brahmaputra has its own specific pollution problems like petroleum refining units contribute most of the industrial pollution load into this river along with other medium and small industries. The 2,900 km long river, the lifeline of the Assam is in bad condition now. The water of the Brahmaputra River in Assam has turned muddy and has changed its colour. It has also been reported that cement mixed in water is creating pollution problems. The Government of Assam is suspecting that dam building activities in China could be a reason for this pollution.

B. River Ganga

783. The water quality of the Ganga is assessed in accordance with the primary water quality standard for outdoor bathing, which is when the Biological Oxygen Demand (BOD) is less than 3 mg per litre, along with other factors. The Ganga river water quality comparison between 2015 and 2021, the BOD level of the river flowing through Uttarakhand (Haridwar to Sultanpur) and Bihar (Buxar to Bhagalpur) was below 3 mg per litre, which falls in the unpolluted category. In the other two stretches of the Ganga flowing in Uttar Pradesh (Kannauj to Varanasi) and West Bengal (Triveni to Diamond Harbour), the BOD level is in the lowest of the pollution category – category-5 (3–6 mg per litre) as per NMCG. As per official data, there was an improvement in 2021 in comparison to 2015, when the BOD of the Ganga flowing through Bihar was in category-2 (7.8–27 mg per litre) and that of the stretch of the river flowing through Uttar Pradesh was in category 3 (3.8–16.9 mg per litre). However, not much change was seen in the BOD level of the river flowing through West Bengal between 2015 and 2021. In 2015, the BOD level between Triveni to Diamond Harbour was in category-5 (3.1–5.8 mg per litre) and in 2021, it remained in the same category with a slight improvement in the BOD level, which was recorded between 1.3 and 4.3 mg per litre. The water bodies that have a BOD level of more than 6 mg per litre are considered as polluted and identified for remedial action (Indian Express, 12 March 2022).

784. The NMCG took up the task of cleaning and rejuvenating the holy river through the launch of several projects. The water is being treated to less than 10 BOD (Biochemical Oxygen Demand). Chemicals and bacteria in the water are being treated separately. The treated water is chlorinated, i.e., 4–5 PPM (Parts Per Million) or milligrams per litre which kills all bacteria in the treated water. A laboratory analysis of the samples found that water quality tremendously improved with growing public awareness and steps taken by the NMCG.

785. The GOI is addressing the challenges of pollution of river Ganga by providing financial and technical assistance. Under Namami Gange Programme (NGP), a number of coordinated activities for cleaning of river Ganga have been taken up. There are three projects being carried out under the NGP. Under these projects, monitoring and surveillance of water quality of river Ganga from its origin to confluence with Bay of Bengal is being carried out. This includes in-depth inspection of GPIs, monitoring of Sewage Treatment Plants (STPs), Common Effluent Treatment Plants (CETPs), groundwater monitoring to assess the impact of CETPs/STPs and major drains falling into the river Ganga and its tributaries. The objective is to inventorize the pollution sources (both point and non-point) and to assess the pollution load being discharged into the river Ganga directly or indirectly through tributaries. The activities carried out under the project during Action taken for Ganga Basin during 2020 for 'Environmental Compensation' for the direct discharge from drains into river Ganga in the five Ganga States were calculated from 1 November 2019 to 31 January 2020. Directions were issued under section 18(1)(b) of the Water (Prevention and Control of Pollution) Act, 1974 to the SPCBs of the five Ganga basin states (Uttarakhand, Uttar Pradesh, Bihar, Jharkhand & West Bengal) that no Authority shall allow the discharge of polluted sewage or polluted effluents directly into a water channel or stream even during monsoon season.

786. In *M.C. Mehta v. Union of India* (AIR 1988 SC 1115), the Supreme Court found that the Municipality of Kanpur was responsible for major pollution in the River Ganga. The court directed that all municipalities along the river course must take action so that pollution could be prevented.

787. In a recent case NGT observed that execution by State authorities is inadequate and the NMCG does not appear to be in a position to take strict measures against non-compliances. Untreated sewage and effluents continue to flow into the River Ganga even after decades of monitoring, still nearly 50% of untreated sewage and substantial industrial effluents are continuing to be discharged in the river or its tributaries/drains, in absence of requisite functional treatment capacity (The Hindu, 24 July 2022).

C. River Yamuna

788. Cleaning of Yamuna is part of the Namami Gange Mission and GOI has been supplementing the efforts of the States for checking the rising level of pollution of river Yamuna, by providing financial assistance to States of Haryana, Delhi and UP in phased manner. Just 2% or 22 km of Yamuna falls in Delhi, but 98% of pollution comes from here due to untreated or semitreated industrial effluents or sewage being discharged into the river. According to estimates made by the CPCB, Delhi generates 3,800 million litres of sewage per day. The over 1,300 km long Yamuna is among the most polluted rivers in the country but provides water to more than half of the national capital. There are eighteen drains that deliver dirty water into the Yamuna, and plans are afoot to tap these drains and divert the dirty water to STPs as these are in place. The treated water from the STPs can then be added to the river so that the flow of the river is also improved. So, no dirty water will be coming into the Yamuna river and its flow will also see improvement. NMCG is starting NGYodha (Namami Gange Yamuna of Delhi area) that will focus on cleaning the Yamuna.

D. River Cauvery

789. The Cauvery river is the source of drinking water for humans and animals, as well as for irrigation in the States of Tamil Nadu and Karnataka. The water samples from the river were analysed for levels of pollutants, and microplastic composition. It was discovered that all chemical pollutants were within permissible safety levels, except for the quantity of DO, which fish breathe in, showing clear signs of hypoxic conditions or reduced oxygen. It may be because of microplastics and other pollutants causing growth defects and skeletal deformities in fish. The study of embryos of zebrafish incubated in these samples in the lab were found them to have growth and skeletal deformities, reduced heart rate, reduced life span, and DNA damage. The damage was attributed to molecules called Reactive Oxygen Species, which are highly reactive chemicals derived from oxygen molecules, in the cells of the fish. These findings may prove helpful in providing valuable insights for treatment of water and the potential health hazards of using KRS-CR water for drinking, fishing, and irrigation.

E. River Godavari

790. Godavari is sometimes also referred to as the 'Ganga of the South'. After every twelve years, a major bathing festival called as Pushkaram is held on the banks of the Godavari river. People feel that taking a bath in the Godavari is sacred and this would wash away their sins. However there is dumping of waste, the flow of drainage water into the river and discharge of effluents from factories and industries pollutes, making its water unsuitable even for irrigation purposes. With the throwing of plastic, photos of gods prepared of glass and cardboard and materials used for prayers including garlands and flowers by the devotees, with the immersion of Ganesh idols made of plaster of paris and chemicals, with mixing of the remains of the dead, the scenario becomes scary. The flowing in of drainage water from Manthani, Godavarikhani and Dharmapuri towns add to a scenario in which the water from the Godavari is polluted and becoming hazardous. Before the construction of the Kaleshwaram lift irrigation project (KLIS), all the waste used to get washed away along with the normal, steady flow of water in the Godavari. Now, as the water is remaining stagnant from Medigadda to Yellampalli reservoirs following the construction of KLIS, the pollutants are remaining stuck in the river.

F. River Krishna

791. Krishna river is one of the longest rivers in the country with its approximate length around 1,300 km (800 miles). This river has several tributaries with Tungabhadra being its largest tributary. In terms of length, Bhima river is the longest tributary of the Krishna river with an approximate size of more than 800 km. The river Krishna and its tributaries are polluted in certain urban stretches due to urban pollution and release of the waste directly into the river. As most of the water of the river is being used for agriculture, it is on the verge of death. The river barely reaches the sea owing to urban pollution and use in sugarcane production. Further, sugarcane mills and refineries release their effluents into the river. The issue of deteriorating water quality of Krishna river is identified by the CPCB and prioritizes restoration of the river Krishna and its tributaries. Discharge of highly alkaline water from the power stations increases the alkalinity of the water, which is already highly alkaline due to the presence of basalt rock formations in the basin.

G. River Mahanadi

792. Mahanadi is lifeline of Odisha state. But Industrial waste and sewage channels of towns and cities on both sides of the river run into Mahanadi. Farmers suffer because of water shortage and industrial units get to suck the river's water.

H. River Narmada

793. Narmada Bachao Andolan is related to this river on which the Sardar Sarovar dam has been constructed which uprooted besides others, Adivasis who have lived along the Narmada river for centuries. The river water is now facing excessive sand mining, on the one hand, and effluent discharge in Narmada and its tributaries, on the other. The Narmada is facing stress from several pollution sources between its origin at Amarkantak and Hoshangabad. Threats are also from religious activities, public gatherings, bathing, and domestic effluent discharges. Approximately 100 km from its origin, agricultural activities in the Narmada watershed are intensive, which also contributes to pollution through surface runoff. Industrial activities, restaurants, and lodges on the river banks also release sewage to the river through small drains. Major towns/cities such as Dindori, Mandala, and Narsinghpur along the river lack STPs, making the river more vulnerable to sewage pollution.

I. River Sabarmati

794. The Sabarmati (By the side of which Mahatma Gandhi lived) is a seasonal river with its flows dominated by the monsoon. It originates from Aravalli Hills, Rajasthan and meets in the Bay of Khambhat in the Arabian sea. It passes through districts like Udaipur in Rajasthan, and Aravalli, Sabarkantha, Gandhinagar, Ahmedabad and Kheda in Gujarat. Its length is 371 km. & total catchment area is 21,674 km^2. Sabarmati river remains highly polluted despite the spending huge amount of funds. The Gujarat High Court reprimanded the Ahmedabad Municipal Corporation and the Gujarat Pollution Control Board for the pollution on the Sabarmati riverfront. The Hon'able Court admonished the officials accountable for the functioning of laboratories in STP, failed to keep a check on polluted water dumped into the riverfront, will be dealt with strictly (The Hindu, 25 October 2021).

J. River Ramganga

795. The Ramganga, a main tributary river of River Ganga, originates from Chamoli town (Uttarakhand) and flows through the Corbett National Park near Ramnagar of Nainital district from where it descends upon the plains and traverses through Bijnor, Moradabad, Rampur, etc., and finally merges with river Ganga in district Kannauj (UP). There are a number of water polluting industries. The polluted river stretch receives considerable amount of wastewater every day from the industries and sewage from different municipal areas which contributes to pollution load and leads to deterioration of its water quality. A high level of pollution prevails in the river during the non-monsoon season and particularly in floodplain tributaries. Anthropogenic sources contribute up to 42% of the dissolved load composition, whereas silicate and carbonate weathering predominantly contributes 93% and 82% of the dissolved load. The total dissolved solids (TDS) during different seasons vary from 67 to 810 mg/L. A decrease in TDS in most of the samples during the monsoon season can be due to the dilution effect caused by high runoff, whereas an increase in the concentration of cations and anions in the non-monsoon season specifies that chemical weathering predominates the dilution effect in the non-rainy days.

III. Bio-monitoring of Rivers/Water Bodies

796. The biological monitoring system is an important and cost-effective tool to maintain and restore the wholesomeness of water quality in terms of ecological sustainability of various designated best uses of rivers and other water bodies. Three of every four river monitoring stations in India posted alarming levels of heavy toxic metals such as lead, iron, nickel, cadmium, arsenic, chromium and copper, according to the State of Environment Report, 2022 from the environmental NGO, the CSE. Of the 588 water quality stations monitored for pollution, TC and biochemical oxygen demand was high in 239 and 88 stations across twenty-one States – an indicator of poor wastewater treatment from industry, agriculture and domestic households.

IV. NRCP and Directorate

797. The National River Conservation Directorate (NRCD), former directorate under the MoEFCC has now became a part of the Ministry of Jal Shakti. The NRCD is implementing the Centrally Sponsored Schemes of National Conservation Plan and National Plan for Conservation of Aquatic Eco-systems (NPCA) for conservation of rivers, lakes and wetlands in the country. Earlier the activities of NRCD were dedicated towards pollution abatement. Considering the successful model of river conservation, demonstrated by the WII, Dehra Dun, under the NGP, NRCD has now amalgamated biodiversity conservation and community participation in the conservation process. NRCD has taken up a nationwide river conservation project, and the rivers Cauvery, Godavari, Periyar, Mahanadi and Narmada were taken as priority rivers. NRCD entrusted WII as a nodal agency for this initiative and initially six rivers viz., Mahanadi, Narmada, Godavari, Periyar, Cauvery and Barak were selected. The project 'Assessment of the ecological status of select Indian rivers for conservation planning' by the WII, in the first phase, aims to spearhead river conservation in identified Indian rivers for biodiversity conservation.

V. Public Participation

798. The large-scale government programmes are generally more successful when citizen participation is at the core. It is also not fair to expect a single agency to measure water quality comprehensively across the country. In India, it is CPCB that undertakes this humungous task, but across the globe, including some African countries, most WQM agencies are democratizing the process of data collection. They are crowdsourcing data by involving communities and other stakeholders. This bottom-up approach reduces the cost, improves comprehensiveness and builds trust on the collected data. A publicly available formal training to certify WQM professionals can support this effort towards incorporating crowd sourced data. The citizens must be made aware about what polluted air is doing to their health. Environmentalists could not really reach the mass until emphasized about the health effects of pollution. Masses cannot sensitize on water pollution until there is increased emphasis on how it impacts their health.

§3. Lakes

799. The lakes in India are spread throughout the country. These are in the Himalayas, the desert region, the plateau region and the coastal region. The main lakes in the Himalayas are the Sisharan Nag, Har Nag and Dudh Nag. The Wular is the largest lake in Kashmir valley, which controls the flow of the Jhelum and other rivers. Besides, Dal and Anchar are other two small lakes in the Kashmir valley. In the Kumaun Himalayas, the Bhimtaal is the largest lake in a series of lakes near Nainital town. The Sambhar Salt Lake in Rajasthan and Chilika Lake in Odisha are the other two large and important lakes in India.

I. National Plan for Conservation of Aquatic Ecosystems

800. Since 2001, the MoEFCC has been implementing the NLCP to conserve and manage polluted and degraded lakes in urban and semi-urban areas. An integrated scheme, The NPCA, combining the NLCP and the National Wetlands Conservation Programme was created to avoid overlap, promote better synergies, and ensure conservation and management work. The new scheme includes conservation and management of lakes and wetlands in the country, including an inventory and information system on lakes and wetlands, a national-level directive on lake and wetlands criteria, a regulatory framework, capacity building at the state government and local body levels, evaluation, and so on. Its goal is to conserve aquatic ecosystems (lakes and wetlands) through the implementation of long-term conservation plans governed by uniform policy and guidelines.

§4. WETLANDS

I. Wetland Conservation Programme

801. Wetlands are lands transitional between terrestrial and aquatic systems where the water table is near the water surface and the land is covered by shallow water. They provide a suitable habitat for fish and other flora and fauna. They act as a buffer against the adverse effects of hurricanes and cyclones, stabilize the shoreline and act as a bulwark against encroachment by the sea, and check soil erosion. To ensure better conservation and management, and to prevent further degradation of existing wetlands the Wetlands (Conservation and Management), Rules, 2017 have been brought in force. These Rules lay down legally enforceable provisions for the conservation and management of wetlands.

802. In India, there is a wealth of wetlands distributed throughout the country in different geographical regions numbering 115 covering twenty-four States and two UT. Most of these wetlands are directly or indirectly linked with rivers like the Ganga, Brahmaputra, Narmada, Tapti, Godavari, Kaveri, etc. Twenty-six sites from India have been declared as Ramsar wetlands sites of international importance. Another six sites are in the process of being designated as Ramsar sites.

II. Ramsar Convention on Wetlands of International Importance Especially as Waterfowl Habitat (2 February 1971)

803. The Ramsar Convention provides the intergovernmental framework for international cooperation for the conservation and wise use of wetland habitat and species. In India, there is a wealth of wetlands distributed throughout the country in different geographical regions numbering 115 covering twenty-four States and two UT. Most of these wetlands are directly or indirectly linked with rivers like the Ganga, Brahmaputra, Narmada, Tapti, Godavari, Kaveri, etc. Twenty-six sites from India have been declared as Ramsar wetlands sites of international importance. Another six sites are in the process of being designated as Ramsar sites.

§5. The Coastal Zone

804. The coastal zones were initially regulated through a notification (dated 9 February 1991) which has been superseded by notification No. 19, dated 6 January 2011, issued under section 3(1) and 3(2)(v) of the Environment (Protection) Act of 1986 and Rule 5(3)(d) of the Environment (Protection) Rules of 1986. This notification was product of national and international developments in the field and in the light of NEP 2006 which declared that there should be 'comprehensive approach to integrate coastal management by addressing linkage between coastal, wetlands and river systems in relevant policies, regulation and programmes'. The Central Government has declared the coastal stretches of seas, bays, estuaries, creeks, rivers and back waters which are influenced by tidal action (on the landward sides) up to 500 m. from High Tide Line (HTL) and land between the Low Tide Line (LTL) and the HTL as CRZ. The HTL is line on the land up to which the highest water line reached during the spring tide.

805. The distance from the HTL will apply to both sides in case of river creeks, and backwater may be modified on a case-to-case basis for reasons to be recorded in writing while preparing CZM Plan, provided that this distance shall not be less than 100 m or the width of the creeks or river or backwater whichever is less. In this notification, certain activities have been prohibited within the different CRZ like dumping of ash or any wastes from thermal power stations whereas other activities have been regulated, and clearance is required for carrying on any activity. The MoEFCC and the Government of the State or UT and such other authorities at the State or UT level have been designated for the purpose of monitoring and enforcing the provisions of the notification. The coastal area has been classified into five zones.

806. In areas between the LTL and HTL, if they are not ecologically sensitive some activities have been permitted like exploration and extraction of natural gas, storage of petroleum products within the existing port limits and harbours and in those areas that have not been classified as CRZ subject to implementation of safety regulations including guidelines issues by the Oil Safety Directorate (S.O.494(E) dated 9 July 1997).

§6. MANGROVES

I. Best Mangroves in India

807. The total mangrove cover in the country stands at 4,921 km^2 and has shown an increase of 181 km^2. Mangrove ecosystems are rich in biodiversity and provide a number of ecological services. They also play a major role in protecting coastal areas from erosion, tidal storms and tsunamis. All the twelve mangrove states have shown a positive change in the mangrove cover, as compared to the last assessment in 2015. Mangroves are salt tolerant plant communities or ecosystems occurring in sheltered coastal areas such as bays, estuaries, lagoons and creeks. Some of the best mangroves are found in India and these are all along the coastline. The main mangrove areas are: North Andaman and Nicobar Island, Sunderbans in the State of West Bengal, Bhitarkanika in the State of Odisha, Coringu, Godavari Delta and Krishna Estuary in the State of Andhra Pradesh, Mahanadi Delta in the State of Odisha, Pitchavaram and Point Calimer in the State of Tamil Nadu, Goa Gulf of Kutch in the State of Gujarat, Coondapur in the State of Karnataka, Achra/Raenagiri in the State of Maharashtra and Vembanad in the State of Kerala.

II. Scheme on Conservation and Management of Mangroves

808. The promotional measures for mangroves and coral reefs are implemented under National Coastal Mission Programme on 'Conservation and Management of Mangroves and Coral Reefs'. The regulatory measures are implemented through CRZ Notification (2019) under the Environment (Protection) Act, 1986; the Wild Life (Protection) Act, 1972; the Indian Forest Act, 1927; the Biological Diversity Act, 2002; and rules made under these acts as amended from time to time. The Government under the scheme for conservation & Management of Mangroves, extend assistance to Coastal State/UTs for implementation of action plans including survey and demarcation, alternation and supplementary livelihood, protection measures and education and awareness activities. The MoEFCC piloted an Integrated Coastal Zone management Project in Coastal stretches of three states namely Gujarat, Odisha and West Bengal, with objective of Conservation and Protection of Coastal resources which included plantation of mangroves as one of the major activities. The FSI assessed Mangrove Cover of the country in three density classes, i.e., very Dense, Moderately Dense and Open Mangrove Cover on biennial basis and publishes the findings in the India State of Forest Report (ISFR). As per the ISFR 2021, the mangrove cover in the country has increased by 17 km^2. in year 2021 as compared to the mangrove cover assessed in year 2019 (10 February 2022, PIB Delhi).

III. National Mangrove Genetic Resource Centre

809. A National Mangrove Genetic Resource Centre has been established at Bhitarkanika in the State of Odisha.

§7. Coral Reef

810. The major coral reef formations in the country are restricted to the GoM, Palk bay, Gulf of Kutch, Andaman and Nicobar Islands and the Lakshadweep islands. While the Lakshadweep reefs are atolls, the others are all fringing reefs. Patchy coral is present in the intertidal areas of the central west coast of the country. The Reef condition is generally poor and declining in near shore waters and areas of high population density. Relatively pristine reefs are located around uninhabited islands or barrier type reefs located away from population centres. Sedimentation, dredging and coral mining are damaging near shore reefs, while the use of explosives and bottom nets in fishing are damaging offshore reefs in specific sites. Although institutions and laws are sufficient in theory to manage and protect the reefs in India, authorities in the field have taken little effective action in implementing these laws.

I. Indian Coral Reef Monitoring Network

811. A National Committee on the Conservation and Management of Mangroves and Coral Reefs was set up in September 1998. The MoEFCC has launched the Indian Coral Reef Monitoring Network to cover activities related to monitoring of health of coral reefs, establish a database network and promote research on the identified thrust areas. On the recommendations of this committee, financial assistance from the UNDP and the GEF has been availed for strengthening the Gulf of Manner Biosphere Reserves and a project relating to the Andaman's Coral Reefs.

II. National Coral Reef Research Institute

812. The existing centre of ZSI at Port Blair has been designated as the National Coral Reef Research Institute. The MoEFCC has also been identified as the National Focal Point of the International Coral Reef Initiative, Global Coral Reef Monitoring Network as well as Coral Reef Degradation in the Indian Ocean. The India-Australia Training and Capacity Building Project on Coral Reefs with Aus-Aid have also been launched.

§8. Marine National Parks

813. The coastal zone of India has valuable ecosystems such as estuaries, mangroves, coral reefs, sea grass beds, mudflats, sandy beaches and many small island ecosystems. These ecosystems and their associated habitats play an important role in the economy of the country. However, man-made and natural pressures threaten these ecosystems and their resources. With the objective of protecting biological diversity and promoting the sustainable use of resources, India has declared three National Marine Parks, namely the Marine National Park (MNP) of the Gulf of

Kutch, MNP of GoM and Wandoor MNP of Andaman. These areas house a large number of endangered, vulnerable and threatened species.

I. Gulf of Kutch

814. During 1980, about 457.92 km^2 of the Gulf of Kutch was declared a National Marine Park. This park is situated along the southern shore of the Gulf of Kutch, Okha eastwards to the vicinity of Khiadia. This includes forty-two islands surrounded by fringing reefs backed by mudflats, sand dunes, coastal salt marshes and mangrove forests, sand and rocky beaches which represent a great diversity of fauna and flora.

A. Biological Diversity

815. Biological diversity of the area is attributed to the varied habitats, which support over 120 species of algae, 7 species of mangroves, about 24 species of mangrove associated flora, about 70 species of sponges, 37 species of soft and hard corals under 24 genera, about 180 species of fish including 8 types of shark, 27 species of prawn, 30 species of crabs, 200 species of molluscs, 3 species of turtle, 3 species of sea snakes, 3 species of mammals, and 200 species of birds.

B. Sustainability Indicators

816. After the declaration of the Marine Park, the area has evidenced an increase in mangrove cover, coral cover and fish catch.

C. Problems and Threats

817. The Gulf of Kutch MPA has been threatened tremendously by various developmental activities such as chemical industries, construction of new ports, and harbours, oil transport, shipbuilding and breaking activities. The majority of coral reefs are buried under mud and sands. Deposition of silt due to mangrove destruction is one of the main reasons of coral loss. New industrial development, especially the establishment of refineries, jetties and expansion of ports and salt works pose potential threats to the park through changing physical, chemical and biological conditions of the coastal ecosystems.

II. Gulf of Mannar

818. The GoM MNP was declared in 1989. Lying between India and Sri Lanka, it covers an area of about 10,500 km^2; it runs along the (mainland) Indian coast to about 170 nautical miles and includes about twenty-one islands.

A. Biological Diversity

819. The GoM reserve covers 10,500 km^2 and has twenty-one islands with continuous stretches of coral reef. In the GoM, one can see the globally endangered dugong, several species of dolphins and whales and three species of endangered sea turtles. The Reserve is home to sea horses, 450 species of fish, hundreds of species of sea cucumbers, sponges, all kinds of corals and species of sea grass found nowhere else. In addition more than 150 species of bird are found on islands in the reserve.

B. Sustainability Indicators

820. The coral reefs of GoM experienced severe degradation during 1980s and 1990s primarily due to rampant mining and destructive fishing. The coast is densely populated and the reef status is also affected by sewage discharge. The coral disease prevalence also increased. However, the reefs of GoM exhibit signs of resilience, especially since 2005 after coral mining was halted and with a reduction in destructive fishing activities.

C. Problems and Threats

821. At present, the MNP is threatened by overfishing and destructive fishing practices; seaweed collection; commercial shell collection; coral mining; poor land use practices; coastal and urban development; harbour and dredging; industrial development and last but not least pollution. The park authorities closely monitor the area through research projects funded by the MoEFCC.

III. The Mahatma Gandhi MNP, Wandoor Andaman and Nicobar Islands

822. The Mahatma Gandhi MNP, Wandoor was notified in 1983 for the protection of marine life. The park is located on the southwestern coast of the South-Andamans, in the Bay of Bengal, encompassing fifteen islands and several islets of the labyrinth group of islands. The park covers a total area of 281.5 km^2. The park is under the overall administrative control of the Chief Wildlife Warden of the Forest Department of Andaman and Nicobar Island Administration.

823. This park ensures that future generations have the opportunity to experience, understand and enjoy areas that have been largely undisturbed by human action over long periods of time. It also provides indigenous human communities living in low density and harmony and in balance with the available resources to maintain their original lifestyle.

A. Biological Diversity

824. The Mahatma Gandhi MNP was established so as to protect the sea turtles, marine lives and the beautiful corals. The landscape of the park is dotted with fifteen rocky islands and is covered with tropical forest. The rich flora and fauna of the Mahatma Gandhi MNP makes this park an ideal destination for the nature lovers. Rich marine life consists of variety of coral reefs, colourful fishes, molluscs, shells, starfish, turtles, salt-water crocodile, etc. The park is home to birds like white-bellied sea eagle, parakeets, Andaman teal, heron, terns, waders and swifts. There are more than 271 different varieties of birds inhabiting the idyllic landscape of Mahatma Gandhi MNP. The park area includes vast stretch of enchanting marine waters, bushy vegetated islands, magnificent coral reefs and sparkling sandy beaches and mangroves.

B. Sustainability

825. In Andaman, all the programmes emphasize on people-centred development and sustainable management of biodiversity. The MPA has been under the control of the park authorities, and the resource utilization is sustainable except certain poaching activities. This protected area is a good model for any other developing country to adopt. The Indian Government also follows the international obligation under the UNCLOS, CITES and CBD which are helpful in managing the micro-level resources of the National MAPs.

C. Problems and Threats

826. The environmental issues relate to removal of sand and dead coral from beaches for construction and deforestation of mangroves for developmental activities. Factors like predation by the Crown of Thorn starfish on corals have been altering the coral reef structure and ecosystem. On Red Skin Island, corals in the reef slope are badly damaged mostly due to boat anchorage. Persistent shell collection has also caused considerable damage to corals on Twins Island and Tarmugli Island. Tourist activities like trampling, overturning the coral blocks, snorkelling and scuba diving have damaged the corals on Jolly Boys Island.

827. The MAPs have international significance for their cultural, scientific, educational and tourism importance. The park authorities take actions so as to prevent overexploitation and monitor the effluents discharged by the industries around the park areas for maintaining nature as much as possible. The authorities are also involved in protecting the livelihood security of the indigenous people and user community through sustainable utilization of the resources and maintaining the area's potential to meet the aspirations of future generations.

Part III. Spatial Planning

r 1. Zoning and Land Use Planning

. Zoning is a land planning process which regulates the built environment creates functional real estate markets. It is done by dividing land that comprises statutory area of a local authority into sections, permitting particular land uses specific sites to shape the layout of towns and cities and enable development. Zoning determines the location, size, and use of buildings and decides the density of city blocks. Zoning allows local and national authorities to regulate and control land and property markets to ensure complementary uses. Land use planning in India came with the emergence of the need for the planned development of towns and cities so as it is sustainable. The planned development is possible only by efficient use of available resources like land, air, water, soil, forests and other natural resources. For achieving efficiency and increasing output land use planning in India gained importance. India supports approximately 16.7% of the world's human and 20% of the livestock population on a mere 2.4% of the world's geographical area. So there is enormous pressure on the land resources which are limited. Land use in India is given in Table 6.

Table 6 Land Use Classification in India (Area in Thousand Hectares)

Land Use (Total Geographical Area is 328.726 mha)	*2016–2017 (P)*	*2017–2018 (P)*	*2018–2019 (P)*
1. Reporting area	308316	307767	307787
2. Forest area	72020	72047	72011
3. Area under non-agricultural uses	27838	27326	27344
4. Barren & unculturable land	16985	16992	17168
5. Not available for cultivation			
(3+4)	44823	44319	44512
6. Permanent pastures &other grazing lands	10340	10338	10376
7. Land under tree, crops & grooves	3124	3167	3154

Land Use (Total Geographical Area is 328.726 mha)	*2016–2017 (P)*	*2017–2018 (P)*	*2[illegible]-2019*
8. Permanent pastures and other grazing lands	10340	10338	1[illegible]
9. Culturable wasteland	12236	12287	1221
10. Other cultivated land excluding follow land (6 to 9)	25702	25792	25749

P means: Provisional.

Source: 'Land Use Statistics 2009–2010 to 2018–2019', Department of Agriculture & Farmers Welfa[illegible] Directorate of Economics & Statistics, Ministry of Agriculture and Farmers Welfare, November 2021.

Chapter 2. Urban and Rural Zoning

829. The policies of urban development and planning in India have come a long way since Independence. The general perception of the policymakers initially was that India is predominantly an agricultural and rural economy and that there are potent dangers of over urbanization which will lead to the drain of resources from the countryside to feed the cities. The positive aspects of cities as engines of economic growth in the context of national economic policies were not much appreciated and, therefore, the problems of urban areas were treated more as welfare problems and sectors of residual investment rather than as issues of national economic importance. This led to deterioration in urban living conditions and gave rise to the problem of cheap dwellings in the form of slums creating environmental pollution. In rural areas as well the pressure on the natural resources, especially land, water and biodiversity, is continuously increasing resulting in their deterioration. In addition to that, the fragmentation of holdings has resulted not only to smaller and unviable units of land holdings but also to intensive cultivation with the use of chemical fertilizers, pesticides, insecticides.

Chapter 3. Statutory Structure and Legal Regime

§1. Constitutional Position

I. The Constitution Seventy-Third Amendment Act

830. This amendment in the Constitution along with the *Panchayats* (Extension to the Scheduled Areas) Act of 1996 entrusts the *Panchayats* with functions like land improvement, land reforms, land consolidation, rural housing and maintenance of community assets.

II. The Constitution Seventy-Fourth Amendment Act of 1992

831. By this amendment, a separate chapter pertaining to ULB was incorporated in the Constitution of India. This chapter redefines their role, power, function and finances. According to this amendment, the ULB, known as Municipal Corporations, Municipal Councils and *Nagar Panchayat* depending on the population are constituted through universal adult franchise in each notified urban area of the country. The *Nagar Panchayat* is provided for an area that is in transition from a rural area to an urban area. A Municipal Council is constituted for smaller urban areas and a Municipal Corporation for a large urban area.

832. An ULB is constituted for a period of five years and if dissolved earlier, an election to reconstitute it shall be completed before the expiration of a period of six months from the date of its dissolution. Not less than one-third of the total number of seats in each ULB shall be reserved for women. The Legislature of a State may, by law, entrust on these bodies such power and authority as may be necessary to enable them to function as an institution of local self-government, including those listed in the Twelfth Schedule.

The Twelfth Schedule of the Constitution has listed *inter alia*, the following functions of ULB:

- urban planning including town planning;
- regulation of land use and construction of buildings;
- public health, sanitation, conservancy and SWM;
- fire services;
- urban forestry, protection of the environment and promotion of ecological aspects;
- slum improvement and upgrading;
- provision of urban amenities and facilities such as parks gardens, and playgrounds;
- burials and burial grounds; cremations, cremation grounds and electric crematoriums;
- regulation of slaughterhouses and tanneries.

A. *Right to Collect Taxes*

833. In order that the ULB can perform the functions assigned to them, the Legislature of a State assigns them specific taxes, duties, tolls and levies and authorizes them to impose, collect and appropriate the same. In each district, a District Planning Committee is constituted to consolidate the plan prepared by the urban and rural local bodies. Similarly for each metropolitan area, a Metropolitan Planning Committee is constituted to prepare a development plan for the metropolitan area. A metropolitan area is an area with a population of 1 million or more comprised in one or more districts and consisting of two or more municipalities or *Panchayats* or other contiguous area, specified by the governor through a public notification to be a metropolitan area.

B. *ULB: Vibrant Self-Governing Institutions*

834. All the State Governments have either enacted new municipal laws or amended the existing laws to conform with the Constitution (74th Amendment) Act, 1992. All the States (except Arunachal Pradesh) have constituted State Finance Commissions and most of the commissions have submitted their reports to the State Governments, recommending significant devolution of resources to ULB. This amendment has made the ULB into vibrant self-governing institutions. This has ushered in a new era of urban governance and urban management in India.

§2. Legislation

835. There are a number of enactments, which deal with zoning, and land use planning and regulate the land holdings in urban and rural areas. There are land-ceiling laws both for urban and rural areas. The building operations in urban areas are regulated so as to prevent haphazard development and also to prevent growth of substandard colonies. The State Government can issue directions with respect to regulated areas. For carrying out any construction, activity approval from the appropriate authority is required.

836. The Constitution of India has assigned the subjects pertaining to the urban areas to the State Legislature. Therefore, every State has its own laws dealing with land and urban planning. Insofar as the urban issues are concerned, the legislative powers of the Union are limited only to the following subjects:

- Delhi and other UT.
- Property of the Union.
- A subject of the State lists which two or more State legislatures authorize the Union Parliament to legislate.
- Amendment of the Constitution of India.

837. In exercise of these legislative powers, the Parliament has enacted the following legislations administrated by the Ministry of Urban Development and on the subjects which State Legislatures authorized the Union Parliament to legislate:

- the Urban Land (Ceiling and Regulation) Act of 1976;
- the Urban Land (Ceiling and Regulation) Repeal Act of 1999;
- the Employment of Manual Scavengers and Construction of Dry Latrines (Prohibition) Act of 1993;
- the NCR Planning Board Act of 1985;
- the Delhi Urban Art Commission Act of 1973;
- administration of Delhi Development Act of 1957;
- the Requisitioning and Acquisition of Immovable Property Act of 1952;
- the Public Premises (Eviction of Unauthorized Occupants) Act of 1971;
- the Slum Areas (Improvement and Clearance) Act, 1954;
- the Special Economic Zones Act, 2005;
- the Real Estate (Regulation and Development) Act, 2016 (RERA).

Some other important legislations which affect land planning are as follows:

- the Right to Fair Compensation and Transparency in Land Acquisition, Rehabilitation and Resettlement Act, 2013;
- the Indian Stamp Act of 1899;
- the Indian Registration Act of 1908.

§3. Salient Features of Legislation

I. The Urban Land (Ceiling & Regulation) Act of 1976 and the Urban Land (Ceiling and Regulation) Repeal Act of 1999

838. This Act of 1976 came into force on 17 February 1976 and was initially adopted by the States of Andhra Pradesh, Haryana, Gujarat, Himachal Pradesh, Karnataka, Maharashtra, Odisha, Punjab, Tripura, UP and West Bengal. Subsequently, it was adopted by six more States namely Assam (25 March 1976), Bihar (1 April 1976), Madhya Pradesh (9 September 1976), Manipur (12 March 1976), Meghalaya (7 March 1976) and Rajasthan (9 March 1976). The act was implemented in sixty-four urban agglomerations having a population of more than 2 lakhs as per the 1971 Census.

839. The Urban Land (Ceiling and Regulation) Act of 1976 was repealed by the Urban Land (Ceiling and Regulation) Repeal Act of 1999 on 22 March 1999. Initially the Repeal Act was applicable in Haryana, Punjab and all the UT. Subsequently, the Repeal Act has been adopted by the State Governments of UP, Gujarat, Karnataka, Madhya Pradesh and Rajasthan. The State Government of Andhra Pradesh and West Bengal have not adopted this Repeal Act so far. This repeal was a significant step towards reforms in the urban land market.

II. Administration of Delhi Development Act of 1957

840. This act replaced the Control of Building Operations Ordinance 1957 by which the Delhi Development Authority (DDA) was constituted. The act defines the constitution, role, powers and functions of the DDA. It defines the development area of Delhi and stipulates that any development of land in this area shall be undertaken or carried out after obtaining permission from the DDA. The DDA prepares the Master Plan and Zonal Plans which regulate the development of Delhi. The act also authorizes the DDA to levy betterment/development charges in respect of the increasing value of the property resulting from the execution of development.

III. Delhi Urban Art Commission Act of 1973

841. By this act, the Delhi Urban Art Commission was constituted with a view to preserving, developing and maintaining the aesthetic quality of urban and environment design in Delhi.

IV. NCR Planning Board Act of 1985

842. By this act, the NCR Planning Board was constituted to regulate the growth and to prepare plans and policies for balanced and harmonized development of the NCR.

V. The Requisitioning and Acquisition of Immovable Property Act of 1952

843. The competent authority of the Union likely to need any property for any public purpose can requisition the same under this act by calling the owner of property giving a fifteen days show cause notice.

VI. The Public Premises (Eviction of Unauthorized Occupants) Act of 1971

844. The act provides for the eviction of unauthorized occupants from public premises and for certain incidental matters. The estate officer, after making such enquiry as he deems expedient in the circumstances of a case, and for reasons to be recorded in writing, may make an order for the eviction of such person(s) who are in unauthorized occupation of public premises.

VII. The Employment of Manual Scavengers and Construction of Dry Latrines (Prohibition) Act of 1993

845. This act was enacted by the Parliament on the authority of the State Legislatures of Andhra Pradesh, Goa, Karnataka, Maharashtra, Tripura and West

Bengal. Subsequently it was adopted by a few other States. The act prohibits the construction and maintenance of dry latrines and employment of persons for manual scavenging of human excreta. Violation of the act is a cognizable offence with imprisonment for a term which may extend to one year.

§4. Initiatives by the Urban Development Ministry

846. Although the Parliament does not have powers to legislate on urban issues, the Ministry of Urban Development has taken the initiative for legal and regulatory reforms in the housing and urban development sector through advising State Governments with model legislation and advising other ministries of the GOI regarding legal reform in areas which have bearings on urban planning and development.

I. Model Legislation

847. The model legislation namely Model Town and Country Planning Act concerning land use planning, property regulation legislation, urban and regional planning and development legislation, etc., was first prepared in 1960 and circulated to all the State Government to help them formulate their respective legislation to bring about uniformity in various State laws and also to simplify the regulations. Later on a revised Model for Urban and Regional Planning and Development Law was brought out and guidelines on Urban Development Plan Formulation and Implementation were formulated in 1991. Some States have already enacted laws/ formulated bills on the basis of this model legislation.

II. Reforms in Related Areas

848. Reforms are required at the various levels to accelerate the implementation of urban development programmes. Concerted efforts are required by all stakeholders to create an environment where a balance is achieved between the private sector's goal to achieve maximum returns and the public sector's goal to achieve social welfare at minimum cost. Such an environment cannot be created over a short span of time and will require sustained effort over a long period. The effort will be worth it as it will reduce the gaps in service delivery and will benefit society in general, and its vulnerable sections in particular. Internal processes are to be improved through the adoption of e-governance systems and the standardization of financial statements. Augmentation of technical and managerial capacity with external handholding support is required. Other reforms are improving monitoring mechanisms and measure services against benchmarks; adopt open data platforms for citizen audits. A strong leadership is required at the city level by empowering mayors and bring all urban planning and administrative bodies in a city under unified command.

Chapter 4. Land Use Planning

849. Town or urban planning in India is relatively new. Planning is done through various types of development plans. One such plan is master plan which is made for urban areas which govern the growth of the urban areas. Other popular plans include Town Planning Scheme. Land use planning is followed for all development purposes which involves assigning the particular activity to a given parcel of land. India being a developing country has its large population engaged in agricultural activity but at the same time with rapid urbanization people are migrating to cities for various reasons like better job opportunities, health and educational facilities, better quality of life and to enjoy urban amenities. Farming in urban areas is not done as it is land intensive and because of this, they rely on the surrounding and the other regions to meet its requirement. The types and nature of activities taking place are vast and needs to be managed. This management of activities takes place by dividing activities into different categories. The activities coming up are on bases of land use of the particular area which is generally given in master plan which governs the development of urban areas. Only the activities which are conforming to the master plan are allowed to take place in that area, so as to avoid conflict in activities and to reduce the negative impacts of different activities. For example, industries are not provided near the residential area to reduce the negative health impact. This management is also done using zoning which involves segregating different activities in different places.

850. The priorities for land use planning and management are set so as to identify and assess 'hot spots' of land degradation so that people derive maximum benefits from the limited resources available. A focus on critical problems on areas where population pressure is causing land degradation and conflicts, and on 'critical interfaces' or boundaries between different land uses, is essential to avoid irreversible damage to the ecosystem.

§1. Consolidation of Holdings

851. The consolidation of agricultural land holdings has been taken up in some States in the name of *chakbandi* by which scattered holdings have been clubbed together. In the States, where it has not been taken up, it requires implementation on a priority basis and speedy completion. The consolidation of holdings in the northern States has shown promising results in terms of per unit area productivity, adoption of production technologies and returns to the farmers.

§2. National Rainfed Area Authority

852. National Rainfed Area Authority (NRAA) under the Ministry of Agriculture and Farmers Welfare, was established as an expert body of Ministry of

Agriculture to provide the much needed knowledge inputs regarding systematic upgradation and management of country's dry land and rainfed agriculture. The mandate of the Authority are:

(i) To prepare a perspective plan, outlining the national strategy and road map for holistic and sustainable development of rainfed farming areas.
(ii) To evolve comprehensive guidelines for all initiatives (schemes, etc.) of different Ministries including externally aided project for promotion of rainfed / dry land farming systems.
(iii) To coordinate and bring convergence within and among agricultural and wasteland development programmes taken up for rainfed areas.
(iv) To identify rainfed areas in different states and prioritize them based on severity, and prepare developmental strategies, including watershed development plans in consultation with states, with a view to nurturing natural resources and promoting welfare of people on a sustainable basis.
(v) To identify gaps in awareness and knowledge level of farmers in rainfed areas.
(vi) To suggest modalities needed to strengthen national and state level institutions/organizations concerned with rainfed/dry land areas; promote inter-institutional/organizational linkages; and establish their responsibility vis-à-vis prioritized watersheds.
(vii) To set the research agenda including a critical appraisal of ongoing programmes and promote diffusion of required knowledge for integrated farming in rainfed areas down to district and field level authorities.
(viii) To evaluate the effectiveness of completed projects, programmes, watersheds, etc., and undertake concurrent evaluation of ongoing programmes.

The NRAA would serve as a knowledge platform and connect research/academic institutions and implementing agencies. It will focus on livelihood opportunities for the landless and marginal farmers in the rainfed area population. One of the mandate given to NRAA is to monitor and evaluate programmes in the rainfed areas, to assess their performance and also to guide the implementation agencies on the short-term and long-term plan with prioritized strategies and suggesting interventions and guidelines which will be beneficial to the rainfed farming community.

§3. Changes in the Land Use

853. Change in land use sometimes in some instances may prove to be environmentally harmful. In the case of *T. Damodar Rao v. Special Officer Municipal Corporation Hyderabad* (AIR 1987 AP 171, 181), it was held that the owners of the area covered can use their property in accordance with law and in conformity with the provisions of development plan. In *M.C. Mehta v. Union of India* ((1998) 7JT 460 (SC)), the court considered harmful effects of transformation of agricultural land to brick kilns and laid down that no brick kiln be permitted if land is less than one hectare.

Chapter 5. National Planning

854. As per Entry No. 18 of the Seventh Schedule (the State List) of the Constitution of India, land including assessment and collection of revenue, maintenance of land records, land management and alienation of revenue, etc., fall under the purview of the State Governments. Thus 'Land' being a State subject falls under the legislative and administrative competence of the States. Land use planning therefore, is the responsibility of the State Governments. As per Article 39 of the Constitution: (1) the ownership and control of the material resources of the country should be so distributed as best to serve the common good; and (2) the operation of the economic system should not result in a concentration of wealth or a means to production to the common detriment. As per Article 243(1) of the Constitution, 'There shall be constituted in every State at the district level a District Planning Committee to consolidate the plans prepared by the Panchayats and the Municipalities in the district and to prepare a draft development plan for the district as a whole.' While the Constitution provided for spatial planning, the national-level activities currently are focused on evolving policies, guidelines and model laws for adoption by the States, disbursing and monitoring assistance/grants/funding, and formulating development plans and policies for UT. In the area of land utilization, there is no single approach currently being followed across the country. Various sectors at central level such as urban, rural, industrial, transport, mining, agriculture follow their own approaches. For example, in the case of rural sector, since nearly 50% of India's population is dependent on agriculture, the sector lays focus on reforms on land acquisition and resettlement and rehabilitation, watershed management and modernization of land records, and there is not yet an approach in place for planning and management of land resources in rural areas.

855. Land use planning and management allows for rational and sustainable use of land catering to various needs, including social, economic, developmental and environmental needs. Proper land use planning based on sound scientific, and technical procedures, and land utilization strategies, supported by participatory approaches empowers people to make decisions on how to appropriately allocate and utilize land and its resources comprehensively and consistently catering to the present and future demands.

Chapter 6. Regional Planning

856. At the time of independence, spatial imbalances and socioeconomic inequalities were prominent in India. To address the adversity, a regional planning and development approach was applied. Numerous regions were identified for development and regional plans were prepared. The Western Ghats regional development programme was a pioneering effort that led to positive outcomes, such as increase in yield of crops due to creation of better irrigation facilities, increase in annual average household incomes, employment generation. Despite the significance, the practice of regional planning became unpopular with time, and the little progress achieved in reducing regional imbalances was adversely affected. Today, in some Indian states, regional (or district) development plans are prepared, however, the implementation and impact of these plans is inadequate. It is important that the prevailing deficiencies in regional development planning are addressed.

857. The fragile ecosystem of the Western Ghats and other hills is a cause for concern. The Western Ghats Development Project and the Hill Area Development Programme are aimed at restoration and preservation of the ecology of identified hill areas. Sustainable use of resources in these areas and preservation of their biodiversity is a prime consideration. The programmes seek to provide a livelihood for the people of the hill areas without disturbing the ecology of the region. Hence projects for the development of minor irrigation, dairy development, animal husbandry, agricultural development, afforestation, non-conventional energy sources and other activities for the generation of employment and enhancing income are being undertaken.

Chapter 7. Local Planning

858. 73rd and 74th Constitutional amendments have brought the third tier of local governance in urban and rural areas. The country currently has twenty-eight states and nine UT which are further divided by districts and blocks. The Eleventh and Twelfth schedule (Article 243G and 243W) of the Constitution explain the jurisdiction of rural (called Panchayats) and Urban Governments. The jurisdiction of rural Government includes agriculture, agricultural extension, rural housing and poverty alleviation programmes; while the jurisdiction of urban Governments includes urban planning including town planning, regulation of land use and construction of buildings, water supply, sanitation and SWM, slum improvement and upgradation and urban poverty alleviation, etc. Urban planning and development administration are commenced under the state legislative background. Local Government or ULB implements the urban development strategies through formation of local plans. ULB is the third tier of governance, directly elected by the people. Planning and development for major cities and urban regions are done by urban/metropolitan/regional development authorities. These authorities are functionaries' institutions under state government. On the local level, the Planning and development department is the body responsible for devising various plans in large cities, as well as for issuing development permits and implementing development among other things. The department is established by State Town Planning Act or individual planning and development department Act. The local planning in rural area is done by Village Panchayats and in urban areas by Nagarpalikas (Municipalities) or such other bodies created locally.

Chapter 8. Municipal Planning

§1. The Master Plan and Development Plan

859. Under Item 8 of the Twelfth Schedule of the Constitution, the responsibility of environmental protection and ecological preservation has been vested with municipalities. Laws have been enacted under the Twelfth Schedule giving power to municipalities in the field of municipal or urban planning; regulation of land use and construction of buildings; planning for economic and social development; slum improvement and upgradation and provision of urban amenities and facilities such as parks, gardens and playgrounds. The local authority prepares a master plan as well as a zonal development plan for a development area. The development area is divided into zones and land use is specified in the master plan. The Zonal Development Plan provides for the allotment of land for parks, open spaces, gardens, etc.

860. Zoning is done to promote local development and for urban planning. Zoning laws deal with the building's construction or for the use of land. In the case of *Delhi Pradesh Citizen Council v. Union of India*, 2006 [131(2006) DLT 189 SC], the Supreme Court outlined the activities which cannot be held in a residential area. Some of which are:

(i) A banquet hall cannot be made in any residential area.
(ii) Any activity that involves the use of hazardous material cannot be carried out in a residential area.
(iii) No liquor shops.
(iv) No Repair shops.

The activities which are allowed in residential areas are hostels, clubs, hospitals, cemetery, vehicle parking. The government also laid down the restriction that the mentioned activities should abide by the noise limit.

In the case, *R.K. Mittal & Ors. v. State of UP & Ors.* [(2012) 2SCC 232-A] the Supreme Court stated that the planning authority has no power to permit a change in the usage of land and if a change occurs in the land use it must comply with the Outside Development Plan. The changes must conform to the Zoning Regulations. This case was related to a residential area. A similar case was, *Dr G.N. Khajuria v. Delhi Development Authority & Ors.* [(1955)5SCC 762], it stated that if a plan was passed to build a public park then only a public park can be built and not a nursery school.

§2. Master Plan of Delhi 2025: Guidelines

861. According to this plan, the population of Delhi will go up to 22 million in the year 2021 from 12.8 million in 2001. This additional population will require 440 km^2 to live on. But even if all the agricultural land and area round the farmhouses is taken over, the total land will not be more than 429 km^2, still short of requirements. This situation will ultimately affect the environment. The future land planning of Delhi has to take this into account.

§3. No Change in the Development Plan

862. The apex courts in a number of decisions have emphasized that once a development plan has been brought into force it must be adhered to and cannot be changed by the implementing authority. The court observed that the protection of the environment is not only the duty of citizens but also an obligation of the State represented by the local bodies (*Damodhar Rao v. S O Municipal Corporation, Hyderabad*, AIR 1954 SC 440).

Chapter 9. Environmentally Sensitive Zones and Industrial Sites

863. Eco-Sensitive Zones (ESZs) or Ecologically Fragile Areas are areas within 10 km around protected areas, National Parks and Wildlife Sanctuaries. ESZs are notified by MoEFCC under EPA 1986. In case of places with sensitive corridors, connectivity and ecologically important patches, crucial for landscape linkage, even area beyond 10 km width can also be included in the ESZ. The aim is to regulate certain activities around National Parks and Wildlife Sanctuaries so as to minimize the negative impacts of such activities on the fragile ecosystem encompassing the protected areas.

864. A number of areas have been declared as ecologically sensitive zones through notification, like the ESZ-Pachmarhi Notification of 1998, the notification to protect and improve the quality of the environment in the Himalayas, notification declaring Dahanu Taluka, District Thane in the State of Maharashtra as an ecologically fragile area. The mapping of environmentally sensitive zones and industrial sites has been carried out. In *Goa Foundation v. Konkan Railway Corporation* (AIR 1992 Bomb. 471), the court upheld developmental activity, that is, building of Konkan railways in public interest even if it may cause some damage to environmentally sensitive zone.

Part IV. Liability Questions

Chapter 1. Liability under Environmental Legislation

865. The basic rules of liability of the State towards pollution emanate from the concept of eminent domain. The individual polluter has liability under specific pollution control legislation, criminal liability under criminal law and liability under tort for nuisance. The rule of eminent domain embodies the principle of control of natural resources in the hands of the State; therefore, the State has a duty to prevent pollution, protect and preserve the ecosystem. This principle is enshrined in the Directive Principles of State Policy provided in the Constitution but not as a part of fundamental rights which are enforceable. However, the apex courts have fixed liability on the State by declaring the right to a healthy environment, a fundamental right under Article 21 of the Constitution of India, considering it as one of the elements of the right to life. The Constitution also imposes a duty on citizens to protect and improve the natural environment (Article 51A(g) of the Constitution). In the process, courts have relaxed the rule of *locus standi* and proof of injury. This relaxation has created a new type of legal action which has come to be known as PIL or SAL as environment affects all. The courts have developed liability parameters on concept of Precautionary Principles, the Polluter Pays, Development Meeting the Need of Present without Compromising the Future needs, Right to Livelihood and Doctrine of Public Trust.

866. General environmental laws such as the EPA of 1986 are enabling in nature and mainly charge a competent authority to provide more specific guidelines and regulations in future. The preamble of the act states that it provides for the protection, conservation, rehabilitation and improvement of the environment, prevention and control of pollution and promotion of sustainable development. The National Appellate Authority Act, 1997 has created appellate authority empowered to hear appeals against orders granting environmental clearance. This Act extends the principle of no fault liability beyond the compensation limits prescribed under the Public Liability Insurance Act, 1991. Earlier the authorities entrusted to enforce under environmental legislation seem to lack the enforcement machinery, and there was an increasing trend that higher courts came down heavily on the enforcing authorities. But after bringing many reform legislation in existence, the situation has improved a lot after the constitution of NGT under NGT Act, 2009.

867. The Supreme Court while describing the scope of the precautionary principle according to which there is a primary duty to take adequate precautions for the prevention of pollution observed that this principle is entrenched in the Constitution as well as in various environmental laws. The Court mentioned that Articles 47, 48-A and 51A(g) of the Constitution, the Water Act of 1974 and the EPA of 1986, where both the precautionary and PPP and special concept of onus of proof were held to be implied.

The courts have successfully isolated specific environmental law principles dealing with liability upon the interpretation of the statutes and the Constitution. Such principles have been traced from the Constitution and are applied even if not explicitly mentioned in the concerned statute.

868. In *Th. Majra Singh v. Indian Oil Corporation* (AIR 1999 J & K 81), the petitioner submitted that the plant in question would be injurious to the health of the residents of the area. It was held that the court could only examine whether the authorities have taken all precautions with a view to seeing that laws dealing with the environment and pollution have been given due care and attention. The court applied the precautionary principle maintaining that it is a part of environmental law of the country.

Chapter 2. Liability under Criminal Law

§1. The Indian Penal Code

869. The IPC, which is a very old legislation, creates various types of liabilities and prescribes punishment for the same. Chapter XIV of IPC deals with offences which affect public health, safety, etc., such as public nuisance, food adulteration, air pollution, water pollution.

I. Public Nuisance

870. A person will be guilty of a public nuisance, if he does any act, or is guilty of an illegal omission, which causes any common injury, danger, or annoyance to the public or to the people in general who dwell or occupy property in the vicinity or which must necessarily cause injury, obstruction, danger or annoyance to persons who may have occasion to use any public right (section 268).

II. Spreading an Infectious Disease

871. In case any person unlawfully or negligently does any act which is, and which he knows or has reason to believe to be, likely to spread the infection of any disease dangerous to life, shall be punished with imprisonment for a term which may extend to six months, or with a fine, or with both (section 269). In case the same act is done malignantly, punishment will be imprisonment for a term which may extend to two years, or with a fine, or with both (section 270).

III. Food Adulteration

872. Adulteration of any article of food or drink, making such article noxious as food or drink, intending to sell such article as food or drink, or knowing it to be likely that the same will be sold as food or drink, is punishable with imprisonment for a term which may extend to six months, or with a fine which may extend to INR 1,000, or with both (section 272).

IV. Corrupting or Fouling Water

873. Voluntarily corrupting or fouling the water of any public spring or reservoir, so as to render it less fit for the purpose for which it is ordinarily used, is punishable with imprisonment for a term which may extend to three months, or with a fine which may extend to INR 500, or with both (section 277).

V. Vitiating the Atmosphere

874. Whoever voluntarily vitiates the atmosphere in any place so as to make it noxious to the health of persons in a general dwelling or carrying on business in the neighbourhood or passing along a public way, shall be punished with fine which may extend to INR 500 (section 278).

VI. Dealing with Poisonous Substances

875. Whoever uses any poisonous substance in a manner so rash or negligent as to endanger human life or to be likely to cause harm or injury to any person, or knowingly or negligently omits to take such precautions with any poisonous substance in his possession sufficient to guard against any probable danger to human life from such poisonous substance, shall be punished with imprisonment for a term which may extend to six months, or with fine which may extend to INR 1,000, or with both (section 284).

VII. Negligently Dealing with Explosives

876. Whoever uses any explosive substance so rashly or negligently as to endanger human life, or to be likely to cause harm or injury to any other person, or knowingly or negligently omits to take such precautions with any explosive substance in his possession sufficient to guard against any probable danger to human life from that substance, shall be punished with imprisonment for a term which may extend to six months, or with fine which may extend to INR 1,000, or with both (section 286).

VIII. Public Nuisance Not Otherwise Covered

877. Section 290 of the IPC is residual in nature and takes care of whatever is not covered under other clauses. According to this section, the commission of a public nuisance, in any case not otherwise punishable by this Code, shall be punished with fine which may extend to INR 200.

Chapter 3. Substantive Rules of Liability

878. Various rules of liability have evolved in pollution-related cases. The most important rule of substantive liability of the State has been that providing a safe environment is a duty of the State and a fundamental right of citizens being an important ingredient of the right to life and personal liberty. Against individual polluters, the principle the 'polluter pays' and 'precautionary principle' have been applied to ascertain responsibility.

The courts have extensively dealt with the questions and issues relating to mining and quarrying, forest conservation, water pollution, gas leak disaster, development projects and the environment, HWs from industries, litigation concerning large dams, protection of livelihood, construction of bridges and environmental degradation. Other active areas were the protection of wetlands, air pollution, water pollution, noise pollution, pollution from animal slaughterhouses, access to environmental information, trade and environment, relocation of the labour force after closure of polluting factories, groundwater management and management of city sewerage system. Out of these developments, a set of liability principles have evolved in the arena of pollution-related jurisprudence.

§1. Deprivation of Life and Personal Liberty

879. Environmental deterioration could endanger the life of present and future generations. Therefore, the right to life has been interpreted in a diversified manner by the courts. It includes, *inter alia*, the right to survive as a species, quality of life, right to live with dignity and the right to a livelihood and has been expressly recognized as a constitutional right.

Article 21 of the Constitution states that 'No person shall be deprived of his life or personal liberty except according to procedure established by law.' The Supreme Court explained that this right has two limbs. First, any law affecting personal liberty should be reasonable, fair and just (*Maneka Gandhi v. Union of India*, AIR 1978 SC 597; *Francis Caralie v. Administrator*, UT of Delhi, AIR 1981 SC 746). Second, the courts recognized several liberties that were not express but implied by Article 21 by reading the directive principal in conjunction with fundamental rights. It is by this second method that the Supreme Court interpreted that the right to life and personal liberty which is a fundamental right includes the right to a clean and wholesome environment as well.

§2. Improvement of Public Health a Primary Duty

880. Article 47 of the Constitution makes it one of the principles of governance that steps are taken for the improvement of public health as a primary duty of the State (*Municipal Counsel Rattam v. Vardhichand*, AIR 1980 SC.1622). In *K. Ramakrishnan v. State of Kerala* (AIR 1999 Kerala 385), the court held that smoking in public places causes positive nuisance. The case concerned the deterioration of the world environment and the duty of the State Government, under Article 21, to ensure a better quality of environment. The Supreme Court ordered the Central Government to show the steps they have taken to achieve this goal through national policy and to restore the quality of environment.

881. In *M.C. Mehta v. Union of India* (1991 AIR SC 813), the Supreme Court dealt with the problem of air pollution caused by motor vehicles operating in Delhi and made several directions to the MoEFCC. This decision indicates that remedies were evolved by the Court itself as those entrusted with the tasks of pollution control failed in their primary duties to control pollution by devising ways and means for the same. However, these remedies seem to encroach and in some cases in fact do encroach on the domain of the executive and legislature.

§3. Duty Not to Dislocate and Disrupt Lifestyles

882. Another expansion of the principle and fundamental right to life is the right to a livelihood (Article 41), otherwise a directive principle of State policy. This extension can check Government actions in relation to an environmental impact that threatens to dislocate and disrupt lifestyles of the people. A strong connection between Article 41 and Article 21 was established in the case of *Olga Tellis v. Bombay Municipal Corporation* (AIR 1986 SC 180). In the Court's view, the following was observed:

> Deprive a person of his right to livelihood and you shall deprive him of his life … Any person who is deprived of his right to livelihood except according to just and fair procedure established by law, can challenge the deprivation as violation of the right to life conferred by Article 21.

§4. Duty of the State and Citizens to Protect and Improve the Environment

883. Article 48A, a Directive Principle of State Policy, provides that 'The State shall endeavour to protect and improve the environment and safeguard the forests and wildlife of the country.' Article 51A(g) imposes a similar responsibility on every citizen 'to protect and improve the natural environment including forests, lakes, rivers and wildlife, and to have compassion for living creatures … '. Therefore, protection of the natural environment and compassion for living creatures has been made the positive fundamental duty of every citizen.

Taking cue from the proactive judgments of the Supreme Court, High Courts have invoked the power of the writ proceedings under Article 226 of the Constitution to deal with environmental degradation as a threat to right to life. In *L.K. Koolwal v. State of Rajasthan* (AIR 1998 Raj 2) while granting standing to the petitioner for challenging the unsatisfactory sanitary conditions in the city of Jaipur, the High Court of Rajasthan held that Article 51A of the Constitution casts a duty of maintaining a clean environment for citizens, it creates a right in his favour to move the court to see that the State performs its duties. In *Attakoya Thangal v. Union of India* (1990 (I) KLT 580) another PIL, the Kerala High Court observed as follows

> Right to life is much more than the right to animal existence and its attributes are manifold, as life itself. A prioritization of human needs and a new value system has been recognized in these areas. The right to sweet water and the right to free air are the attributes of the right to life. These are the basic elements which sustain life itself.

§5. Public Trust Doctrine

884. The application of public trust doctrine to protect and preserve the environment is another aspect of the right to life. This doctrine enunciated by Professor Joseph Sax requires affirmative state action for effective management of resources and empowers citizens to question ineffective management of natural resources, and that the State as trustee of all natural resources, was under a legal duty to protect them. The courts applied the public trust doctrine considering it not only as an international law concept, but also as one, which is well established, in the national legal system of India. In *M.C. Mehta v. Kamal Nath and Others* ((1997) 1 SCC 388), the court added that '[it] would be equally appropriate in controversies involving air pollution, the dissemination of pesticides, the location of rights of ways for utilities, and strip mining of wetland falling on private lands in a state where governmental permits are required'. In both *M.I. Builders Pvt. Ltd* (*M.I. Builders Pvt. Ltd v. Radhey Shyam Sahu* AIR 1999 SC 2468) and *Th. Majra Singh* (*Th. Majra Singh v. Indian Oil Corporation* AIR 1999 J&K 81), the court reconfirmed that the public trust doctrine 'has grown from Article 21 of the Constitution and has become part of the Indian legal thought process for quite a long time'.

885. In *Bakir Ali Rangwala v. State of M.P. through Principal Secretary & Ors.* [Original Application No. 11/2022 (CZ)], the NGT held that 'Article 21 of the Constitution of India protects not only the human rights but also casts an obligation on human beings to protect and preserve a specie becoming extinct, conservation and protection of environment is an inseparable part of right to life. In *M. C. Mehta v. Kamal Nath and Others* (1997) 1 SCC 388, the Court enunciated the doctrine of "public trust", the thrust of that theory is that certain common properties such as rivers, seashores, forests and the air are held by the Government in trusteeship for the free and unimpeded use of the general public. The resources like air, sea, waters and the forests have such a great importance to the people as a whole, that it would be totally unjustified to make them a subject of private ownership. The State, as a custodian of the natural resources, has a duty to maintain them not merely for the benefit of the public, but for the best interest of flora and fauna, wildlife and so on. The doctrine of 'public trust' has to be addressed in that perspective.'

§6. Duty to Develop Without Causing Pollution

886. Three basic elements of implementing sustainable development are equitable utilization of natural resources by the State, economic development of the people without causing pollution and the right of the people to development. The Supreme Court of India mentioned the principle of sustainable development and tried to balance the social, economic and ecological aspects. It was a challenge to deal with polluting industries such as the leather factories because of conflict between economic benefits from the industry and harm caused by pollution (*Vellore Citizen Welfare Forum* case, AIR 1996 SC 2715). The court concluded that although the industry generates foreign exchange and provides employment to a large number of people, industry has 'no right to destroy the ecology, degrade the environment and pose a health hazard'.

887. In *People United For Better Living in Calcutta – Public and Another v. State of West Bengal and Others* (AIR 1993 Cal. 215), the petition was filed to prevent encroachment of wetlands in Calcutta. The Calcutta High Court opined and observed that: 'There should be a proper balance between the protection of the environment and the development process: the society shall have to prosper, but not at the cost of the environment and in the similar vein, the environment shall have to be protected but not at the cost of the development of the society.'

§7. Duty to Take Positive Measures

888. The right to life guaranteed by Article 21 of the Constitution includes in its ambit the right of enjoyment of pollution-free water and air for full enjoyment of life by the citizen. The right to a wholesome environment has been recognized as part of the fundamental right to life. The municipalities and governmental agencies entrusted with the tasks of dealing with pollution could no longer rest content with unimplemented measures for the abatement and prevention of pollution. They may be compelled to take positive measures to improve the environment, and paucity of funds cannot be taken as a plea to run away from their principal and basic duty in this respect (*Subhash Kumar v. State of Bihar*, AIR 1991, SC 420).

§8. Precautionary Principle

889. The court laid down the meaning of the precautionary principle (PP) in *Vellore Citizen's Welfare Forum* ((1996) 5 SCC 647 at 658). It stated that environmental measures, adopted by the State Government and the statutory authorities, must *anticipate, prevent and attack* the causes of environmental degradation. The court followed the definition provided in the Rio Declaration. It was observed that where there are threats of serious and irreversible damage, lack of scientific certainty should not be used as a reason for postponing measures to prevent environmental degradation.

Part III. Spatial Planning

Chapter 1. Zoning and Land Use Planning

The court again followed the 'anticipate, prevent and attack' approach in the *M.C. Mehta* case wherein the precautionary principle was invoked to prevent construction within 1 km of two lakes located near Delhi, and the principle was accepted as a part of the law of the land.

890. In the (*Taj Trapezium* case (1997) 2 SCC 353), the Supreme Court ordered a number of industries in the area surrounding the Taj Mahal to relocate or introduce pollution abatement measures in order to protect the Taj from deterioration and damage. Following the decision of *Vellore Citizen's* case and *Indian Council for Enviro-Legal Action* case *(Vellore Citizen's Welfare Forum* (1996) 5 SCC 647; *Indian Council for Enviro-Legal Action v. Union of India* (1996) 3 SCC at 247), the Supreme Court described the PP principle as environmental measures which must 'anticipate, prevent and attack' the causes of environmental degradation.

891. In the *S. Jagannath* case (*S. Jagannath v. Union of India and others* (1997) 2 SCC 87), the precautionary approach was relied on to curtail commercial shrimp farming in India's coastal areas. The commercial users of agriculture lands and salt farms were discharging highly polluting effluents and causing pollution of water. Normal traditional life and vocational activities of the local population of the coastal areas were being seriously hampered.

892. An application of the PP is found in the *Suo Motu Proceedings in Re: Delhi Transport Department* ((1998) 9 SCC 250) where the Supreme Court dealt with air pollution in New Delhi. In the Supreme Court's view, the precautionary principle has to be followed by State governments in controlling pollution.

893. In *A.P. Pollution Control Board v. Prof. M.V. Nayudu (retd.)* (AIR 1999 SC 812) where the case dealt with the setting up of an industry for the production of castor oil derivatives, the Supreme Court reaffirmed the customary status of the precautionary principle. The PCB of Andhra Pradesh brought the case against an individual and added that the principle is entrenched in the Constitution as well as in various environmental laws. The court accepted the observation supplied by the *Vellore* case that the precautionary principle is a part of customary international law, but it is still evolving and applies according to the situation and circumstances of each case. The burden of proof in environmental cases is reversed and the 'burden as to the absence of injurious effect of the proposed action is placed on those who want to change the *status quo*'. The person who wants to maintain status quo by maintaining a less polluted state should not carry the burden of proof and the party who wants to alter it by carrying on some activity must bear this burden (*See* C.M. Jariwala 'Complex Enviro-Techno Science Issues: Judicial Direction, 42 *Journal of Indian Law Institute* (JILI) 29 January–March 2000)'.

894. In the Research Foundation (*Research Foundation for Science, Technology and Natural Resource Policy v. Union of India* AIR 2012 SC 2627) case, the honourable Supreme Court stated that ship breaking cannot be allowed unless the company adheres to the precautionary principle. The Supreme Court in 'Court on It's Own Motion' case (*Court on Its Own Motion v. Union of India* (2012) 12 SCC

497) pointed out that precautionary principle belongs to the core value of Article 21 of the Constitution. In Odisha Mining case (*Orissa Mining Corporation Ltd. v. Ministry of Environment and Forest* (2013) 6 SCC 476), the FAC represented the apex court that precautionary principle is the only principle available to check the irreversible damage to the environment. In G. Sundarrajan case (*G. Sundarrajan v. Union of India* (2013) 6 SCC 620) the Supreme Court held that precautionary principle is applicable to prevent the future environmental degradation. In the State of Tamil Nadu case (*State of Tamil Nadu v. State of Kerala* AIR 2014 SC 2407) held that the application of precautionary principle means there must be scientific uncertainty regarding irreversible damage to the environment, therefore, competent public authority must anticipate and prevent such damage by attacking the cause for such environmental damage.

I. A Land Mark Judgment

895. In the case of *T.N. Godavarman Thirumulpad v. Union of India* (2022 Live Law (SC) 467), the Supreme Court delivered a landmark judgment on the precautionary principle. In this case, the clearance for doubling the railway line between Castlerock (Karnataka) and Kulem (Goa), was revoked by laying emphasis on the principle of sustainable development and the precautionary principle. The proposed railway line passed through protected and non-protected forests and a major tiger corridor. The petitioner's claim was based on the lack of a comprehensive impact assessment by NBWL before granting clearance to the project. They also relied on the Central Empowered Committee's (CEC) detailed impact study, which underscored the adverse impacts of the project on the surrounding biodiversity. However, Rail Vikas Nigam Limited (RVNL), the project proponent, submitted that the doubling of the railway line will cater to the projected increase in traffic from Karnataka to Goa. It highlighted that a comprehensive biodiversity and environmental assessment of the project had been undertaken by the Indian Institute of Science, Bengaluru. Furthermore, it submitted that state-of-the-art mitigation measures would be undertaken to prevent damage to the environment and that under-bridges and over-bridges would be constructed to ensure safety of animals crossing the railway lines.

A. *Judicial Background of Precautionary Principle*

896. The court's interpretation and application of the precautionary principle in this case amalgamates spread-out jurisprudence on the principle, reconciles conflicting positions, and streamlines its application. Here, it is crucial to understand the judicial development of the principle. In 1996, for the *Vellore Citizens v. Union of India* case (regarding the pollution caused by discharge of untreated effluents in Tamil Nadu), the Supreme Court imported the principle into Indian environmental jurisprudence for the first time. It stated that where there exists a threat of serious or irreversible damage to the environment, lack of scientific evidence should not preclude regulatory measures to protect environment and human health. The burden of proof to prove that the activity is environmentally harmless lies on the proponent. Thus, as per the Court, the principle is a tool to regulate situations of scientific uncertainty. However, in this case, there was no supervening scientific uncertainty with respect to the impacts of the impugned project, yet the Court applied the principle. Following suit, in the *A.P. Pollution Control Board v. Prof M.V. Nayudu* case (regarding the establishment of an industry), the adverse impacts of the project were certain, the Court applied the precautionary principle to prevent its establishment. In many cases that followed, the principle was applied inconsistently, regardless of the existence of a state of scientific uncertainty. Therefore, the judicial application of the principle over decades has blurred the boundaries between prevention and precaution.

B. Supervening Scientific Uncertainty

897. Thus T.*N. Godavarman* case is a forward move in streamlining the interpretation and application of the precautionary principle. A primary reason for this is the clarification that the principle is 'based on scientific uncertainty'. In other words, it comes into operation when there is supervening scientific uncertainty about the impacts of the project on the environment. Applying this jurisprudence, the Supreme Court launched an enquiry into the impacts of the impugned project and established that there is prevailing scientific uncertainty. In doing so, it emphasized that RVNL's impact assessment was cursory and incomprehensive. Furthermore, it considered CEC's report which highlighted that the state-of-the art mitigative measures proposed by RVNL, could not possibly be implemented. The court interpreted this contradiction and held that the mitigation measures are 'not clear'. The court has successfully dispelled the ambiguity surrounding the principle's application. In this case the argument that the project had already attracted significant economic investment, did not steer the court's decision. This is in a stark contrast to the decision in the case of *Narmada Bachao Andolan v. Union of India* wherein, *inter alia*, major economic investment made in the dam, was a factor considered by the court while allowing its expansion, despite the absence of a comprehensive impact assessment.

C. Assessing the Proportionality

898. The court did not explicitly refer to the doctrine but engaged in a proportionality assessment while revoking the clearance. It analysed the environmental risks posed by the project (although uncertain) against the projected economic growth. Employing an ecocentric approach, it said that environmental protection includes protection of the environment for its own sake. The environmental risks include threats to non-human environment – the fact that human environment is unaffected by such threats does not dilute the 'value' associated with such risk. Thereafter, considering the contentious nature of the projected growth, the court revoked the clearance until further comprehensive studies were conducted. The court even allowed the project proponent to submit a fresh proposal. A detailed proportionality assessment of the like, considering every economic and environmental interest, is a unique and notable precedent. Particularly, the court's clear recognition of the intrinsic value of the non-human environment is a significant step forward in mainstreaming ecocentrism. Where there is doubt, environmental interests shall take precedence over economic interests. A possible implication of this jurisprudence is that any protectionist measures could be taken regardless of the economic consequences.

§9. Polluter Pays Principle

899. The National Environmental Policy 2006 identifies and indicates that there is a need to move to a strong civil liability mechanism which is based on the polluter pay principle instead of a criminal penalty mechanism. In the case of *Vellore Citizen Forum v. Union of India* (AIR 1996 SC 2715) 'polluter pay' principle was applied. In this case, a PIL was filed by the petitioners on the grounds that the tanneries and other industries were discharging untreated effluents into the River Palar in Tamil Nadu. 35,000 hectares of agricultural land has become either totally or partially unfit for cultivation according to Tamil Nadu Agricultural University Research Centre. It was held that the industries have to pay compensation to the villagers for the damage caused by them and also compensate for the restoration of the environment.

900. The courts adopted an innovative approach by propounding the PPP as a part of the national legal system (*Indian Council for Enviro-Legal Action v. Union of India* (1996) 3 SCC 247). In *Vellore Citizen's Welfare Forum* (AIR 1996 SC 2715) dealing with the environmental pollution and health hazard caused by the tanneries, the court affirmed the PPP as a rule of customary international law. In *M.C. Mehta v. Kamal Nath and Others* ((1997) 1 SCC 414), the same view was adopted. It also endorsed the absolute liability regime laid down in the *H-Acid* decision as an integral component of the PPP.

901. The PPP is one of the three key principles upon which the NGT relies for delivering decisions. As per section 20 of the NGT Act, 2010, while passing any order, decision or award, the Tribunal shall apply three core principles, including the 'principles of sustainable development, precautionary principle, and the polluter pays principle'. Adhering to these principles has been essentially underscored to ensure that the decisions of the Tribunal not only take care of the current environmental nuisance but also try to ensure a sustainable future. The PPP is important for determining punitive costs of damages from environmental violations caused by industries or individuals. The principle is applied to ensure that the costs of mitigating environmental damage are internalized by the industry or the individual found liable, and not externalized. The principle has the potential to play an important role in taking environmental concerns seriously and shaping the performance of industries and make them adopt environmentally responsible practices.

902. In the Vellore decision, the cost of remediation was transferred from the government to the polluting industries. It observed that 'Remediation of the damaged environment is part of the process of 'Sustainable Development' and as such the polluter is liable to pay the cost to the individual sufferers as well as the cost of reversing the damaged ecology.' The court applied the PPP in cases related to accidental pollution and environmental damage caused by industrial waste and ordered compensation for the harm caused as well as the obligation to pay for the preventive control.

In *M.C. Mehta (Tanneries) v. Union of India and Others* ((1997) 2 SCC 411), the Supreme Court ordered that the one who pollutes the environment must pay to reverse the damage caused by his acts. The court ordered the unconditional closure of the tanneries and payment of compensation by them for reversing the damage and for rights and benefits to be made available by them to their workmen. The Supreme Court has held that PPP envisages 'precautionary protection against environmental hazards by avoiding or reducing environmental risk before specific harm is expected'. Thus it has become a part of the principle of sustainable development (*Research Foundation for Science (18) v. Union of India* (2005) 13 SCC 186; also see, *Tirupur Dyeing Factory Owners Association v. Noyal River Ayacutdars Protection Assn* (2009) 9 SCC 737; AIR 2010 SC, 3645).

§10. Rule of Absolute Liability

903. If an industry or enterprise is engaged in some inherently dangerous activity and that activity is capable of causing catastrophic damage then the industry officials are absolutely liable to pay compensation to the aggrieved party or parties. It cannot be pleaded that all safety measures were taken care and that there was negligence on the part of industry. They will not be allowed any exceptions and cannot put up any defence like that of 'Act of God' or 'Act of Stranger. This is doctrine of absolute liability whereas in strict liability, the defendant can plead for exceptions. So the Doctrine of Absolute Liability prevents the defendants from taking any defence. The enterprise will be held responsible for all possible damages or consequences resulting from the activity. The element of escape which is an essential in strict liability may be ignored here as this restricts the application of this Doctrine as often incidents may arise where escape of the dangerous thing like poisonous fumes may not take place outside the industry premises but may damage the workers inside. In this case, the workers' right to compensation will not be ignored. Therefore, the extent of this principle is to be applied in a wider context ruling out the element of escape.

904. In *M.C. Mehta v. Union of India* (A.I.R. 1987 S.C. 1086) the Supreme Court was dealing with claims of leakage of oleum gas from one unit In Delhi. Due to this leakage, one advocate and several others had died. An action was brought against the industry through a writ petition under Article 32 of the Constitution by way of a PIL. The judges in this case refused to follow the Strict Liability Principle set by the English Laws and came up with the Doctrine of Absolute Liability. The court then directed the organizations who had filed the petitions to file suits against the industry in appropriate courts within a span of two months to demand compensation on behalf of the aggrieved victims.

905. In Bhopal Gas Tragedy (*Union Carbide Corporation v. Union of India* (1991) 4 SCC 548), there was leakage of methyl-iso-cyanide (MIC) poisonous gas from the Union Carbide factory in Bhopal which led to a major disaster and over three thousand people lost their lives. The effects were so grave that children in those areas are born with deformities even today. The Court applying the principle of 'Absolute Liability' held the company liable and ordered it to pay compensation to the victims.

906. In *Indian Council for Enviro-legal Action v. Union of India*, AIR 1996 SC 1446, a PIL was filed under Article 32 of the Constitution voiced protests of the petitioners over the presence of industries that was causing large-scale environmental pollution and endangering the lives of the villagers who resided in the vicinity of the industries. The court upheld the Doctrine of Absolute Liability stating that the polluted environment must be restored to a pollution-free one conducive for healthy living by utilizing antipollution scientific appliances. The expenditure so incurred in this process must be paid by the industries even if their properties need to be attached for this purpose. The industries were made absolutely liable for paying monetary damages for restoration of the environment.

Chapter 4. Duty to Preserve for Future Generations

907. The duty to preserve and protect the environment is a duty that is owed not merely to present but extends also to future generations. Mankind consist of the human race as it exists today and also as it will in the future. The necessity of preserving the environment for the present generation as well as for future generations has been expounded and accepted. For example, in the cases dealing with reserved forests, the court decided the cases based on the need of the present generation and rational use of natural resources. The notion of equity has been connected with the concept of public trust and depended on the people's right to enjoy a healthy environment.

The *Vellore Citizens' Welfare Forum* (*Vellore Citizens' Welfare Forum v. Union of India* (1996) 5 SCC 647 658 paragraphs 11–13) recites the Brundtland Commission definition of sustainable development 'which meets the needs of the present without compromising the ability of the future generations to meet their own needs'. In *People United for Better Living in Calcutta v. State of West Bengal* (AIR 1993 Cal 215 at 227), it was stated that: 'The present day society has a responsibility towards posterity for their proper growth and development so as to allow posterity to breathe normally and live in a cleaner environment and have consequent fuller development.'

Chapter 5. Balance Between Development, Planning and Environment

908. In the *Goa Foundation and another v. Konkan Railway Corporation* (AIR 1992 Bom 471), the court held that no development is possible without some adverse effect upon the ecology and environment, but the project utility cannot be abandoned and it is necessary to adjust the interests of the people as well as to maintain the environment. A balance has to be struck between the two interests, and this exercise must be left to the persons who are familiar and specialized in this field. It gave priority to sustainable use of natural resources and to a right to a healthy environment for the present, and to a certain extent, to future generations. The national environmental policy and legislation reflect the concern for a balance between development, planning and the environment.

With respect to large projects, the court has restrained itself from going into technical and scientific aspects. In matters and projects which involve intricate questions involving science and engineering, the Supreme Court observed that it does not possess the requisite expertise to deal with it (*Tehri Bandh Virodhi Sangharsh Samiti in the State of U.P. and others* (1990) (2) scale 1003).

Part V. Juridical Actions of Individuals

Chapter 1. Civil Action

909. There are various ways and categories of judicial actions and corresponding legal remedies available to individual citizens. There can be action under constitutional provisions, judicial review of administrative actions, civil litigation, criminal prosecution, private or citizen suits under environmental statutes and through administrative action.

910. Pollution is a civil wrong. By its very nature, it is a tort committed against the community as a whole. A person, therefore, who is guilty of causing pollution has to pay damages in the form of compensation for restoration of environment and ecology (*M.C. Mehta v. Kamal Nath* (2000) 6 SCC 213). Civil actions against environmental problems in the common law system are based on the law of tort. The torts related to environmental pollution liability are negligence, trespass, nuisance and the rule of strict liability as laid down in *Rylands v. Fletcher*. Under this, a person who has suffered personal injury or damage to property can sue for damages. But such damage is required to be proved; otherwise, the action will fail. However, an intentional trespass is actionable per se that is, without any proof of damage. Besides the damages, another remedy available under the law of torts is injunction.

§1. Private and Public Nuisance

911. There can be two types of nuisance, one affecting private individuals, which can be termed as private nuisance and the other affecting the public and termed as public nuisance. The common law actions of nuisance, negligence and the rule in *Rylands v. Fletcher* are resorted to by civil litigants in the matter of individual disputes relating to environmental matters. A five judge Constitution Bench of the Supreme Court of India has ruled that industries which are engaged in inherently dangerous and hazardous business cannot rely on the exceptions to the rule in *Rylands*, and that they are strictly and absolutely liable to compensate for the damage caused by them.

Chapter 2. The Criminal Procedure Code

912. Sections 133 and 144 of the CrPC prescribe the procedure for handling public nuisance.

§1. Powers of Magistrates to Remove Obstruction or Nuisance

913. A District Magistrate or a Subdivisional Magistrate or any other Executive Magistrate empowered in this behalf by the State Government, on receiving the report of a police officer or other information and on taking such evidence (if any) as he thinks fit, considers the following:

(a) that any unlawful obstruction or nuisance should be removed from any public place or from any way, river or channel which is or may be lawfully used by the public; or
(b) that the conduct of any trade or occupation, or the keeping of any goods or merchandise, is injurious to the health or physical comfort of the community, and that in consequence such trade or occupation should be prohibited or regulated or such goods or merchandise should be removed or the keeping thereof regulated; or
(c) that the construction of any building, or the disposal of any substance, as is likely to occasion conflagration or explosion, should be prevented or stopped; or
(d) that any dangerous animal should be destroyed, confined or otherwise disposed of.
    such magistrate may make a conditional order requiring the person causing such obstruction or nuisance, or carrying on such trade or occupation, or keeping any such goods or merchandise, or owing, possessing or controlling such building, tent, structure, substance, tank, well or excavation; or owing or possessing such animal or tree, within a time to be fixed in order to take the following actions;
(e) to remove such obstruction or nuisance; or
(f) to desist from carrying on, or to remove or regulate in such manner as may be directed, such trade or occupation, or to remove such goods or merchandise, or to regulate the keeping thereof in such manner as may be directed; or
(g) to remove, repair or support such building, tent or structure, or to remove or support such trees; or
(h) to destroy, confine or dispose of such dangerous animal in the manner provided in the said order.

If he objects so to do, to appear before himself or some other Executive Magistrate subordinate to him at a time and place to be fixed by the order, and show cause, in the manner hereinafter provided, why the order should not be made absolute.

Any order duly made by a magistrate under this section shall not be called in question in any Civil Court.

§2. Powers to Direct and Abstain

914. The order passed by the magistrate has to be served on the person against whom such order has been passed (section 134). On service, the order is to be complied with (section 135); otherwise, a penalty will be imposed as prescribed under section 188 of the IPC (section 136). The magistrate is authorized to issue injunctions in cases where urgent action and measures are required and necessary (section 142 of the CRPC). It goes to the extent that in urgent cases of nuisance or apprehended danger, the magistrate can issue an order directing to do or abstain from doing something as per the provisions of section 144 of the CrPC, the full text of which is given below:

144.

(1) In cases where, in the opinion of a District Magistrate, a Sub-divisional Magistrate or any other Executive Magistrate specially empowered by the State Government in this behalf, there is sufficient ground for proceeding under this section and immediate prevention or speedy remedy is desirable, such Magistrate may, by a written order stating the material facts of the case and served in the manner provided by Section 134, direct any person to abstain from a certain act or to take certain order with respect to certain property in his possession or under his management, if such Magistrate considers that such direction is likely to prevent, or tends to prevent obstruction, annoyance or injury to any person lawfully employed, or danger to human life, health or safety, or a disturbance of the public tranquillity, or a riot, or an affray.

(2) An order under this Section may, in cases of emergency or in cases where the circumstances do not admit of the serving in due time of a notice upon the person against whom the order is directed, be passed *ex-parte*.

(3) An order under this Section may be directed to a particular individual, or to persons residing in a particular place, or to the public generally when frequenting or visiting a particular place or area.

(4) No order under this Section shall remain in force for more than two months from the making thereof:

Provided that, if the State Government considers it necessary so to do for preventing danger to human life, health or safety or for preventing a riot or any affray, it may, by notification, direct that an order made by a Magistrate under this Section shall remain in force for such further period not exceeding six months from the date on which the order made by the Magistrate would have, but for such order, expired, as it may specify in the said notification:

(5) Any Magistrate may, either on his own motion or on the application of any person aggrieved, rescind or alter any order made under this Section, by himself or any Magistrate subordinate to him or by his predecessor-in-office.

(6) The State Government may, either on its own motion or on the application of any person aggrieved, rescind or alter any order made by it under the proviso to Sub-Section (4).

(7) Where an application under Sub-Section (5) or Sub-Section (6) is received, the Magistrate, or the State Government, as the case may be, shall afford to the applicant an early opportunity of appearing before him or it, either in person or by pleader and showing cause against the order; and if the Magistrate or the State Government, as the case may be, rejects the application wholly or in part, he or it shall record in writing the reasons for so doing.

915. The public nuisances can be prevented by filing a case before the magistrate by passing an injunction order. However, these proceedings are not punitive but remedial. The (*Supreme Court of India in Suhelkhan Khudyarkhan v. State of Maharashtra* (2009) 5 SCC 586). The condition precedent for application of section 133 CrPC is that the conduct of trade must be injurious to the health or physical comfort of the community. There must be imminent danger to health or physical comfort of the community in the locality in which trade or occupation is conducted. It is not intended to settle private disputes. The remedies for private nuisance under the EPA are as follows:

(1) abatement;
(2) damages; and
(3) injunction.

916. In order to obtain an injunction, it is to be shown that the injury complained of as present or impending is such as by reason of its gravity, or its permanent character, or both, cannot be adequately compensated in damages and has to be prevented. There can be another category of actionable future nuisance when the likely act of the defendant is inherently dangerous or injurious such as opening a shop dealing with highly inflammable products in the midst of a residential locality. It has been held that in spite of the provisions in the Water and Air Acts, section 133 CrPC can be called in aid to remove public nuisance and thus, avoid hardship to the general public (State of *M.P v. Kedia Leather and Liquor Ltd.* (2003) 7 SCC, 389).

§3. Preventive Powers under the Police Act of 1861

917. Section 30 of the Police Act of 1861 provides that the District Superintendent of Police may prescribe routes for a procession. The persons convening any assembly shall apply for a licence if such assembly if uncontrolled, may likely cause a breach of the peace. Music may be regulated on the streets on the occasion of festivals and ceremonies.

The police has been conferred power of arrest (section 34 of the Police Act) *inter alia*, for the following:

(a) Obstructing passengers and causing inconvenience or danger to the public.
(b) Throwing of dirt on streets.
(c) Negligence in protecting dangerous places.

Chapter 3. Actions Prescribed under Specific Legislation

918. Under the Air (Prevention and Control of Pollution) Act of 1981, the Water (Prevention and Control of Pollution) Act of 1974 and the Environment (Protection) Act of 1986, the court can take cognizance of the offences on a complaint by the PCBs or its authorized officers. In addition to the State machinery, a private individual, after giving notice to the Board can institute proceedings against an offender who violates the penal provisions and prosecute for offences under these acts.

The CPC 1973 also allows two or more private citizens to file a suit for public nuisance, with the leave of the court, even though they have not suffered any special damage. Section 133 of the Code of Criminal Procedure empowers the executive magistrate to make an order for the removal of a nuisance. The Supreme Court in the *Ratlam Municipality* case held that any citizen can initiate proceedings under the above provision, if it is found that the municipal authorities are not discharging their statutory duty of providing drainage and other sanitary facilities.

Chapter 4. Access of Citizens to Apex Courts

919. To weed out the non-serious litigant, as a general rule, only the aggrieved party is allowed to move the court which is called *locus standi*. The concept of *locus standi* has an important role in private law litigation, but with the growth of public law, the scope of environmental litigation has widened, especially in the judicial review of actions impacting on the environment. Since environmental harm is a common concern for all people, this is to be checked as allowing deterioration to continue unabated is not in the public interest. Thus, there is a need to recognize someone who comes forward on behalf of the people some of whom may not have access to higher judiciary because of paucity of resources. Groups or associations of people committed to protecting the environment can take up the matter before the court. In this way, court was able to look at the matter from the point of an environmental problem to be solved rather than a dispute between contesting parties. Most of these cases have been brought under Article 226 of the Constitution in the High Courts and under Article 32 in the Supreme Court.

The court has thrown open its doors to citizens out of concern for social causes when the executive and legislature lag behind. The development of PIL is a judicial response to social necessities, in the background of inability of the executive and legislature to take care and provide a healthy environment. However, the orders passed by the courts in PIL have been a moving force for quick administrative action and may even evoke a political process in conjunction with the public opinion generated. This can ultimately lead to corrective measures through the legislative process.

920. In *Subhash Kumar v. State of Bihar* (AIR 1991 SC 420), it was held that the 'Right to life is a fundamental right under Article 21 of the Constitution and it includes right of enjoyment of pollution-free water and air for full enjoyment of life.' It further ruled that 'if anything endangers or impairs that quality of life, in derogation of laws, a citizen has a right to have recourse to Article 32 of the Constitution for removing the pollution of water or air which may be detrimental to the quality of life'. Under Article 32, the Supreme Court can issue writs for enforcement of fundamental rights of the citizens and can be invoked by a citizen against the State.

Delay and laches on the part of the petitioner may defeat the PIL. In *Narmada Bachao Andolan v. Union of India*, the Supreme Court Observed: 'just because a petition is termed as PIL does not mean that ordinary principles applicable to litigation will not apply. Laches is one of them. We cannot disturb a third party interest created on account delay. Even otherwise also why should the court come to the rescue of a person who is not vigilant in his right'. Further, with respect to litigant of doubtful integrity bringing PIL, the Supreme Court observed that 'howsoever genuine a case brought before a court by a PIL be, the court has to decline its examination at the behest of the person who, in fact, is not a public interest litigant and whose bonafides and credentials are in doubt.' (*T.N. Godavarman Thirumulpad (98) v. Union of India* (2006) 5 SCC 28; AIR 2006 SC 1774).

Chapter 5. Administrative Remedies

§1. Administrative Bodies

921. There are a number of administrative bodies to deal with pollution matters. These bodies have been created under various enactments and by the apex courts for certain specific purposes. The CPCB, the SPCB and the PCC are responsible for implementing the legislation relating to prevention and control of pollution. These bodies also make rules and regulations which prescribe the standards for emissions and effluents of air and water pollutants and noise levels. The CPCB provides technical services to the ministry for implementing the provisions of the Environment (Protection) Act of 1986. There is the NEAA established under the NEAA Act of 1997 (22 of 1997) which hears appeals with respect to the restriction of areas in which any industrial activity shall not be carried out or shall be carried out.

§2. The Committees

922. The Supreme Court not being satisfied with the working of the authorities created under the pollution control laws, constituted committees from time to time to deal with specific environmental issues. A Supreme Court Monitoring Committee oversees the quarrying and mining operations in the Doon Valley whereas the related cases before the Supreme Court have been disposed of. The Supreme Court in *Andhra Pradesh Pollution Control Board v. Professor MV Nayudu* (AIR 1999 SC 812) emphasized the importance of the judicial approach by observing 'Of paramount importance in the establishment of environmental courts, authorities and tribunals is the need for providing adequate judicial and scientific input rather than leave complicated disputes regarding environmental pollution to officers drawn only from the executives.'

923. Despite the existence of these bodies, water is dirty, air is foul and all the concerned citizens are worried as to where it will lead. The PCBs in the country charged with the responsibility of controlling and monitoring pollution could not overcome their own problems relating to men, money and infrastructure so as to perform their functions in an efficient and effective manner. Compliance remains poor in some States. In practice, the boards have found it difficult to move effectively against offenders. Virtually nothing can be done without court intervention in some form or another, by one party or the other.

§3. Administrative Action and Judiciary

924. Courts generally avoid upsetting the administrative decisions so as to maintain the doctrine of separation of powers. As the Government began to involve itself in non-traditional fields, it began to affect the rights of the common man resulting in an unprecedented growth of public law litigation. This necessarily involves the challenge of Government decisions and policies.

A liberal rule of *locus standi* in judicial review makes all administrative sectors of the executive open to judicial scrutiny. There was also a feeling that the fear that the judiciary is constantly looking over their shoulders will make civil servants nervous and defensive in their actions and less willing to exercise discretion. In fact in some instances, this has happened or affected the functioning of the executive. In planning and development-related matters, judicial review may jeopardize and bring the entire process to a grinding halt. Since judicial review touches on the areas of policy of the Government, it is likely to be used and sometimes used as a tool in the hands of the parties in opposition to embarrass the Government.

Therefore, judicial review cannot be viewed as a panacea for all the problems of pollution. The threat of action for contempt of court may force the administration to implement orders passed by the court, but frequent intervention by the courts is likely to lead to demoralization of the administration. Further, it brings about a tendency for the judiciary to consider itself a 'super executive', upsetting the balance of constitutional distribution of powers. But in cases where the political and administrative processes fail to deliver goods, citizens look up to the courts for redressing grievances. Hence, the judiciary is justified in intervening and waking up the executive.

§4. Hierarchical Relationship

925. The authorities created under various environmental legislation such as the CPCB, SPCB, PCC lay down the pollution standards and parameters in their respective sphere of activity. These authorities are charged with the function of issuing consent orders or authorizations and have also to oversee their implementation. The directions given by the Central Government are binding on the CPCB. The directions of the CPCB and State Government are binding on the SPCB. In the event of any inconsistency with respect to direction issued by the CPCB and State Government, the matter can be referred to the Central Government.

The CPCB can make an application to court for restraining apprehended pollution and to give directions to any person, officer or authority. Besides, any consent order can be challenged in the National Environment Appellate Tribunal. Matters relating to conservation of the environment can be taken to the court as is evident from certain provisions of specific laws in relation to the environment, under the CrPC and CPC. The Supreme Court and High Courts have allowed the taking up of matters related to the environment as an infringement of fundamental rights and under PIL.

§5. Types of Recourse Bodies

926. The recourse bodies for redressal of environment-related wrongs are administrative, quasi-judicial and judicial in nature. The bodies charged with the responsibility of issuing consent and granting approval discharge their function either independently or in consultation with the MoEFCC.

I. Central Pollution Control Board

927. The CPCB is an autonomous body of the ministry set up in September 1974, under the provisions of the Water (Prevention and Control of Pollution) Act of 1974 and later was entrusted to oversee air pollution. It coordinates the activities of the SPCBs and PCCs and also advises the Central Government on all matters concerning the prevention and control of environmental pollution.

II. State PCBs

928. The Water Act of 1974 institutionalized the pollution control machinery by establishing the SPCBs which were later on also authorized under the Air Act to look after air pollution. Now in every State there are State PCBs. The SPCBs achieve their objectives of pollution control and protection of the environment through the following three instruments:

(1) consent to establish producing units (NOC);
(2) consent to operate; and
(3) setting standards for air and water pollution.

The specific functions of the SPCBs include the following:

(a) formulation of preventive measures;
(b) laying down standards;
(c) technology development which is environment friendly;
(d) control of pollution through inspection of industrial units;
(e) regulation of location of industries;
(f) disposal of HWs; and
(g) collection and dissemination of information on the prevention and control of pollution.

929. The SPCBs are very important bodies in the scheme of implementation of pollution control laws. The functioning of SPCBs has been reviewed by various committees and study groups. These studies highlight the need for adequate financial backing. Through these studies, it has become clear that SPCBs have an inherently weak setup, and they have a large number of part-time members. Pollution control is a scientific and technical job but many of the boards are staffed, even headed, by non-technical people. Even civic authorities, against which the boards are sometimes required to act, find representation on these boards.

III. National Green Tribunal

930. The Government brought into force on 18 October 2010 the NGT Act 2010. The Act provides for establishment of an NGT for the effective and expeditious disposal of cases relating to environmental protection and conservation of forests and other natural resources including enforcement of any legal right relating to environment and giving relief and compensation for damages to persons and property. This Act has been brought in the background of UNCED held at Stockholm in June 1972, and at Rio de Janeiro in June 1992 with a view to provide effective access to judicial and administrative proceedings, including redress and remedy in view of involvement of multidisciplinary issues relating to the environment. The NGT is a specialized body armed with necessary expertise to handle disputes involving multidisciplinary issues. The Tribunal is not bound by the procedure laid down under the Civil Procedure Code, 1908 (CPC) and is guided by principles of natural justice.

The other complimentary rules and orders brought in force so as to give NGT a practical shape are the NGT (Manner of Appointment of Judicial and Expert Members and Procedure for Enquiry) Rules 2010; the NGT (Removal of Difficulties) Order, 2010; the NGT (Practice and Procedure) Rules, 2011.

IV. The Loss of Ecology (Prevention and Payments of Compensation) Authority for the State of Tamil Nadu

931. This authority consisting of a retired Judge of the High Court and two members and one Member Secretary has been constituted in compliance with the Honourable Supreme Court's order dated 28 August 1996 in Writ Petition (Civil) No. 914 of 1991, namely, *Vellore Citizens Welfare Forum v. Union of India and others*, *see* Notification S.O.671(E) dated 30 September 1996: the Loss of Ecology (Prevention and Payments of Compensation) Authority for the State of Tamil Nadu, to deal with the situation created by the tanneries and other polluting industries in Tamil Nadu. The tenure of the authority has been extended up to 30 October 2004.

V. Environment Pollution (Prevention and Control) Authority for the NCR

932. The Central Government (*see* Notification S.O.93(E) dated 29 January 1998) constituted the Environment Pollution (Prevention and Control) Authority for the NCR. The authority is empowered to exercise the powers under section 5 of the Environment (Protection) Act of 1986 for issuing directions for compliance relating to violation of standards for quality of the environment, emission or discharge of pollutants and to take all necessary steps to control vehicular pollution, restriction of industries causing environmental pollution and monitor the progress of an action plan drawn up by the Ministry on Pollution in Delhi as contained in the White Paper on Pollution in Delhi with an Action Plan.

§6. Right of Complaint

933. The environmental legislation contains provisions which confer the right on citizens to question authorities for non-compliance of environmental standards.

Under section 19 of the EP Act of 1976, a court can take cognizance of any offence on the complaint of any person, provided that other requirements under the section are met.

I. Civil Action

934. The question of right of complaint assumes importance in the case of individuals who litigate in civil action. The civil remedies available to individuals in environmental matters are damages, injunctions or declarations. Courts examine whether the plaintiff has suffered damage or is exposed to a potential damage. Civil remedies are by and large remedies in private law. Therefore, the plaintiff must have a direct nexus with the injury alleged.

II. Criminal Prosecution

935. In criminal prosecution, the role of individuals is wide in nature. But it is not necessary that the one who initiates prosecution is an affected person. Therefore, the law allows a public-spirited individual to set the criminal prosecution in motion when an offence is noted by that individual.

III. Environmental Legislation

936. Environmental legislation treats certain activities as offences. But the right of private citizens to initiate prosecution for such offences is circumscribed by the requirement of prior notice to the authorities before they take up the matter before the court.

937. Any person seeking relief and compensation for environmental damage involving subjects in the following legislations may approach the NGT:

The Water (Prevention and Control of Pollution) Act, 1974.
The Water (Prevention and Control of Pollution) Cess Act, 1977.
The Forest (Conservation) Act, 1980.
The Air (Prevention and Control of Pollution) Act, 1981.
The Environment (Protection) Act, 1986.
The Public Liability Insurance Act, 1991.
The Biological Diversity Act, 2002.

938. The Tribunal has jurisdiction over all civil cases involving a substantial question relating to environment. Additionally, any person aggrieved by an order/direction of any of the Appellate Authorities under the legislations mentioned above can also challenge them before the NGT. Engaging an advocate is not necessary.

Aggrieved parties may approach the Tribunal in person by submitting an application in the required format. The decisions of the Tribunal are binding. The Tribunal's orders are enforceable as the powers vested are the same as in a civil court under the Code of Civil Procedure, 1908. The Tribunal has powers to review its own decisions. If this fails, the decision can be challenged before the Supreme Court within ninety days. The Tribunal is an open court and its proceedings can be attended in person.

IV. Class Actions or Representative Actions

939. Before Independence, environmental problems were not very significant. The pollution of water in streams and rivers was the only conceivable form of environmental harm which affected only a very small number of persons. But now, the magnitude of the problem transcends rivers and streams and pervades into other media affecting the entire population. As people began to realize the gravity of the situation, groups, associations and organizations with the object of protecting the environment were formed. They invoked legal remedies and took up matters before the court. The citizen suit enables a private citizen to initiate proceedings for violation of legal provisions and for compelling the authorities to enforce statutory provisions.

940. The citizen suit provisions in environmental legislation in India enable any person to institute criminal prosecution for the offences mentioned in those laws, besides the provisions in the IPC relating to pollution. Section 133 of the Code of Criminal Procedure may also be used by a citizen who wishes to initiate proceedings for environmental pollution. In the *Ratlam* case, the Supreme Court said that local citizens had standing to approach the executive magistrate for removal of a public nuisance. The court observed that basic amenities like cleanliness are human rights, and that the same has to be respected by the State by providing such amenities.

A. *Procedure under the CPC*

941. Order I Rule 8 of the CPC 1976 provides for representative action when the class has numerous members and when they have the same interest in the suit. It permits any member to join the class if that person wants to pursue. Order I Rule 8 of the CPC prescribes that notice be published in a newspaper having circulation in the place where the members of the class reside, or that notices be served if persons are ascertainable. Suits filed under Order I Rule 8 of the CPC cannot be compromised or settled until the court issues a notice to all members of the class. The decree in such cases has binding force on all the members of the class.

942. The provision in Order I Rule 8 of the CPC was successfully employed by the Supreme Court of India in PIL against pollution of the river Ganga wherein the court directed the issue of a notice under Order I Rule 8 of the CPC, treating the case as a representative action by publishing the gist of the petition in the newspapers in circulation in northern India, and calling upon all industrialists and municipal bodies having jurisdiction over the areas through which the River Ganga flows, to appear before the court and to show cause against the petition. Likewise, in the Bhopal tragedy, the GOI filed a class action suit on behalf of all the victims according to the provisions of the Bhopal Gas Leak Disaster (Processing of Claims) Act of 1985 by which the Government assumed jurisdiction.

B. Protection of Public Interest

943. The people approach the courts in environmental matters only when they are left in the lurch by the administrative and political processes of the country and have no recourse to any other authority. PIL, class actions and representative actions are special procedures evolved by the Supreme Court and High Court which enable a class of persons or environmental groups with the same interest to sue or to be sued. In present day industrial development where mass production and mass consumption are inevitable, a large number of persons may become aggrieved about a common occurrence affecting all of them in a similar fashion. When such persons are too numerous to be joined together easily, class action is the most economical, fair and efficient way of making justice available to that class. In the case of environmental damage, since all injured persons have identical interests and since their grievances are common, class action or PIL are the most suitable forms of litigation for redressing their grievances.

Chapter 6. Judicial Remedies

944. In India, various legislations relating to the environment have been passed. Almost all these laws have their separate mechanism for dealing with the problem of environmental pollution. This has resulted in a multiplicity of forums and authorities for the settlement of disputes and enforcement of pollution control measures. Individuals can also invoke the jurisdiction of the courts for enforcement of measures of pollution control through the filing of writs in High Courts and the Supreme Court of India, claiming civil remedy in tort, invoking provisions of the CPC, prosecution under the CrPC, filing a suit for damages or injunction.

945. The most common remedies offered by the courts to deal with pollution are directions, injunctions and compensation. The courts have even taken *suo motu* cognizance and actions have been initiated, if the matter is of public importance. In order to provide complete justice, the court even took account of a letter sent by a public-spirited person (1990 (Supp) SCC 77), a memorandum (O.P. NO 6721 of 1992, Kerala), and a newspaper article (AIR 1992 pat 86).

946. The judiciary issued directions to fill the gaps in existing laws and have created expert committees in several environmental litigations. A special committee was constituted to monitor air quality and traffic congestion ((1998) 9 SCC 93), the archaeological survey was directed to set up an automatic monitoring system ((1998) 3 SCC 381); the court directed the subordinate green bench to monitor compliance with the previous order ((1997) 2 SCC 411 and (1998) 9 SCC 448).

947. The courts have also made several directions on unconditional closure of tanneries and relocation (*M.C.Mehta (Calcutta Tanneries Matter) v. Union Of India* (1997) 2 SCC 411); payment of compensation for reversing the damage, payment of costs required for the remedial measures, necessary measures to be adopted by the relevant ministry to broadcast information relating to the environment in the media, attracting the attention of the Government where there is a necessity of legislation, etc.

§1. The Court System

948. India has a well-developed judicial system for dispensation of justice. The Supreme Court at New Delhi is the highest court. There are High Courts in the States, and cases of the UT are also looked after by these High Courts. The Supreme Court and High Courts have appellate jurisdiction. The writ jurisdiction and enforcement of the fundamental rights also lie with the Supreme Court and High Courts. The judgments of the Supreme Court and High Courts are important sources of law because decisions of the Supreme Court are binding on all the courts of India and decisions of the High Courts are binding in the same High Court and have persuasive value in the High Courts of other States. The Supreme Court and High Courts can issue directions or orders or writs including the writs in the nature of habeas corpus, *mandamus*, prohibition, *quo-warranto* and *certiorari*.

949. A hierarchy of subordinate courts functions under the High Courts. In each district, which is a subdivision of a State, there is District and Sessions Court presided by a District and Sessions Judge being the highest judicial authority in the district. In some States, *Panchayat* courts also function, which decide disputes of a petty and local nature.

I. Supreme Court

950. The Supreme Court has original, appellate and advisory jurisdiction. The exclusive original jurisdiction of the Supreme Court extends to disputes between the GOI and one or more States or between two or more States. The Supreme Court also functions as a Court of Appeal with respect to any judgment, decree or final order in civil, criminal or other proceeding from any High Court in the territory of India.

Under Article 32 of the Constitution, the Supreme Court can issue writs for the enforcement of fundamental rights against the State. Besides this, the Supreme Court has original jurisdiction in any dispute arising between the following:

(a) between the GOI and one or more States; or
(b) between the GOI and any States or States on the one side and one or more States on the other; or
(c) between two or more States.

II. High Courts

951. The High Courts are the highest courts in the State and carry out the judicial administration of the State in addition to their function as a court. These courts acting under Article 226 of the Constitution can issue directions, orders or writs including the writs in the nature of habeas corpus, *mandamus*, prohibition, *quo-warranto* and *certiorari* for the enforcement of fundamental rights and for any other purpose.

The High Courts have power of supervision over all subordinate courts in the State (Article 235). They can call for returns from such courts, make and issue general rules and prescribe forms to regulate their practices and proceedings. They also prescribe the manner and form in which book entries and accounts shall be kept.

III. Subordinate Courts

952. The subordinate courts deal with all disputes of a civil or criminal nature in accordance with the powers conferred on them. These courts follow the procedure prescribed under the CPC 1908 and the Code of Criminal Procedure 1973 and some local statutes. After a direction by the Supreme Court, a uniform designation has been brought about with respect to judicial officers throughout the country. These designations in descending order are the District or Additional District Judge, Civil

Judge (Senior Division) and Civil Judge (Junior Division) on the civil side. On the criminal side, these designations are Sessions Judge, Additional Sessions Judge, Chief Judicial Magistrate and Judicial Magistrate.

The members of the State Judicial Services are governed by rules and regulations framed by the respective State Governments in consultation with High Courts in the exercise of power conferred under proviso to Article 309 read with Articles 233 and 234 of the Constitution.

§2. Judicial or Administrative Recourse

I. Writ Jurisdiction

953. The Constitution of India has established a powerful judiciary which is perhaps the most powerful in the world. The Supreme Court and High Courts are bestowed with the extraordinary writ jurisdiction to protect the rights of the people, which has been used by the courts time and again to serve the cause of environment protection. Even policy and technical or procedural constraints have not prevented the courts to provide remedies in environmental matters.

954. The writ jurisdiction is available against the State under the Constitution, and it has emerged as most preferred mode for citizen groups compelling the State to observe and enforce environmental protection measures. The writ jurisdiction of the Supreme Court can be invoked for enforcement of fundamental rights of the citizens enshrined in Part III of the Constitution. The High Courts can exercise this jurisdiction not only for the enforcement of fundamental rights but also for any other purpose as well. It has become easier for the courts to permit invocation of writ jurisdiction because of the fact that the right to a safe, clean and healthy environment has been held to be a component of the fundamental right to life guaranteed by Article 21 of the Constitution of India.

955. In *Municipal Council Ratlam v. Vardhichand* (AIR 1980 SC 1622), the Supreme Court extended the remedial right for a traditional legal concept like public nuisance to cases pertaining to environmental pollution and a duty was imposed on the State to provide a clean environment. By liberally interpreting the right to life – a constitutionally guaranteed fundamental right, the Supreme Court has expanded its ambit to include in it the right to a healthy environment.

A. *Exhaustion of Remedies Available in Special Legislation*

956. In the *Ganga Pollution Cases* (AIR 1988 SC 1033), the Supreme Court held that although the closure of tanneries may bring unemployment, loss of revenue, but life, health and ecology have greater importance to the people. The court passed comprehensive directions to various authorities charged with the task of pollution control under Article 32 of the Constitution despite the availability of remedial mechanism under the Water Act.

B. *Constitution of Green Benches*

957. In *Vellore Citizens Welfare Forum v. Union of India* ((1996) 5 SCC 647), the Supreme Court had held that 'the right of a person to a pollution-free environment is a part of the basic jurisprudence of the country'. In this case, the Supreme Court asked the Chief Justice of Madras High Court to constitute a 'Green bench' to deal with the pollution of water and other environmental matters. Such benches are also functioning in Calcutta, Bhopal and in some other places.

C. *Judicial Review*

958. The primary and first instance regulation of the environment is achieved through the administrative agencies established by law. It is necessary that deeds and misdeeds of such agencies should be controlled. In common law, countries individuals aggrieved by the acts of administrative agencies can approach courts for review of such administrative decisions. Courts intervene in the administrative decisions of the executive, if those decisions are *ultra vires*, unreasonable, *malafide*, inconsistent with the rules of natural justice and suffering from procedural irregularities. The technique of judicial control of administrative action is used to protect citizens from unbridled or uncontrolled exercise of power. This control is achieved by the mechanism of issuing writs like *certiorari*, *mandamus*, prohibition and *quo-warranto*. Courts can also issue injunctions against the reckless exercise of power by the Government and its agencies.

Basically judicial review in India is aimed at judicial control of administrative actions. The primary concern of the courts is whether the administrative action has violated any statutory provisions and the established principles of law such as natural justice. In India, there is a written Constitution which is the fundamental law of the land; therefore, courts test the legality of the actions of administrative agencies on the touchstone of the constitutional provisions.

II. Action under the CPC

959. Under section 91 of the CPC, two or more citizens may apply to the District Court for leave to file a suit for declaration and injunction and for some other remedies in respect of a public wrong. A private person who suffers a special damage by reason of a public nuisance may bring an action for damages under common law, which has been recognized by the CPC as well. The claim may consist of a claim for damages or removal or abatement of the nuisance in question. In *Aamina Sadat Ali v. Municipal Board* (AIR 1980 All 376), the right to seek the removal of a public nuisance was specifically recognized. Section 91(2) of the CPC provides the following provision in this regard. 'Nothing in this section shall be deemed to limit or otherwise affect any right of suit, which may exist independently of its provisions.'

§3. Right of Action

960. Access to justice is now well recognized as a human right and part of a civilized existence. In a modern legal system, justice is delivered through the process of courts. Therefore, people look to the courts for justice when they feel or apprehend that they have not been justly dealt with. Courts do not open their doors to everybody: rather they screen complainants to see whether or not they have the proper standing and interest. *Standing to sue* or *locus standi* is the legal capacity to challenge an act or decision. The concept becomes complex in those environmental cases which deal with the interests of the general public.

I. Public Interest Litigation

961. Individuals affected by environmental problems may feel reluctant to approach a court because of financial difficulties, lack of environmental awareness, ignorance of proceedings and apprehensions about the outcome. Thus the role of public-spirited individuals and environmental associations attain significance. They increasingly espouse the cause of affected individuals or class of individuals and challenge environmentally unsound decisions. Against this backdrop, the Supreme Court came up with the concept of PIL when it reckoned the fact that a large number of the people due to their poverty, illiteracy and remoteness from the seat of power are silently suffering injustice even in matters relating to their fundamental rights guaranteed by the Constitution. Thus, the court, as a matter of judicial policy, began to accept petitions filed by public-spirited individuals and organizations seeking relief for problems of a public nature mainly of environmental deterioration.

II. Sufficient Interest

962. Article 14 of the Constitution provides that all are equal before the law and shall be accorded equal protection of the law. Equal protection of the law means that all persons in like circumstances shall be treated alike and no discrimination shall be made in conferment of rights or imposition of liabilities. The environmental groups resort to Article 14 to quash arbitrary municipal permissions for activities like construction that are contrary to development regulations or plans. Article 14 is also used to challenge Government sanctions for mining and other activities with adverse environmental impact. The applicant is allowed access to the judicial process if he has 'sufficient interest'. It is worth mentioning that the absence of any specific rule of standing is one of the reasons behind the development of PIL in India.

963. The Supreme Court has been vigilant in identifying litigation motivated by self-interest. *Chhetriya Pardushan Mukthi Sangharsh Samithi v. State of U.P.* (AIR 1990 SC 2060) and *Subhash Kumar v. State of Bihar* (AIR 1991 SC 420) are two instances where the cases were dismissed when the court discovered that the petitioners who filed PILs were motivated by a personal grudge against the respondents. The Supreme Court has gone to the extent of imposing cost for abuse of process of law (AIR 2006 SC 1774, 1784).

Therefore, the court allows only public-spirited individuals and organizations to approach it in pursuit of a matter of public interest, especially those concerning persons in a disadvantageous position. The court examines facts through the commissions appointed by it, rather than merely relying on the versions presented by both sides through affidavits. The verdict often comes in the form of directives to the executive agencies to cure the maladies. The court directs the unwilling executives to discharge their duty in tune with the spirit of the law.

In a *Mehta series* case, the issue was whether the petitioner who was not a riparian owner could be granted standing to move for prevention of nuisance for pollution in the River Ganga. The court held that he was a person interested in protecting the lives of the people who make use of the waters of the river and so could move. In the court's view, in PIL, it is reasonable to allow any person to instigate proceedings on behalf of the community at large.

§4. Environmental Groups and Associations

964. When the gravity of environmental hazards became increasingly perceptible, courts felt the need for strict enforcement of environmental legislation. By invoking the power under Article 32 of the Indian Constitution to protect fundamental rights, the Supreme Court has given relief to the petitioners – both individuals and environmental organizations. Disregarding the traditional concepts of *locus standi*, the court entertained a new genus of litigation, viz. PIL for protecting the fundamental rights of the people.

I. Evolution of Environmental Groups

965. The history of environmental groups can be traced back to the 1960s. Publication of books like *Silent Spring* by Rachel Carson persuaded the world community to be concerned and think about the problem of pollution and environmental deterioration caused by industrialization. In the US, public-spirited persons formed associations with a view to protecting the environment from the harmful effects of industrialization and unplanned development projects.

In the next decade of the 1970s, there was a boom in the growth of environmental organizations all over the world. Some have grown as worldwide organizations, well equipped with scientific and technological knowledge and facilities for research. These organizations take up environmental causes and approach the court on behalf of the general public.

966. In India, environmental groups like the 'Chipko' movement which existed in the distant past have attracted the attention of the world. Members of that group physically hugged the forest trees to prevent them from being cut down by the forest timber contractors. Tehri Bandh Virodhi Sangharsh Samiti campaigned and launched a popular movement against the environmental destruction and loss of habitat for nearly ten million people because of construction of Tehri Bandh in the State of Uttaranchal. Sasthra Sahithya Parishad in the southern State of Kerala forced the authorities to drop a proposed hydroelectric project which would have drowned a rare rain forest known as Silent Valley.

II. Letters, Newspaper Reports as Writs

967. Even a complaint written as a letter addressed to the court by the aggrieved persons or public-spirited persons began to find its way to the courts, to be taken up as a new case. The Supreme Court in this crusade against environmental deterioration proceeded on the premise that a clean and wholesome environment is a prerequisite to enjoy the right to life enshrined in the Indian Constitution as a fundamental right of all persons. The court treated mere letters as petitions. The notable examples are *Bandhua Mukti Morcha v. Union of India* (AIR 1984 SC 802) and *Rural Litigation and Entitlement Kendra v. State of U.P.* (AIR 1985 SC 652) which were the harbingers of a new trend. When the limestone quarries in the Mussorie Hill range were found to be creating an imbalance to ecology and a hazard to a healthy environment, the Supreme Court, in a PIL by the Kendra, ordered a major part of the quarrying activities to be closed down. In a few subsequent PIL cases, the court recognized the right to environment and invoked the power under Article 32 of the Constitution to issue appropriate orders and directions.

968. The series of PIL cases instituted by a public-spirited lawyer, Mr M.C. Mehta, in the Supreme Court set a glorious precedent. One *Mehta* case (*M.C.Mehta v. Union of India*) concerned the closing down of a chlorine plant of Shriram Industries. The one known as the *Oleum gas leak* case was decided by a five judges Constitutional Bench of the Supreme Court. In view of the gravity of the legal questions under consideration, granting *locus standi* to the petitioner, the court held that there is absolute liability on the hazardous industries.

III. Environmental Groups Launching Criminal Prosecution

969. There is no legal prohibition for environmental groups to initiate criminal prosecution in India, as the policy of law is to permit any person to set criminal prosecution in motion subject to, in some cases, certain prerequisites. Citizen suit provisions in the environmental legislation of India contemplate only criminal prosecution against the offences specified therein. When environmental groups seek civil action and judicial review, courts examine whether they have the requisite *locus standi* or not. The pronouncements of the courts in India on the question of *locus standi* are quite often guided by the circumstances of each case.

IV. Success Stories and Achievements

970. On an action initiated by an environmental NGO, the Supreme Court on 12 February 1997 issued a direction to the MoEFCC to take the necessary steps by 1 April 1997 to implement the relevant laws banning the use and dumping of hazardous and noxious substances by industrial units throughout India.

In another case by an NGO, 'Research Foundation for Science', the Supreme Court warned the MoEFCC that if the top officers concerned did not measure up to their duties and enforce the provisions of the Environment (Protection) Act of 1986, the court would be constrained to record a 'judicial finding of failure to perform their duties against them' and that the court would also ensure that the judicial finding is recorded in their service records.

In cases of public nuisance, members of such organizations can, with the leave of the court, resort to the provisions of section 91 of the CPC for the relief of injunction and declaration or such other appropriate reliefs, even though no special damage has been caused to the members of such organizations. In addition, in public nuisance cases, courts have also recognized persons in the locality and the neighbouring residents as having *locus standi* for injunctions and declarations.

Selected Bibliography

Books, Journals and Papers

Ghosh S. (ed.). *Indian Environmental Law-Key Concepts and Principles*. 1st edn. Hyderabad: The Orient Blackswan, 2019

Gopalkrishnan, V. *Ethical, Legal and Social Issues Facing Capture Fisheries*. https://www.eubios.info/EJ103/EJ103E.htm

Jaswal, P.S. & J. Nishtha. *Environmental Law*. 3rd edn. Haryana: Allahabad Law Agency, 2009

Leela Krishnan, P. *Environmental Law in India*. LexisNexis: Butterworths India 2018

Malik, M.R. *Environment and Pollution Laws*. Delhi: Professional Book Publishers, 2010

Mohanti, S.K. *Universal's Environment and Pollution Laws*. Delhi: Universal Law Publishing, 2014

'Ozone Cell': www.ozonecell.com

Shastri Satish, C. (Prof.). *Environmental Law*. 4th edn. Lucknow: Eastern Book Company, 2012

State of India's Environment 2014, 2019, 2022, Centre for Science and Environment, New Delhi

Tiwari, H.N. *Environmental Law*. Haryana: Allahabad Law Agency, 2016

Turnaround – Reform Agenda for India's Environmental Regulators – 2009. Centre for Science and Environment. 41, Tughlakabad Institutional Area, New Delhi 110062

Waste Management in India, Shifting Gears, ASSOCHAM, 2017.

The World Bank Report on Environmental and Social System Assessment (ESSA)-Transforming India's Public Health Systems for Pandemic Preparedness (P175676) dated 4 May 2022

Government Publications

Annual Report 2020–2021, Ministry of Environment, Forests and Climate Change, Government of India, New Delhi

Annual Report of Niti Aayog 2017–2018, 2018–2019, 2021–2022

Annual Report 2021–2022, Ministry of Housing and Urban Affairs, Government of India

Auto Fuel Vision and Policy 2025

Selected Bibliography

Mashelkar R.A. Dr '*Auto Fuel Policy Report*'. Ministry of Petroleum and Natural Gas, 2000

National Environment Policy (NEP) 2006 published by MoEFCC

G.S.R. 281(E) dated 7 March 2016

Pollution Control Acts, Rules and Notifications issued thereunder, CPCB, MoEFCC, April 2021 (http://www.cpcb.nic.in)

State of the Forest Report, 2017

The National Forest Policy 2018

Third National Wildlife Action Plan for 2017–2031

Razzaque Jona Dr, Human Rights and the Environment: the national experience in South Asia and Africa, joint OHCHR-UNEP Initiative on Human Rights

Index

The numbers here refer to paragraph numbers.

Index

www.ingramcontent.com/pod-product-compliance
Lightning Source LLC
LaVergne TN
LVHW011110300926
849160LV00008B/333
* 9 7 8 9 4 0 3 5 3 3 8 6 5 *